I0225544

Jesus' Africa

Patience Museveni Rwabwogo

Foreword by H.E. Yoweri Kaguta Museveni

First Edition: June 2023

Published by Nsemia Inc. Publishers (www.nsemia.com)

Cover Concept: Author

Cover Illustration: Sezi Jedidiah Nuwewenka

Cover Design: Linda Kiboma

Layout Design: Linda Kiboma

Project Consultant: Matunda Nyanchama

Note for Librarians:

A cataloguing record for this book is available from

Library and Archives Canada

978-1-989928-22-6

"For whoever would come near to God must believe that God exists and that He is the rewarder of those who earnestly and diligently seek Him."

- Hebrews 11:6

Dedication

For My Yeshua

My life truly started when I found You. It is in You that I have found my eternal place, my purpose and my passion. Thank You for always loving me, always seeing me and never giving up on me. This is my magnum opus to You.

For Daddy and Mummy

You are my heroes. It all began with you and I honour, bless and thank you for all the love you poured into my life and the many sacrifices you made for me. I pray that you are proud of the person I have become.

For My Havel

The day we met started the most beautiful adventure. What a blessing that after all these years I still feel like a bride. Thank you for keeping your promise.

For My Mumutiine Rubanza, Kendagaano Nganzi, Judah Nyentsya and Gigi Hadarah

You bring so much joy and fulfillment to my life. Each of you is a perfect gift from God to us and the world. I am so excited to see how Yeshua is growing and preparing you to make your mark in the world.

For Mo, Tash and Na

You have been there for me all through the years and the changing seasons of life. Thank you for walking, sharing, laughing, growing, learning, crying and always praying with me. Thank you for being the keepers of our collective History.

For Covenant Nations Church

You are the greatest church in the world. Thank you for graciously walking this journey of faith together with so much love and patience. It is in serving God and you all that I stumbled into my destiny. This is our story. May we live to see the fulfillment of God's Word.

Acknowledgements

I want to thank, in a special way, everyone who has had a hand in not only the writing and compilation of this book but more so the life and journey behind it. Writing the book has taken three years but the journey behind the story has taken many more years. I honour and appreciate everyone who has mentored, encouraged, corrected, guided, listened to and spoken into my life from my childhood.

I thank my parents, Daddy (Mzee) and Mummy (Maama) for their unwavering love and support all through my life. I thank them for being present parents who enjoyed, loved and encouraged me to follow the unique path that God had for me. So much of who I am today is because of the unconditional love and grounding they gave to my siblings and me from childhood. I thank and honour you for being the best parents, friends, confidantes, cheerleaders, counsellors and guides.

I am indebted to my siblings, the amazing (and historical) 3K's, Mo, Tash and Na. Thank you for always being there for me, to encourage, laugh, cry and be witnesses to the many milestones of life. My life has been richer and more joyful because of your friendship and love. Thank you, Tash and Na for reading this manuscript and offering valued input.

I am grateful to my many nephews and nieces who have filled our lives with so much joy, laughter and love. Each of you is a blessing and you have so many gifts and talents. I can't wait to see what God will do in and through you to impact your generation.

Thank you to my friends Nukuri Kamugasha, Gloria Omaswa, and Allen Kagina, for your love, encouragement and support in my life and during the writing of this book. Thank you for your helpful insights in the editing process.

I thank my many family and friends who have stood in the as intercessors for me and my family over the years. Auntie Penina Kyembabazi, Auntie Jane Kyishakye, Annette Butukaine Ndegyeya, Dr. Bonita Kafureka Mugarura, Mrs. Nicole Tshani, Analiza Twahirwa, Nkamuzaara Rwehabura and Jerusalem Kebede. I wouldn't be able to carry out my ministry as a preacher of the Gospel without your constant prayer covering. Thank you for your prayers for me, especially during the writing of this book.

I send my gratitude to the elders of Covenant Nations Church; Mr. and Hon. Asiimwe, Dr. and Hon. Okia, Mr. and Mrs. Sekaran Vellasamy, Mr. and Mrs. Tshani, Mr. and Mrs. Kaguhangire, Mr. and Mrs. Kagina, Mr. and Mrs. Kamya, Mrs. Peace Mahoro and Mrs. Peace Byaruhanga. Thank you all for your unwavering support, encouragement and love over the years. I appreciate and value each of you and the unique gifts and talents you carry, thank you for helping to carry the weight and responsibility of the work of the ministry and for adding so much joy, laughter and colour along the way. I thank the leadership team of Covenant Nations Church, without whom I would not be able to do the work of the ministry. I cannot mention all of your names, but I recognize and deeply appreciate the support and service that I have received from all of you.

I am indebted to Mr. Andrew Nabende from Covenant Nations Church, who was instrumental in transcribing the audio messages from Jesus' Africa. Thank you for your diligence and commitment to excellence in what you do.

Words of gratitude go to my younger brother Sezi Jedidiah Nuwewenka for his excellent work on the design and artwork for the cover of the book. Thank you Sezi for allowing God to use you in the area of media and communications. You perfectly capture, through design, what I see and perceive in the spirit.

To my assistant and church administrator, Ms. Jean Namara, thank you for wearing the numerous hats you wore and doing whatever is necessary to get the job done for the glory of God. I greatly appreciate your quiet commitment, tenacity, integrity and heart of service.

I thank my friends and family who have shared their testimonies and teachings in this book. Dr. James Magara, whose teaching on remitting the sins of slavery was foundational for chapter 13. I thank Mrs. Lorna Magara, Mrs. Natasha Karugire, Mrs. Allen Kagina, my husband

Odrek Rwabwogo, Pastor Tom and Kate Hess from Israel, Rev. Jim Olson from St. Paul, Minnesota, Pastor Nsembe from the Democratic Republic of Congo and Prof. Jang Saeng Kim from Korea.

I thank my editor and publisher from Nsemia Publishing, Dr. Matunda Nyachama; thank you for taking this project on and walking every mile with me to see that we completed the whole process and stayed true to the original intent of the book.

In a very special way, I am indebted to the many mentors that God has used along the way to teach, guide, mentor and encourage me. Some I have known personally, and others I have known through their teachings. God has used them all to help me grow in my knowledge of God and to help me further along this journey of faith. The great healing evangelist and prince of God, T.L. Osborn and his wife Daisy. God used them mightily to preach the gospel in great miracle crusades in Uganda in the 1980s when Uganda was just emerging from years of war and devastation. Their ministry was key in my mother's salvation, and it was Daisy Osborn who gave me my first Bible. Over the years I have been so blessed by their teaching ministry and by their demonstration of the absolute power of God, with signs and wonders following.

I thank Creflo Dollar, a great teacher of the Word of God from Atlanta, Georgia. I visited the World Changers Church International in the United States on several occasions and was greatly blessed by his teaching ministry.

I thank my dear friend and elder brother, Bishop Joshua Lwere, the General Overseer of the National Fellowship of Born Again Churches, who has been of tremendous support to me as a minister of the Gospel in Uganda. We have partnered in the work of the ministry many times and I have benefitted from his vision, integrity and commitment to the cause of the Lord Jesus Christ in the nation.

Arthur Burk, of Sapphire Leadership Group, I thank you sincerely. Your landmark teachings on the redemptive gifts of cities and nations as well as teachings on deliverance and cleansing of the land have given us the language and tools to deal with sometimes complex generational issues. Thank you for being a pioneer in this field and showing that it's a blessing to be spiritually dangerous.

I thank, in a special way, my dear friend Rev. Dr. Arthur Rouner (RIP), a man that modelled love, humility and complete devotion to the Lord Jesus Christ in his daily life. I thank Arthur and his beloved wife Molly, for being my friends, surrogate parents and mentors. God used Arthur, to cast his father's mantle of encouragement over me, in the early days of ministry when I was feeling very discouraged and wanted to give up. I wouldn't have made it this far without Arthur's love and friendship when I most needed it.

I thank the great man of God, Pastor E. A. Adeboye (Daddy G.O.) and his beloved wife Mrs. Folu Adeboye (Maama G.O.). Pastor Adeboye carries an Elijah mantle and anointing for this generation and I have learnt more from observing and listening to his messages than I have from any other minister of the Gospel. God is using him to do staggering things in these last days, and I have been personally built up by his commitment to evangelism, humility, true worship and holiness.

I thank our children: Mumutiine Rubanza, Kendagaano Nganzi, Judah Nyentsya and Gigi Hadarah; you are my joy. Each of you is a special gift to us and the world, and I thank you for making every single day pure bliss and filled with pleasure. Thank you for allowing Imma to follow God's path for my life and for encouraging me along the way.

I must thank my husband, Odrek; thank you for providing the spiritual covering for me to serve the Lord wholeheartedly. I know that I wouldn't be able to do what the Lord has called me to do without your love, support and constant encouragement. Thank you for always believing in me and challenging me to run my race with joy. During the writing of this book, you have given invaluable advice and guidance.

Finally, even if I had a thousand tongues, I would never be able to thank my Lord and Saviour, JESUS, my YESHUA. You saw me when I didn't see myself and You called me by my name. Thank You for all You are that cannot be captured in words. My one prayer is that my life would be pleasing to You and that You fulfil Your greater purpose through me. In all things be glorified!

A Review of Jesus' Africa

Whenever dealing with *any* situation, problem or circumstance, the only way to *properly* approach it, is to go to the root (source) of the dysfunction. To do anything else would only serve as efforts of futility. Why, you may ask? Because it would leave us, not addressing the problem, but trying to *solve a symptom!* The fallacy of this effort is that symptoms can be anesthetized or *medicated* to give the impression that one is not sick, while the real issue (the root cause) has yet to truly be addressed!

Nothing demonstrates this truth more than the *disconnect* that exists in the *so-called* Church and amongst blacks in other parts of the world and their relationship with blacks in Africa ...and we are ALL family! As Jesus is to be "The Great Unifier" of us all, yet in His body we find more divisiveness. This is not by *coincidence.* The adversary had a plan.

PATIENCE RWABWOGO, with a burden for those of African descent in the Body of Christ, has taken a **deep dive** into the cause of this malady that has the whole of Christianity *stuck* in a malaise of mediocrity, medicating symptoms having *"... a zeal of God, but not according to knowledge."* [Romans 10:2] Thus, the cause of the calamity is never addressed.

I wept as I read through this. This is a heart-wrenching read that *forces* the reader to refuse to settle for what has been accepted as normal.

> *"The whole head is sick and the whole heart faints. From the sole of the foot even to the head,* ***there is no soundness in it,*** *but wounds and bruises and putrefying sores;* ***They have not been closed or bound up,*** *or soothed with ointment. Your country is desolate your cities are burned with fire;* ***Strangers devour your land in your presence;..."*** _ *Isaiah 1:5-9*

I highly commend Minister Patience. She is a **sword** in the hand of the LORD in this season. Further, I highly recommend this literary work. It will **shake up** all who are *"... at ease in Zion."* [Amos 6:1]

> *And even now* ***the ax is laid to the root of the trees.»*** _ *Luke 3:9*

Dr. James "Bamidele Sturdivant
Senior Pastor Faith United Ministries
Maryland, U.S.A

Table of Contents

Dedication v

Acknowledgements vii

A Review of Jesus' Africa xi

Foreword 1

1. Prologue 9

2. Seeing Africa Through Jesus' Eyes 15

3. A Voice in the Wind 37

4. Africa the Bookend of Biblical History 47

5. The White Council 61

6. My People 93

7. Walk in the Dark with Jesus 109

8. The Edomite Spirit 135

9. Mr. Wonderful 153

10. The Call 179

11. Good Hair 239

12. Soldier 253

13. Remitting the Sins of Slavery 289

14. A Troop is Coming 307

15. The Need for a Return 329

16. Marrying the Land 345

17. The Joseph Company 367

18. The Crossing....383
19. The Glorious Church....395
20. Rebuilding Africa's Walls....409
21. Testimonials....453
About the Author....475

Foreword

By some coincidence, my children were born on dates of either global or national importance. Muhoozi was born on the 24th of April, 1974 at Ocean Road Hospital in Dar-es-Salaam. Early the following day, I excitedly rang His Excellency Samora Machel, at his residence in Kurasini, to tell him the good news about my family. He answered the phone but requested me to call him on subsequent days because, at that moment, he was busy listening to radio news from Lisbon, Portugal, where a revolution against the Fascist Government of Marcel Caetano was taking place. Therefore, Muhoozi (whom we affectionately called *Mwoogi* as a child) was born just a day before the great date of April 25th, 1974, the day of the Portuguese Revolution that initiated the collapse of the Portuguese Empire in Africa that had lasted 500 years.

The revolution in Portugal, led by middle-level army officers such as Otelo Saraiva de Carvalho, Vasco Goncalves and others, acting behind the elderly Spinola, was a great victory for the African anti-colonial fighters in Angola, Mozambique and Guinea-Bissau, not to forget the islands of Sao Tome and Principe. The independence of Mozambique the following year, 1975, was decisive for our struggle in Uganda. Although Frelimo, on the request of Mwalimu Julius Nyerere, had trained 3 batches of officers of our group, Fronasa, the one that turned out to be most useful, was the one I directly supervised while training at Montepuez between 1976 and 1978. It is that group of 28+1 that created the Fronasa Army of 1979 and, eventually, the NRA (National Resistance Army) and UPDF (Uganda People's Defense Forces).

Natasha (affectionately called *Kukuru* as a child) was born on the 12th of March, 1976 at Kilimanjaro Christian Medical Centre (KCMC) in Moshi when I was teaching at Moshi Co-operative College.

By some coincidence, it was on the 12th of March, 1985, that I separated from the powerful Mobile Brigade, commanded by Salim Saleh, at Kawumu, on my way to the historical journey across Lake Victoria, through Kenya to Sweden and Libya to get arms that would assist us, not only to defeat the government in Kampala but also to have the capacity to control the whole country quickly, to avoid chaos.

By March 1985, the war in Uganda had entered the stage of strategic equilibrium. With 2500 rifles and 4000 fighters and officers, we were too strong for the Government forces to defeat us, but we were also not strong enough to go on a strategic counter-offensive. I re-entered Uganda at Mutukula from Tanzania in September 1985, having secured 800 rifles and one million rounds from Muammar Gaddafi of Libya and 5000 rifles and one million rounds of ammunition from Mwalimu Nyerere. These 6000 rifles and two million rounds of ammunition from our brothers of Libya and Tanzania, plus some small quantity from our brother Samora Machel, plus huge equipment we were capturing, enabled us to stage a six-phase strategic counter-offensive.

In phase one, we disarmed all the detachments that were in the Luwero Triangle area such as Ngoma, Kiboga and others.

In phase two, Saleh overran Mubende barracks and proceeded to Fort Portal that had peacefully surrendered to our forces of the Western axis.

In phase three, Saleh's force, jumping off from the Fort Portal area, swept all the way to Katonga River, besieging the Masaka Barracks as Chefe Ali's force besieged the Mbarara Barracks.

In phase four, after defeating all the Uganda National Liberation Army (UNLA) counter-offensives on the Katonga Bridge (September to December 1985), our forces crossed the bridge and established a defensive line along the Kampiringisa (Kampiringitsa)-Kibibi-Buloba line.

Phase five started on the 17th of January, 1986 when there was a general offensive by all the forces to capture Kampala and on the western axis. The forces aimed at capturing Masindi; Kampala was captured on the 26th of January, 1986.

Phase six happened when we sprang from Kampala and launched a general offensive through Jinja-Mbale-Soroti and others, on the Eastern axis and from Masindi to Dimu-Karuma-Arua and others, intending to reach the international borders of Uganda in the East, North and North West.

Therefore, my departure from Kawumu on the 12th of March, 1985, was an event of great historical significance in Uganda and a date on which my daughter Natasha was born.

Patience (affectionately called *Pusi* after a Pussycat as a child) was born on the 9th of May, 1978 and, as everybody knows, the 9th of May is Victory Day- which is celebrated in Europe to commemorate General Jodl of the German Army's surrender to the Allied Forces in the Second World War.

Diana (affectionally called *Kinini* as a child), was born on the 30th of June, 1980, that date being the Independence Day for Congo-Kinshasa, Rwanda and Burundi.

All the children have *ebikubyo* and *ebiziniro* (pet and praise names). Muhoozi is *Mwoogi*, courtesy of Mzee Tito Okello, our neighbour in Upanga, Dar-es-Salaam. He had a problem pronouncing the letter "z" as most traditional Acholis have. Muhoozi's other praise name is *Rureeta-eyokyeero* (the one who brings reinforcements).

Natasha, *Nyinanchwende Karugire*, is *Kukuru* (as if she is my grandmother). Patience *Kokundeka*, on account of her face that would cause a lot of *embabazi* (parental feelings), is *Pusi* after a Pussycat, also called *enjaangu, kamunyamire, ifuro, entuuru* (wild cat) *nyamyorobo*, etc. Diana Kyaremera, is *Kinini* (the good thing). *Kinini* is the only one of our children that was born when we came back to Uganda in 1979. She, therefore, rebalanced the numbers of the Ugandan-born in the family, otherwise the Tanzanian born family member had outnumbered us - 3 vs 2. Now it became three vs. three. She was born in a hospital in London. She is quite an independent girl and I am gratified that she is now broadening the base of wealth creation both in the areas of tourism and farming.

All these children are now grown and making positive contributions to society in their fields of choice.

The Foreword here is for Patience's book titled *Jesus' Africa*. Patience, was only 11 months when I received Maama Janet and the children at Entebbe Airport, in mid-April 1979, after the defeat of Idi Amin. She was a big, quiet and pleasant baby with a lot of hair, with dark linings above the cheeks, which would have resulted into *ebitarira* (sideburns) if they were boys. This is typical of all of them.

In school, she was a super performer, emerging among the topmost 32 in the whole country in the Senior Four examinations in 1995 and making it to the Dean's List at the University of Minnesota, a large university in America with tens of thousands of students, as she points out in the book.

I always treat my children equally and never boss them around. Rather, I engage them in discussions on all matters of interest. I did not like the regime of our parents of beating (*kuteera*), haranguing (*kutonganisa*) or even mocking (*kutsyorira*); nor did I think it necessary or useful.

Whenever, therefore, I had time with them, I would give them as much information on all matters of interest as I had. When we came from the bush in 1986, I would always take them to our farm in Rwakyitura every end of the year, if not more frequently. There, we would walk on the farm, follow the cows or walk in the midst of the maize crop. In Entebbe or Nakasero, I would pass by their rooms every morning to wake them up. I have carried on this practice such that, even with the grandchildren that are twelve years old and above, they have the 8 km walk with Grandpa whenever they are on holiday from school.

When I was doing all this, I did not know how much of it the children were absorbing. Apparently, the children were absorbing a lot, according to Patience's account in this book.

My little contribution to Patience's development was, apparently, my political struggles and my absences from home when they were growing up, but also points from my speeches in public and in private.

There is, for instance, the advice I gave to a dinner guest, in her presence, who was complaining about the sectarian politics in his country of origin. My answer to the guest was for him to establish who had the just cause in their country. This is a long-standing doctrine of the National Resistance Movement/National Resistance Army (NRA/NRM). We only fight for just causes and never engage in causes of aggression, chauvinism, and the like.

The other contribution to her development was, apparently, our walks on the farm. There, she saw the cattle, smelt the sweet aroma of the land when the rain fell and enjoyed the protection against the light rain under my jacket, together with her sister, Diana. That event is stuck in her memory.

According to her in this book, the result of all this was to create a person who has become her own boss all these years since she graduated from university. I am very proud to read those words. She has gone back, to tread in the paths of her ancestors: Kaguta, Kabuguma, Kashanku, Kyamukaanga, and the others. Her ancestors never worked for either the pre-colonial kingdoms or for the subsequent regimes (colonial or post-colonial), except as soldiers to defend the area where when mobilized by the chiefs. I am, actually the first of the Kyamukaanga lineage to work for the government, partly because the ideas of the private sector, after independence, were not concretized. As well, it is partly on account of the political crisis created by the ideological disorientation of the political players at the time. She, indeed, reveals that being self-employed has enabled her to look after her young children flexibly because she does not have to abandon them to go to work as an employee. Her husband and herself, have gone seriously into dairy farming and processing. Together with some Israeli co-investors, they have built a milk processing factory in Rushere. If my trips with the children to the farm contributed to the creation of this entrepreneur, then I am most gratified.

However, Patience is not yet done, if you only read what I have written in this Foreword up to place. There are three additional aspects, you must prepare for.

She has a deeply personal religious conviction and the voices she keeps hearing from above; a deep understanding of the scriptures, their interpretation and their conveyance to us, the not so involved; and she is a passionate Christian patriot and Pan-Africanist cadre. Patience, several times in the book, like when she was coming back from school as narrated in Chapter 3, *A Voice in the Wind*, hears this Voice from above when it tells her to "Follow Me." Then, on another occasion, the Voice tells her not to study medicine but political science and University. Then, the Voice told her to go to Buikwe and do evangelism work and more.

I have never had the experience of hearing voices, but I, sometimes, get dreams and inner voices within me. Whatever it is, there is no doubt that, for instance, in the Buikwe issue, Patience's group did great work against witchcraft and superstition in that area. I am, therefore, most pleased that after 146 years of the advent of Christianity in Uganda, I have got a pastor/priest in my family for the first time.

All and sundry, please, remember that, since time immemorial, the Kyamukaanga lineage has been cattle keepers and soldiers, when mobilized by the chiefs for their unprincipled wars. Here is some historical context: up until the 1400s, much of Uganda was ruled by the Bachwezi Dynasty. This covered areas of Bunyoro, Ankole, Buganda, and Karagwe in Northern Tanzania, Eastern Congo and the Omutara region of Rwanda. When the dynasty collapsed, smaller kingdoms emerged such as Bunyoro (ruled by the Babiito), Buganda(ruled by the Barangira) and Nkore (ruled by the Bahiinda).

Nkore covered the areas of present-day Nyabushozi, Lyantonde, Ibanda, Kashari, and small parts of Rwampara, Isingiro, Bukanga and Sheema. The rest of what is present-day Ankole was populated by the same people but called Mpororo. Mpororo covered Igara, Mitooma, Kajara, Rusheenyi, parts of Rwampara, Ruhaama, Isingiro, Kigezi, Rukungiri and the Omutara region of Rwanda. This area was ruled by the Bashambo clan and the people were called Bahororo. The Banyabatumbi were forest dwellers who lived in the Imaramagambo Forest. The area from Bushenyi to Rukungiri was called Butumbi and the people who lived in the forest were called Banyabutumbi. As a child, I heard stories of how the chiefs mobilized warriors, one of whom was my grandfather Kashanku, to raid the Banyabutumbi. This is an example of how the chiefs divided and distracted the population on non-issues instead of focusing on uniting the people under common causes.

Apart from this distraction, my family was always involved in wealth creation, which was primarily cattle rearing. I am, therefore, most pleased to have, for the first time, a pastor who is also a wealth creator in my family.

The second aspect is the incredible insight and knowledge of the Bible that Patience has. I never knew that the descendants of Esau and Lot, are not Israelis. Although it was repeated to me for the 14 years I was involved in learning the Christian scriptures (1952-1966), nobody ever told me, nor did I detect it myself, that the descendants of Esau became the Edomites and those of Lot became the Moabites and Ammonites and that they are not among the Israeli descendants. I knew something about Ismail and his mother Hagar, producing the Arabs, but I never knew the information about Esau and Lot and their descendants. To hear that Herod, the King that wanted to kill Jesus, was an Edomite, a descendant of Esau, who continued the vendetta of his ancestor and Jacob, is most amazing. Salutations to Patience for dispelling my ignorance.

The third aspect is Patience the Christian Patriotic, Pan-Africanist cadre and a passionate one. She backs up her patriotism and Pan-Africanism with the Bible.

She quotes the Bible where she points out that, from one man, God created many nations and gave them their places of habitation and their boundaries. The quotation in Acts 17:26 goes as follows, *"From one man He made all the nations, that they should inhabit the whole earth; and He marked out their appointed times in history and the boundaries of their lands."*

Therefore, the idea of empires is a pagan idea. I have heard Bishop Lwere making the same point. Bravo, Patience.

However, Patience, a Christian patriot and Pan-Africanist is not yet done. She brings out the spirit of Esau, who sold his birthright voluntarily in exchange for a morsel of food (*ekitoongye kye eby'okurya*). Patience makes a powerful point that the Africans, led by the myopic and ego-centric chiefs, who were busy fomenting wars among themselves instead of uniting to fight the imperialists, sold their birthright by so doing. They incurred the Edomite curse because they carried the same spirit as Esau. Jacob was a thief. He cheated Esau twice, by exchanging *ekitoongye* (the morsel of food) for his birthright and by deceiving the blind Isaac to give him the blessing of the firstborn by wearing the skin of an animal. The message Patience brings is that if you do not defend your birthright, your blessings too can be stolen. And God can transfer the blessings, which belonged to you, to another.

The book brings out the four aspects of Patience's character.

The first one is Patience the entrepreneur building on the heritage of her Kyamukaanga lineage of cattle keeping and self-sufficiency. The second is Patience the deep Biblical scholar - the first in my family to do so. Third is Patience of the deep spiritual conviction as a Christian and the Voice she hears from above that turns out to be true e.g. the Buikwe mission. Fourth is the passionate Christian Patriot and Pan-Africanist that has rightly identified the Esau spirit of selling the African birthright and the resulting Edomite curse of being traitors and parasites in the service of foreign interests and the need to fight and defeat these parasites.

The religious angle of Patience's life is, in large part, due to Maama Janet (affectionately called *Ginga* by the grandchildren). When she got her own communication with God, she became passionate and her devotion was noticed by the children and, in turn, influenced their own spiritual development. I thank her for that.

God bless Patience's book and work.

Yoweri K. Museveni (Gen.rt)
PRESIDENT of Uganda
24th April 2023.

1. Prologue

Berlin, 1884-1885

In November of 1884, German Chancellor Otto von Bismarck invited mainly European leaders to Berlin for a conference to address a matter of growing concern. Among them were the leaders of France, Britain, Portugal, Spain, Italy, Norway, Denmark, Sweden, Russia, Belgium, the Austro-Hungarian Empire, America, and the Ottoman Empire. To be discussed at the conference was the division of the African continent, a process later dubbed "The Scramble for Africa".

It is most notable that not a single African king or chief was invited to this meeting where the continent of Africa was to be carved up like a cake. , The Sultan of Zanzibar would later be ridiculed for seeking to be invited to attend the meeting to represent his and his people's interests.

The Berlin Conference had three main interests:

1) To secure the commercial interests of the industrialized nations present in the room and especially their need for raw materials;

2) To resolve the matter of the Congo Free State that had been established by King Leopold II of Belgium; and

3) To promote the development of the "native peoples".

This last point, I believe, was appended as an afterthought to save face and show that there was some altruistic purpose for the land grabbing and that claiming the lands belonging to African peoples was for the good of the Africans themselves.

The truth, however, is plain. In the eyes of these powers, Africa was seen as a no man's land and up for grabs by whoever could lay claim to it. The sovereignty of the African nations, their kings, chiefs and their peoples was never discussed or even considered as it would be a roadblock to their diabolical schemes. King Leopold of Belgium had, in essence, led the way. As well, his contemporaries in Europe were anxious to establish their replicas. In their view, Africa was a playground for them to send out expeditions and hoist their flags.

The Berlin Conference set in motion actions and decisions that generations of Africans are still dealing with today. The boundaries that were drawn, with states, invented from thin air, forced together peoples from different ethnic groups and separated others. The European colonial system sought to invent African traditions and culture to replicate the feudal systems of their home countries. They created social hierarchies of class and assigned different positions to ethnic groups, pitting one ethnicity against another. Those societies and chiefs that collaborated with the colonialists were rewarded. Those who resisted in an attempt to preserve their freedom were punished.

Mwalimu Julius Nyerere said of the effects of the Berlin Conference, "Artificial nations were carved out by the Berlin Conference and today we are struggling to build these nations into stable units of human society. We are in danger of becoming the most balkanized continent of the world."

After the Berlin Conference, the map of the continent took on the colours of the flags of the colonizing powers, foremost being Britain, France, Belgium, Germany and Portugal.

After World War II, the independence movement gained momentum in Africa, with more Africans agitating and even taking up arms to fight the colonial powers in search of freedom. Slowly, but surely, the flags of the colonial powers were lowered. In their place, national flags were hoisted as nation after nation in Africa became independent. Ghana was the first in 1957 and the most recent country to become independent is South Sudan in 2011. The map of Africa changed drastically from displaying the colours of the colonizers to displaying our national flags.

However, if getting political power from the colonizers was all it took to regain control of our destiny as African peoples, then we should have gained that at the time of independence. Our collective journeys have shown that when you finish dealing with the external enemy you must deal with the internal one too. Our history has shown that each country has had to deal with a complex colonial legacy and that this legacy that pitted brother against brother has deep roots. And problems linger on with Africans faced by multiple problems from multiple directions, both internal and external.

What if the landscape we need to change the most is the one in our hearts and minds and our connection to God, each other and the land that God has given to us? It is a question I have spent many years of my life seeking to answer. By the Grace of God, I have found some of the answers to these questions as I have sought the Lord in my own life. My experience has taught me that as I have been reconnected to my God spiritually; He has restored my identity and my relationship with Him, with others and with my land. Maybe the most important flag is not the one that is hoisted over sovereign states but the one in our hearts. The question of which King rules in our hearts and which spiritual Kingdom we belong to is a fundamental one we must all consider.

The King we serve determines how we serve, lead and love others. The spiritual Kingdom we belong to determines the set of values that we espouse and how we live out those values in our spheres of influence.

Isaiah 9:6-7 declares:

> *"For to us a Child is born, to us a Son is given, and the government shall be upon His shoulders, and His Name shall be called Wonderful Counsellor, Mighty God, Everlasting Father, Prince of Peace. Of the increase of His government and of peace, there shall be no end, upon the throne of David and over his kingdom to establish it and uphold it with justice and with righteousness, from the latter time forth, even forever more. The zeal of the Lord of hosts will perform it." – Amplified Bible*

This scripture speaks of a Kingdom and Government to come in the latter times, whose ruler or King is the Lord Jesus Christ. Isaiah prophesies that the characteristics of this Kingdom are justice and righteousness even as the throne of God is founded on these very principles.

> *"Righteousness and justice are the foundation of Your throne, mercy and loving-kindness and truth go before Your face." – Psalm 84:14*

The Kingdom which the prophet Isaiah is speaking of is not a political entity but rather a spiritual one. It has no geographical boundaries except the boundaries of men's hearts. The Kingdom of God speaks of the spiritual domain where the Lord Jesus Christ reigns as King of kings and Lord of lords. When we accept the Lord Jesus into our hearts as Lord and Saviour, we become citizens in that eternal Kingdom. Our condition as citizens in that Kingdom is characterized in Romans 14:17, "After all the Kingdom of God is not a matter of food and drink, but instead, it is righteousness, peace and joy in the Holy Spirit."

Finally, this Kingdom is characterized by liberty or freedom as shown in 2 Corinthians 3:17, *"Now the Lord is the Spirit and where the Spirit of the Lord is, there is liberty (emancipation from bondage; freedom).*

The Lord Jesus Christ did not come to create a theocracy here on earth. He specifically said before His death that if He had come to create a natural Kingdom, His followers would have fought to keep Him from being arrested. The leaders of the Crusades, the so-called "holy wars" and the Inquisitions that sought to coerce and murder people into the Kingdom were as far away from the Kingdom of God as those they sought to convert. Where the Kingdom truly exists in the lives of God's people, its fruits are clear: liberty, emancipation from bondage, righteousness, justice and peace. Is this not what we all want?

Why have we seen so little of the Kingdom of God demonstrated in the world today? Why did the colonizers, who supposedly espoused the values of the Kingdom, propagate such an evil and diabolical scheme that brought bondage and not freedom to Africa?

That is a big question that I do not believe we can dissect fully in a few paragraphs, but I will share my humble beliefs. The majority of the colonizers were driven not by the Spirit of God but by carnal self-interest. Even many (not necessarily all) of the missionaries who came to "spread the Gospel" saw themselves as servants of their national governments sent out to civilize the "savages" and extend political control to give their home governments more leverage over Africa. I believe that it wasn't truly about souls but about hegemony; and who rules and over how many.

The Kingdoms they sought to propagate were natural ones looking for resources such as gold and other raw materials in the guise of "spreading the gospel." In the process, were there some good things done like the building of schools and hospitals? Yes, but these were a by-product and not the end goal of their purpose of coming to the continent.

Look to the present and ask ourselves how well we, the African Church, have fared since then. I would honestly say, not much better; and for a plethora of reasons.

These are some of the questions and issues I grapple with in this book which I hope will bring a better understanding and establish the context of the present circumstances. However, the book is not about trying to pin blame on one group or another. Rather, it is about us, as the Church in Africa, learning to take responsibility for ourselves and the people and land God has entrusted to our stewardship.

Recently, I read author Eric Metaxas's great account of the life of Martin Luther, the German monk who led the Reformation in Europe. I was struck by many things in the book. The one that struck me most was in the epilogue, where the author, in enumerating the many benefits of the reformation, writes that God used Martin Luther to help the Church in Europe mature. Out of this maturing of the Church came the reformed ideas and mindset that created the new Europe and much of the Western world that we see today. The focus on individual rights for all, more humane treatment of workers, scientific discovery versus superstition, a strong work ethic and much more were a direct result of the reformation of the Church.

The concept of maturity is worth understanding and applying accordingly. Maturity is when people no longer behave like children who need to be scolded or guided by others. Maturity is when we intuitively know the right thing to do and do it consistently, steadily and with little fanfare. Maturity is when we stop pointing the finger at all the world and look inward and draw a line in the sand and say, "from now onwards..."

There have been books and books written about the legacy of our colonial past and slavery, and rightly so. Just like there are books written about the holocaust or the bombing of Hiroshima and Nagasaki during World War II. But it is my humble belief that it is up to the true Church in Africa, those who belong to the Kingdom of the Lord Jesus Christ, to say with quiet conviction, "that was then, but today, the Kingdom of God is here." And through each of us, God can work to reconcile our land and people back to His original purpose and plan. I pray that the Lord helps us to become mature people, a mature Church and a mature Kingdom. It is my firm belief that then and only then can God's perfect redemptive plan and purpose be fulfilled in Africa. Then and only then will we be **Jesus' Africa.**

2. Seeing Africa Through Jesus' Eyes

A garden so green
Where water rains clean
And animals roam without names
And love was a girl
Who walked through the world
And passion was pure as a flame
In the back of our minds
Is a time before time
And a sad irreversible fact
We can't seem to think why we left there
And we can't seem to find our way back

All of us are homesick for Eden
We yearn to return to a land we've never known
Deep is the need to go back to the garden
A burning so strong
For a place we belong
A place that we all know is home

Have you ever just cried
For no reason why
Like a child who's been left on his own?
We can't quite explain
The confusion or pain
So you live with a heartache alone
In the back of your mind
Is a place and a time
And an image of what should have been
And you know you won't be happy

Till you find your way back there again
We were made to live in His perfect love
We were meant to walk in His Grace
And we'll never feel we are home again
Till we see Him face to face

All of us are homesick for Eden
We yearn to return to a land we've never known
Deep is our need
To go back to the garden
A burning so strong
For the place we belong
To rest at His feet
In fellowship sweet
A place that we know is home

Homesick for Eden,

– A song by Paul Smith from the album *Back to Who I Am.* 1989

Why is this book called "Jesus' Africa?"

To answer this question I have to go back a few years to the beginning of my Call from the Lord and the vision God showed me at the founding of Covenant Nations Church.

Between 2005 and 2006, a period of one year, the Lord gave me His vision for Africa. I saw a vision of the continent of Africa and in the beginning, the continent was very dark. Then I heard a Voice say **"out of what was called darkness, will come a great light." The Lord said, "this light will come from within you**."

I then saw someone blowing a trumpet, specifically a ram's horn (*shofar*) and, as the person blew the trumpet, a small light started shining out of Uganda. It initially started as a very small light and then continued to grow brighter and brighter and spread across the whole country until the whole country was filled with bright light. Then the light spread beyond Uganda to the other countries in Africa until the whole continent was filled with brilliant light. Once the entire continent was filled with light, the light continued to grow in strength and intensity and went out to the other nations of the world. The light followed a particular pattern, starting from one small point and then emanating out in concentric circles. Each circle would then shoot light out to another point and wherever that light landed it emanated out from that point. This process continued until the whole world was filled with this beautiful bright light.

I asked the Lord in the vision, "why is the light coming out of Uganda? Is it because I am Ugandan and You are speaking to me?"

The Lord answered, "**No, Uganda is the heart of Africa, and just like a man is changed when his heart is changed, so as Uganda aligns with My redemptive purpose it will have a domino effect in the rest of Africa."**

Finally, I asked the Lord, "Who is that person blowing the trumpet?"

The Lord answered, "**you are the one blowing the trumpet**."

This was the founding vision and word for Covenant Nations Church (CNC). That word has been incubated in CNC all these years since the Lord planted the church. However, I sense that the Lord is releasing this word to the nations of Africa and even to the world during this season.

From the Bible, we see that, just before a time of great deliverance, there would be a counter-attack or a shaking in an effort by the enemy to derail or to stop God's redemptive purpose from being fulfilled on the earth.

Let us look in the Old Testament at the account of Moses who was a great servant of God. God raised Moses to deliver the children of Israel from bondage in Egypt. Moses was born in a time of great persecution of the children of Israel in Egypt. The persecution was executed by a king who did not know Joseph, a man God had used mightily for the preservation of the known world. The new king did not recognize the great things that Joseph had done to preserve Egypt and the people of the world. Instead, the king hatched a demonic scheme to kill all the Hebrew boys born at that time. The king thought that this act would keep the population of the Hebrews small and ensure that they remained weak and subservient to the Egyptians.

Despite the great persecution that arose and the many little Hebrew boys that were killed, God had arranged a way to preserve a Hebrew baby who was going to grow up to become a deliverer. What I find even more amazing in this story is the absolute sovereignty and resourcefulness of God, in that He preserved the boy Moses in the house of his greatest enemy, Pharaoh. God preserved Moses in the house of the man who was killing Hebrew boys in his generation.

Imagine that, for 40 years, it was Pharaoh that fed, clothed, educated and protected Moses, the man God raised to deliver the Hebrews. This shows that God can preserve us even in the face of great danger. God's plan prevailed. The shaking and persecution that arose against God's people were not able to derail or destroy the plan of God. Right on time, as God had prophesied to Abraham 430 years prior, He delivered His people out of bondage.

In the New Testament, the same thing happened on a larger scale in the life of Jesus. At the time that Jesus, the long-awaited Messiah was to be born, the devil put in place an evil plan to kill all the Jewish boys under the age of two. It is the same thing the enemy was anticipating; something great, something big was going to happen. Therefore, the devil tried to truncate the redemptive plan of God for the world.

The enemy could not tell who the Messiah was or to which family the Messiah would be born, but he knew that there was something great about to be realized in the world. A Saviour was to be born, not just for the deliverance of the nation of Israel, but for the world - Salvation was coming to the world. God preserved Jesus the Son of God in the face of great danger and peril. God hid His Son away until the danger and persecution had passed.

These two examples in the Bible show that whenever God is about to release something great on the earth, and especially for the deliverance and salvation of many, there is always a counter-attack. There is always an attack to counter the purposes of God in the world.

However, since God's plan must come to its fulfilment and culmination, He makes a way despite the many machinations of the enemy.

God's purpose can be compared to a freight train that is moving at 100 miles per hour. No matter what you try to put before that train to stop or derail it, the train will keep on moving. The train is moving so fast that you either have to get on the train or get out of its way. As the train heads towards its destination, God's plan must come to its fulfilment and culmination. God has a million ways to preserve, deliver and save His people.

I believe that God's redemptive plan for Africa is being revealed at this time. God has prepared deliverance for His people not only in Africa but also in the world.

Since the year 2020, because of the global pandemic caused by the Covid-19 virus, there has been unprecedented shaking all around the world. The pandemic has redefined how we work, how we educate our children, how we travel and even how we meet to worship God. We have seen great institutions and global brands simply collapse under the uncertainty of these times. Tensions in cities and nations have led to riots, protests and general unrest. Countries around the world have seen a very high loss of life as a result of the Covid-19 pandemic. The health sector across the world has experienced unprecedented strain.

There has been a shaking of all that can be shaken. Despite all this, I believe this shaking is not for our destruction but for our establishment.

Acts 17: 26 says thus:

> *"And He made from one common origin or one source one blood all the nations of men to settle on the face of the earth having definitely determined the allotted periods of time and the fixed boundaries of their habitation their settlements their lands and their abodes so that they should seek God in the hope that they might feel after Him and find Him although He's not far from each one of us."*
> *– Amplified Bible*

This means that God determined ahead of time the boundaries, the lands, the habitations, the settlements and the times that all people and groups would live on the face of the earth. God made, from one common origin, one blood, one source all the human families, nations and ethnic groups.

He made them from one common source and He determined the boundaries of their habitations and the times, the epochs and the eras in which they would live. God did this so that people should seek Him, so that they may find Him since He is not far from each one of us. This means that each nation or ethnic group has a specific redemptive purpose. God determined ahead of time where the Africans, Europeans, Arabs, Asians and the different ethnicities all over the world would live and their specific times and seasons. Why? So that each group would seek Him and find Him. That means that there is a redemptive purpose for each people group, nation, and continent.

Africa's Redemptive Gifts

In this book, we will be looking specifically at Africa because the word that the Lord gave to me is specific to Africa. Let us, therefore, delve a little deeper to study the redemptive gifts of Africa that we can glean from the Bible. Africa and the African people have a very unique place in the Word of God and you only have to read the scriptures to see that Africa plays a pivotal role in the Biblical account.

1. The Gift of Increase

In the book of Genesis 46:1-3, we read the story of Jacob as he is contemplating going down to live in Egypt. Egypt was the global superpower of its time, and the patriarchs and the children of Israel stayed in Egypt at different times and for different reasons. Whether it was during times of famine or brief sojourns the patriarchs and the children of Israel often visited Egypt.

This scripture speaks of a time when Jacob was going to Egypt because of the intense famine in the land of Canaan. Jacob had heard from his sons that Joseph was alive and was the Prime Minister of Egypt. He was going to relocate his whole family from Canaan, the land of God's promise, to Egypt indefinitely. Jacob would eventually die in Egypt. He was well advanced in years and, understandably, apprehensive about what this journey meant for him and the future of his family. He was a bit unsure about whether he should go to Egypt. I believe he sensed that there was something different about this journey he was about to make.

Genesis chapter 46: 1- 3 that:

> *"so Israel made his journey with all that he had and he came to Beersheba and offered sacrifices to the God of his father Isaac and God spoke to Israel in a vision of the night and He said, 'Jacob, Jacob,' and he said, 'here am I,' and He said, 'I am the God of your father, do not be afraid to go down to Egypt for I will there make of you a great nation.'"*
> *– Amplified Bible*

Jacob and his family went to Egypt. They were 70 people in all - a fairly large family but by no means a nation. The seventy people included Jacob himself and the four generations of his sons, grandchildren, great-grandchildren and great-great-grandchildren. Four Hundred years later, this family of seventy people had grown into a nation of millions of people.

There was something supernatural about their sojourn in Egypt. God wanted to accomplish a time of great increase for the people of Israel. In the book of Exodus, it says that they increased, became great in number and their population grew at a higher rate than that of the Egyptians. This unusually high population growth caused the Egyptians to fear them. There was something supernatural about their time in Egypt. There was supernatural empowerment to increase. Population growth is not something that just happens. There have to be certain conditions that are conducive to allowing it to happen. However, even the best environmental conditions, and the passage of time, cannot explain the exponential growth of this family.

God said, "I will make you a great nation there." Genesis 46;3. They went in as a family and they came out as a nation. If you look at any given family tree and go back four generations, you may find that there is consistent and steady growth from the ancestors to the posterity. The children of Israel saw a dramatic growth of their population within four generations that they had not seen in the previous four generations, from Jacob going back to Haran. From the three generations from Jacob to Haran, the family had grown to the size of seventy people. But from the time of Jacob to the time of Moses, the population grew exponentially into the hundreds of thousands and even millions.

Generally speaking, population growth is the difference between the number of people who are born and the number of people who die. If more people are born than those who die, the population growth is positive and vice versa. The population growth of the children of Israel in Egypt was not only positive but it was a steep rise in population.

That rapid population growth is one of the first redemptive gifts of Africa. Why did they have to come to Africa? Why did they have to come to Egypt? Why couldn't this have happened in the Promised Land? They needed to be incubated and to be in an environment where they could increase supernaturally and I believe that's one of the first redemptive gifts that God has bestowed on Africa. Today, the population of Africa is over 1.2 billion people. In addition people of African descent in the diaspora number in the hundreds of millions, therefore God has indeed blessed and increased our population numerically. There is a reason for this and we need to harness the great potential that our youthful population offers to position Africa for growth.

2. A Gift of Wealth

Africa is a place of wealth; it's a place of supply, with a land that is vast and which stretches as far as the 'eye can see'. It is also a land that has mild temperatures and wonderful weather, a land that has large tracts of arable land, forests, mountains, lakes and rivers. It is a land of blessings. It is a land of great supply and people can increase and grow numerically with ease, and that is exactly what happened for the children of Israel.

Africa is also very wealthy in terms of natural resources. It has plenty of minerals like gold, silver, and precious stones like diamonds, tanzanite and metals like iron, bronze and copper. In addition, the land is rich in raw materials such as rubber and timber. The land produces crops such as cotton, coffee, tea, timber, cocoa and much more. All these, and more, were available in Africa in such large quantities that the citizens of Egypt were clothed with them. The citizens of Egypt were wealthy and it was this very wealth that God planned to transfer to Israel on the night of the Passover.

After the 400 years of bondage in Israel had elapsed, God started orchestrating events to raise Moses as the deliverer of His people. After 40 years in the wilderness, at the age of eighty, God called and commissioned Moses to go and deliver His people from the hand of Pharaoh.

God spoke to Moses ahead of time and told him what would happen:

> *"So I will stretch out my hand and I will smite Egypt with all my wonders which I will do in it; and after that he will let you go. And I will give these people favour and respect in the sight of the Egyptians; and it shall be that when you go, you shall not go out empty-handed. But every woman shall solicit of her neighbour and of her that may be residing at her house jewels and articles of silver and gold, and garments*

which you shall put on your sons and daughters; and you shall strip the Egyptians (of the belongings due to you)." – Amplified Bible

In speaking to Moses, God promises to transfer the wealth of Egypt to the children of Israel. Note that there was great wealth in Egypt. We don't see this level of wealth in the land of Canaan. God had placed a great deposit of wealth in Africa to build His Kingdom. God prophesied 400 years earlier that He would transfer wealth to His people and bring them out with great possessions.

How did He know there was great wealth in Egypt? He was the One who put the wealth there for His purposes. He put the wealth there and He could transfer it out of Egypt when He needed to.

In my opinion, Africa is God's bank account, His storehouse. From African history, it is clear that much of the gold that is covering buildings in the capitals of Europe was mined in Africa. The jewels that adorn the crowns of the kings and queens of Europe were mined in Africa. God deposited great wealth in Africa.

Our primary products such as cotton, coffee and tea are the raw materials that fuel the industries of the world. The cotton that we grow makes the garments that clothe the world. Therefore, the same resources that existed in Biblical times are there today. In the book of Exodus 25: 1-9, we see God calling the children of Israel to give generously for the building of the first Tabernacle. Earlier, we noted how there was a wealth transfer and a lot of material resources went into the hands of God's people in order for them to build the Tabernacle.

God showed Moses the pattern of the Tabernacle on Mount Sinai and all the materials that they needed to build the Tabernacle were going to come as offerings from the people. These offerings were material resources that they obtained in Egypt. God instructed Moses to speak to the children of Israel and take an offering from every man who gave it willingly and ungrudgingly:

"with his heart, he shall take an offering. This is the offering that you shall receive from them gold, silver, bronze, blue, purple, scarlet, Rams skin, dolphins skin oil for the light stones, precious stones for the breastplate." Exodus 25:1-7; – *Amplified Bible.*

I believe that God blessed Africa with wealth for the purpose of building His Kingdom. God has placed great wealth in Africa not for misuse, abuse, corruption or self-aggrandizement, but rather for the building of His kingdom. As such, when we have a paradigm shift in our thinking we shall begin to tap into this redemptive gift of using the vast resources that God has given to Africa for the building of His kingdom in the earth.

3. Strategic Leadership

The third redemptive gift that we discover as we look at Africa through the Bible lens is the Gift of Strategic leadership. We need to reiterate that the name "Africa" was not in use until the time of the Roman Empire. In the Bible, the continent of Africa is called many names including Egypt, Ethiopia, Cush, Put, and Cyrene.

In Genesis 41, we read the account of Joseph and his interaction with Pharaoh, the king of Egypt. Pharaoh had two dreams that he couldn't understand. He sent for all his wise men and told them the dream to see if they could interpret it for him but they all failed. Finally, the cupbearer remembered how Joseph correctly interpreted his dream while he was still in prison and mentioned this to Pharoah. Joseph was hastily summoned to come before Pharaoh to hear his dream.

What is interesting about this story is that it shows the power of a strategic relationship between the spiritual and the natural authority. Joseph represented spiritual authority or the wisdom which comes from the Spirit of God, while Pharaoh represented political authority. The two working together brought a strategic partnership which we rarely see replicated in the world today.

Sadly, today, Christians compartmentalize life into the spiritual vs the natural world and yet I believe God intended that the spiritual realm should provide and give unique wisdom and insight into the natural realm.

God gave Pharaoh the dream, but Pharaoh didn't understand the dream. He needed somebody who had the Spirit of God in him to interpret the dream. Why didn't God just give the dream to Joseph? I believe that God didn't simply give the dream to Joseph because He envisaged a partnership between the political leadership, which Pharaoh represented and the spiritual leadership which Joseph represented, working together for the transformation of the nation. This unique dynamic between the two bases of authority unlocked great breakthroughs and innovations for Egypt and the world. This was the first time that the Bible highlighted that kind of strategic leadership. I believe that it is a blueprint for transformational leadership for the world in order for us to tap into the strengths and anointing of both realms.

In the life of Joseph, God gave a picture of strategic leadership where spiritual and natural leadership work hand-in-hand instead of against each other for the good of the nation. There needs to be strategic leadership of the spiritual and the natural to see the blessing of Africa unlocked on a large scale. At the time, strategic leadership preserved the known world when famine was very severe and all the people came to buy food from Egypt. Egypt became the storehouse of the world, something that was only possible because of the strategic leadership that Joseph brought to Pharaoh.

Today, Africa is experiencing a spiritual revival. Everywhere you visit the continent, you will find a vibrant and growing Church walking in the power of the Holy Spirit. However, I believe that God is pouring out His Spirit not only for spiritual awakening and salvation but more so for the reformation of our nations. I believe that, as more Christians awaken to this truth, they will begin to apply the unique wisdom and gifts of the Holy Spirit within them to interpret and solve the complex problems our societies face.

4. The Gift of Being a Store House

With the unique strategic leadership exhibited by Joseph and Pharaoh, a blessing was released that averted what would have been a catastrophe for the world. At the time, Egypt was the only place in the world that had food. All the nations came to Egypt looking to buy food during the seven lean years. I am amazed that God prepared Joseph all those years to deal with essentially a problem of food security. His main life's work was to administer food and thus preserve the world.

In modern times, I see a large number of well-meaning international organizations that are grappling with some of the complex problems of society. I wonder why the problems are never fully dealt with and resolved once and for all. With all our technological advancements in the world in the areas of science, agriculture, irrigation and so on, why is it that the problems of hunger and famine are not solved completely? It seems to me that the vision of the agencies is to merely alleviate or lessen the pain but never to solve the problem. Joseph used the wisdom of God to manage the food supply and store food during the good years so that there would be a plentiful supply in the lean years. It seems almost too simple! However, I find that truth is profoundly simple; it is lies that are complicated. I believe that God is speaking to Africa in our times. In many nations in Africa, we have bumper harvests, adequate seasonal rain and fertile soils, but are we implementing a strategic vision or are we simply eating tomorrow's food today? Are we implementing a higher vision to produce enough food to be a storehouse for our region and the nations of the world?

I believe that part of Africa's redemptive purpose is not just for producing food but other resources as well. We have so much water and such a wealth of natural resources but we need a strategic vision, insight and the wisdom of God to begin to unlock the redemptive gifts of Africa. Food security, to be a storehouse for the world, was something that God used Africa to do in the past and I believe that God is calling Africa to again fulfill this purpose in our times.

5. The Gift of Prayer and Intercession

The fifth redemptive gift that I believe we possess in Africa is the gift of prayer and intercession. I have been in prayer meetings around the world where many people from different nations gather. I always find it interesting that believers from other parts of the world talk about the prayer and intercession of Africans. They often speak about how Africa leads the world in the area of prayer and intercession. When Africans pray, they generally tend to experience more perseverance, travail and depth in prayer and intercession. It is routine for African Christians to spend many hours a week in overnight prayer coupled with fasting. If you have ever visited the prayer mountain in Uganda, it is not uncommon to see people praying and fasting for days or weeks with seeming ease and they possess grace enabling them to do that. There is a sense of being anointed or empowered to pray and intercede for others.

Genesis 44: 15- 34 gives the account of the family of Jacob being ripped apart by jealousy. Jacob's seven sons plotted to kill their brother, Joseph. This was due to intense jealousy and rivalry among the brothers. The origin of the problems was that Jacob's two wives were sisters and they both competed for the love and affection of their husband. In addition to polygamy, this family had other issues such as jealousy, sibling rivalry, mistrust and mistreatment by in-laws among other things, yet this was the family that was in covenant with God.

In the grip of jealousy, Joseph's brothers sold him into slavery in Egypt and then lied to their father that he was killed by a wild animal. Meanwhile, Joseph was taken as a slave to Egypt and endured great hardship and injustice for years, but God was with him. Finally, God raised him to be the Prime Minister of Egypt. As fate would have it, a severe famine hit the land of Canaan. The brothers were sent by their father, Jacob, to buy food in Egypt where they come face to face with their long-lost brother. Joseph immediately recognized his brothers, although they never imagined that the brother they sold into servitude was now the second most powerful man in Egypt. To test whether his brothers had changed or were still the same selfish and hateful men who sold him into slavery, Joseph devised a clever plan.

He instructed his servants to put his cup into Benjamin's sack which meant that Benjamin was going to become Joseph's slave. What happened in this emotionally charged moment is something amazing. This family that had experienced so much pain and loss of the family relationship, suddenly came full circle. Judah stepped forward representing the firstborn of the family and interceded on behalf of Benjamin's life. Here is what it says in Genesis 44:33

> *"Now therefore, I pray you, let your servant remain instead of the youth a slave to my lord, and let the young man go home with his brothers. When he sees that the lad is not with us, he will die; and your servants will be responsible for his death and will bring down the gray hairs of your servant our father with sorrow to Shoel."* – *Amplified Bible*

This is a very powerful portrayal of what true intercession means. It is not rote words or mechanical repetition. It is far from a mere religious observance. Judah's is a deeply emotional act; standing in the place of another and crying out for God's mercy. He stood and interceded for his brother Benjamin. He actively took his place and asked for the punishment that was Benjamin's to be placed on him. Recall that this was a family that had previously worked very hard to see the death of their brother, Joseph, whom God preserved. But now there was a complete transformation in the family. They had come full circle and recognized after years of pain the role of the family. Now the role of these brothers was to pray - interceding for one another. This intercession or stepping in to take the place of his brother, is what broke the long-standing schism in the family. It finally brought repentance, tears, restoration and the revelation that Joseph was alive! It took a higher level of intercession to restore the family.

I believe that, through Africa, God wants to unlock a higher level of intercession for the restoration of families, marriages, cities and nations. There is something unique that God has placed in Africans to lead in prayer and intercession that goes into a deeper dimension and that brings breakthrough and restoration.

6. A Place of Refuge

Africa and Africans appear all over the Bible, both in the Old and the New Testaments. Through this chapter, we are taking a journey to look at our continent through Biblical lenses and to learn what gifts the Lord has embedded in our spiritual DNA as Africans. One of them, I believe, is to be a place of refuge.

In Jeremiah 42: 14 -19 God spoke to the children of Israel who had fallen into sin and warned of the judgment that was to come. In those days, Egypt represented a place of safety and refuge from the horrors of war and privation. Often, God chastised the children of Israel and told them not to put their hope or trust in Egypt. Why? Because Egypt represented a place of stability, refuge, economic provision and supply. Many times, the children of Israel relied on Egypt to be their protection and safety in hard times.

In this account, God through the prophet Jeremiah instructed the children of Israel to go to Babylon and submit to exile and the Babylonian king. However, the children of Israel wanted to go to Egypt because Egypt represented a place of plenty, refuge and safety. Egypt also represented a place in which they put their confidence and trust. However, God warned them saying, "don't go down to Egypt." Why? Because He didn't want them to put their confidence in another nation or system; He wanted them to put their trust in Him alone.

I have learnt over time that the enemy will often attack us at our place of blessing or even at our place of destiny. That means the very thing we are meant to be is where we experience the greatest attacks from the enemy. Even though the devil loves to cast himself in the character of the anti-God or opposite of God, the truth is that the devil is nowhere near God. God is the Creator of all things, and the devil is a created being, a fallen archangel in the league of Michael and Gabriel. That being said, the devil cannot simply create new things; all he can do is work to pervert what God has already created.

We see redemptive gifts in Africa, whether it is increase, wealth, strategic leadership, food security, or using our resources for the building of the kingdom and being a place of refuge. In each of those gifts, the enemy has worked hard to pervert that gift into a counterfeit.

It is sad to say that the conditions we see in much of Africa are counterfeit to the true redemptive purpose of God. For instance, instead of food security, we see famine or hunger in many nations even when those nations are well endowed in terms of arable land and rainfall. The economic resources that God blessed Africa with have for centuries been siphoned off through all kinds of diabolical arrangements whether it is colonialism, neo-colonialism or unfair trade practices and corruption. Strategic leadership is something that is perverted many times, even though many nations talk about good governance. I believe that the redemptive purpose of Africa is to show the world what strategic leadership looks like. Instead, Africa has struggled in the area of leadership for decades so much so that poor governance and lack of servant leadership have been some of the great obstacles in our path to development. As a result, the world keeps giving African nations condescending lectures about what form of government they must adopt. That is a perversion because, according to the Bible, it is Africa that has the redemptive gift to be able to reveal and teach something new that unlocks the blessing of God on the earth.

Africa, instead of being a place of refuge for many people, sadly supplies a disproportionate number of refugees to the world. Whether it is people who are going on boats or planes. How do we correct the problem? Well without going into details, I believe that we need to have a paradigm shift. If the Bible is our foundation, then let us return to our roots as Africans. Let us choose to believe what God's Word says about us as opposed to what the world says about us. If we believe God's Word to be true then let us begin to act in line with what we believe and rise to the level of our beliefs rather than settling for the low expectations of those who have a vested interest in keeping Africa down.

How do you tell whether something is counterfeit? The easiest way to tell whether something is counterfeit is to bring the original or genuine artifact. There is a way that the original looks as opposed to something that is a replica or that is fake. I believe that the only way that you can reveal what is a counterfeit or what is a perversion is to go to the original.

If we use the example of Africa being a place of refuge as opposed to an exporter of refugees; I have a personal experience with this since I have experienced both being a refugee and welcoming refugees into my country. I was born in exile in Tanzania when my father was involved in the struggle for liberation in Uganda and I spent my formative years in exile. When the war ended and my family returned home the nation embarked on the reconstruction of a country that had been devastated by decades of civil war. As Uganda stabilized, some countries in our region experienced political instability such as Rwanda, Burundi, the Democratic Republic of Congo and South Sudan. Uganda opened her arms to receive hundreds of thousands of refugees who were fleeing instability at home and today Uganda is home to about one million refugees from the region. These refugees can find refuge and rebuild their lives from the devastation and ravages of war and instability. In 2021, when the United States chaotically withdrew their armed forces from Afghanistan, many civilians were left exposed to danger especially those who had worked closely with the Americans. The U.S. government asked Uganda to temporarily host a few thousand Afghani families because of the track record that we have for welcoming refugees. I was very proud to see that God had turned around our story so that we who had once been refugees were now giving refuge to those who desperately needed it. I believe that because of God's redeeming work in Uganda, we are seeing our nation begin to walk in her redemptive purpose. I believe the same can happen for the entire African continent if we will partner with God to see our nations align with God's purposes.

The Uganda Youth Forum

As a teenager, I was blessed to attend the youth conferences that were organized by Mama Janet Museveni in the 1990s when HIV/AIDS ravaged our land. At the time, the HIV infection rate was at its peak in Uganda. Many of my generation attended the conferences which were organized under the banner of the Uganda Youth Forum. The main purpose of the conference was to teach and empower young people to make better choices in the area of sexual purity. However, what was interesting is that they did not spend a lot of time talking about HIV, AIDS, and sexually transmitted diseases. Nor did they dwell much on religious dos and don'ts. Instead, the conferences focused on teaching young people about their identity in Christ. They put a lot of focus on sharing the great plan that God has for us, the good future that He was preparing for us. They painted a portrait of an amazing life that God wanted to give us only if we are obedient and made a commitment to follow His path. Only then would we be able to reap the tremendous blessings in the future for example by not engaging in premarital sex and waiting until we were married.

This message resonated with many young people and as a result, they were able to make decisions that forever impacted their lives. Why? Because when you show someone the original (the truth), they can reject counterfeits, perversions, and what they are not.

I believe that the enemy has for so long tried to convince Africans that the counterfeit is who we are. The world has coined specific terms to describe Africa such as poor, developing, emerging markets, underdeveloped and so on. We are grouped into clubs of the rich vs. the poor, the haves vs. the have-nots. Depending on which category you fall in, there is a certain status quo that you are told to accept. And this message is constantly reinforced by international agencies such as the UN, World Bank, IMF and others. It is similar to giving a person a straight jacket and asking them to get comfortable with it. I reject the standard that the world has set for Africa and I refuse to have my boundaries set by the very same people that have a vested interest in keeping that status quo intact.

The Bible speaks of God's original intent, His purpose from the foundation of the world. As we study the Biblical account, we try to paint a picture of Africa through Jesus' eyes. Through the eyes of the Lord, Africa is a place of incredible beauty, wealth, leadership, productivity, growth, material supply and spiritual authority. This is the original; this is who we are according to God's plan.

Therefore this perversion, this counterfeit, that the enemy keeps trying to ram down our throats is a lie and must be rejected as such. I believe that at this time there is a shaking that is going on around the world. The true redemptive plan of God for Africa is being revealed. I believe that God is going to continue to reveal that Africa is a big player in God's end-time Redemptive plan. To fully align with this plan, we have to become aware of who we are first of all; our identity in Christ, the redemptive plan of God and be busy in the work of reformation in these last days.

Prayer

Heavenly Father I want to thank You for Your Word. I especially want to thank you for the times in which we are living. It is a time of great shifting. There are things that You are moving and changing and there are structures that are falling and there are new structures that are rising.

Heavenly Father I pray that in this season You will remove the scales from our eyes and help us to see ourselves through Your eyes. I pray for the light that You prophesied that is going to come out of Uganda. The light that You showed us so many years ago and that light is going to come out of Uganda and go out into Africa and the world. You said that out of what was called darkness would come a great light. Out of that place that was despised, overlooked, denigrated and exploited, out of that place would come a great Light. Heavenly Father, let Your light begin to shine. I pray that as this word goes forth, Lord let Your light shine, let us begin to see as You see. Let us begin to connect with our true identity and may You unlock the redemptive purposes in all of us and all of our nations so that Your kingdom purposes may be established. In Jesus' mighty name, Amen.

3. A Voice in the Wind

"Here I am! I stand at the door and knock. If anyone hears My Voice and opens the door, I will come in and eat with that person, and they with Me." - Revelations 3:20; – Amplified Bible.

I encountered the Lord Jesus Christ personally when I was eleven years old. At the time, I was in Primary Five. On my way home from school one day, I had a simple but profound encounter with Jesus. Up until then, I had a nominal understanding of God and faith. My mother had given her life to the Lord a few years earlier. Her conversion was dramatic and impacted our family life deeply. Most nights, we would pray and sing hymns as a family. There was the real knowledge that God was a part of our daily life. My mother prayed about every detail of our lives, and the reality that she relied on and waited on the Lord for His answers to prayer was evident to us all. I recall my mother listening to worship music routinely. Most mornings and evenings we heard Integrity and Hosanna's worship music playing in her room.

All this time, God was around me but not in my heart. I had never surrendered my life to Him; people often mistake coming from a Christian family for being a Christian yourself. The Lord was very clear even to the Jews that they shouldn't put their hope in being "the children of Abraham", saying that the LORD could raise descendants of Abraham from the stones. God has no "grandchildren," only sons and daughters and therefore coming from a Christian family, or having parents who are believers, doesn't in any way guarantee us eternal life in Heaven. God desires to have a personal relationship with all of us and He invites us all to become His children.

That day in November 1989 started like any other day at Kampala Parents School, the school I and my sister attended in Kampala. Each day we had to wake up at the crack of dawn to make the long journey to Kampala to go to school.

That day, I went to school with my younger sister Diana, as usual. After a long day at school, we got in the car to make the 45-minute journey home to Entebbe. School days were long and gruelling. During the car ride home, if Diana and I weren't talking or listening to music on the car radio, we often just nodded off for a brief nap.

On that fateful day, Diana had fallen asleep in the car. As for me, I sat looking out the window, my mind wandering and not thinking about anything in particular. In the silence of that moment, I heard a Voice, a still small Voice.

The Voice said, "**Follow Me**." I looked around me for the source of this unusual voice. My sister was still sleeping peacefully beside me and all else in the car was unchanged. The driver was looking at the road straight ahead and so was the soldier who was sitting in the front passenger seat. All was quiet and still, but I knew I had heard something.

I looked out the window again, but this time cautiously and holding my breath. Again I heard that Voice, "**Follow Me.**"

I held my breath! There it was again, a Voice I couldn't hear audibly, but distinctly heard in my heart. I looked up through the open roof of the car at the sky and clouds as they passed by. I saw nothing unusual!

"Who are You?" I asked in my heart.

The Voice answered me saying He was the Lord Jesus and He wanted me to follow Him for the rest of my life. He said He would be My Friend and lead me on the right path all my days.

Even though I was quite young, I completely understood what the Voice was telling me. It was clear what I needed to do.

I looked up again at the clouds rolling by through the open car roof and I answered in a whisper, "I will follow You, Jesus..."

That was all I said and, immediately, my heart flooded with peace and joy. It was a joy and peace that was unexplainable.

There I was sitting in the same position I usually sat in the same car I usually rode in, but something profound had taken place. I felt a Presence come into my heart that I had never experienced before. He was in my heart and I felt so much joy!

When we got home, I emerged from the car as a new creation, although I didn't fully understand what had just transpired.

From that day onwards, my life was radically transformed. The only way I can describe it in my child's mind is that I found a Friend in Jesus. Jesus was so real to me and our friendship was and still is more real than the chair I am sitting on as I write this chapter. My love for Jesus grew as I got to know Him and experience Him every day. I loved spending time alone in His Presence.

Often after school, I would run to a quiet room so I could talk to Jesus and share with Him everything that I had faced that day. I spent hours on the floor worshiping and praising Him. In these times He would speak to me and guide me on everyday matters of my life. As a child, most of my concerns had to do with school, friends, and everyday struggles that children usually experience. What I find amazing now, as I look back on those precious early days, is that I never got the impression that the Lord was simply indulging me or listening to me in the condescending way that adults sometimes listen to children. When I was in His Presence, I felt that I was the only person in the world and He listened to all my endless ramblings, fears and prayers. He listened with interest and with so much love, and He always answered me.

That same year, the evangelist Daisy Osborn visited Uganda for a crusade with her husband T. L. Osborn. After the crusade, Daisy Osborn came to visit my mother and pray with her for our family and the nation. After visiting us, she gave my siblings and me each a gift of a Bible and a music tape or cassette as they were called then. She gave us all gifts of music tapes from contemporary Christian artists; Carmen for my older brother Muhoozi, Twila Paris for my older sister Natasha, Amy Grant for me and Sandy Patty for my younger sister Diana.

So now that I had my very own Bible, I read it voraciously. It was as though I had an insatiable hunger that only grew as I delved deeper into the Word. The more I knew the Lord, the more He satisfied my soul; and the more He satisfied me, the more I hungered for Him. Reading the Bible became like food for my soul and oxygen to my spirit. If I missed my daily reading or devotional time, I would feel the effect on my mood. I would feel vulnerable and irritable as though I wasn't properly prepared for the day. When I had time with the Lord, I felt like I was wearing impenetrable armour, and that nothing could come against me.

"But what does someone so young have to pray about or worry about?" one may ask.

The truth is my prayers were concerned with childish things that confront all children of that age. However, it gave me a foundation for experiencing God. As I prayed, He answered; and the more I prayed, the more I got to know God for myself. I experienced Him, I knew Him by experience.

What was I praying for? Oh that I would pass my Primary leaving exams and get accepted into the secondary school I wanted to attend. I prayed that my house would win the sports competition or the drama competition. I prayed for my friends and shared all the ups and downs of my friendships.

Looking back, it all seems very childish and silly, and yet the most amazing thing was that the God of the Universe, the Ancient of Days, not only listened, and paid attention, but He answered me with His characteristic style, flair and power!

I remember one time when I was in primary school, I was praying desperately that our House would win the drama competition at the end of the term. I participated in some songs and dances, but the competition was quite stiff from the other three houses. Our colour was green and our house mascot was an elephant. The other three houses' colours were blue, yellow and red, and each with its animal mascot. After the performances by each house, all of us children left the assembly area to allow the judges time to make a decision.

I remember vividly that I climbed the stairs to the top floor of one of the classroom blocks. I stood by the stair rail dressed in my green shirt, blue shorts and knee-high socks, looking anxiously towards the assembly hall where the judges were still deliberating.

I remember praying to God to help our House win against all the odds. Again I heard that still small Voice. He said, **"I will show you a sign."** Immediately I saw a flock of white birds called egrets rising above the school buildings and flying in the clear blue sky above me. As I was looking with amazement at the birds with their white wings reflecting the afternoon sun, I heard an uproar of cheers and applause coming from the students in the assembly hall. A few moments later, I saw my fellow green housemates running out of the hall, jumping, whooping and cheering! Our house won the tournament that year and went on to win again for many years after that.

The reason I remember that experience to this day is not because our house won the competition. Indeed by God's Grace, I have won greater awards than a house musical competition. I remember that experience because the eternal God entered into that moment in time to meet me at my point of need, to hear, to answer and to personally set His seal of approval on something that I needed.

Since that day, whenever I see a flock of white egrets flying, I know it is His secret sign to me saying, **"I see you, I hear you, I love you."**

Over the years, God has spoken to me countless times, but always in His characteristic still small Voice.

Fast forward a few years later when I was preparing to do my Ordinary Level Certificate examinations at Mt. St. Mary's Namagunga. The LORD again led me by His Voice during that stressful season. Any student who has gone through the Ugandan educational system knows that great emphasis is placed on passing certain examinations to carry you to the next level of your educational journey - starting from the Primary Leaving Certificate (PLE), the Uganda Certificate of Education (UCE), and the Uganda Advanced Certificate of

Education (UACE). All these are the gatekeepers of education in our nation and passing the exams is an important rite of passage for students. Recently there have been many reforms taking place in the educational sector and also more options for parents and students as they look for the right fit for their children's learning styles. However, in 1995 when I was in Senior 4 there was one track and so the pressure to ace the examinations was on.

I always enjoyed school and learning, but I was never the kind of student who would wake up at 4 am and read by candlelight; nor would I manage to sit outside in the cold to read by the veranda light or put my feet in cold water to stay awake at night to read. I watched many of my fellow candidates do this and many other things to get that additional study time apart from the regular study times of class and prep.

Since I wasn't cut out to study that way, and it seemed that was the necessary price to pay to succeed in "Cantab" as we called the examinations, I was very worried about my chances of passing my examinations. The Lord spoke to me about this and told me to not compare myself to my classmates who were going that route. He encouraged me to put my "blinkers" or "blinders" on, so to speak, and focus on the path that He had for me and not worry about the rest. Blinkers/blinders are used for racehorses to keep them focused on the path ahead of them and to prevent them from getting distracted by the horses running in the lanes beside them. The racehorse trainers know that when the competition is between the horse and the track and not the horse and other horses, the horse stands a better chance to run its race and win. So God told me in essence, "Stop looking at your classmates, run your race, do it your way, the way that works for you."

What did that mean for me? Well, it meant I woke up and spent my normal time in prayer before getting ready for breakfast and class. I attended my classes and studied after class and during prep time. But after prep, I rested and slept until early the next morning. On weekends I studied in two-hour periods taking a break after the two hours. In the evening, I would take time off to do something that helped me relax like listening to music or reading something simply for pleasure. I loved reading about the history of Israel and following military heroes like Moshe Dayan, David Ben Gurion and Benjamin Netanyahu. So in my spare time, I read books I liked before switching back to studying. On Sundays I rested and had a lighter load, taking more time to praise and worship God, and spending time listening to my music just to refresh my spirit. Then I would revert to my study time again for the rest of the day. This regimen worked for me and gave me a kind of pace or cadence that didn't overwhelm me or cause burnout.

As the dreaded examinations drew near, the pressure intensified, and this was evident by the proliferation of discussion groups or circles that would congregate in different areas around the school such as the crack circle (study circle), lower field, upper field, dormitory verandas and any other patch of green around the school. In these study circles, there were always the very annoying girls who seemed to enjoy causing alarm to other students by letting us know the questions that might come in the examinations. They would hear one word mentioned in one circle and go find another group and say, "Oh my gosh have you guys revised titration or Ghana or the St. Lawrence Seaway, these guys are saying they might ask about it in the examinations." To which the listeners would scramble to open their books and textbooks to go over what the girl had said "might come" in the examinations. The said girl would then proceed to another group to spread alarm and dismay in another group and so on. All this served to do was to heighten an already stressful situation. In essence, the girls would not study because they were full of anxiety about what they felt they hadn't studied and the amount of time they had to cover all the material.

Again here the LORD spoke to me clearly and said, "**stay away from the study circles, study by yourself, or with one or two people who share your perspective.**"

For the entire time I prepared for my examinations, I studied alone or with my best friend Nukuri, who understood my study style and we were able to have a flowing routine together without causing each other anxiety. She too detested the fear and anxiety that ruled some of the study circles and had a rhythm more similar to my own.

As we started writing the examinations, the Lord spoke to me again He said, **"always be the last to enter the examination hall and stand a good distance away from the last person so you cannot hear what they are saying."** The Lord led me this way because, even at that point, certain students would use the last minutes before the examination started to cause anxiety and bring stress to other students by asking them answers to questions right before going into the examination room. So for the whole examination period, I always kept to the back of the line. I was the last one to enter the examination room and so I never heard any of the conversations shared by other students before we entered the hall.

Finally, the Lord spoke to me about focusing my mind on Him before every exam, He said I "should fix my mind on Him and He by His Spirit would bring all things to my remembrance." I learnt how to practice focusing my mind on Him and, by the time I entered the examination room, I was in the Presence of the LORD. Writing the examinations was a peaceful, joyful and calm experience because the Lord's Presence surrounded me. Every time I came out of a room, I knew He was with me; His Presence was so real to me.

God carried me through the weeks of examinations on His eagle's wings. At the end of it, He spoke again. He said, **"Now cast this care on me. Surrender it to Me and do not try to carry it by worrying about the results of your examinations."**

I learnt then that when you have completed something with the Lord, it is wrong to continue worrying about it because you have been walking by faith and He wants you to roll the complete care of it on Him. So after finishing writing my examinations, I rolled the care of it on the Lord and never worried about how I would perform. I left it in His hands and was in complete peace. We had a wonderful farewell dance from school and there was the euphoria of being free of the gruelling school schedule of studying and writing examinations after four long years! My long vacation, or "vac" as we called it, was absolutely amazing; I enjoyed every minute of it.

One afternoon, my father came home early from his office. As I went to greet him, I saw that his face was beaming with the biggest smile I had ever seen. He started giving me the thumbs-up sign with both of his hands raised. I didn't understand what he meant. When he reached the top of the stairs, he said he had to carry me on his back and started doing it! I laughingly asked him what was going on. He insisted on carrying me on his back.

After the laughter and joy of that moment, and as other family members gathered on the landing of the steps wondering what the commotion was about, my father finally showed us what he was carrying in his hands. He opened the national newspaper that had a list of the 50 best-performing students in the country in the Uganda Certificate of Education (UCE). He pointed to my name as being among the best-performing students in the country; I had the second-highest grade in my school.

I was completely blown away! As we all hugged and cried tears of joy and thanksgiving, I remembered my Father, my Heavenly Father! He had carried me on His eagle's wings; He had walked with me every step of the way. He had taken the girl who didn't wake up at 4 am, the girl who didn't put her feet in a basin of cold water all night and taught me how to study and put my blinkers on and run my race with joy. My Heavenly Father taught me how to be "me" in the area of my education, to find my path, and to follow Him. The victory was beyond what I could have ever hoped for or dreamed of; it belonged to Him, and I knew He did it! He led me as always with His gentle, still small Voice.

It has been many years since I first heard that still small

Voice; it has been the greatest power and influence over my life. That Voice has guided me on the right path as He promised, He has helped me avert disastrous choices and decisions and has encouraged, edified, corrected and inspired me. All through, that Voice has spoken to me about my own life, my family's, and strangers. He has spoken to me about marriage, raising children, running a business and His purpose for cities and nations. That Voice and the LORD behind it are the Guiding force of my life and He has never failed or led me the wrong way. I bless the day that I first heard His Voice calling me in the wind.

4. Africa the Bookend of Biblical History

"Revival isn't a spectacular event in the clouds. It's in your own life. Revival doesn't require big meetings with famous speakers. Revival begins with you." – Festo Kivengere.

I came of age in the 1990s and, like anyone who comes of age in a particular era or a decade, you always feel that those were the best of times or the "good old days." The 1990s were truly interesting times and I believe that some of the best music and the best movies that we have were made during that time. One of the great movies made in the 1990s that helped to awaken the political or black consciousness of that generation was titled *Malcolm X*[1], starring Denzel Washington, a role he played to critical acclaim. He did it very well and many young people, especially many Africans and African Americans identified with him and were immensely impacted by that movie.

I enjoyed it. However, I only had one problem with the movie.

Many are familiar with the story of Malcolm X. He was one of the civil rights leaders in the 1960s in the United States of America. He converted to Islam after being imprisoned in the very racist system in the South. While he was in prison he received a revelation, an epiphany and as a result, he converted to Islam and started following the teachings of the Nation of Islam under the leadership of Elijah Muhammad. Today the Nation of Islam is led by Louis Farrakhan. In the movie, Islam is depicted as the natural choice for African-Americans because of the unity, acceptance and universal brotherhood that Islam purportedly gave to its followers.

Christianity was depicted as something to be rejected as the "religion of the oppressor." One part of the movie that was quite funny was where Malcolm X gets into an argument with

1 *Malcolm X* 1992 film directed by Spike Lee and Martin Worth starring Denzel Washington.

a chaplain in prison who tries to convince him that Jesus Christ was "of course white with blond hair and blue eyes." He showed Malcolm X a picture of "Jesus" that was hanging on the wall of the prison, where Jesus was depicted as a white person.

That posed a dilemma for me. I agreed with the premise of the movie and many of the writings and teachings of Malcolm X and other Civil rights leaders and the Black Consciousness Movement, especially concerning the unconscionable treatment of blacks in America. However, I fundamentally disagreed with the view that there is a natural religion for Africans or that Christianity represented the "religion of the oppressors" and thus must be rejected wholesale. To be clear there has been great evil perpetrated in the name of Christianity and God. From the Crusades, and the Spanish Inquisition to slavery and even Colonialism. I am not discounting the fact that there has been great evil done in the name of Christianity and the name of God. Jesus even prophesied, in John 16:2," They will put you out of the synagogues *and* make you outcasts. And a time is coming when whoever kills you will think that he is offering service to God."

The great failures of 'religious' people, in the name of God, do not replace the foundation of our faith which is the Person of Jesus Christ. Christianity is not a religion *per se*. It is a kingdom and the state of being of the people in that kingdom is righteousness, peace and joy in the Holy Ghost. (Romans 14:17) Jesus did not come to bring religion to the world; He came to bring us into a right relationship with God. When He came preaching, He said in Matthew 4:17, "Repent for the kingdom of God is at hand." Jesus came to establish a kingdom and to make us sons and daughters of God. He came to give us access to the Kingdom of God.

The Bible declares in 1 John 3:1, *"Behold what manner of love the Father has given to us that we should be called the sons of God."* That is what Jesus came to give us. He came to give us the right relationship with our Heavenly Father, God.

Therefore if people are practicing unrighteousness, Jesus said, "you will know them by their fruits."(Matthew 7:16) It is not by what they say, what their culture is, how they dress and what language they speak; something that could be termed "cultural Christianity." But Jesus said you will know true believers by what they do. What are their fruits? Is it righteous? Is it peaceful? Is it joyful?

Therefore people who are practicing unrighteousness are not part of the kingdom that Jesus came to bring. They are not doing the will of God no matter what "religion" they claim to follow. The question is: should Africans reject a relationship with Jesus because Christianity is the "religion of the oppressor" that came with the colonizers or the missionaries or the slave traders? The only way we can answer that is by looking at what the Bible says. Many people have different opinions including the generation that liberated Africa from colonialism; the independence generation of the 1950s and 60s. Some of those great leaders had the same opinion and the same point of view that "since Christianity was the religion of the Western countries which colonized Africa, therefore, it was a religion of the oppressors that should be rejected as such."

Africans who aligned with this belief found it easier to accept Islam or even revert to animism or African traditional beliefs, than the worship of the One True God.

I believe the Bible is our foundation and our final authority, and so I want to answer this question from a Biblical perspective. Let us hear what the Bible says so that I am not simply stating my own opinion.

What does the Bible have to say about Africa's role in God's redemptive plan? Or how is Africa depicted in the Bible? Did Christianity and faith in Jesus Christ come through the missionaries, through colonizers and through the people who came to Africa with a different agenda?

1. A Refuge

Let us look at Matthew 2:13-20 where we find the story of the birth of Jesus. It is also the first time we see Africa in the New Testament. It is very early on in the book of Matthew chapter 2 this is after Jesus was born in Bethlehem and God sends a word to Joseph in a dream to get up and leave Bethlehem and take the baby Jesus and Mary to a safe place.

The Bible says in -(Matthew 2:13-15:

> *"Now after he had gone, behold an angel of the Lord appeared to Joseph in a dream and said, Get up! (Tenderly) take unto you the young child and His mother and flee to Egypt; and remain there till I tell you (otherwise), for Herod intends to search for the child in order to destroy Him. And having risen, he took the Child and His Mother by night and withdrew to Egypt. And remained there until Herold's death. This was to fulfil what the Lord had spoken by the prophet, out of Egypt have I called my Son (Hos 11:1)") – Amplified Bible.*

At that time, Jesus was at his most vulnerable stage, probably, being between the ages of two and five. The Lord said to Joseph in the dream, "get up and flee!" Can you imagine the Son of God running for His Life or running for security? That's exactly what happened. Jesus and his parents fled Israel and they found safety, refuge, sustenance and shelter in Africa – Egypt. Jesus, the Son of God in His time of vulnerability found a safe haven in Africa!

This means Africa partnered with the greatest will and purpose of God on earth that was being worked out through Jesus. The salvation of the world hung in the balance. The salvation of the world and the new covenant, ratified in the Blood of Jesus, depended entirely on Jesus' life, ministry and death on the Cross being fulfilled. God needed a safe place for His Son, and He chose Africa for that fulfillment to happen.

Time and again, as we read the scriptures, it is clear that Africa's role has been to partner with God's redemptive plan at crucial times. At critical times, Africa comes to the forefront to play that redemptive purpose. So Joseph and his family stayed in Egypt until King Herod, who posed great danger to baby Jesus, died. Following Herod's death, the family relocated back to Israel.

2. Via Dolorosa

In the New Testament, the second time that we see Africa coming to the forefront is at the arguably most critical stage in the life and purpose of Jesus on earth: on His way to the Cross.

In Luke 26:23-26, we see Jesus in the final and the most important moment of His life on earth. He came to this earth to die for our sins. His whole purpose of coming to earth was to die and to be a sacrifice, the Lamb of God. That is what we celebrate on Good Friday, Easter and Passover. Jesus was that perfect Lamb of God, the Lamb that God had chosen.

Try and picture this: Jesus is on His way to the cross. He has already been judged, flogged, and beaten within inches of losing His life. He is tired, bleeding profusely and weary. However, He still has a way to go to the place of the crucifixion.

Every person who was going to be crucified was supposed to carry his cross. But Jesus was so weakened because of the whipping and torture that he could not carry His cross to the place of Crucifixion. The two criminals who were going to be crucified alongside him had not gone through that same ordeal as Jesus had. As such, they were able to carry their crosses. But Jesus had already gone through so much before the Crucifixion that he did not have the strength to carry the cross to Golgotha.

Take another moment to consider this: This is what Jesus was born to do; He was born to be the sacrificial Lamb of God. All that He had done in His 33 years on earth had brought Him to this point, the ultimate point for the sacrifice. It is why He came to earth, but He still had a way to go to the Cross. He couldn't carry the Cross Himself as he was substantially weakened; I imagine He stumbled many times under the immense weight of those wooden beams.

The Roman soldiers had a dilemma; who was going to carry the cross? Who was going to help Jesus to carry the cross the distance to Golgotha? Who was going to help Him to get to that place of fulfillment of destiny? At that moment, all of history was hanging on that one decision. The Roman soldiers looked around and different groups of people were following Jesus in the procession to the Cross.

We know from the Bible that there were several women, and the disciples of Jesus who ministered to Him and followed Him everywhere He went. They were mourning, weeping and watching from a distance. These obviously could not be called upon to carry the Cross. Apart from the physical weight of the Cross and the fact that no one woman could carry the weight alone, there was also the fact that crucifixion was a gruesome experience. There was a lot of blood and gore and most likely the Roman guards didn't think that women could manage this horrific experience.

As well, there were religious people: the Pharisees and Sadducees who were looking on with disdain and gloating with pride. They were relishing in this final "victory" that they believed they had won over Jesus. But the Pharisees and Sadducees could never carry the Cross. This is because they were marked by the religious spirit which is one of the most deadly spiritual strongholds. That spirit was responsible for killing Jesus. This spirit was and still is so dangerous because it cloaks itself in religiosity & piety and yet it is completely anti-God and opposed to the will of God. This deadly religious spirit magnifies man's will above the will of God.

The Pharisees had a religious spirit that would never allow them to carry the cross. They were of no help in these circumstances.

The other group in the procession was Roman soldiers. From a practical standpoint, it would appear that the Roman soldiers would be the obvious choice to carry the cross because they were in charge of the process, and Jesus was in their charge.

Why didn't they choose one of the Roman soldiers to carry the cross?

The Roman Empire as a civilization was marked by pride and a sense of superiority to other people whom they deemed inferior. They despised the Jews and no Roman in their right mind would ever carry the cross for a Jew. As well, for them, crucifixion was the lowest kind of punishment reserved for the worst criminals. Roman citizens were not subjected to that kind of death; even if they were being punished for committing crimes they were never crucified. Crucifixion was reserved for foreigners; for the Romans, it was a symbol of great shame & humiliation to the victim.

I can imagine the leader of the soldiers who was leading the procession looking around and suddenly his eyes land on a man, Simon of Cyrene or Simon the African. Simon was from northern Africa in present-day Libya, just west of Egypt. He had come to Jerusalem to worship. In Mark chapter 15 the Bible mentions the name of his two sons Alexander and Rufus. Simon of Cyrene, or Simon the African, was probably someone who had converted to Judaism and had come to Jerusalem at the time of Passover to worship God. The crucifixion of Jesus caused a great uproar in the city of Jerusalem. Simon of Cyrene had probably heard about the great prophet, Jesus Christ, His wonders and His miracle-working power. Then suddenly he hears that Jesus is being led away to the place of crucifixion. Whether as a bystander, or a sympathizer, Simon was there.

Then it happened! A Roman soldier picked Simon to help Jesus carry the Cross the rest of the way. Simon, a man from the African continent, ended up carrying Jesus' cross for the journey to the site of the crucifixion, Golgotha.

I believe that the person who carried the cross of Jesus the remainder of the way to the place of crucifixion is not only partnering with God's redemptive plan, the plan of salvation of the world but is someone who is uniquely positioned. I don't think that God chose just anybody to do this work. Let us remember that God is a purposeful God; everything He does has a reason and a purpose. Indeed, looking at the life of Jesus from His birth until His ascension, nothing happened by chance. Everything was divinely orchestrated and I believe the choice of Simon was no different.

As such, Africa helped to carry the cross to fulfill the purpose of God for the salvation of mankind. The Bible says that Jesus appeared to many people, apart from the disciples following his death and subsequent resurrection. This did not take place by happenstance. It was orchestrated by our Father in Heaven.

In my mind, I believe that one of the many people that Jesus probably appeared to be Simon of Cyrene. I can imagine Jesus encountering Simon of Cyrene and the conversation they would have. What would Jesus say to him? What kind of unique exchange would take place between somebody who helped you at the darkest point in your life but also at the point of you fulfilling your purpose? We will never know some of these details, at least not on this side of eternity. However, whatever the case, Simon of Cyrene is a clear example of an ordinary man who, for a moment in time, stepped into the eternal plan of God's Redemption.

3. The First Gentile Convert

The Church was born on the day of Pentecost as recorded in Acts 2. The birth of the Church began the age of Grace that we are still living in today. With the coming of the Holy Spirit, the church began to grow and the Gospel spread like wildfire.

As the church grew rapidly, there was the preaching of the Gospel in Jerusalem and Samaria.

Even as it spread like wildfire among the Jews, it hadn't yet been preached among the Gentiles, the non-Jews.

In Acts chapter 8:26 we meet Philip who was one of the Deacons of the early church in Jerusalem. Here is what the bible says in (Acts 8:26-28):

"But an angel of the Lord said to Philip, rise and proceed southward or at midday on the road that runs from Jerusalem down to Gaza. This is the desert (route), so he got up and went. And behold, an Ethiopian, a eunuch of great authority under Candace the queen of Ethiopians, who was in charge of all her treasure, had come to Jerusalem to worship. And he was (now) returning, and sitting in his chariot he was reading the Prophet Isaiah." – Amplified Bible

An Ethiopian!

At the time of the early Church the word "Africa" was not in use. However, we all know that Ethiopians are Africans.

An African in the time of the New Testament church was going to Jerusalem to worship and he was reading the book of the prophet Isaiah.

That seems to completely go against the narrative that the first time Africans ever heard the gospel and the God of the Bible was with the coming of the missionaries. Yet here is an Ethiopian, an African, reading the word of God almost immediately after Pentecost, after the Ascension. This is early church history. It completely flies in the face of typical commentary that the gospel arrived in Africa with the coming of the missionaries.

Imagine this: the African official eunuch who had great authority under the queen of Ethiopia was seated in his chariot, reading the book of Isaiah. At that time, the Holy Spirit told Philip to go forward and join the chariot accordingly. Philip ran up to the eunuch and heard the man reading the book of the prophet Isaiah. The eunuch asked whether Philip understood what he was reading. Then Philip asked how it was possible to do so unless someone explained to him and guided him in the right way. At that time, the eunuch earnestly requested Philip to come up and sit beside him, now this was the passage of Scripture that he was reading,

"Like a sheep, He was led to the slaughter and as a lamb, before its Shearers is dumb so he opens not his mouth in his humiliation he was taken away by distressing an oppressive judgment and justice who can describe or relate

the wickedness of his generation for his life is taken from the earth and a bloody death inflicted upon him." - Isaiah 53:7-8; – *Amplified Bible.*

The African eunuch was, of course, reading about the crucifixion of Jesus which had only recently taken place and he asked Philip to explain to him what this scripture meant.

Philip then proceeded to announce to him the good news of the gospel of Jesus Christ. The African eunuch was then baptized by Philip and returned to his country with great joy. According to the Christian tradition, the eunuch was the first African convert and he returned home, bringing along the gospel to his country and people. Therefore the preaching of the gospel came to Africa through the mouth of a fellow African for the first time. I believe this was the beginning of the Orthodox Church. Many other traditions speak about Mark the disciple of Jesus Christ. Mark was of that same stock, bringing the gospel into Egypt and Libya and founding the Coptic Church that still exists today.

4. Missionaries

If I were to ask who the greatest missionary apostle of all time was, most people would agree that it was the Apostle Paul. As well, he is the only one of the apostles who was sent to spread the gospel to the Gentiles and went out on great missionary journeys. All the other apostles remained in Jerusalem because they were called to the house of Israel.

Paul was called to the Gentiles – essentially, called to go to the world. So he travelled far and wide in his missionary journeys, going as far as Asia Minor and Europe.

Thinking about missionaries raises the question of who sends the missionaries out. For example, we can ask who sent Paul out to spread the gospel. Who commissioned him? Who laid hands on him in prayer?

In Acts 13:1-3 it says thus:

"Now in the church (assembly) at Antioch, there were prophets (inspired interpreters of the will and purposes of

God) and teachers: Barnabas, Simeon who was called Niger (Black), Lucius of Cyrene, Manaen a member of the court of Herod the tetrarch, and Saul. While they were worshipping the Lord and fasting, the Holy Spirit said, 'Separate now for me Barnabas and Saul for the work to which I have called them.' Then after fasting and praying, they put their hands on them and sent them away." .– Amplified Bible.

It is in the church in Antioch where believers were first called "Christians". It was a great church filled with devout saints of God. There were prophets and teachers in the church. Before they sent Paul out on his missionary journey, they gathered to pray over him.

Who were the leaders of the church in Antioch? Acts 13 mentions the names of the key church leaders as being Barnabas, Simeon who was called Niger (meaning black), Lucius of Cyrene, Manaen and Saul.

Two of the five elders, leaders of the church in Antioch, were Africans, one named Simeon who was called Niger (Black) and another Lucius of Cyrene.

So this whole idea that the first time that the gospel came to Africa was through the missionaries is misplaced. It is very recent at the turn of the 19th Century and misleading at that. There were African believers in the early church. Indeed the Bible is explicit in showing that there were African Christians who prayed and consecrated Barnabas and Saul under the guidance of the Holy Spirit.

We know a lot about Barnabas and Saul(Paul). We also know about Paul and Silas. However, we do not know as much about the African Christians who sent them out.

Why is this important?

A couple of years ago the Lord gave me a word that one of the redemptive gifts of Africa is to send out missionaries to the nations of the world. He led me to Acts 13:1 and showed that two of the leaders who consecrated Paul, the greatest missionary, were from Africa. Therefore, one of the redemptive gifts of Africa is to send out missionaries to the world.

The signs are clear, which explains why, today, anointing to preach the gospel and send out missionaries to the world is very strong in African people. If you look at the largest churches today, be they in Africa, Europe or anywhere else around the world, you'll find Africans at the centre of their leadership.

The largest evangelical church in Ukraine, of all places, is led by Pastor Sunday Adelaija, a Nigerian. As well, many large (in some cases the largest) churches in Europe are led by Africans. Indeed, if we look at the church globally, we can see that there is an explosion of a revival led by Africans. Why? I believe that it is in alignment with God's redemptive purpose. It is something that has always been within the spiritual DNA of Africans but it needed to be awakened. The time has come for that awakening!

I believe that we're going to see much more revival in the years to come. I believe that we will see Africa begin to send out more missionaries to the rest of the world that so desperately needs to hear the truth of the saving power of Jesus Christ.

5. The Restoration of the Holy Spirit.

The Day of Pentecost marked the birth of the church. With this birth came the promise of the Father that the disciples have been waiting for; The Holy Spirit arrived with power and fire. In that instance, the church was born and has been stewarded for the past 2000 years under the power of the Holy Spirit. The New Testament Church was a church on fire for God and filled with the power of the Holy Spirit.

That said, the church has had to ensure substantial trials and tribulations. Over the years and centuries that followed the gift of the Holy Spirit was lost, in part because of the mixing of pagan religions with Christianity.

I believe the Holy Spirit was quenched because of the sin that entered into the Church. The Bible warns us, "do not quench the spirit"(1 Thess. 5:19). Why? Because the Christian life and the work of Ministry are impossible without the Holy

Spirit. Without the ministry of the Holy Spirit, Christianity would be a dead religion with no life.

A time came when God wanted to reintroduce the Holy Spirit or restore the gift of the Holy Spirit to the church. In doing so, He looked for somebody to use to achieve that purpose. The person that He chose to begin to restore the gift of the Holy Spirit to the body of Christ was a son of former slaves, a man called William Seymour.

William Seymour was born in 1870 in the south of the United States. He didn't have any formal training or education as a young man. However, he learnt how to read by reading the Bible. It is said that he was always searching for God. He used to have dreams and visions and was very sensitive to the Holy Spirit. In the end, God powerfully revealed Himself through this very humble man. The baptism of the Holy Spirit was restored to the body of Christ through the revival on Azusa Street in Los Angeles that was led by William Seymour.

This came about when William Seymour had been invited to lead a small Church in Los Angeles. As they kept on seeking God and praying and waiting on God's move, God restored the gift of the Spirit - speaking in tongues and great testimonies. The testimonies of the Azusa Street revival are mind-boggling when you listen to them. There are miracles, signs and wonders. The book of Acts came to life again according to the testimonials from Azusa Street. What is written in the book of Acts are the kind of things that were experienced in the Azusa Street revival.

William Seymour was a very humble man who lived a life in which he completely surrendered to God and, through him, the Holy Spirit was restored to the body of Christ. If you are a believer who has been baptized in the Holy Spirit you have to look back and thank the son of former slaves whose surrendered life and quest for God restored to the body of Christ the gift of the Holy Spirit. Isn't that such a great spiritual heritage?

Therefore, I believe that there is a redemptive purpose for Africa, as we have seen from the scriptures that we've gone through. In these, we see from the Bible that the redemptive purpose of Africa is to partner with God's Will on earth.

My prayer is that the Church in Africa will awaken to our spiritual heritage and calling. I believe God is calling Africa to arise and take her place in the kingdom, to take her place and in God's end-time plan.

Prayer

Heavenly Father, we want to thank You very much for Your word, we want to thank You that the entrance of Your word brings revelation and my prayer is that as we hear Your Word, new revelation and light will illuminate our paths. Father, I thank You that You gave Africa and Africans a unique spiritual héritage, a unique place to partner with what You are doing on the earth, to partner in the life of Your Son, in His ministry and His destiny on earth and that even today you have a unique purpose for Africa to play. So Father I pray that You awaken the church in Africa to our true spiritual heritage.

We ask that You take away spiritual blindness and help us to see that You have called us to be front and centre in Your redemptive plan for the nations. Father, we ask that You'll empower the church in Africa to preach the gospel and to send out missionaries to the world because that is part of our calling.

Father, we pray for revival in our nations and to see the move of God and the Holy Spirit in the nations of the world. That is what you have called us to. Lord, we're praying for a resurrection of Africa's identity and spiritual heritage in Christ and we're asking that the truth of who and what You created us to be will never again be covered, diminished, or forgotten but identified and claimed. Lord, connect us to our spiritual heritage and past so that we can embrace our future.

In Jesus' Mighty Name.

Amen.

5. The White Council

Rutetera rwa guri mwoongo (The apple doesn't fall far from the tree). - Runyankore proverb

I was born the third child in a family of four children. Being the middle child in a close-knit family has its unique lessons and blessings. As I have grown older, and particularly since I became involved in church ministry, I have found a new appreciation and respect for the simplest of things in life called family and home. As a child growing up, it seemed to be the most ordinary of things: parents, siblings, and a place called home. However, time, years and maturity have taught me that what seems ordinary is usually anything but ordinary, and what we take for granted, in the end, is of paramount importance. As I have counselled and prayed for people, young and old, I have found that most things, good or bad, begin at home. I have observed that, when you see a confident, secure in their skin, kind and generous person, it is most likely that the person grew up in a loving and secure home environment. I have also observed the opposite to be true; when you see an insecure, petty or wounded person, often it is because the person lacked a secure and loving home environment.

This is why I am eternally grateful to God for the family that He gave me because so much of who I am is because of who they are and the values I learnt from my parents and siblings growing up. It is in this spirit that I share my unique experience with my family, the place where my journey began and the foundation from which I spring.

The Visionary

My earliest memories of my father start when I was around four or five years of age. This may sound strange to some who have never experienced the agony of separation from their parents. I am thankful that the separation from my father occurred when I was still very young and so the impact of his absence wasn't too strongly felt.

I was born at Muhimbiri Hospital in Dar-es-Salaam, Tanzania on the 9th of May 1978. My father came to see my mother and me at the hospital and the very next day, he left for Mozambique for military training. Our early years as a family were a patchwork of movements and separation from my father. Before I reached the age of seven, I spoke three different languages. I was always learning a new language at every new stop we made or the "home" that we stayed in. When we moved to Sweden in 1983, my memory and understanding as a child were just beginning to form. Our world revolved around my mother and my siblings. My home was wherever my mother was. Luckily, my mother was a master at making a home seem like the most wonderful, safe and inviting place on earth. I never once felt there was anything unusual about our family situation. Maybe I was too young to notice, or maybe my mother did such an excellent job of being both father and mother to us, that I didn't know I was missing something or someone.

One day in our little apartment in Gothenburg, Sweden, I heard everyone shouting and calling us to come and watch television. There was an important interview on the news and my older siblings called me and my younger sister who was playing in our room to watch it. We sat on the carpet in front of the television. The news programme was in Swedish. On the TV, I saw a man speaking. He was wearing a green camouflage uniform and sitting in the middle of a jungle. My aunt, Alice Kaboyo, who lived with us told us that this was our father. Everyone quietly watched and listened, including my mother who seemed transfixed by the interview and followed it intently. I looked at her to take my cue on what I should make of this new information.

As I looked back and forth from my mother's face to the TV, I heard the Swedish presenter saying that this man was a guerilla leader. Now in my child's mind, I didn't know what a guerilla leader was. I understood it to mean he was a leader of the "gorillas" like Tarzan. After all, maybe that's why he was wearing green and in the jungle.

After that interview, I was very interested in knowing more about this person they said was my father. It was the first time I remember thinking about my father. After seeing him in the interview on TV, I found that I often daydreamed about this man called my father. This happened especially at bedtime, when the mind wanders between sleep and consciousness. I imagined meeting him in the jungle where he lived and telling him all my stories of the day. His face was imprinted on my mind. I only had to close my eyes and there he was. My father.

One day, I asked my mother which direction Uganda was from Sweden. She explained to me that Uganda was in a south-westerly direction and that there were seas and oceans in between. Now every night before I slept, I imagined myself walking out the door of our apartment building, down the stairs to the street, then following a south-westerly direction until I reached the sea. I imagined myself boarding a ship and then walking some more, even driving in a car until I finally arrived in Uganda. I imagined myself taking that same direction until I reached the jungle where my father lived and found him. That one thought of finding my father in the jungle stayed with me for a long time. Always before I slept, I would see his face as I did on the television.

I was a very happy child; we all were. At that young age, your life revolves around the main people in your life. For us, that was our mother. As long as she was with us, all was peaceful and the world was as it should be. The interview on television brought into play that there was another important person in our lives, but he appeared more like a phantom or dream in the night. All day, every day, I was busy, active and happy. I never imagined that, one day, I would meet my father, not in a faraway jungle as I had dreamed, but right there at Skolsparet 63, Hjalbo, where we lived.

In the spring of 1985, our quiet sleepy life in Sweden was blown wide open when my father stepped out of our dreams into reality. I remember it was a weekend because we were allowed to watch television in the morning on the weekends. We had two children visiting us from the neighbourhood. John Peter and Tracey were two American children who were the same age as my sister Diana and I. I do not recall clearly what we were watching on TV, but it must have been some Saturday morning cartoon or children's show. The doorbell rang and my sister Natasha went to answer the door. We were sitting down on the carpet, as we often did, our eyes glued to the TV. My mother and aunt were with us in the living room, seated on the living room sofas. Suddenly, we heard my mother scream uncontrollably and what followed was, simply put, pandemonium. We turned and sat up to see the cause of my mother's screams and saw a man coming into the hallway dressed in a light-coloured blazer. My mother was crying and hugging this man who was now in the room. My aunt Alice was also crying, and we the children were simply spellbound by all the drama. We had never seen our mother react that way before.

John Peter, our little American friend, asked courageously, "what is going on here?"

To which my aunt Alice replied, "Don't you see, their father has come back from the bush."

To which John Peter replied, "we're getting outta here!" And he and Tracey made a hasty exit to leave our house to all the noise, excitement and tears of joy.

And just like that, my father crashed into our world. I was very excited by this new person in our home because he quickly became the centre of attention. He brought great new energy and fun to our home. One day, we returned from school and found he had bought us all new bicycles. He took us hiking on the trails in the forests around our neighbourhood. I remember he also loved to play football and took the time to organize a football match for the neighbourhood children. At home, it seemed like there was this boundless energy and excitement. My sister Diana and I would take turns being carried on his back. He would twirl us around in circles and we would squeal in pure joy. Our father coming home felt wonderful and life with him was very exciting and full of joy.

My father's presence in our home also showed that there was something that we were missing as children, only that we didn't know we were missing it. It was like there was a dad-shaped hole in each of our hearts, and when he came home to us, that hole was filled.

When my father came into my world, I stopped dreaming about him. I knew the real person and didn't have any more need for dreams. People usually focus on the need that growing boys have for a father at home. I am sure that boys have a special need for their fathers to teach them how to be men and to help them in their transition from childhood to adulthood. However, I think that all children, both boys and girls, need the presence of their fathers for vastly different reasons. When my father came back to us, even at such a young age, he brought with him a sense of security. I am not talking here of merely physical safety but, even more than that, emotional, spiritual and psychological safety. There was a sense of being covered or protected. I had never felt unsafe without my father; we had a very happy upbringing even before he joined us. But when he came home to us, I felt as though nothing in the world could go wrong because he was with us. It was as though we were living with Superman; he was the biggest, strongest, wisest person and when he was home, the world was right.

My father stayed with us in Sweden for some time and then had to leave to return to Uganda. This was hard because, now that we knew him, it was hard to go back to life before we knew him. His presence had awakened something in us all, and we could not return to life without him. By the Grace of God, our separation this time was not long. In February of 1986, we finally said goodbye to our adopted home in Sweden and returned home to Uganda for good.

When we reunited with our father, it was pure joy and bliss. Now we could see him every day. He would tell us stories of *ishekatabazi,*[1] which is Runyankore folklore teaching moral

---

1 C. B. Katiti *Ishe-Katabazi: Traditional Stories of the Ankole People of Uganda.* Fountain Publishers, 1948/2004

lessons through the engaging and humorous stories of the man by the same name. No matter how many times we heard the same stories, we never grew tired of hearing them just one more time. My father genuinely enjoyed fatherhood and spending time with us; probably he was making up for the lost time. I recall vividly that he always called us to count his exercises in the morning, and taught us how to do military-style drills. He also taught us karate and different self-defence stances.

One of the foundational things I learnt from my father is my identity. That deepest of questions, “Who am I?” “Where am I from?”

My dad felt it was extremely important for children to know who they are and where they were from. He wanted us to be grounded and to know who we were as Ugandans and Africans. One of the ways we imbibed this ethos was by spending a lot of time with him at our country home called, Rwakyitura. It was from this quality time with him on the land and looking after cows that I developed one of my great passions. Over the years, I have come to appreciate my love for cows. I'm not sure if I love cows that much because they remind me of the time I spent with my dad or if it is a distinct passion on its own. The two are so intertwined that I'm not sure whether I can separate them now. However, what I know, for sure, is that it was with my father that I gained a deep love for the land and cows.

I have a very vivid memory of one such time in Rwakyitura. We were there together as a family on holiday from school. I was probably seven or eight years old, and my sister Diana and I had tagged along with my dad to go see the cows. We had a daily routine where we usually went very early in the morning before daybreak and then again in the evening to see the cows. This day was like so many other days and I don't think I would have remembered it specifically if it were not for one special memory frozen in time.

I remember I was wearing pale pink dungarees with light blue stars and tennis shoes. I loved those dungarees and felt very smart in my outfit. We stood under a tree and watched as my father spoke to the herdsmen about the herd. Suddenly, the skies opened and a gentle rain started falling. My sister and I huddled together under the tree. We hadn't expected it to rain and hence didn't bring an umbrella. My father was wearing his characteristic herdsman gear which consisted of walking boots, a windbreaker jacket, a hat and a long walking spear. He was completely sheltered from the rain but when he noticed us huddling under the tree to be sheltered from the rain, he came to help us. He pulled us both close to him and covered us with the same jacket he was wearing. We were safe and warm, like little chicks safe and close to their brooding mother. My father continued directing work from under the shade of the tree and my sister and I enjoyed the warmth and safety of being hidden in our father's jacket. We talked to each other and watched what was going on from that safe and warm vantage point.

I remember distinctly the wonderful scent of the soil as the rain fell gently on the earth. It is an intoxicating scent that I have always loved. That moment lasted a few minutes until the rain abated and we continued watching the cows grazing, but it will always be frozen in time in my mind and heart. At that moment, all the things I greatly love mingled together in a powerful amalgam. The love for and connection I have with the land and our cattle-rearing tradition, which has been passed down for generations, together with being with my father. This moment, fused together, evokes a powerful emotional and spiritual response.

My father was such an important part of introducing me to this wonderful world and it is such an integral part of who I am as a person. I am not sure if I love the land and cows because of my father, or if it is my passion, apart from him. Whatever the answer to that is, what I know is that he introduced me to that wonderful world that is so connected to my past, who I am as a person, and my identity. I learnt so much about the land and cows by simply observing him and being close to him as we walked the land together while we were children. He taught us the colours and physical attributes of the different breeds, how to identify high milkers and the desired qualities for breeding Ankole cows. By the time I was twelve years old, I went to the cows by myself every day while on holiday. By the time I was sixteen years old, my siblings and I went to the farm even without our parents and checking on the cows was the big assignment there. Finally, years later when I was married and my husband and I were praying about what sector of business we should focus a bigger portion of our attention on; after prayer and contemplation, we came back home to the land and the cows. We chose to focus on dairy and beef farming with value addition for both beef and dairy processing. Today, our dairy products are exported to many countries in the region and, by the Grace of God, we are working to have our beef processed and exported to the region and other markets.

My father is a visionary as a leader; he has always seen a Uganda and an Africa that few others saw or believed could exist. He has worked his whole life and sacrificed so much to see that vision become a reality. God has used him to do great things to give people hope that Uganda and Africa can become what God always intended them to be.

As a father, the image of him covering my younger sister and me from the falling rain is an apt image of the man he has always been for us and many others in our nation. He is not just our father, but he is a father to the nation. By the time we returned from exile when he was still in his early forties, people called him "Mzee" which means "old man" or "senior person." I think calling him "Mzee" back then was not so much about his biological age as much as a term of respect and honour from the many people that he was leading. He has the mantle of a father and by the Grace of God, he has used that mantle to be a covering to millions of people in Uganda and beyond.

Talking about my father wouldn't be complete without mentioning his legendary sense of humour. Growing up with my dad was always fun because he always made us laugh. He and my mother were intentional about spending quality time with us. Even though they were very busy, I don't remember them as being busy or preoccupied. When they were with us at home they were always present in the moment.

My dad was also quite forthright about discussing all matters with his children, sometimes embarrassingly so. He wasn't shy about broaching all subjects with us because he wanted us to know that we could always talk to him about everything. He talked to us about the birds and the bees and he poked fun at what he deemed undesirable behaviour such as having a boyfriend. Even though we would cringe at these talks, we also laughed and knew that we could always talk to our parents about everything and anything. They placed strong boundaries around us but they also gave us wings to fly.

My father possesses a spirit of wisdom which I believe is a gift from God. King Solomon prayed to God for wisdom so that he could adequately govern God's people and God answered his prayer. I believe God has given my father a gift of wisdom so that he can serve God's people in Uganda, Africa and the world. In pivotal times in my own life, my father has spoken into my life and helped me to make better decisions, or encouraged me in the decisions I was already making if they were good. He also has a gift for teaching and is a teacher at heart. I have been with my dad on some of the most tiring and gruelling campaign trails, where it is late and everyone is tired, worn out and hungry and my father is speaking to the umpteenth meeting. I am always humbled and amazed at how he will always take the time to listen to what the people are saying and start to teach them. He never underestimates or underrates people's opinions; he gives them full weight and hearing and always hopes to convince people of the rightness of his position through patient teaching. This has always been his approach whether it is to parenting or revolutionary ideology. He understood early in his life that, when a person is convinced of the rightness of a position or action, they are very easy to lead. As compared to the case where someone isn't convinced and you try to lead them through other means.

As a father, his approach was always to talk to us, to explain and to allow us to conclude for ourselves. Often, even when we disagreed, we always felt heard and validated. Mzee is an astute student of history and his character is such that he feels that the right position will always win in the end, regardless of the opposition. He possesses the courage of his convictions that he feels on a cellular level and I believe on a spiritual level so that he is resolute and determined in the path he takes.

Once, many years ago, my parents hosted a guest and invited us to join them for dinner. By this time we were grown and married with homes of our own, but it is always a blessing to come home and spend time with our family. During the dinner, their guest complained about a situation in the guest's home country and sought counsel on how Mzee would deal with the situation. The situation their dinner guest was describing was one of factionalism in the politics of their home nation and they wanted to know what he would advise. I will always remember my father's response. He said, "First you must have a just cause.."

The guest was surprised because they thought he would address the position of the factions but, instead, he focused on the guests' position and whether it was meritorious enough to get broad buy-in from people of different backgrounds. That simple answer gives a glimpse into Mzee's heart and the fact that he believes in the justice and truth of what he does, and that is the driving force of all the sacrifices and work he has done all his life. He believes that his is a just cause and that it will prevail because it is right.

Finally, my father is a man of mercy. I believe that this speaks to his fear of the Lord. The Bible declares in Micah 6:8:

> *"He has shown you O man what is good. And what does the Lord require of you, but to act justly, to love tenderly and that you walk humbly with your God." – Amplified Bible*

The Bible says that we should forgive others so that God would forgive us and that we should be merciful so that we too may obtain mercy. My father has demonstrated this principle of mercy and forgiveness in his personal and political life. I believe that God has blessed him for walking in mercy and I pray that it has helped heal some of the old wounds of division that existed in our country because of our turbulent political history.

If I had a difference of opinion with my father when I was younger and spoke out of turn, when I returned and repented to him, I would find that he had already forgiven me. He was more concerned about having our relationship back to its usual place than over my misdeed. I remember once when he was very angry because I pierced my ears without his permission. Even then he forgave me and our friendship was quickly restored. His heart is like that of the father in the story of the prodigal son in the Bible, he yearns for a relationship with his children and is quick to forgive whenever we do anything wrong.

Two scriptures always remind me of my father and his unparalleled influence on not only my life but the lives of so many Ugandans and Africans.

2 Samuel 23: 3-5:

> *"The God of Israel spoke, the Rock of Israel said to me, When one rules over men righteously, ruling in the fear of God. He dawns on them like the morning light when the sun rises on a cloudless morning when the tender grass springs out of the earth through the clear shining after rain. Truly does not my house stand so with God? For He has made with me an everlasting covenant, ordered in all things and sure. For will He not cause to prosper all my help and my desire?" – Amplified Bible*

Psalm 37:37:

> *"Mark the blameless man and behold the upright, for there is a posterity for the man of peace." – Amplified Bible*

The Saint

From my earliest memories, my mother was always there. She is like the cedar tree, tall, stately enduring, incorruptible.

When I was a young child, she framed my world. Everything I knew and understood came from her. Her presence was the one constant in a world that was always changing. Even when we moved from country to country, changing homes, schools and languages, she was always with us and she provided the security and stability that we all needed. Wherever she was, was home for us.

My mom has always been an exceptional homemaker. She excelled at making every place we lived, warm and inviting. We never imagined that there was anything we lacked or that somehow our situation was different from other people's. Even though she was undoubtedly under intense stress, pressure and uncertainty, we never felt it. For us, the world was as it should be because she was with us. It is only when I grew up that I understood how incredibly brave and strong my mother was in those difficult days. She is a warrior, a fighter and a queen all in one. She has always carried herself with immense dignity, whether it was carrying groceries in Sweden, driving her old red Datsun car in Nairobi, or meeting heads of state when we returned to Uganda; she has never really changed.

I always knew that my mother was beautiful; in a way that most children think their parents are the best at everything. Her hands are elegant and her fingers are long and beautiful. Whenever I had a temperature or a headache, her hands were always cool to the touch and whenever she placed her hands on my forehead I always felt better. Her straight nose with nostrils that flare to warn you of her disapproval or anger, was something we always talked about as children. Her tall and dignified stature meant we could always see her even in a crowd of people. She always smells wonderful, and her perfume stays with you long after she has left the room. She is also the most particular person I know. She wants things done with excellence, whether it is making your bed, keeping the house or running a business or organization.

In our home growing up, my mother was the law, the jury and the judge. If you landed yourself in trouble, she would be the one and only person you would have to face. She was very strict about how she wanted to raise her children and ensured that we all knew it. The *kanyafu* or rod was not far away in case she needed to give a good spanking to any one of us. However, I think the simple fear of possible spanking kept us out of mischief. I was the middle child and so by the time I came along she was a little more accommodating in terms of actually spanking us, but we still dreaded getting into trouble where we might get spanked. What she didn't achieve with spanking she more than made up for in lecturing both young and old. Her lectures could make you cry faster than spanking. Now that I am a mother myself, I completely understand why my mother maintained her strictness with us.

First, raising children without their father while in exile and then after our return to Uganda, growing up in the State House, she wanted to make sure that she instilled in us the values that she had grown up with. She wanted us to grow up to be normal, well-adjusted people who would thrive in the world on our own. So she was strict and we often didn't understand the reasons behind some of her rules.

Often, when I was young, I didn't understand why my mother did or said some things. Some things she said, and did, baffled me outright. I would file them away in my mind as "mom-isms", things my mother said or did that I didn't understand but accepted because she was my mother. One such mom-ism was that she never allowed us to go to other people's homes for birthday parties or other events. We cried and bewailed our existence but she held to her position. Every time we told her that we wanted to visit a friend from school she would answer, "Be friends with your siblings." It was so perturbing that I finally stopped trying to understand the meaning behind it. As a mother now, I completely understand what she meant and what she was trying to teach us. She wanted us to develop friendships amongst ourselves first and then we would have a basis for other friendships. That one mom-ism alone has reaped huge dividends for us as siblings because we grew to become great friends with each other over the years.

Another baffling mom-ism happened when I was around 12 years old. I loved babysitting my aunt's and uncle's children, and we had plenty of relatives having children and coming home to visit us. Out of the many, there were a few favourite aunts and uncles that we all especially liked. One day, I learnt that one of my favourite uncles was going to christen their young children. Since I especially liked this uncle, I imagined that I would be picked as a godmother at age 12. As the day of the christening drew closer, I grew disappointed as I heard those who were asked to be godparents. Needless to say, I wasn't asked to be a godmother and that news completely devastated me. My mother found me sullen and morose and asked me what was wrong. I explained to her my disappointment at not being considered to be a godmother. She sympathized with me because she knew how much I loved babies, but then she laughed and said, "oh don't worry, you'll be a godmother to your siblings' children."

Now telling a 12-year-old that she will have children and be a godmother to her siblings' children is like saying she will go to the moon. I was completely perturbed by this mom-ism and felt my mom didn't understand the gravity of the situation. Here I was explaining to her that this was my last chance to be a godmother and she was talking about being a godmother to my siblings' children. But this mom-ism also came to pass a few years later when we all got married and had our own families. So my mother was right in the end.

When my mother was thirty-seven years old, she had an encounter with the Lord Jesus Christ and surrendered her life to Him. That simple quality decision had a monumental impact on her own life and by extension our lives as her children. Her faith and walk with God have been evident for all to see and her devotion to God is deep and genuine. My mother doesn't just preach her faith, above all, she lives it. Since the day she became a Christian, she has been a pilgrim on a journey with the Lord. Her single and highest purpose is to be pleasing to the Lord and to fulfill His will for her life.

In doing this she walked away from many things that the world offered and she chose the road less travelled. In seeking to obey God, she became a servant to all, to the vulnerable, to orphans, rural women and youth. She gladly takes up the mantles that others disdain because her eyes are not on the world but on God and Heaven. To every task and assignment from God, she brings the same single-minded devotion, focus and excellence. She attacks every task whether small or great with the same tenacity, integrity and focus. Take the case when she was appointed Minister for Karamoja, an area in Uganda that had lagged behind the nation in terms of development. This was a fact acknowledged by much of the population so much so that when we were in school our teachers would say, "we will not wait for Karamoja to develop," if a student was taking a long time to finish their work. This region of the country was isolated both geographically and socially and lagged in many areas like education of children, security and economic development. Karamoja was so disdained by other parts of the country that once another minister turned down the appointment to be Minister for the area because he saw it as a demotion.

When Maama was appointed Minister for Karamoja, she welcomed the role with her characteristic focus, work ethic and humility. She started spending long periods in Karamoja getting to know the people and understanding their problems. She championed their causes and focused more national attention and important government programmes on developing the area. She camped in Moroto, the major town in the area and daily toured the people's lands and projects in the sweltering heat. She was instrumental in getting the Bible translated into the Karamojong language, a first for the great people of this area. She prayed for God to send rain to the semi-arid region and God answered her prayers and sent an abundance of rain and people planted food crops. Maama pioneered agricultural projects and the first housing projects in the area. Through her work, the government secured water for livestock, educated the children, built road networks and connected the region closer to the rest of the country. Karamoja was forever changed because of the servant leadership that Maama brought to the area. The people of Karamoja loved and received Maama with open arms because they recognized the genuineness and integrity of her heart. She loved them and they loved her in return. The elders of Karamoja gave Maama the special name, *Nyakiru*, which means "the one who brings rain," in celebration of Maama's faith and service to their community.

Since our family returned from exile in Sweden, people young and old started calling my mother, *Maama.* This special name spoke more about the spiritual mantle she wears than her biological age because she was a young woman in her thirties at that time. The nation has called her *Maama* because she carries the generational anointing to nurture, love, protect and serve others, especially those who are vulnerable and overlooked by society.

It would be remiss to write about my mother and not talk about her lifestyle of prayer. This would be a topic for a whole other book. My mother has lived a life of prayer in such a fundamental way that it shapes everything she does. From as far back as I can remember, my mother has woken up at 3 am to have her prayer time with the Lord. Wherever she goes, she sets up her prayer room or more aptly put, her "war room." This is because my mother's prayers have helped shape the destiny of not only our family but that of very many families, communities and the entire nation. In her war room, there is her prayer chair, usually an armchair, a table that carries her many Bibles and prayer journals and sometimes her CD player for her worship music. She has countless prayer journals with prayer lists that span decades, and in those prayer journals you realize how a lot is settled in the place of prayer, countless battles are won, disasters averted and blessings secured in that powerful place of prayer. In Maama's prayer closet, the Lord speaks to her through the reading of the Bible, a word of knowledge and dreams and visions. God has often revealed things to

Maama in the place of prayer for her to pray about them. Maama is a spiritual gatekeeper and watchman over the walls of our nation.

The Bible declares in Psalms 24:3-10:

> *"Who shall go up into the mountain of the Lord? Or who shall stand in the Holy Place?*
>
> *He who has clean hands and a pure heart, who has not lifted himself up to falsehood nor sworn deceitfully. He shall receive the blessing from the Lord and righteousness from the God of his salvation. This is the generation of those who seek Him, who seek Your face O God of Jacob. Lift up your heads , O you gates and be lifted up you age abiding doors, that the King of glory may come in. Who is the king of glory? The Lord strong and mighty, the Lord mighty in battle. Lift up your heads o you gates; yes lift them up you age abiding doors, that the King of glory may come in. Who is this King of glory? The Lord of hosts, He is the King of glory." – Amplified Bible*

Maama has been able to go up to the mountain of the Lord in prayer because she strives to have clean hands and a pure heart. She commits to travelling in the light by walking in love toward others and forgiving while also asking for forgiveness. Even when enemies have fought her and spoken ill of her, she forgives and chooses to walk in love. As such she has a tremendous spiritual authority to speak to the gates to open for the King of Glory to come in. That is the reason why favour and blessing follow Maama wherever she goes and in whatever she does.

One day, that I remember vividly is when we were all back at home from school as young people, my mother called us into the living room where she was sitting. She was in a serious mood and we didn't know what she wanted to talk to us about. She went on to share with us that she was grateful to God for all He had given to her in blessing her with children. She said that she would always pray for our success, academically and in every other facet of our lives. Yet, she said that while success on earth was great, her highest prayer for all of us was that we would be counted worthy to have our home together in Heaven. My mother, who is a stoic woman, became emotional when she said, "The most important thing is that I find you there." We all cried together and hugged her and prayed together and the moment soon passed.

I will never forget that day and what Maama shared with us because it reveals the heart of the matter, the foundation of all things in life and in my mother's life. The truth is that this life is a precursor to the next life, to eternity. The decisions we make in our lives on earth determine where we will spend eternity, either with our Lord Jesus Christ or separated from God. That is the heart of my mother's life, she is a saint. She walks this earth as a pilgrim, serving and loving God and waiting for the Blessed Hope of our triumphant reunion with our Lord and Saviour. Maranatha! (Even so, come Lord Jesus!)

Finally, I remember hearing a message many years back from Creflo Dollar, a wonderful preacher of the Gospel. He said that God's people should find themselves in the Bible instead of some statistics in the world, just like Jesus found Himself in the Bible in Luke 4:21, where Jesus said, *"Today, the scriptures have been fulfilled while you are present and hearing."*

I think we can all find ourselves in the Word of God as the Holy Spirit breathes life and brings revelation to us as we study the Bible. One place that I definitely know was written for Maama is Proverbs 31:

> *"Many daughters have done virtuously, nobly and well (with the strength of character that is steadfast in goodness) but you excel them all.*
>
> *"Charm and grace are deceitful and beauty is vain (because it is not lasting) but a woman who reverently and worshipfully fears the Lord, she shall be praised.*
>
> *"Give her of the fruits of her hands, and let her own works praise her in the gates of the city." – Amplified Bible.*

The 4K's

I do not know whether it was by accident or grand design, but each of the children in our family has a name beginning with the letter "K." By this, I mean the middle name given to us by our parents apart from our first names. My older brother's name is Kainerugaba, my older sister's name is Kainembabazi, my name is Kokundeka and my younger sister's name is Kyaremera.

Our parents also have middle names beginning with the letter " K." My father's middle name is Kaguta which was his father's name, and my mother's name is Kataaha, which was her father's name. For us children, our middle names evolved over time and so when we were in our teenage years, we began to call ourselves the 3K's when referring to just the girls, or 4K's when referring to all of us children in our family. Since we were very close growing up, we always missed each other very much whenever we were separated for any amount of time. During such times, we found a way to keep the sense of being close to each other despite the distance. There is a constellation of stars called Orion's belt, which is also known as the Three Kings or Three Sisters. Orion's belt consists of three stars that form a straight line in the night sky. In Arabic, the stars together are called Alnizam which means "string of pearls" and no doubt describes the appearance of the stars in the night sky.

The component stars have Arabic names, the first being Alnitak which is a triple-star system and is much bigger than the sun. The second star is called Alnilam, and it is a supergiant star and it is an anchor for other star classifications. The last is called Mintaka which is a double star which also shines much brighter than the sun.

These stars are always perfectly aligned and shine brightly in the night sky. Whenever we looked at Orion's belt we thought of each other, the 3K's, my sisters and I all aligned perfectly. No matter how far apart we are, we can always look up at the night sky and see Orion's belt and remember each other and the special bond we share. When all the 4K's are together, it is always a blast. When we were younger, it was like bringing down the house with laughter and staying up all through the night talking and having fun.

When all the 6K's were together, we called it the "white council" or a perfect union of all family members. When the white council is together, we talk, laugh and share wonderful memories. In my recollections, our life was very simple, our parents didn't focus a lot on gifts or material things. They provided for our education and needs, but the true gifts we shared were love, friendship and a close bond as a family. That was what made every homecoming so special; it was the time, the love, and the warmth of being together as a family.

*****

For my siblings and I, our camaraderie and tight-knit bond go back as far as I can remember. My brother in my memories was my hero, the adored older brother who could do no wrong. He was funny, kind and very protective of his sisters. From childhood, and especially when we were in exile in Sweden, he was very conspicuously the only boy in a house full of girls and women. Being the only boy and the firstborn, I believe he learnt early on that he needed to be there for his sisters and our mother.

I recall vividly one such occasion when we were on the playground in our neighbourhood. I was very young, maybe five or 6 years old, which would have made Muhoozi around nine or ten years old. I was climbing some ropes when suddenly an older boy started climbing the rope after me and swinging it violently back and forth. I was terrified that I was going to fall off or, worse, that he would get to where I was and push me off. I clung to the rope in complete terror until suddenly out of nowhere, my big brother saved the day. Muhoozi held the rope steady on the ground and gave the bully a good tongue lashing telling him to leave me alone. Needless to say, I was rescued from that experience and went on my way happily grateful to have a big brother. When he was young, he loved Michael Jackson's music and had a big poster of the pop star on his bedroom wall. Like many boys in the 1980's he wore white socks, black shoes and a glove in one hand to imitate Michael Jackson. He had all the records and hits of the pop star and learned how to do the moonwalk and the dance moves from the popular song *Thriller*. We all thought it was very cool and were an eager audience for him and his friends.

As Muhoozi grew, his love for God deepened and permeated every area of his life. He loved the Bible and stories of larger-than-life Biblical characters like King David and Moses. But above all, he loved the Lord Jesus and enjoyed watching the 1977 movie, *Jesus of Nazareth*[2], with Robert Powell starring as the Lord Jesus. As his relationship with the Lord matured, he became an evangelist and would share the gospel with anyone he felt needed to know the Lord. This could be his friends but often he preached the gospel to adults who were much older than he was.

He also had the role of designated storyteller or comedian. I cannot even remember what we always found so funny with his 'tales', but during the holidays we would stay up into the wee hours of the morning laughing and cackling at some stories he was sharing with us. These stories were about his friends at boarding school, their teachers and whatever adventures they had gotten up to at school.

During our holidays, we always went to our country home, Rwakyitura. In our small home, we children shared the same room well into our older teen years. Therefore, we had plenty of time to hear stories, talk, laugh and stay up late at night. Usually, our parents told us to go to bed, but after a while, they just left us to stay up talking for as long as we wanted. I will always remember the wonderful times we shared. When the generator was switched off, because it was late, we kept talking in pitch darkness and used a torch if we needed to move around in the dark.

---

2 *Jesus of Nazareth.* 1977 TV show. Cinematography by Armando Nannuzzi and David Watkin. Starring Robert Powell as Jesus.

My brother grew into a very handsome young man and this became a blessing and a problem for us his younger sisters; a blessing because we loved and were proud to have such a wonderful and handsome older brother, but the problem came with the girls who liked him and wanted to get to know him through us. If Muhoozi's school was coming to our boarding school for inter-school activities, I noticed that the older girls were very gracious and lenient with us. It finally dawned on me that they probably wanted us to mention them when he came, but for us, it was all good fun.

Muhoozi always had a tight-knit group of friends since he was a boy. These friends became extensions of our family over the years and many of these friendships have stood the test of time. From his childhood in Kenya, his close friends were Jimmy Bageire, Sammy, Joey and Maggie (Weya). When we returned home to Uganda his band of brothers grew to include Michael Pinto, Siwa, Cedric Babu, Julius Kategaya, Phillip Rukikaire and Sam Mpuuga.

As he has grown, my brother has taken on many mantles and roles, including husband, father, soldier and general. But I always tell him that, in my heart, he will always be a man after God's own heart, that young man who sought to live for God and please him with all his heart.

*****

My older sister Natasha, the second K in our group, has always been the communication hub in our family. She is the one who articulates clearly her ideas, thoughts and feelings and those of everyone around her. As a child, she was precocious, speaking at an early age and having a grasp of things beyond her years. She also inherited a propensity for more drama than any of the rest of us children. She had a way of telling stories in such a dramatic way, always acting things out so much that everyone would be spellbound.

I remember when we were children in Sweden, Natasha had somehow made up the story that she could fly and that she had flown over our neighbourhood. She convinced all the children in the neighbourhood that this had truly happened. When the children discounted her story, she said that she would repeat this great feat for their benefit on a certain predetermined night. All the children came to our home and crowded into one of our rooms. With the lights off, she would demonstrate this great feat of flying.

Everything was set, the day and the venue agreed. The only problem was that Natasha couldn't fly and she needed a sidekick to pull off this great feat of pretending to fly so that her story would remain intact. The greater problem was that she asked me to be her sidekick, which was not a good choice and ended up causing more problems than it solved. She made me practice my part in the elaborate drama and warned me against giggling or doing anything that might give away the story. I agreed and I wanted to do it so that I too could be admired as having been part of the flying story.

That evening our friends from the neighbourhood came. Our brother Muhoozi brought his friends and they all piled into the room sitting on beds and standing up against the wall. Natasha was hiding in the closet dressed in a long white night dress. She had chosen this on purpose so that her feet wouldn't be visible so that when she stood on tiptoe and pretended to fly, she would be believable. My role was to hold up the torch and do some special effects to make it look like she was flying off the ground. It seemed simple enough, only I wasn't so gifted in acting and I cracked under the pressure. I opened the closet door and whispered that everyone was ready, she gave me the go-ahead to turn off the lights in the room and put on the torch which I did. Then she came out and did the most dramatic display of flying, waving her hands and speaking in a weird voice. I couldn't help it, but I did the very thing she warned me not to do. I started giggling. I tried to hold it in but finally broke into fits of laughter. The children switched on the lights and our elaborate charade was over.

Despite our disappointing show, somehow the legend of Natasha flying lived on and she even coached other children on how they too could fly.

On another occasion, my sister and a group of friends formed a gang called the "Lietree Gang." It was very popular to form a "gang", although what we meant by "gang" was simply a group of boys or girls that agreed to some rules, secret passwords and some rivalries with other groups. The girls always had rivalries with the boys' gangs. Our brother Muhoozi and his friend had a gang called, "The Scorpions," and they were cool. Apart from the whole Michael Jackson effect, their group was bigger and they seemed to do cool things like ride bikes and go climbing the hills around our neighbourhood.

So Natasha and her friends made a group, there weren't that many in the gang, maybe four girls altogether. Diana and I used to tag along to the gang meetings although technically we were too young to join the group. One day, Natasha's friends gave her an ultimatum that her little sisters could no longer join the meetings unless they too had been initiated into the group. What was the initiation? Well, you had to have a snail, which was the symbol of the group, walk on your hand! Natasha had put in a good word for me to be allowed to join the group, but I had to have the snail walk on my palm. I was terrified of snails and thought they were the most disgusting things ever, but I really wanted to be part of the gang. So I accepted and the important day dawned when I was to have the snail walk on my hand. Our meetings usually took place on the steps of our apartment buildings, so we sat on the steps and one of the girls brought out the special snail. She placed it slowly on my palm and I felt its sluggish body begin to move on my hand. I screamed and shook it off!

With that, I had committed the cardinal crime and Natasha had to plead for me to be allowed into the group despite my poor performance. Finally, they let me in based on my sister's good word. But I would cause them to regret their decision very soon after.

One day, the Lie Tree gang decided to have our meeting up on the rocks around our neighbourhood. So we walked up the rocks and brought along our special snail in its matchbox home. One of the girls took it out of the matchbox and put it under a leaf so that it wouldn't be burned by the afternoon sun. As we talked and took notes in our secret diary, suddenly we heard the giggling and laughing of the rival boys' gang. They had been spying on us all along and now they jumped out of the bushes and started running around us laughing and making noise. In the pandemonium that ensued, and in our effort to get our things and leave, I accidentally stepped on the special snail that was hidden under the leaf. I was mortified when I heard the crunch of the snail's shell underneath my sneakers. I quickly told the rest of the girls and they were beyond heartbroken. Our special snail had died and I was the one who killed it!

We held a burial for the special snail and soon had to find another one to replace it. I was amazed that I wasn't thrown out of the gang. It was all on account of my big sister who made sure that, even though I had broken all the rules and failed to do a single thing right, I was her baby sister and no one was going to throw me out.

As my sister grew, she evolved from a dramatic and talkative little girl. Her relationship with the Lord brought out the heart of a worshiper that she has. She also loved art, painting, sketching, writing and music. Whenever we came home for the holidays, we read books to each other. Somehow we loved hearing the sound of our voices as we read to each other. We would read 800-900 page books to each other, taking turns to read them. Natasha was always best at reading to us because her voice was so expressive and animated. One holiday, she read Frank Peretti's *This Present Darkness* for us. I remember that story to this day.

Another thing we always did before returning to school after the holidays, was we would write long letters to each other and place them on our pillows. In this digital age, the art of writing letters is sadly disappearing, but it was such a wonderful tradition that lasted long into our older years. These letters reinforced our relationship as sisters. We encouraged each other, shared inside jokes and loved on each other. These letters were a long-held tradition and I think, in some way, they reaffirmed our relationship and our interdependence on each other. We are not only sisters, more than that we are forever friends by the Grace of God.

Natasha also had the gift of making friends wherever she went. In primary school, she had a big group of friends who became a permanent fixture in our lives. On birthdays and some weekends, all these friends would visit and it would be great fun for us all. Her big group of friends included Lillian Nagenda, Priscilla Egadu, Enid Rukikaire, Ishta Kyambadde and Josephine Wapakhabulo. On these weekends, the girls would arrange dance shows complete with special effects and cool costumes. My younger sister Diana and I loved tagging along as the audience for any of these home productions and we thought they were the coolest girls ever. In secondary school and university, Natasha made even more friends who became part of our family. Maria Ngatunga, Nancy Gassim and Mukami Mwanike were her great friends and became an extension of our family. Because we were a tight-knit unit as a family, each child's friends often developed friendships with the other siblings as a result of the amount of time we all spent together. These friendships have stood the test of time and are a testament to the gift to love and nurture people that Natasha possesses. She is a beautiful person both on the outside and inside and has always been a cheerleader in my own life.

My sister has gone on to wear many mantles in her life, that of a wife, mother, artist, author and filmmaker. However, in my heart, she will always be a beautiful romantic. Growing up it was a running joke that we could always tell a movie that Natasha would like. If it was not a nail-biting thriller, it had to be an epic love story with a brave protagonist preferably riding a horse with soaring Celtic music. That is why Mel Gibson's *Braveheart*[3] which portrayed the epic story of William Wallace, the Scottish noble who rebelled against England's King Edward in the C13th, was her undisputed favourite movie for many years in a row. God has helped her discover her own epic love story closer to home and it is a love story for our continent Africa, and

---

3 *Braveheart.* 1995 film directed and starring Mel Gibson; based on the poem *The Wallace* by Blind Harry.

the brave protagonists that have fought and continue to fight for our freedom and liberty. Natasha is using her many gifts and talents to introduce these stories to a new generation of Africans and to inspire them through art, film, music and culture.

*****

My younger sister Diana is the fourth K and the only sibling I have who is younger than me. As such, she has always had a special place in my heart and life. I do not know when I got it into my young mind that it was my role to mother my little sister, but as far back as I can remember I was very clear on that being my role. Even though we are only two years apart, I always felt that I was the mother hen and it was my role to shelter, protect and look after her. We shared a room from the time we were babies until I was twenty-two years old. That is when I graduated from University and left her in Minnesota to return to Uganda. As such, I shared more time with Diana than I did with any other person before I got married.

When we were little children in Sweden, we shared a room and before going to sleep I would tell her to dream of butterflies, flowers and horses. If she had scary dreams she would wake up and call my name. I would soothe her by telling her again to dream of only butterflies, flowers and horses. We were each other's playmates and confidantes; We laughed, fought and shared everything.

Diana and I attended a kindergarten called "Dogis" at the home of a Swedish teacher called Lisebet. In the morning, our mother dropped us off at Dogis and we spent the whole morning there until early afternoon. Then we walked home together, round the corner and over the hill until we got to our apartment. I was only six years old and Diana was just four years old, but we somehow always found our way home safely. When we got tired walking up the hill on our way home, we would put our arms around each other and supported each other up the hill until we finally got home. On arriving home, it was always easy to know if our mother was already home because we could smell the aroma of food cooking when we opened the mail slot in the door. When she opened the door for us, and we fell into her waiting arms, we knew we were safe and home.

One day, we went to Dogis as usual and when the day was done, we made our way home as we always did. When we climbed the stairs to our apartment and looked through the mail slot in the door, the house was quiet and there was no one home. This was the first time we ever came home before our mom got back from her Swedish class programmes. This posed a huge dilemma for us. What should we do? We couldn't walk back to Lisebet's because that was too far and we couldn't go out and play because it was deep winter and it was too cold outside. We were both dressed head to toe in our winter overalls, with hats, mittens and winter boots.

So we sat on the steps outside our apartment and waited for a while. To pass the time we started playing in the playground in front of our apartment block. It was the middle of the day and there weren't many other children there. Finally, tired and hungry, we decided to go and check if perhaps our mom had returned home. Thankfully, by God's Grace when we got back to our door and opened the mail slot, we heard the sound of our mother busy cooking in the house! She was home! When she opened the door and her two babies narrated the account of how they were stranded at the front door, she hugged us and helped us get out of all the winter clothes.

Diana and I have had many more adventures together in our years. To begin with, we shared the experience of being the "younger ones" although she was the baby of the family. We experienced much of life in those early years by hearing the tales that our older brother and sister shared at night before we went to bed. When we returned to Uganda, for the first couple of years, we all shared one big room. Muhoozi and Natasha had their single beds, and Diana and I shared one double bed. At night we snuggled together in our bed and giggled as we listened to the amazing stories shared by our siblings. They were all so funny and exciting and we actively listened to every word in the dark. One of the games we loved to hear them play was a game that asked which of your favourite singer/actor would you save if you could only save one person and the other person would fall into a chasm of fire and die. Natasha loved to ask Muhoozi this question, and the contest was always between Janet Jackson, who was the clear favourite and Sheena of *Sheena Queen of the Jungle*[4]; the corny 1980s movie about a white girl who grows up in the African Jungle and can call on animals to come to her aid. We always giggled as Natasha asked this question over and over and Muhoozi always capitulated to saving Janet Jackson and poor Sheena 'fell to her death in the chasm of fire'.

Diana has always been an animal lover. She kept dogs, cats, rabbits and any other animal she could get her hands on. But her clear favourite pets were dogs. I love dogs too but not in the same way that Diana does.

When we were at University in Minnesota, she used to watch a TV show called "Dogs 101" almost every day. This show details the different breeds of dogs, their history, pedigree and the advantages of one breed versus another. After some time, Diana made up her mind that she wanted to get a dog of her own and she had seen an advertisement on TV about a store called Petsmart. She begged me day after day to go with her to Petsmart to look at the breeds of dogs and see the one she could buy for herself. This went on for a while. Finally, I agreed and we made time to go and visit Petsmart. This was way before Google became prominent and you couldn't just search out venues and locations on the Internet. We also didn't have a car, so we had to go by taxi cab far out of town to the nearest Petsmart store in the suburbs. When we got to the store, Diana excitedly went in and I followed her. We were both shocked to find that the store did not carry pets as its name eluded, but rather they sold pet accessories and care items. So there was dog shampoo, dog brushes, dog food and other pet accessories but no actual pets. I was mortified

4 *Sheena, Queen of the Jungle.* 1984 film starring Princess Elisabeth Bagaya of Toro and Tanya Roberts. Based on the book *Sheena, Queen of the Jungle* by W. Morgan Thomas.

and I let her know it. We had gone all that way and there weren't even pets there! To return to campus, we had to call a taxi and wait close to an hour for one to finally come and pick us up. That story has gone down in our history as the "Petsmart incident" and I never let her hear the end of it.

Amongst us the girls or 3K's, we have something we call the "vault." This is just the imaginary place of our archived history together or our stories. So when we experience something that only we understand or find funny, we file it away in the vault and only bring it out when we want to reminisce on all our past adventures and escapades.

One such story that went into the vault happened when we were both at university. It was the end of my sophomore year and Diana's first year. At the end of the term, students had to return the items they rented from the school like refrigerators or any other such items. We rented a refrigerator at the beginning of the school year and were planning on returning it.

In renting the refrigerator there was an agreement signed between the student and the dorm whereby the student paid a deposit of $300 and a safety deposit of $10. On returning the refrigerator, the school returned the safety deposit of $10 if the fridge was in good working condition. I, however, had misread the contract and thought I would be receiving the $300 back when I returned the refrigerator. I had even earmarked that money to help me pay for something else as we moved out of the dorm. I was also very excited because this was our last year in the dorm and I was looking forward to having more space and privacy in the new year.

So Diana and I waited outside the dorm with our miniature refrigerator for the pick-up truck that was scheduled to arrive. Diana asked me about the other expense and I assured her that I had it covered because I was going to use the refund from the refrigerator deposit. Finally, the truck arrived driven by a big gruff looking driver who proceeded to load the refrigerator onto the truck. I waited confidently for him to finish loading so that he could sign for the receipt and then hand over the $300. The driver did exactly that, only when it came time for him to hand over the money, he reached into his pocket and pulled out a wrinkled $10 bill. I looked at the money and then at the driver with the most perplexed look ever and Diana who was beside me almost burst out into laughter. She said she wished she had a camera to take a picture of the look I had on my face. Finally, I recovered enough to ask the driver where the rest of the money was. He looked surprised and asked me which money I was referring to. I unfolded my contract and showed him the $300 on the contract. He agreed and then found the clause of the contract that stated that the safety deposit of $10 would be refunded at the end of the term if the refrigerator was in good condition. He said, "there's your $10." It was my mistake; I had completely misunderstood and misread the contract. That one episode went into the vault and whenever anyone has the kind of perplexed look that Diana purports that I had that day, we say they had the 'refrigerator look'.

Diana studied history and antiquities at university and she has always been interested in the development of cultures and civilizations. She is an astute businesswoman who is working hard to redefine the tourism sector in our country. Her quiet, gentle, demeanour belies her inner indomitable spirit.

Diana has grown to wear many different mantles in her life; that of wife, mother, conservationist and advocate. But in my heart and mind, she will always be the silver girl; a beautiful, kind, generous, funny and intelligent person who possesses great strength of character and moral fortitude. The silver girl represents someone who shines from the inside out because Diana possesses an intrinsic poise and elegance that makes her shine without being flashy. She is my sister and forever friend and I am so thankful to God for the blessing that she is to our whole family.

*****

My family continually grows to include more and more people. God has blessed me with an ever-expanding circle of spiritual sons and daughters, fathers and mothers, brothers and sisters. But my family, the white council, are the first ones who taught me how to love and to be loved. They gave me my roots and wings to fly. We are not a perfect family, we have flaws as human beings and we all make mistakes but our home has always been a place of love and acceptance. And along this wonderful, miraculous, journey of life, the white council members are always there, to witness, to cheer, to encourage and to celebrate. I honour them all, and I bless God for giving me a home built on His amazing Grace.

6. My People

Isaiah 19:24-25:

"In that day Israel shall be the third, with Africa and with Assyria (in a Messianic league) a blessing in the midst of the earth. Whom the Lord of hosts has blessed, saying, Blessed be Africa My people and Assyria the work of My hands and Israel My heritage." – Amplified Bible

I was a student of Political Science and Development Studies at the university. I recall that, in lectures, professors would talk about the political and economic powerhouses of the day. They would talk about the Asian Tigers of the East, with a focus on the growing influence of China. With the fall of the Soviet Union, a decade earlier and the explosion of growth in technology use with the advent of the internet, there was a tremendous discourse on the power of globalization in turning the world into a "global village" and the inevitable hegemony of the West.

As I sat in those lecture halls, from my vantage point as an African, it almost seemed as though there was a blanket of invisibility over Africa. When I would ask questions about Africa's role in global geopolitics, my professors would simply be at a loss. It seemed as though Africa was this big invisible elephant in the middle of a room that no one understood. Even in terms of intellectual discourse, Africa was often silent; I would often read the thoughts and ideas of foreigners which were often skewed and misrepresented Africa's historical and current position. I would leave my lectures upset and go to my room. There, I would fall on my face and cry to the Lord. As I cried, my heart had just one question, "Are we not also Your people?"

I asked this because I felt as though all the peoples of the earth were represented and had a voice in the affairs of the world except Africa. It took many years before God fully began to answer the deepest questions and yearnings of my soul.

Acts 17:26-27 reads,

> *"And He made from one common origin, one source, one blood, all the nations of men to settle on the face of the earth, having definitely determined their allotted periods of time and the fixed boundaries of their habitation (their settlements, lands and abodes), so that they should seek God in the hope that they might feel after Him and find Him although He is not far from each one of us." – Amplified Bible*

This scripture reveals that God has a redemptive plan and purpose for all the peoples of the earth. God, in essence, predetermined, for all, where they would live, where their lands would be and the times, seasons and epochs in which they would live.

Therefore, we can conclude that God determined that Africa would be for the African people. The scripture adds that there is a connection between the land and the redemptive purpose of people.

Why is that important? Because God gives land as an inheritance. If we look at the Biblical context of the children of Israel, it is very clear that the land of Israel was part of the covenant that God made with them.

This is what it says in Genesis 15:17-18:

> *"When the Sun had gone down and a (thick) darkness had come on, behold, a smoking oven and a flaming torch passed between those pieces. On the same day, God the Lord made a Covenant (promise, pledge) with Abram, saying, To your descendants I have given this land, from the river of Egypt to the great river Euphrates- the land of." – Amplified Bible*

The children of Israel were exiled twice in their history - first to Babylon and after the destruction of Jerusalem by the Romans. But God's Word is sure. Just as He had promised that the land was theirs even when they had gone into exile for many years - the first exile for 70 years and close to two thousand years the second time - God returned the Israelites to their land because that was their inheritance.

A good question to ask is whether this is unique to the children of Israel. Or is this part of the larger relationship that God has with humankind?

God was simply being true to His Word and His character in giving the children of Israel their land as an inheritance. The land that God gives has an everlasting lease; a lease that never expires.

However, when the people of the land sin, it brings judgment on the people and the land.

The Old Testament shows very clearly the effects of sin on the life of a people in relation to the land. The children of Israel experienced foreign domination, slavery and exile as a result of their sin. But God, in His mercy, eventually restores people as He did to the children of Israel and they returned to their land. In this respect, the children of Israel were eventually restored to their land in 1948 with the birth of the State of Israel. God, from the time that He made the covenant with Abraham, kept His promise of giving them the land. Land is an important part of people in fulfilling their redemptive purpose.

I have observed that people who have been forcibly removed from their land experience a kind of spiritual orphanhood or mourning that doesn't end.

By forcibly removed, I mean that they did not leave their land willingly, they did not emigrate or go to live in another land for different reasons. When people are forcefully removed from their land against their will, through war or forced exile, there is something that comes into the spirits of those people. They are overtaken by something akin to grieving for what they have lost.

This is true of the Native Americans who lost their lands forcibly with the coming of the Europeans into what they called the 'New World,' the Americas. It is also similar to the case of the Aborigines of Australia and the Africans of South Africa. The same is true of the African peoples of Namibia, Zimbabwe, Angola and the Kenyan Highlands, who were forced off their lands to make room for white settlers.

The people who are forcibly removed from their lands also experience deep psychological, emotional and social problems. They often suffer from substance abuse such as alcoholism, drug addiction, depression and deep sadness and melancholy. This kind of grieving, sadness and mourning continues for generations.

It says in Psalm 137,

> *"By the rivers of Babylon, there we the captives sat down and wept when we earnestly remembered Zion. On the willow trees in Babylon, we hung our harps. For there they who led us captive required from us a song with words, and our tormentors and they that wasted us required of us mirth saying, 'Sing one of the songs of Zion.' How shall we sing the Lord's song in a strange land? If I forget you or Jerusalem, let my right hand forget its skill." – Amplified Bible*

The Jewish captives in Babylon went as far as to say that they couldn't sing the songs of the Lord, the songs of Zion in a foreign land. They were traumatized by being torn from their land which was made worse by their captors' seemingly making light of their pain by asking for the songs of the Lord. Even as they were exiled to Babylon, their hearts were set on Jerusalem. In the subsequent captivity after A.D. 70, the Romans under Titus sacked Jerusalem, and the Jews were scattered to the four corners of the earth. The prayer "Next year in Jerusalem" was often quoted. This kept their hope of returning to their land alive for generations.

How about Africa? How does that apply to Africa?

There are Africans on many continents in the world. This is the case whether it is in the Americas, Europe or the Caribbean. How did Africans end up there? They came to be in those places - not as immigrants, refugees or tourists. The people of African descent in the Diaspora were taken there as slaves.

The case of slavery is vastly different from that of immigrants who move to a new land in search of opportunity. Lessons from human social development tell us that it takes immigrants three generations to move from the lowest social economic rung on the ladder to a medium or higher rung in the socio-economic ladder. That means that if your grandfather immigrated to a new land by the time you got to the third generation that family would have moved from the lowest point in the socio-economic ladder to a medium or higher place in the socio-economic ladder. That is the general trend in social development.

The story is markedly different for slaves as happened to Africans that were taken to Europe and the Americas.

Take the condition of African Americans, as a case in point. It is clear that after 400 years since they were forcibly taken as slaves, their position in no way compares with that of say the Irish, Japanese or Chinese immigrants to the Americas. African Americans, a minority in the US, represent the highest percentage of people incarcerated in prisons. In 2018 the percentage of African Americans less than 18 years of age living in poverty was 30%, a rate that is more than double that of whites in the same demographic.

The median household income of African Americans as of 2021 is $45,000 which is significantly lower than that of whites which is $70,000 in 2021. The unemployment rate amongst African Americans (16%) is more than double that of white Americans (6%). Infant and maternal mortality rates are also significantly higher than that of white Americans.

In addition, African Americans experience the highest cases of police brutality and violence compared to any racial group in that country. In addition, murders and homicides are higher in African American neighbourhoods than in white neighbourhoods.

African American families are more likely to be led by single parents and, overwhelmingly, do not have fathers in the home.

Why is this so?

Many historical reasons are responsible for these negative trends. To enforce slavery as a system, the social fabric of

African American society had to be broken down and destroyed. Slaves had no control over their lives, bodies, families and children. The uncertainty of life and the fact that the slave owner controlled every aspect of a slave's life scarred and traumatized the family unit especially. The image of African American men and women was also greatly denigrated, demonized and ridiculed. Finally, we cannot properly grasp the effects of generations of violence performed continuously on a group of people by another.

All these and many other reasons describe the roots of the problems that African American communities are still grappling with today. This greatly impacts the quality of family life and thus the children being raised and the future generations.

If the majority of men of a certain age are in prison then you will find that most families are led by women. As well, a majority of children are born out of wedlock. That makes family life very unstable and as a result, they get caught in a vicious cycle that repeats itself from generation to generation. Breaking out of this cycle seems insurmountable. Although there are some success stories, they are usually the exception and not the rule.

So this is the unfortunate picture of just one group of descendants of Africans outside of Africa in these other continents where Africans were taken as slaves.

The situation varies to some degree for those Africans taken as slaves to South America, Europe or the Caribbean but, generally speaking, the condition of the Africans has lagged behind other people groups in terms of social, political and economic development.

*****

Back to my questions in University: as I wrestled with these difficult questions, and the soul searching it birthed in my heart, I continually cried to the Lord, "Are Africans not your people?"

Many years later, the Lord finally answered this question through the Book of Isaiah 19:19-25.

My heart's cry was, "How come the case of Africa is different? How come you can have Chinese immigrants into a new land and, over these generations, you see a shift or upward mobility? You can have Italians, you can have Irish, you can have Jews, and you can have all these different people groups but this group - Africans who were brought as slaves - why is it that their condition is different? Why is it so different? Why is it such a stark contrast? What is the difference between us and other people? Are we not also Your people?" this is what it says in (Isaiah 19: 19-25):

"In that day there will be an altar to the Lord in the midst of the land of Egypt (Africa), and a pillar to the Lord at its border. And it will be a sign and a witness to the lord of hosts in the land of Egypt (Africa); for they will cry to the Lord because of the oppressors, and He will send them a saviour, even a mighty one, and he will deliver them. And The Lord will make Himself known to Egypt (Africa), and the Egyptians (Africans) will know (have knowledge of, be acquainted with, give heed to, and cherish) the lord on that day and will worship with sacrifices of the animal and vegetable offerings; they will vow a vow to the Lord and perform it. And the Lord shall smite Egypt (Africa), smiting and healing it; and they will return to the Lord, and He will listen to their entreaties and heal them. In that day there shall be a highway out of Egypt (Africa) to Assyria (Middle East), and the Assyrians will come into Egypt (Africa) and the Egyptians (Africans) into Assyria, and the Egyptians (Africans) will worship (the Lord) with the Assyrians. In that day Israel shall be the third, with Egypt (Africa) and with Assyria (In a Messianic league), a blessing in the midst of the earth, Whom the Lord of Hosts has blessed, saying, Blessed be Egypt (Africa) my people and Assyria the work of my hands and Israel my heritage." – Amplified Bible

When I read that, the Lord spoke to me at a very personal level. It was almost as though He came down from His throne to have a good heart-to-heart chat with me; father to daughter, one on one. He said, "I have not called you cursed. I have not called you what the entire world has called you."

From the scriptures, He showed me that He has called Africa "blessed" because He said, "blessed be Africa." Second, God showed me that He has called Africa "My people." God spoke to me clearly and said, "never again ask Me that question: 'Are we not also Your people?'" He assured me from His word that Africans are not just His people but they have a very unique redemptive purpose on earth. According to Isaiah 19, this redemptive purpose is linked to the Messianic league that will be established on earth to usher in the Return of the King Jesus to earth.

I believe that what God has in store for Africa in these end times is truly amazing and it is a unique time for Africa's redemptive purpose.

So if we are blessed and if we are His people, why has Africa suffered so much at the hands of so many? Why have there been so much pain and so much loss inflicted on Africans both externally by other people but also internally, self-inflicted? I believe what the Bible says in Luke 12:48 "….For whom much is given, of him shall much be required…"

There is a great spiritual and physical deposit of blessing that the Lord gave to Africa and so the failure to steward that deposit has brought great devouring and even judgment. I want to clarify that; what is it that has led to so much devouring? If we look at our history as the African continent, some historical events have had unprecedented impacts on our past and our present – one is slavery and the Second is Colonialism. As a believer, I did not see the significance of slavery and see the impact beyond it being a historical event. For years I viewed slavery as a horrific event in our past, tragic and unfortunate. However, I did not see its spiritual impact on our past, present and more importantly our future.

In 2017 the Lord began to download into my spirit His revelation that truly astounded me. The Lord spoke to me and He said the root of corruption is the same as the root of slavery. He went on to say that it is, "the Esau spirit."

As I have said before, I had always viewed slavery as a historical event but never thought it had a spiritual or natural impact on the present-day lives of the church or African nations. As such, I couldn't deny what I was hearing the LORD say. Corruption, which is a modern-day problem facing Africa, was connected to an ancient horrific event. The Lord revealed that unless we dealt with the root causes of this spirit we would only be dealing with the fruits or the symptoms and not dealing with the foundational issues.

With one word, God brought slavery out of the history books and into my present day. I started to pray and study all I could about the historical roots of slavery.

In Genesis 25:29-34, we read the following:

> *"Jacob was boiling potage (lentil stew) one day when Esau came from the field and was faint (with hunger). And Esau said to Jacob, I beg of you, let me have some of that red lentil stew to eat, for I am faint and famished! That is why his name was called Edom (Red). Jacob answered, Then sell me today your birthright (The rights of the firstborn). Esau said see here I am at the point of death; what good can this birthright do to me? Jacob said, swear to me today (that you are selling it to me); and he swore to (Jacob) and sold him his birthright. Then Jacob gave Esau bread and stew of lentils, and he ate and drank and rose and went his way. Thus Esau scorned his birthright as beneath his notice." – Amplified Bible*

Esau and Jacob were the twin sons of Isaac, the son of Abraham, the father of our faith. According to the Jewish tradition, Esau as the firstborn was entitled to the birthright and inheritance. The second son would also get a blessing from his father but it would be subservient to the blessing of the firstborn.

Being cognizant of this the Israelites took pains to establish who was born first as the condition for the blessing. Why? Because the one who comes first has a legal and spiritual claim to inheritance but also to the blessing and that blessing – that fatherly blessing would establish or uproot an individual.

> *"Now behold when the time came for her to be delivered, there were twins in her womb. And when she was in labour, one baby put out its hand and the midwife took his hand and bound a scarlet thread on it, saying this baby was first born..." Genesis 38:27-28 – Amplified Bible*

Esau was the firstborn and thus legal heir and he had a double portion of the inheritance. However, because he took his inheritance lightly or he despised it he did not understand the enormity of what he was doing. His younger brother Jacob understood that there was no way he would get the inheritance and blessing unless there was a transaction or an exchange.

The transaction had to take place because Esau is the one who possessed the inheritance and only Esau could give it. What's so interesting is that Esau sells his inheritance to his brother for a bowl of stew. He in essence gives away what is priceless in exchange for a cheap meal. Esau "sold" his birthright, his position, his blessing and his inheritance. Jacob could not have stolen it, if Esau hadn't first sold it because he despised it.

The Lord revealed that the root of the "Esau Spirit" was that Esau despised his inheritance; he took it as a light thing, and he didn't esteem its worth. This was an unequal transaction; one far outweighed the other. Esau sold something eternal and priceless to gain something temporal and cheap. He gave away his destiny, future, and the destiny of his descendants for a simple meal.

What happens after this transaction? Once the birthright is sold, the blessing is easily seized.

Genesis 27: 26- 37 says thus:

> *"Then his father Isaac said, come near and kiss me, my son. So he came near and kissed him; and (Isaac) smelled his clothing and blessed him and said, The Scent of my son is as the odour of a field which the lord has blessed.*
>
> *"And may God give you of the dew of the heavens and of*

the fatness of the earth and abundance of grain and (new) Wine; Let peoples serve you and nations bow down to you; be master over your brothers, and let your mother's sons bow down to you. Let everyone be cursed who curses you and favoured with blessings who blesses you. As soon as Isaac had finished blessing Jacob and Jacob was scarcely gone out from the presence of Isaac his father, Esau his brother came in from hunting. Esau had also prepared the savoury food and brought it to his father and said to him, Let my father arise and eat of his son's game, that you may bless me. And Isaac his father said to him, Who are you? And he replied, I am your son, your firstborn, Esau. Then Isaac trembled and shook violently, and he said, Who? Where is he who has hunted game and brought it to me, and I ate of it all before you came and I have blessed him? Yes, and he shall be blessed. When Esau heard the words of his father, he cried out with a great and bitter cry and said to his father, Bless even me also, O my father! (Isaac) said, Your brother came with crafty cunning and treacherous deceit and he has taken your blessing. (Esau) replied, is he not rightly named Jacob (the supplanter)? For he has supplanted me these two times: he took away my birthright and now he has taken away my blessing! Have you not still a blessing reserved for me? And Isaac answered Esau, Behold, I have made (Jacob) your Lord and Master; I have given all his brethren to him for servants and with corn and (new) win have I sustained him. What then can I do for you, my son?" – Amplified Bible

Esau recognized that twice he had lost out to Jacob, but he only had himself to blame. Jacob did not have the power to possess his birthright if Esau had not sold it. Esau lost his position and rights as a firstborn - the blessing follows the birthright once he had sold his birthright the blessing was violently and cunningly stolen. Jacob took up a new position that was formerly not his own and Esau took up a new position and it came with second-class status.

One may wonder why all the fuss about simple words, but the father's blessing was a powerful spiritual transaction that established seniority and the pathway for blessing. What happened between Esau and Jacob was the dispossession of Esau in favour of Jacob.

Esau's lineage and descendants, who came to be called the Edomites, were eventually wiped out; the nation of Israel and the covenant were established through Jacob. The State of Israel that we see today and all the Jewish race over the face of the earth are descendants of Jacob. Jesus Christ the Son of God came from the house of Israel, the house of Jacob.

Therefore, Esau was completely dispossessed of his blessing and his inheritance. Eventually, his descendants were wiped off the face of the earth. This is a dire situation, Esau completely lost his place. He lost what was his right as a firstborn because he sold his birthright. Remember that only through selling one's birthright could one lose the rights of a firstborn.

Africa's Birthright

What does the term "Birthright" mean in the African context?

In the case of slavery, African kings and chiefs sold out their birthrights when they sold their people for the trinkets they received from slave traders. The slave trade would never have flourished or even worked without the active collaboration of the African kings and chiefs. What happened? African chiefs and kings would raid other people and take them to the coast, sell them to middlemen and those middlemen would eventually sell the captured Africans to the European slave dealers. The African kings thought that they were selling "other people" because they never sold their subjects but rather the people they raided from neighbouring villages or rival ethnic groups. How tragic and myopic it was for our kings and chiefs to sell human beings, brothers and sisters, sons and daughters for mere trinkets. People were sold in exchange for cloth, cowrie shells, mirrors and guns.

They, like Esau, sold what was eternal for the stew of the day!

They despised their birthright and sold it for what was commonplace. Remember that, once the birthright is sold, the blessings that come with it can be violently and cunningly seized. After selling our African brothers and sisters into slavery, our independence and freedoms were violently and cunningly stolen. This happened through colonialism and the oppression that followed. In the African context, financial resources and wealth flowed freely and continue to flow out of Africa to the colonial powers.

There are many great scholarly accounts of the great injustice perpetrated by the Europeans through colonialism and later neo-colonialism. Walter Rodney in his landmark book, *How Europe Underdeveloped Africa,* gives an in-depth account of the impact of colonialism on the continent. The illegitimate meeting known as the Berlin Conference of 1878, organized by Chancellor Otto von Bismarck, brought together the European powers that were fighting for dominance on the African continent. There was no African representation at that meeting. It was not attended by a single African king or chief. What ensued was the "scramble for Africa", the race to seize African territory and exploit her resources. Consequently, European powers carved up the African continent like a cake into hastily drawn-up states or territories, created for the sole purpose of serving the colonial powers as a source of raw materials. The development of Europe came at the cost and underdevelopment of Africa. Africa's economy, society and culture were disrupted to serve the colonial powers and came with a devastating price tag whose effects reverberate to date.

Even after decolonization and the fight for Independence on the continent, the global structures of oppression remain albeit in a more subtle way. There may not be foreign flags flying in Africa, but they pull the strings in other ways such as through predatory economic policies, unequal trade that disenfranchises the primary producers and enriches their economies, interference & meddling in the domestic affairs of African countries and working behind the scenes to keep Africa, poor, disunited, weak and distracted with petty differences.

The Spirit Behind Corruption

Africans are free moral agents that have agency just like any other human beings on the earth. We must take responsibility for our wrong actions that have brought untold harm and pain to our communities. It is only by coming to terms with our failures in the past that we can work to avoid those same wrong choices and their tragic consequences today and in the future. In the past, our chiefs sold the destinies of millions of Africans for the greedy gain of the moment. Today, men and women are still grappling with the consequences of these choices. In African government bureaucracies today, we have new chiefs and kings who are doing the same thing that our chiefs and kings did generations ago. They sit in air-conditioned offices and sign away the destinies of their people through contracts and kickbacks, padded invoices and bribes. They have titles such as "Minister, Commissioner, Permanent Secretary, and so on..." They are big men and big women, but they are still exchanging what is eternal for the soup of the day.

We must recognize that no one can steal our blessings unless we first sell our birthright. As such, it is time for us to go to the root of the matter and take responsibility for our actions, both in the past and in the present.

This in no way removes or diminishes the responsibility of those foreign actors that have actively fought against African advancement. They have their overwhelming burden of guilt which they are reluctant to own up to. They have failed, time and again, to show any trace of morality and even higher Christian virtues of those who call themselves followers of Jesus.

But that is not the point of this book. We must look into our hearts, and settle these matters right in our hearts. We must stand in the gap and repent for the sins of our ancestors and our sins, as a people, that keep us from possessing our birthright and inheritance.

Repossessing our birthright? What does that mean for us today?

I believe that the Lord has begun to reveal all these hidden truths at this time because it is indeed His appointed time for Africa. In August 2019 the world commemorated the 400th year since the first African slaves were taken to the Americas. It is a 400-year gate of time.

I believe that the Lord started revealing these things ahead of time because He wants us as the church to capture this gate of time.

Here are the words from Genesis 15:13-14:

> *"And (God) said to Abram, know positively that your descendants will be strangers dwelling as temporary residents in a land that is not theirs (Egypt), and they will be slaves there and they will be afflicted and oppressed for 400 years. But I will bring judgment on that nation whom they will serve, and afterward, they will come out with great possessions." – Amplified Bible*

From these words, it is clear that God prophesied to Abraham what would happen to his descendants many years into the future. He told Abraham that his descendants will be strangers in a land that was not theirs for 400 years. Does it mean that you can be living in a place for 400 years and be a stranger in that land? Consider the people of African descent who were taken as slaves into all these continents and have lived there, are citizens, have built homes and raised families; is it possible that they can be strangers in a land that they have lived in for 400 years?

That was the case for the children of Israel. Is that the reason why they do not possess the land and are strangers even though they have lived there for so long? It says they will be afflicted, they will be oppressed for 400 years. So 400 years is a gate of time. As soon as the 400 years were over, it was as if God had a calendar, a divine appointment. At exactly that time God raised Moses to begin the process of the deliverance of the children of Israel.

I believe that in this season God is especially visiting Africa and not just Africans in the continent but people of African descent around the world. This word that the Lord has kept hidden all these years, He is beginning to reveal at this time because there's a great deliverance, a great freedom, a great restoration at hand.

Prayer

Heavenly Father we thank you because you are a God of mercy and compassion and the multitude of your mercies. We Africans, in this time Lord, have long cried out to you for the Mercy and salvation of our nations. In your time you have remembered us and this is your great day of visitation.

Father I pray that you will forgive the great weight of our sins as a people for we have sinned against you and each other we ask that in this season you will deliver us from the enemy and the oppressors that have long pursued us.

Father may you judge the nations that have plundered Africa for so long. We ask

that you will begin the healing of our hearts, our minds, our spirits and of our land. Please make us great people. In Jesus' mighty name Amen.

7. Walk in the Dark with Jesus

Where are You taking me, why are we turning here?
This road is strange to me, this path is not so clear
It must be the place where my doubt turns to faith
Where I close my eyes and take Your hand.

I'd rather walk in the dark with Jesus
Than to walk in the Light on my own
I'd rather go through the valley of the shadow with Him
Than to dance on the mountains alone
I'd rather follow wherever He leads me
And go where none before me have gone
I'd rather walk in the dark with Jesus
Than to walk in the Light on my own.

I've made some plans You know
Mapped out a strategy
Can somebody tell me where did the seasons go
Have You forgotten me?
But I've heard the darkest hour is just before dawn
And wherever You are the sun will shine, shine

I'd rather walk in the dark with Jesus
Than to walk in the Light on my own
I'd rather go through the valley of the shadow with Him
Than to dance on the mountains alone
I'd rather follow wherever He leads me
And go where none before me have gone
I'd rather walk in the dark with Jesus

Than to walk in the Light on my own.

There will be shadows but I won't be shaken

Because You have never forsaken a vow

No, No, You've never failed me before this I know

And Jesus You won't fail me now, No, No

– Song by Wayne Watson from the album *Beautiful Place*, 1993.

After my ordinary level examinations, my greatest desire was to apply directly to university as my older sister Natasha had done. Both my older brother and sister were in university and I wanted nothing more than to follow them and be done with secondary school. I spent all my time looking for university prospectuses and searching for degree courses that I could study. Any university, in any place, was better in my opinion than going back to boarding school in Namagunga. Four years in my opinion was more than enough for me. I had had my fill of boarding school and was ready for the wider world or so I thought. I was ready to put all my energies into finding a good university and convincing my parents that, at age 17, I was ready for independence.

The interesting thing about walking with the LORD is that after some time, you get a sense of when He is with you and when He isn't. However, I am stubborn by nature and always thought that I could convince my Heavenly Father to agree with me and back my plans. In this situation, I could sense early on that He wasn't with me in my desire to not return to boarding school. I couldn't for the life of me understand why God couldn't see that I was so done with boarding school that I did not want anything more to do with it.

I was finished with "self-reliance" which meant digging fields in the school garden and doing housework which meant washing hundreds of plates and cups in the school dining room. I was finished with clearing weeds on walkways, fetching water, peeling *matooke* (banana plantains) and cassava and getting the starch stuck on my hands! So I was on a mission to get out of boarding school and I was confident I could get God to agree with me.

I researched several universities in different countries and felt that I had zeroed in on the courses I liked. I armed myself with prospectuses and all the options I considered available and of interest to me. I knew that my long vacation was coming to an end soon and, therefore, a decision about where I was going for my A-levels would be coming up. I started quietly lobbying my parents.

I am thankful that we always had a good relationship with our parents, and felt that, whatever the situation, we could always share our minds and hearts with them and that they would always give us a fair hearing.

My parents listened to me as I continually brought up my plans of not going back to Namagunga and, instead, apply to university. They listened but they never gave me their answer. As the countdown to the end of the vacation drew closer, I became desperate and continued to badger them for an answer. Indeed, even when it was a few weeks before school opened, there was no decision on my case and no change of heart in sight from my parents.

Then one morning my father called me to his room and asked me to sit on his lap. That wasn't a good sign, it meant that he was going to give me some bad news and wanted to lessen the disappointment by comforting me.

I did as instructed. I sat on his lap. Then he explained to me that it was very expensive to have three children in university at the same time. He added that both he and my mother did not feel that I needed to skip my A-level years at that point. He said they had decided that I should go back for two more years in Namagunga.

Two years! It felt like an eternity! My eyes started tearing up; I felt the blow of shattered hopes and expectations. As tears run down my cheeks, I sobbed saying I could not handle two more years in boarding school.

My father answered lovingly that two years in Namagunga would not kill me. After all, he had fought in the bush war for thirteen years and he was no less a person than others.

I felt convicted by his words and dried my tears. I agreed that I would go back to Namagunga and "do my time," so to speak. The disappointment and dashed hopes were, for me, a lot to take! My long holiday wound up not with me packing my suitcase to go to university but rather me packing my tin box to go back to boarding school.

I arrived back at school on the appointed day. Our headmistress, Sister Cephas, an Irish Franciscan sister who had dedicated her life to the education of girls in Namagunga, warmly welcomed us all back. She asked me if I was happy to be back at school. I dared to mumble something incoherent like, "not really."

Sister Cephas, or "Capui" as she was nicknamed by the students, was a luminous figure in our lives in Namagunga. She was feared and respected by all the girls, and we all wondered what her hair looked like under the customary brown veil that she wore. As O-level students, we all made fun that Capui was everywhere and saw everything that happened in the school, and if you did something wrong, you would be sure that Capui would find you.

It was only after leaving Namagunga that I properly grasped what an amazing human being Sister Cephas was and how much of an impact she had on our lives. She was a devoted woman who lived a life for a higher purpose of service to God and the community. It took great courage and bravery to leave her country to come to Uganda especially during the turbulent years of war in the 1970s and 1980s to serve as a headmistress. Sister Cephas' main goal was to properly educate and prepare girls for the lives they would lead after Namagunga. As a Franciscan sister, her motivation was not money or financial gain of any form, but spiritual and social impact. And so, for all the years that she was the headmistress of Namagunga, the school class sizes remained relatively small, and the services and facilities were well maintained. Above all, the moral and spiritual development of the girls was above par.

Every Namagunga girl wears a badge of honour and she is distinct in the way she comports herself, speaks and indeed lives. Namagunga graduates are among the leaders of our community and society today, and whenever you see a woman who speaks and carries herself with dignity and confidence, she is most likely a Namagunga product. That is Sister Cephas' legacy to the world, a Franciscan nun who neither married nor had children, but who raised a generation of incredible daughters. She lived, imbibed and passed on the motto of the school, *Per Scientiam Ad Virtuem*, which means "Through Knowledge to Virtue."

Sister Cephas retired from Namagunga many years ago and returned to her home in Ireland. However, whenever she has the chance to visit Uganda, the Namagunga old girls from around the country, in a heartbeat, will be there to receive and honour her, and in a congregation of Namagunga girls, the blessing of St. Francis is always sung.

However, back then, when I returned to Namagunga in mid-1996, I didn't see all these wonderful virtues of my school environment. Indeed hindsight is 20/20! At that time, all I could see was two more years of drudgery. Yes, life as an A-level student had its benefits compared to those at O-levels. Since the A-level numbers were small, we had the conveniences of a larger hostel space compared with the crowded dormitories of the juniors. In Senior 5, two girls, or at most four, shared a cubicle in a hostel. In addition, the hostels were open all day. As such, you could always retire to your room after class. We were also allowed the luxury of having a kettle to boil water and make tea or coffee, or even boil water to take a shower. This was the high life fp schooling; no more cold showers in the morning.

In theory, we also had indoor plumbing. Practically speaking, though, this didn't always work. As such, even seniors had to use the unbearable pit latrines just like the rest of the school. Also, there was 'no lights out' time because, as seniors, we constituted the school government which meant we ran the show. So life as a senior wasn't as bad as I had imagined.

Going back to Namagunga was also a great chance to be reunited with my friends from my O-level class and make new friends from those that had newly joined the school from other schools for their A-levels.

Now that I was a senior, I had a little more time to breathe and think about what contribution I wanted to make to school life. In Senior Five, the student government was chosen with ministers and deputy ministers elected to key positions. Electing officials for student government was an exciting time for seniors who wanted to stand for any specific positions. Girls had to campaign amongst their classmates and show why they were the best candidates for the different posts.

All this was fun and good. However, I had no interest in holding a position in the student government. My interest was to start a school newspaper. So, while some of my friends were campaigning for the school government, I was speaking to a few girls about what it would take to publish a school newspaper. To do so I needed to gain the approval of the headmistress, Sister Cephas, and the school administration. The school had never had a newspaper before and so Sister Cephas happily approved our plans.

First, I constituted a small team of girls, many of them my friends and classmates. They had varied interests such as history, politics, current affairs and sports. The paper, according to our plan, would be issued every two weeks to give us time to gather different stories. Bear in mind that this was in the 1990s and I had never actually worked on a computer at all. We had one computer at school which was safely stored in the school library under the care of the librarian. One couldn't just go and ask to use the computer at any time one wished. As such, we had to be tactical. We had to gauge whether the librarian was in a good mood or not. We would then go and greet him politely and then kindly ask, if it wasn't too much trouble for him, if he could help us to type up our paper and print it out for us. This happened every two weeks and the effort to meet the print deadline was real.

We also agreed to distribute our paper outside the dining hall which was where the whole school population congregated every day for meals. There was no cost to buy the paper so it was the school bearing the cost of the printing of the paper. In the week before the paper was to be issued we made handmade flyers about what readers would expect that week in the columns. As the editor, I had a column in the paper called *Seanachai* which means "storyteller" in Gaelic. It was my fun way to write fictional stories and share them with our audience.

Before we launched the paper we had to agree on a name. As a team, we all contributed ideas and finally narrowed on *Dawn 2000*. It sounds cheesy now, but you must understand that this was 1996. The year 2000 was the millennium that held expectations, including, as some thought, people wearing space suits and driving flying cars! At the time, *Dawn 2000* was truly futuristic in our imagination!

When we had our first edition ready, we approached Sister Cephas about launching the newspaper at the assembly with the entire school body present. She kindly acquiesced and everything was set for the occasion.

On the day of the launch, we had the whole student body present. Then Sister Cephas shared a few words congratulating us on starting the first school newspaper. We had one newspaper bound in a beautiful red ribbon and a scissor for the symbolic act of opening our first edition. Sister Cephas kindly obliged and cut the ribbon! Everyone applauded. So there it was! We were officially launched, and now started the hard work of churning out a paper every two weeks along with all the other school workload we had.

I continued to work on the newspaper for the rest of my stay at Namagunga. It was a wonderful creative experience to work with amazing, talented girls to get our newspaper out every two weeks. Even with very limited resources, we drew on the intelligence and organizational skills of our group of girls and had a lot of fun doing it. I am not sure if the school continued with the newspaper after I left, but I like to think of it as my contribution to student life at Namagunga.

*****

I was blessed to make wonderful friends in my years in Namagunga. The bonds of friendship forged during those pivotal five years have, by the Grace of God, stood the test of time.

In my senior year, my friends and I started a weekly fellowship that we called *Bencho*. This name arose simply because we met on a bench on the field opposite our hostels. The bench wasn't long enough to carry all of us, so we added a mat on the grass. That way some of us could sit on the mat while others sat on the bench. The Bencho Group consisted of my friends Nukuri Mizero, Annabelle Katembwe, Gloria Omaswa, Kristine Kallemera, Kobusingye Kilonsi (RIP), Juliana Mukasa, Jean Rwomwijhu and Olivia Byanyima.

We consistently met and fellowshipped every week, times that became treasured memories for all of us. We laughed, cried, and shared different aspects of our lives and our relationships with God. We encouraged each other to continue on our journey with the Lord despite the many different problems we encountered along the way. This core group of friends has since spread across the country and even the world; marriage, work and others callings have taken us in vastly different directions. But whenever we come together, as the whole group or just a few of us, the spirit of Bencho encourages us all to keep on going on this journey of faith.

At school, all seemed to be going well as the months slowly moved on. However, in my heart, I knew that the LORD wasn't happy with me. Since my disappointment of not being allowed to go to university, I was simply coasting along. I was disengaged with my classwork and not working as hard as I normally did. In class, my mind would wander into daydreams I found more interesting than the "boring" subjects I had in front of me. I did my studies and attended class, I was physically there but my heart and mind were not present.

One day as I was studying in a room alone, the Lord confronted me about my attitude. I was shocked that God wasn't happy with my behaviour. I mean what more did God want from me? I was obedient to my parents, I was doing my school work, and I was there, what more did God want? The Lord spoke to me clearly, saying, **"I want you to trust Me."**

As He spoke these words, I felt tears welling up in my eyes, I started talking back to God, "I trusted You but You didn't come through for me."

He answered, "**That is not trust**." The Lord showed me that, if I had truly trusted Him, I would have let Him decide for me where and when I should go to university. Instead, I made the decision and wanted Him to rubber stamp it. I was shocked to hear His Voice, very gentle and kind but firm and strong. He said, **"To trust Me is to surrender, to give your desires to Me and trust that I will do the best thing for you."**

His words sunk deep into my spirit like rain on dry ground. I was broken and sorry for my attitude. I knew He was right, I hadn't trusted God. I wanted my way and, when I didn't get it, I was offended at God.

The dam burst and an avalanche of tears poured out. I repented to the Lord for my attitude, for taking His goodness for granted, and for despising the blessings He had given to me. I realized that I was not grateful for the blessing of a loving family, parents who supported me, a wonderful school community, friends that cared for me and above all, the blessing of knowing God as my Friend. I repented and felt the healing power of His forgiveness wash over me. I knew that I had taken a lot for granted and had been very ungrateful. I listened to a worship medley that day by Twila Paris and understood for the first time what the words meant.

Sometimes my little heart can't understand,

What is in Your Will and What is in Your Plan,

So many times I'm tempted to ask You why,

But I can never forget it for long, Lord what You do could not be wrong,

So I'll believe You even when I must cry.
Do I trust You Lord?
Does the north wind blow
Do I trust You Lord, does the river flow?
You can see my heart, You can read my mind
And You've got to know I would rather die
Than to lose my faith in the One I love,
Do I trust You?
Do I trust You Lord?

– Song by Twila Paris from the album *A Heart that knows You,*1992.

This song accurately captured what I felt at the time. Many times we forget that the walk of faith is truly a walk of faith. There are times when we don't know exactly where the Lord is leading us or where we are going. There are many things the Lord asks us to do that don't make sense to the natural mind. Those are the times we must choose to trust the Lord, to trust His love and His heart for us, that He would never lead us into hurt, pain or trouble.

My dear friend Nukuri walked in on my crying fest and I shared with her what the Lord had just shown me. I confessed to her that all that the Lord spoke to me was true and right and that I had decided to make a change. From then on I consciously 'reconnected' with school, with my work and my teachers. I got my head out of the clouds and came back into my world of school and life. I gave it my all that I could, all my focus and attention, and all my energy and love. In the end, I was much happier for it than before.

I realized that I loved Namagunga and that it was one of the greatest places I had experience with; it had given me a lot and taught me very many lessons. I loved the way the sun rose over the morning hills of the tea plantations opposite the school. Every morning, as I walked to class, I could see the mist hanging over the hills like a veil. It was beautiful and captivating. I loved the green fields and the space that we had to walk all over the campus. I loved the traditions that we had and the love, laughter and poignant memories that we all shared. I loved my teachers who invested a lot into all of us, who gave of themselves and challenged us to strive for greater heights. I loved my friends who would forever be a part of my life and journey. I never would have met them if it were not for this magical, wonderful, special place called Namagunga. I loved my school, it was a part of me and I was blessed to have experienced it.

As we came to the end of my Senior Five year, I geared up for Senior Six which would be my final year in Namagunga. With it would com the final Uganda Advanced Certificate Examinations and bidding farewell to our beloved school. As I prepared mentally for this year, I packed all my textbooks and study notes so that I could study during the holidays.

On arrival at home, my parents told us that my younger sister Diana and I would be travelling with them to attend the graduation of our older sister Natasha. We were elated to go and celebrate this huge milestone in the family. We also wanted to see her university and meeet her friends who, up until then, we had only seen in pictures and heard about in letters. I knew that I still had to study during the trip. As such, I packed my books figuring that I would get some time to revise while on the trip.

My sister Natasha's graduation was wonderful. Our whole family and many friends were present and we were filled with pride when they called out her name and she walked across the stage to be awarded her degree. We hollered and cheered in as dignified a way as we could, not wanting to embarrass our parents and relatives with the noise. In the evening, there was a big graduation dinner for the graduates with music and dancing. We were a big group of girls all together, my sisters, her friends, and our cousins who were also attending university in the same city. My older brother, Muhoozi, who was also preparing for his graduation, came to the graduation and so the group was complete. Muhoozi, as the oldest child and leader of our group, was always adored and loved by us girls. He was a protective, loving and very funny big brother and having him with us made everything perfect.

During those wonderful days of celebration, my parents called me to their hotel room to share something important with me. This time my father didn't invite me to sit on his lap but what he shared with me completely caught me off-guard. He said that, together with my mother, they had been thinking about my education. Since my older siblings were graduating from university, he said, they were now open to my going to university as well. My father went on to say that he had met the dean of the Humphrey Institute at the University of Minnesota, in the USA, who visited Uganda for some work. During the meeting, my father asked him about the possibility of me applying to the university as an undergraduate.

I was completely dumbfounded and speechless. I had long given up the hope of going to university before completing my A-levels. In the proces, I had embraced my time at Namagunga wholeheartedly. I didn't know how to process what they had just told me. As such, I simply asked how it could be possible since I was now preparing to sit my Senior Six examinations. My father replied that I didn't need to go ahead with the examinations since the university would accept me on my O-level or High School Certificate.

"So what should I do now? Will I be going back to school after the holidays?" I asked.

Both my parents said that I wouldn't go back to school after the holiday break but instead should work on my applications and prepare to go to university in the fall of that year. My talk with my parents ended and I returned to my room completely speechless. I couldn't believe what they had shared with me.

Minnesota had been in my dream for years. My friend Nukuri and I had long dreamed that I would go to the University of Minnesota and her to Pennsylvania, so we could visit each other. However, now now following the news from my parents, I was in a complete daze and a little conflicted. Before, when I was desperate to leave Namagunga, the Lord told me to stay; now when I was completely at peace with staying at Namagunga, He opened the door for me to move on to university. I was confused and unsure of what to do next. What did this mean? What about my friends at Namagunga and the strong bonds we had created among us? Would I leave them and go to university on my own?

The Lord spoke into my confusion and calmed the storm in my thoughts, He said, **"I told you that if You would trust Me, I would open doors for you that no man can close. I am the One opening this door for you, all you have to do is walk through it."**

That was all I needed to hear!

Again there flowed tears of joy, shock and amazement. God was so good to me! So faithful and true! At that stage, my heart became quiet and still; I had no words to speak to articulate what I was feeling and the emotion in my heart. All I could think of was, 'God you are God; You are My Father, You love me and I have no words to thank You!'

Our time at the graduation ceremony soon came to an end and I returned home with the same bag of books I had carried along to study. Everything had changed now and, as all my friends prepared to go back to school for their Senior Six, I stayed home to work on my university applications. I applied to the University of Minnesota, Twin Cities, as a pre-medical student. In August of 1997, I got my acceptance letter and there was not enough praise music in the world to capture my heart of praise to God. He had done it again!

I went back to school to say goodbye to my friends and my beloved school, Sister Cephas and to the place that had been my whole world for five years. It was a bittersweet time; saying goodbye with tears, letters and songs of farewell taught me that to walk into a new season means closing an old season. Many times it is hard to let go of the old in order to receive the new. However, when we walk with God, we trust that when He opens a new door it is because He has taught us all that He wants to teach us in the old season. At that moment, it is time to move on. I said goodbye to Namagunga and all my friends and looked forward to a new chapter of my life opening up in Minnesota.

Minnesota On My Mind

The word alone speaks volumes in my life. It speaks of a time, a season, a moment in time when the Lord took me out of my familiar world and surroundings so that He could do greater work in me. Minnesota, is that wonderful world of snow, cold and ice, the land of ten thousand lakes, prairies and rivers. Minnesota is the land of Native American nations like the Sioux, also known as the Dakota, the Chippewa and the Ojibwe. The name 'Minnesota' means *Clear Wa*ter, because of the rivers and lakes that crisscross the land. The name Minneapolis, which became my new home, comes from the Native American word that means waterfall or the *City of the Waters*. Everywhere in Minnesota, there were reminders that this beautiful land belonged to and was home to great Native American nations. Thousands of years before the coming of the Europeans, their tribes lived on the land and hunted game on the open wild prairies. My spirit welcomed and found a home in this land. It reminded me so much of my beautiful homeland, Uganda, a land that the rivers and lakes divide.

I arrived in Minnesota in the Fall of 1997, ready to embrace the new season that the Lord had opened up to me. I was very grateful that my mother made the long journey to take me to school and help me settle into the new environment. I remember noticing the change as soon as we boarded the Northwestern flight from Amsterdam to Minneapolis. Northwestern, an international airline, had its hub in Minneapolis so it was very convenient to connect directly instead of transiting through other cities. As soon as we got on the flight, I knew we had switched to American standard sound because Americans generally speak very loudly. The plane was full of Americans and, in particular, those from the midwest in their khaki shorts, drinking Coca-Cola with a lot of ice and talking loudly. We could hear the conversations of almost everyone on the flight because everyone spoke very loudly. It was strange behaviour I thought; we couldn't understand why they were shouting, for instance.

Apart from the loud conversations, I felt comfortable in my new environment. Minnesotans are generally open and friendly people with a small-town attitude even in a big city like Minneapolis. Everyone said hello and asked a lot of personable questions. People were warm, friendly and welcoming.

We landed in Minnesota to find that the summer was in its last glory days before the coming of the fall change of seasons. The first night, when we checked into our hotel, I looked out over the skyline of this new city. I knew no one in this sprawling metropolis and, to make matters worse, I heard police sirens blaring in the streets below. My mind raced back to all the police movies I had watched and wondered how I was going to manage to live in this city where police were chasing criminals. My mind got the better of me and I remembered Eddy Murphy in the movie *Beverly Hills Cop* and Mel Gibson and Danny Glover in *Lethal Weapon* chasing down hardened criminals. This was my reality now, I imagined. My mother was going to leave me here in this strange place to face it all. That night, we gathered to pray and my mother chose a song from our traditional songbook called the *Zabuli* or Psalms. I believe she was led by the Spirit to choose a song that quickly became my favourite. The song in Runyankore, our language, said, *"Yesu nangira ati, Tindikutsiga wenka* (Jesus says I will never leave you alone).

Those words were of great comfort and consolation to me, especially one verse that said, *"Omu mwirima ndindidi we nandaganisa ati Ndya guma hamwe naiwe, Tindikutsiga wenka"...*(Even in the deepest darkness Jesus promises He will always be with me, He will never leave me alone.)

I asked my mother what the word *ndindindi* meant and she replied, "in the deepest darkness." The verse said that, even in the deepest darkness, Jesus will be with us.

What a wonderful comfort that song was to me. The Lord spoke to me through that song to let me know that, yes, even in this new and strange new city with police cars blaring in the night, the Lord would be with me. It gave me new courage to face this new world knowing that my Lord and Friend Jesus would still be with me.

The orientation week went by in a blur as I ran around the big campus to register for classes and attending different events for freshmen. Finally, the day came for me to move into my dorm. My mother escorted me with my suitcases and a little dorm furniture, like a reading lamp, nightstand and other items. My mother was shocked to find that, unlike us, most other students hadn't packed their clothes in suitcases or any kind of bags but rather they simply threw their clothes with the hangers into their cars or in giant boxes and moved in with them. So, as we met in the hallways, I was the only one with a suitcase; everybody else just brought in their clothes on hangers or in giant boxes or even trash bags! I could see that my mother wasn't impressed and it gave her cause for concern. I could 'hear' her unsaid thoughts, "where am I leaving my daughter? With people who don't even pack their clothes properly?"

That was just one of the lessons of the differences between Americans and Ugandans or Africans. I found over the years that there were many differences because Americans are very independent-minded. They are more focused on the individual, and not necessarily the community or society. In African culture people are generally very social, and do things because that is what society expects of them. It can be aptly summarised in the word *ubuntu* which means "I am because we are." As such, we are very much influenced by cultural norms while in America there is a strong, independent spirit of self-sufficiency and individuality.

There were many other shocking differences I would see such as roommates who never cleaned the rooms, never made their beds or did any kind of organizing their personal things. I marvelled at my floor mates who would wake up and not even wash their faces before going down to the dining hall, sometimes bare feet and sometimes just wearing socks, or in pyjamas and with dishevelled hair. I got used to seeing my fellow students looking like they had jumped out of bed and grabbed their book bags and ran to class.

All this shocked me at first, but then I soon got used to it. Interestingly, my dorm mates made fun of me for making my bed *every* day like I was in the army. They spoke about how my bed had rose bedspreads and my side of the room was always impeccable. I couldn't help being organized and clean. First, I am a neat freak. Also, I had had five years of boarding school where we had to maintain a certain level of neatness or else we would be punished. In Minnesota, I was an anomaly, a strange person who was unnecessarily clean, neat and organized.

Before leaving for Uganda, my mother introduced me to a few of her American friends. These were wonderful friends like the Reverend Arthur and Mrs. Molly Rouner, Bob and Kathy Junghans and their daughter Ashley, and Mr. and Mrs. Ed Schuh who was the Dean of the Humphrey Institute.

These friends became like my extended family during my time in Minnesota, especially during my freshman year when I was trying to get my bearings and acclimatize to life there. They invited me for Thanksgiving Dinner and took me out to watch basketball games, concerts and other events. They invited me to church, and their family events. They took me to my driving test when I wanted to get my driver's license and did many other things for me. They were my family and they helped me adjust to life so far away from home. I will forever be grateful for those dear friends and the love they showed me. I am also thankful that our friendship has endured long after I left Minnesota and came back home.

Reverend Arthur Rouner was the one we asked many years later to come and officiate at our wedding ceremony when my husband Odrek and I got married. He graciously accepted and made the long journey to attend the wedding. When Arthur went home to be with the Lord in December of 2021 I grieved his passing deeply because he was a dear friend to me and my family. I am thankful that I had the privilege of knowing him and that my friendship with his family endures to this day.

I am eternally grateful Aunt Peninah Kyembabazi, a dear friend and colleague of my mother's, for helping me through my early days in America. She stayed with me during my first year in Minnesota and her presence made all the difference in helping me adjust to life away from home. Her love, friendship, sense of humour and generosity of spirit were such a blessing to me and I cannot thank God enough for her life.

God showed me that the whole world belongs to Him and that He always has many "people in this city." As He said to the Apostle Paul in Acts 18:10, when He is leading us, He makes many divine connections that endure for many years.

*****

I threw myself into studies and the new life in college with great enthusiasm. I loved my lectures and the courses I was registered for. I joined the university as pre-med class. I had compulsory science classes but was also free to choose some elective courses in other areas. One of the things I found difficult at university was the way the professors always asked for my opinion on issues. I had gone through all my years of school without teachers asking me what I thought personally about what I was studying. At school back in Uganda, we were taught to regurgitate what the teacher or the textbook said. We were not encouraged to have independent thoughts or opinions. 'What do you think?' was the question I dreaded most at university in Minnesota. Then I would think to myself: why are you asking me what I think? I am telling you what the textbook says. The professor would double down and ask pointedly, "yes I know what the textbook says, but what do you think?"

It was such a hard question to answer. I didn't know what I thought because I had never really been asked about my thoughts as a person. I had all along thought that my opinion was irrelevant as long as I gave the "right" answer.

Through this experience, my professors showed me that there was a whole unexplored world in my mind and heart that I hadn't permitted myself to articulate. For the first time, I started thinking, "what do I think? What do I think about myself, and my place in this world? What do I think about Uganda, my home, in Africa? What do I think?" When the lid was lifted I found that what lay underneath was a volcano of emotion, passion and a search for my identity in this world. Why was I here? What was my purpose and what was I supposed to do?

I found that I had deep questions about myself and especially my identity as an African. For the first time in my life, I read my father's book, *What is Africa's Problem?* The search for answers took me to libraries all over Minneapolis and St. Paul, the Twin Cities. I looked at old footage of the early independence fighters like Patrice Lumumba of Congo, Amilcar Cabral of Guinea, Samora Marchel of Mozambique and the African thinker Franz Fanon. I read books by African American authors like Frederick Douglass, Sojourner Truth, W. E. B. Dubois, and Booker T. Washington. I read books about Africa from such authors as Walter Rodney who wrote How *Europe Underdeveloped Africa.* I also read American authors like Thomas Paine with his *Common Sense* and more contemporary ones like Thomas Friedman and David McCullough.

In doing all this, I was searching for my identity, my place, and my worldview amid the big ideas that have shaped and continue to shape the world.

In the midst of all that, I felt a deep conflict in my heart. I realized that, the more I searched for answers, the further I was walking away from the safety of the known path that I was on to become a medical doctor. I had dreamed of being a doctor since I was a little girl. I had planned all along that it was the path I would take. However now, with this whole world to explore, I wasn't sure that medicine will be my destiny. I felt like I was at a fork in the road and that I would have to make a decision soon. This realization made me very scared of the unknown and the path I felt the Lord was calling me to. I wanted the safety of the known, and the conventional path that made sense to my mind. Yet, in all that, I felt the Lord calling me to the road less travelled. I had walked with the LORD long enough to know that He wasn't with me on my choice to study medicine. I could feel it in my heart but tried very hard to ignore it. This time I would fight for my way; God would give me my way this time, I thought. Right?

*****

In the fall of 1998, together with my friends, we went away from the city to spend a weekend in a cabin in the northern part of the state. It was a beautiful season when all the leaves turned orange, yellow and red. The air was crisp and fresh. Our friend's cabin was beside a lake and so we had a wonderful time going out on a boat and just enjoying the scenery. We spent the time taking long walks and hanging out together. By that time, my younger sister Diana had joined me as well as my best friend Nukuri. We also went with another Mexican friend called Scarleth, my aunt Penina and our hosts. It was a refreshing time to pause and take a break from the busy pace in the city and just enjoy time together.

One morning before we left the cabin, I woke up early to go and sit by the lake and pray. My sister and our friends were asleep as we were all sharing one room in the cabin. There was a rough wooden bench by the lake on which I sat alone in the gathering light of the morning. There was a hushed silence, a stillness in the air around and over the lake. The Lord was there. I could feel His Presence surrounding me. I didn't speak a word; I just closed my eyes and allowed His Presence to envelope me. Then He spoke, **"You are not going to be a doctor."**

As I heard those words, fear and panic gripped my heart. Here He was doing it again, changing my plans, changing my direction. I said, "Lord, this is what I knew I wanted to be my whole life since I was a little girl." Then in my mind's eye, He showed me two roads. One of them was wide and clear and free of any encumbrances. The other was more like a small path that went into the forests. It was by no means clear, wide or easy. It was a small rough path off the beaten road. The Lord spoke to me and showed me the small path, He said, **"I am on this path. If you choose this path I will be with you."**

I asked Him, "what if I choose the other path?"

He answered, **"I will still be your God and you will be my child, but you would have missed your purpose."**

I sat there quietly in the morning light. Tears started rolling down my cheeks as I felt the pain of letting go of my dreams and desires to heed the Lord's call. During the pain, something strange happened. I felt God's comforting glory cover me. God knew I was letting go. I was surrendering to Him and He enveloped me in His cloud of glory. The cloud of glory is like a great big hug from God. In that moment, He enveloped me and I cried, but tears changed from tears of pain to tears of wonder and worship. God was here; He was sitting with me on that bench and He loved me. It was a glorious moment in time; a moment when Heaven touched Earth and God wiped away my tears. He said, **"I will be with you."**

I said, "the way I will know that You are with me is if my parents agree with this decision; then I will know that You have gone ahead of me." Then I asked, "If I change my major from medicine, what should I study?"

The Lord answered, **"I will show you."**

Many years later I understood what the Lord was essentially asking of me that day. The Bible says in John 12:24,

> *"I assure you most solemnly, unless a grain of wheat falls into the earth and dies, it remains just one grain; it never becomes more but lives by itself alone, But if it dies, it produces many others and yields a rich harvest. Anyone who loves his life loses it, but anyone who hates his life in this world, will keep it to life eternal." – Amplified Bible*

Jesus said in Luke 9:23-24,

> *"If any person wills to come after Me, let him deny himself, disown himself, forget lose sight of himself and his own interests, refuse and give himself up and take up his cross daily and follow Me. For whoever would preserve his life and save it, will lose it and destroy it, but whoever loses his life for My sake, He will preserve and save it." – Amplified Bible*

The Apostle Paul put it this way in Philippians 3:7-8,

> *"But whatever former things I had that might have been gains to me, I have come to consider as loss for Christ's sake.*

> *Yes furthermore, I count everything as loss compared to the possession of the priceless privilege of knowing Christ as my Lord and progressively becoming more deeply and intimately acquainted with Him. For His sake I have lost everything and consider it to be mere rubbish in order that I may gain Christ." – Amplified Bible*

What does all this dying and hating your life mean?

It doesn't mean that you physically die or that you hate your life, but rather that you allow your flesh, the old man, and the old nature to be crucified so that the new spirit man may live. There is a constant war over your life as to who will reign, the spirit or the flesh. The flesh cannot be pacified; it must be crucified through surrender and laying down our will for God's will.

That day at the lake, I felt like a part of me was dying and yet another part of me was becoming stronger. The flesh, the old me that wanted my way independent from God, was dying so that my spirit man could live and God's will and purpose for my life were magnified. How does it feel? It is painful as any believer who walks with God knows, but I have come to realize that it is a necessary pain. Jesus paid the ultimate price when He laid down His life for us on the Cross. Was it painful? Yes, and it was unlike any other pain that any human being will ever experience. But was it necessary? Yes, Jesus needed to lay down His life so that, through Him, we all could become sons and daughters of God. Every child of God and follower of Jesus will be asked to lay down their lives so that God's purposes can be magnified in and through them. He, in essence, is asking us to do what He did daily so that the power of His life can be demonstrated through us.

*****

I left the cabin after that weekend knowing that I had experienced Jesus in a way I never had before. I was still not sure what the Lord had in store for me, but I was sure He was with me.

The next holiday, when I came home from college, I knew that I had to share what God was speaking to me with my parents. I prepared accordingly and waited for an opportune time to let them know that I felt God was leading me to change my major. I truly believe that parents are God's representatives on earth and have the authority to open or close doors in the lives of their children. To their eternal credit, my parents have only ever opened doors that needed to be opened in my life and closed doors that needed to be closed. They have operated in line with God's will for my life always; for that, I am eternally grateful.

After a long discussion with them, my parents intimated that they wanted all their children to follow the path that they have chosen and not force us to make choices to please them as our parents. I said I believed this change was what the Lord was leading me to. They agreed with my change of plans and supported my decision. When I went back to college the following year, I changed my major from Pre-Med to Political Science and Development Studies. As I made that decision and started taking classes, I felt the Lord's wind in my sails. He was leading me, spurring me on. I didn't know where I was going, but I knew that God was with me.

I loved my new courses and revelled in the discourse I had with my fellow students and professors. In my second year, I joined the Model UN and loved attending conferences around the country and interacting with other students who had the same interests in nation-building as I did.

In my second year, my friend Nukuri and I also joined the Reserve Officer Training Corps (ROTC) at the University of Minnesota. This is a special programme offered at universities that trains college-educated men and women for possible careers in the active army, army reserve or National Guard.

I was part of this programme for two years and I loved every minute of it. It is a programme that you go through alongside your degree course and so all your time is taken up with classes and drill training. I learnt a lot from my time in the ROTC, lessons about teamwork, organizational and time management and the extraordinary discipline it takes to be part of the army. We met great men and women in the military and many of our lecturers and supervisors had been in active combat. Every weekend, come rain or shine, Nukuri and I had to jump out of bed, get washed and be in our uniforms ready for training, including running halfway across campus to our headquarters. When we arrived there we had to quickly ensure that our shoes were shining and our uniforms were clean and sparkly before our parade and drill. It was a nasty experience to get shouted at by your drill inspector when you made a mistake so we made sure we were always there on time and ready for inspection.

Today, I often tease my children when I find that their rooms are not clean or their beds not made perfectly, by saying, “you need some time in the army to straighten you out.” Joking aside, my time in the ROTC was some of the most rewarding times that I had in university. After my junior year, I ended my time at ROTC and also the model UN as I was preparing for my final year and graduation.

In my senior year, I was on course to graduate and so I spent most of my time preparing for and writing my senior paper or dissertation. The subject I chose was the development of two African countries, Botswana and Somalia. The two attained independence around the same time, but their trajectories as nations went in vastly different directions: Botswana was a stable country with a thriving economy versus Somalia which became a failed state. The reality of the impact of a failing nation on her people was not far removed from me since Minnesota was home to one of the largest populations of Somalis outside of Somalia. I thoroughly enjoyed doing my research for my paper, which included personal accounts and interviews with Somali elders in the community.

Researching and writing my senior paper consumed all my time as I stayed in contact with my professor. Finally, I submitted my senior paper and was delighted when my professor gave me a glowing report and commendation. I graduated from the University of Minnesota in May of 2001 with a degree in Political Science, Development Studies and a minor in Child Psychology.

My graduation ceremony was a glorious, wonderful celebration of the amazing Grace of God, and His Faithfulness to His Word and His promises. God even added the cherry on the cake when I graduated on the Dean's List in a University of tens of thousands of students. My family and friends came from near and far to share that special time with me. My younger sister, Diana, and my older sister Natasha who was now married to Edwin Karugire and expecting her first baby, travelled from Uganda to be with us. They came with a dear friend Susan Muhwezi who made the long journey from Uganda to be with me on that special day. My dear aunt Hope Nyakairu also came from the UK to be there and other dear friends who lived in the U.S. My brother Muhoozi's wife Charlotte, who was also pregnant with her first baby, also attended my graduation along with her sister, Shartsi Musherure. I was happy to see my friends Bob and Kathy Junghans and their dear daughter, Ashley, present as well. My friends, the Kamunanwire family, Ambassador Perez and his wife Caroline and their daughters, Malaika and Bahati, travelled from New York as did another friend Richard Kabonero who worked at the Uganda Embassy in Washington, D. C.

God showed Himself to be my bright morning star in the land that I was afraid of at first. He illuminated my path and made a Way for me in a strange land. He revealed Himself to me in a deeper way and His purposes for my life. Surely, the earth is the Lord's and the fullness thereof! Minnesota will forever be a special place to me because God met me there in a new way. Today, I have two throw pillows in my home with the fun inscription, "My heart is in Minnesota." Granted, my heart is firmly in Uganda, but Minnesota will always have a special place in my life.

I have learnt, through those sometimes trying and difficult moments when you can't see the forest for the trees, to close my eyes and take Jesus' Hand trusting that He knows His purposes and plans for me and He has never failed me before and He will never fail me.

8. The Edomite Spirit

"Humankind has not woven the web of life. We are but one thread within it. Whatever we do to the web, we do to ourselves. All things are bound together. All things connect."
- First Nations Chief Seattle, 1854

My husband and I are farmers and we know that, once you uproot a plant, the fruit will eventually dry up because you have cut off the roots that nourish and sustain the fruits.

In the chapter titled *Remitting the Sins of Slavery*, I share how the Lord showed me that the root of corruption was the same as the root of slavery, which was the Edomite spirit. Dealing with slavery is a process and we will have to have more and more teaching in the body of Christ and identificational repentance focused around the issue. It is not a one-time event; it is a process.

I believe that there will have to be more repentance on a larger scale within the body of Christ in Africa and also with our brothers and sisters of African Descent around the world.

In this chapter, we will delve a little deeper and look at the fruit of this root which is the sin of corruption. I will not spend much time going into the history of post-colonial Africa because I feel we all know the basic history of our countries and it is obvious that corruption is something that many African countries face and continue to grapple with.

Is corruption a uniquely African problem? Do other countries deal with corruption or is it particularly endemic in Africa?

The dictionary definition of corruption is 'dishonest or fraudulent conduct or behaviour by those in positions of power or authority, typically involving bribery.'

It could be somebody at a lower level of authority or somebody in a very high-level position of authority and power. At whatever level corrupt conduct takes place, it is still corruption. Corruption is not an African problem alone. All countries in the world deal with corruption on some level, whether they are in China, India, Russia, South America, Europe or the United States. It is a problem that manifests in different levels of sophistication and adapts to the environment it faces.

I remember reading Thomas Friedman's *The Lexus and the Olive Tree: Understanding Globalization*[1] where the author delves deep into the problem of corruption and particularly regarding *kleptocracies,* societies whose systems are riddled with corruption. He told a funny story which I will share with you about two government ministers who were visiting each other, one was an African minister and the other was an Indian Minister. You probably know where this is going, but bear with me.

So the African minister visited the Indian minister in his home and noticed that he had a lavish home and lifestyle. It boggled the African minister's mind how all this was possible. He finally gathered the courage to ask his counterpart how he could afford such an extravagant life on his ministerial salary. The Indian minister looked around to see that no one was within earshot and then pointed to a half-built bridge in the distance. He said smugly, "you see that bridge over there in the distance." The African minister looked out of the window and realized there was a half-built bridge in the distance. The Indian minister then pointed at himself with a smile and said, "fifty percent." By this, he meant that the bridge wasn't completed because fifty percent of the budget was stolen by this minister to build his lavish home. The African Minister nodded in understanding.

A year later the Indian minister visited the African minister in his country and he finds that his counterpart is living an even more extravagant lifestyle than he is. The African minister owns a lavish home, sports cars and fancy clothes. The Indian minister is amazed and he asks his colleague, "How are you able to afford this lifestyle on just a small minister's salary?"

---

1 Thomas Friedman. *The Lexus and the Olive Tree: Understanding Globalization*, Ferrar, Straus & Giroux, 1999.

The African minister looked at him knowingly and smiled. Then pointed to a murram road in the distance and said, "you see that highway over there."

The Indian minister followed his gaze into the distance and didn't see anything but an old murram road. He replied, "I don't see any highway, only a murram road."

The African minister smiled and pointed to himself and said, "100 percent." By this, he meant that the entire budget for making the highway had been embezzled to give him his luxurious life.

This was supposed to be a joke but it pokes fun at a very serious situation that we have to deal with as a society. Whereas the problem of corruption isn't specific to Africa, I believe that the spiritual roots of the sin make it more endemic in Africa and therefore more difficult to fight naturally. It is a spiritual problem that must be dealt with in the spirit realm first.

The Edomites?

Who were the Edomites? What is the Edomite curse? What does it mean? I'll try and answer these questions.

The Edomites were the natural descendants of Esau, Jacob's twin brother. He was the firstborn and thus the blessing and birthright of the firstborn legally belonged to him. However, he sold his birthright to Jacob. In that transaction, he sold what was spiritual and of eternal significance for what was temporal. After Esau sold his birthright to his brother for a pot of stew, Jacob then went on to steal his brother's blessing by conniving with their mother Rebecca to trick Isaac, their father. Esau ended up supplanted by Jacob and from then on a bitter feud between the brothers began.

The Edomites harboured great animosity, hatred, resentment and bitterness towards the children of Israel who were in essence their brothers. At every opportunity, they fought against Israel and constantly allied themselves with the enemies of Israel. The Edomites lived on Mount Seir and God gave them their inheritance even before He gave the children of Israel the Promised Land. God ensured that all the descendants of Abraham had their lands and He did not allow the Israelites to invade those lands even during the conquest of Canaan.

It is chronicled in the book of Joshua that God distinctly forbade the children of Israel from fighting against the descendants of Esau - the Edomites. He forbade them from fighting or dispossessing the Moabites and the Ammonites who were descendants of Lot because God saw them as brothers. How do you dispossess your brother? God commanded them not to disturb, meddle, or enter their land without their permission. God respected the relationship of brotherhood and the connectedness of family ties even though four hundred years had gone by.

The children of Israel obeyed God's Word and did not disturb the Edomites, but the reverse wasn't true. The Edomite curse came into effect over the generations as the Edomites continued to harbour bitterness and resentment against their brothers. The modern-day word for this is "tribalism." Tribalism is essentially when we actively work for the benefit of those who are members of our ethnic group or tribe at the expense of those we consider outside our ethnicity or tribe.

In the book of Obadiah 1:6-15, it is clear that the Edomites in spirit and practice saw themselves as enemies of Israel. This status quo remained even until the New Testament when King Herod sought to kill baby Jesus. He was the descendant of Esau and hence an Edomite. The feud that started with Esau and Jacob continued and strengthened throughout many generations until it affected the life of Jesus, the Son of God. There was an Edomite who was seeking His destruction.

Obadiah prophesied that judgement and destruction were coming against the Edomites in Obadiah 1:6-15:

> *"6 How are the things of Esau (Edom) searched out! How are his hidden treasures sought out!*
>
> *"7 All the men of your Confederacy (your allies) have brought you on your way, even to the border; the men who*

were at peace with you have deceived you and prevailed against you; they who eat your bread have laid a snare under you. There is no understanding (in Edom, or) of it.

"8 Will not I in that day, says the Lord, destroy the wise men out of Edom (men of) understanding out of Mount Esau (Idumea, a mountainous region)

"9 And your mighty men, O Teman, shall be dismayed, to the end that everyone from Mount Esau will be cut off by slaughter.

"10 For the violence you did against your brother Jacob, shame shall cover you, and you shall be cut off forever.

"11 On the day that you stood aloof (from your brother Jacob) – on the day that strangers took captive his forces and carried off his wealth, and foreigners entered his gates and cast lots for Jerusalem - you were even as one of them.

"12 But you should not have gloated over your brother's day, the day when his misfortune came and he was made a stranger; you should not have rejoiced over the sons of Judah in the day of their ruin; you should not have spoken arrogantly in the day of their distress.

"13 You should not have entered the gate of My people in the day of their calamity and ruin; nor have reached after their army and their possessions in the day of their calamity and ruin.

"14 And you should not have stood at the crossway to cut off those of Judah who escaped, neither should you have delivered up those (of Judah) who remained in the day of distress.

"15 For the day of the Lord is near upon all the nations. As you have done it shall be done to you; your dealings will return upon your own head." – Amplified Bible

In this account, the Lord judged Edom for the sin of not being their brother's keeper. God was displeased that the Edomites rejoiced and relished in the calamity and misery of the Israelites. God said they did violence against their brothers and because of that, shame would be their portion.

God said the Edomites stood aloof from their brothers when they were under attack and allied themselves with Israel's enemies to cut them off and dispossess them. Even though what was happening to Israel was God's direct judgement on the nation, He was still displeased that those who would have been compassionate and merciful; instead rejoiced at the calamity of their brothers.

Eventually, Edom was completely cut off and the descendants of Esau were wiped off the face of the earth. What started with Esau selling his birthright developed into the Edomite curse on his descendants. The Edomite curse represents a perversion of human relationships between those who should have a familial, brotherly relationship. What God expected was brotherhood and what the Edomites exhibited was tribalism. Edomites were the brothers of the Israelites but instead, they wished the Israelites ill and worked actively for their downfall. They stood aloof from the pain of their brothers and allied themselves with their enemies to destroy them.

What does that mean in the context of Africa?

What the Lord revealed to me was that just as the Esau spirit was the root of slavery, the Edomite curse is the root of corruption. How does tribalism work? God considers all the people of a nation or people group as brothers, and He expects us to be our brothers' keepers.

Remember from the beginning we were building on the foundational scripture Acts 17:26 which says:

> *And He made from one (common origin, one source, one blood) all nations of men to settle on the face of the earth, having definitely determined (their) allotted periods of time and fixed boundaries of their habitation (their settlements, lands, and abodes). – Amplified Bible*

God determined the boundaries of our habitation. In God's eyes, He sees all Africans as brothers just as he saw the Edomites, Moabites, Ammonites and Israelites as brothers

–people from the same family. Even though they didn't all worship God since it was only the children of Israel who had that covenant relationship, God intended that they should be governed by a sense of brotherhood. That is why He forbade the Israelites from invading their lands.

God sees tribalism as a sin and judges it. Tribalism works to sell out our brothers to their enemies. Selling out our brothers is not only in the context of slavery when there was actual trading in human beings but also in the present-day situation, it is selling off what belongs to your brothers - selling off their destiny, their futures and their opportunities. When you misuse the resources of the nation or the community for your own personal, or private benefit then you are selling out your brothers.

Corruption pits brother against brother. It makes enemies of brothers. One group of people or one "tribe" are made to benefit because of their access to power. The people who are close to power are considered to be the legitimate beneficiaries of the resources and all others are seen as 'the other' or 'the outsider'. This means that if a person is in a position of authority or influence he will use that position to further the goals of a specific group of people he considers "his own" at the expense of the others.

If we look at it in the context of Africa and take the example of South Africa, the Zulus are the biggest tribe by population and are often pitted against smaller tribes. In Nigeria, you have the Yoruba tribe that has a big majority and so they are pitted against the Hausa, or Ibos, the Southerners versus the Northerners. If we look closer to home in Kenya, the Kikuyu are a big tribe that is pitted against the Luo. In Sudan, before the independence of South Sudan, it was the Arab North versus the African South. With the birth of the youngest African nation of South Sudan, the majority of Dinkas are pitted against the smaller tribes. In Uganda, there are so many different tribes it could be Baganda versus Acholi or Banyankole versus Banyoro or Bagisu or whatever. It always pits one group against the other.

On another level, the definition of the "tribe" can encapsulate people who are not necessarily of the same ethnicity but who have the same beliefs, values or ethos. Sometimes the Edomite curse brings together a group of people who may not necessarily have the same background in terms of ethnicity or language but they are united by the same beliefs, values, and culture. Class in Africa is a phenomenon that must be understood deeper. We have career politicians whose goal is to use their political offices as a means to fleece the population of resources that belong to the people. The political class or elites conspire with those of their class to undermine the rights and needs of the people they are elected to serve. Therefore, the Edomite curse unites them to do wrong regardless of their ethnic background. They are brothers in that they are united by a negative mindset and they use that unity to strip away the rights or the benefits that are due to the larger community.

The East African Revival

This principle positively was in operation during the Great East African Revival that swept across the region starting in the mid-1930s. People who became Christians during the revival became part of a spiritual or Kingdom culture that overshadowed the cultures they were born into. Christians from different ethnicities or even nationalities became one; they would call themselves brothers and sisters. In Luganda, a local dialect, they used the term *Owoluganda* which means, "a person from the same family or clan." In Runyankole, another dialect, the Christian brethren coined a similar term, *Oweishemwe*, which means "having One Father."

The power of the saving Grace of God united people of vastly different backgrounds and made them brothers. They sang a universal anthem called, *Tukutendereza Yesu*, which simply means "Praise Jesus." Similar to the New Testament Church, wherever the Christian brethren or *Balokole* travelled, they stayed in the homes of their fellow Christian brothers and sisters regardless of their different ethnicities. The culture of the kingdom of God has the power to melt even the strongest and most rigid of barriers and divisions. God's Kingdom culture supersedes and overshadows all our differences and has the power to unite us if we allow Him to work in our hearts and transform us from the inside out.

Secret Societies

On the negative side, the kingdom of darkness also can unite people who have no biological or cultural connection under the banner of evil. We see this play out in cults and secret societies like the Freemasons[2]. This is very dangerous because unlike Christians who are open about their faith and belief in the Lord Jesus Christ; members of secret societies are sworn to secrecy and perform all their rituals in the dark. These people can deceive others into thinking that they have the interests of their community at heart but the reality is that they have a higher allegiance to the "brotherhood" of their cult and the evil forces that they serve.

Here is the word as written in Isaiah 5:20-23:

> "*Woe to those who call evil good and good evil, who put darkness for light and light darkness, who put bitter for sweet and sweet for bitter! Woe to those who are wise in their own eyes and prudent and shrewd in their own sight! Woe to those who are mighty heroes at drinking wine and men of strength in mixing alcoholic drinks!- Who justify and acquit the guilty for a bribe, but take away the rights of the innocent and the righteous from them!" – Amplified Bible.*

"Woe" is the strongest word to describe and spell out a curse and judgment from God. In this scripture, the Lord condemns those who call what is evil good and what is good evil.

In line with our discussion on corruption, sadly in many quarters of our society, there is almost a sense of resignation or acceptance that corruption is a necessary evil. Some think

2 An international order (men only) established for mutual help and fellowship with elaborate secrecy and secret ceremonies.

that as long as you can get away with it or figure out "how to work the system" for your benefit then you are wise, shrewd and smart. Those who strive to do the right thing are viewed as simpletons, naïve and unrealistic. They are circumvented in the greasing of elbows and making deals because they are seen as unsophisticated, wide-eyed suckers who don't know how to get things done. This is an acceptance of evil and a calling of evil good and good evil. The Lord heaps judgment and condemnation on those who exchange what is good for what is evil. God is, in essence, saying just because society condones certain actions doesn't make them right in God's sight.

Therefore, with the Edomite Spirit, with corruption, there should always be the question of 'who is my brother?', the person that I am supposed to watch out for. We have seen that God's perspective is different. It isn't only the people that you are directly related to who are your brothers, but rather God sees us all as brothers and sisters with a deep responsibility towards each other.

We have also seen from the scriptures that God's standard of righteousness doesn't keep pace with popular culture. Just because our society is resigned to evil doesn't make it good or acceptable in God's sight. If something is wrong and goes against the rights of the innocent - the majority, then it is evil and stands judged by God.

The Time for Restitution has come

Genesis chapter 15: 13 – 14:

> *"And (God) said to Abram, "Know positively that your descendants will be strangers dwelling as temporary residents in a land that is not theirs (Egypt), and they will be slaves there and will be afflicted and oppressed for 400 years. But I will bring judgment on that nation whom they will serve and they will come out with great possessions."*
> *– Amplified Bible*:

God prophesied to Abraham that his descendants would go to Egypt and would be enslaved for 400 years. The 400 years was a unique gate of time and the Lord said He would bring them out and judge the nation that had enslaved them. God also said He would bring them out with great possessions. Fast forward to 430 years later, on the night of the first Passover, in the space of one night, there was a transfer of wealth from Egypt to the children of Israel. Why was there a transfer of wealth? It is because the children of Israel had been working as slaves - working with neither pay nor benefits for 400 years. But in one night the wealth of Egypt was transferred from Egypt to the children of Israel. These were their rightful wages and benefits that they had worked for but had never been paid because of the injustice of slavery. What does that mean for Africa at this gate of time? It is 400 years since the beginning of the slave trade taking Africans to the Americas. Could restitution and a wealth transfer be coming to African nations and people of African descent?

James 5:1-4.

> *"COME NOW, you rich (people), weep aloud and lament over the miseries (the woes) that are surely coming upon you. Your abundant wealth has rotted and is ruined, and your (many) garments have become moth-eaten. Your gold and silver are completely rusted through, and their rust will be a testimony against you and it will devour your flesh as if it were fire. You have heaped together treasures for the last days. (But) look (here are) the wages that you have withheld by fraud from the labourers who have reaped your fields, crying out (for vengeance); and the cries of the harvesters have come to the ears of the Lord of hosts." – Amplified Bible*

The Name of the Lord of Hosts in the Hebrew language is "Jehovah Sabaoth" which means "the Lord of heaven's armies."

Let us try and unpack what God is declaring in His Word. Here God is speaking to the wealthy, specifically those who have acquired their wealth through fraudulent means. Slavery is a fraudulent way to acquire wealth, and so is corruption. God is forewarning those who have become wealthy through unjust means that they should weep because their wealth will testify against them. What will the wealth say? It will say to its owners, "you acquired me by defrauding the poor, by stealing the labour of hundreds of thousands of men and women for generations. Therefore, prepare to weep for great miseries are coming upon you."

What is woe or misery to somebody who is rich and who has gotten wealth fraudulently? It is that wealth is going to leave them. Just like a bird, it will get wings and take flight and be transferred to others; its rightful owners.

The scripture goes on to say that the wages that have been held back fraudulently, the gold and silver have rusted. Why? Because it was meant to pay people their hire and was held back. So it will no longer serve its masters but will be transferred to its rightful owners. We need to understand that God's Word is forever settled.

God's Word says in 1 Timothy 5:18, *"the labourer is worthy of his wages."*

Therefore, if you have withheld the wages of the labourer whether it is one year or four hundred years, there comes a day of payment. I want to declare in the Name of Jesus that payday is here! The labourer whose wages have been held back fraudulently whether it's through slavery or corruption, payday is here in the Name of Jesus.

The scripture says that the cry of the labourers who reaped your fields are crying out for vengeance and the cry of the labourer has come to the ears of the Lord of Hosts. That means that the cry of the labourers has come to the ears of the Lord who is in charge of heaven's armies. It is a fearful thing to be in the hands of God. There is misery and there is woe coming upon the unjust and fraudulent systems of the world.

I believe in this season the cry of the labourers has come to the ears of the Lord of hosts and the Lord is judging the unjust systems of the world. This is good news for people that have been disenfranchised by these evil systems. It will happen in Africa, whether it is related to slavery, or to the unjust systems that have been propagated in Africa since slavery, such as colonialism and neo-colonialism and right up until the present day. I believe we are coming to a day of restitution.

Zacchaeus

Our little daughter loves the story of Zacchaeus from the Bible. The short man couldn't see Jesus and ended up climbing the sycamore tree to get a glimpse of the Savior. When our daughter was younger she loved to sing a nursery song about Zacchaeus: "*Zacchaeus was a wee little man and a wee little man was he. He climbed up in the sycamore tree for the Lord he wanted to see. And as the Saviour passed that way He looked up in the tree. And He said, 'Zacchaeus you come down coz I'm going to your house today.' Zacchaeus was a wee little man and a very happy man was he For he had seen the Lord that day and a very happy man was he." - Cedarmont Kids Songs 1995.*

This little children's song hides powerful truths that we adults often fail to grasp.

The story of Zacchaeus is often shared in Sunday school messages much like the story of Noah and the ark. At its heart, Zacchaeus' story is one of restitution and it is important to share that side of the story. There are descendants of the people who have benefitted from the unjust systems of this world and who want nothing more than to be free of the sense of guilt and condemnation that they constantly feel. Even though many are saved and have a relationship with the Lord Jesus, there is a shame that they carry in their hearts because of the many wrong things perpetrated by their ancestors on other peoples.

Many years ago when Covenant Nations Church was still a young church meeting in our home, I received a visiting group of British missionaries from the City of Liverpool. These missionaries were led by a lady who shared with me the intense burden of guilt and shame that they carried because their city was the centre of the British slave trade. It was in Liverpool that the slave ships arrived and human beings were traded and carried like cargo before they set sail for the Americas. God had not yet awakened me to this immense burden and pain of the history of slavery and I could only sympathize with this dear woman as she prayed with deep pain and groaning for God's mercy and forgiveness for the sin of slavery.

At that time I wondered why it affected her so much since she was not guilty of harming anyone. But later on, I understood that, in spiritual matters, often if it is not dealt with, future generations carry the burdens of sins they didn't commit. After all these years I understand the burden they carried and the reason she came with a broken spirit to repent to me, an African.

That is why the story of Zacchaeus is important. Zacchaeus had profited from his work as a tax collector, extorting huge sums of money from his people. He was wealthy but he was despised by the people around him. When Jesus came to his town, he ran to see Him but because of his small stature, he couldn't see Jesus and had to climb a tree to get a glimpse of Him.

Here is what it says in Luke 19:1-10:

> *"When Jesus reached the spot, He looked up and said to him, "Zacchaeus, come down immediately. I must stay at your house today." So he came down at once and welcomed Him gladly. All the people saw this and began to murmur saying, "He has gone to be the guest of a sinner."*
>
> *"But Zacchaeus stood up and said to the Lord, "Look, Lord! Here and now I give half of my possessions to the poor, and if I have cheated anybody out of anything, I will pay back four times the amount."*
>
> *"Jesus said to him, "Today, salvation has come to this house, because this man, too, is a son of Abraham. For the Son of Man came to seek and save the lost." – Amplified Bible*

It is important to note that Jesus announced that salvation had come to Zacchaeus' home when he made restitution to all those he had cheated and defrauded of their goods. It means that salvation is not only about receiving Jesus into our hearts! That is the beginning. Full salvation is making things right with those we have wronged or mistreated. Those people who murmured against Zacchaeus would not be able to discount the genuineness of his faith once he made restitution for his past actions. I am sure they welcomed him and received him back as a brother because he had done the right thing.

Restitution is an integral part of the process of salvation and allows for true healing to take place. Please note I am not using the word "reparations" which is generally understood to be compensation given to offset an abuse, injury or injustice. Reparations have taken the form of affirmative action, settlements, monetary payments and scholarships. Restitution is a Biblical principle and not a man-made one, it is about making things right in God's sight and not in man's minuscule vision. Restitution can only be led by the Spirit of God and genuine repentance for the wrong or injury done. Restitution opens the door for genuine healing because it deals with the root of the problem- the restoration of the relationship, of what was lost because of the injury or injustice. It isn't about balancing the scorecard which can never be balanced because of the wrong done. It is about building a bridge and seeking to restore or return the person to a condition before the injury was done. That is the heart of restitution and I believe that is what the Lord desires of all His people.

My Brother's Keeper

If the Edomite curse is a perversion, what is God's perspective? How does God want us to see ourselves? How does God want us to relate to each other?

Genesis 4:9 -10 says:

"'Where is Abel your brother?' And he said, 'I do not know. Am I my brother's keeper?' And (the Lord) said, 'what have

you done? The voice of your brother's blood is crying to Me from the ground." – *Amplified Bible*

God asked Cain, "where is your brother?"

Cain's answer was defensive, "Am I my brother's keeper?"

God asked Cain about his brother because God is Love and the foundational principle of our faith is love for God and love for each other. In God's perspective, love of our neighbour is normative, that is the springboard of all blessings. If we love our brothers, we are concerned for their welfare, we cannot rejoice at their calamity, and we cannot profit at their expense. God asked Cain, "where is your brother?"- meaning "how is your brother doing?" I believe God is still asking us that question today.

Malachi 2:10 says:

"Have we not all one Father? Has not one God created us? Why then do we deal faithlessly and treacherously each against his brother, profaning the covenant of (God with) our fathers?" – *Amplified Bible*

God is our Father, God is the Father of us all and therefore we should not deal treacherously or betray the interests of our brothers.

Matthew 12: 46 -50 says:

Jesus was still speaking to the people when, behold, His mother and brothers stood outside, seeking to speak to Him. Someone said to Him, Listen! Your mother and Your brothers are standing outside, seeking to speak to You. But He replied to the man who told Him, Who is My mother, and who are My brothers? And stretching out His hand toward (not only the twelve disciples but all) His adherents, He said, Here are My mother and My brothers. For whoever does the will of My Father in heaven is My brother and sister and mother! – *Amplified Bible*

Jesus was saying that his brothers and sisters were not merely the people in his family. Those whom He considered His brothers were those who obeyed the will of His Father in heaven. That means that Brotherhood in God's perspective is not about those who are related to us. It is a larger view of those who are under the will and the purpose of God Matthew 23: 8 says, *"......you are all brothers."* And finally Hebrews 2: 11 says, *"......all have one (Father)......"*

On one end of the spectrum, is a perversion – the Edomite curse where you have no concern, no care for your brother, or even actively working for his destruction.

On the other end is God's perspective, where we are our brother's keeper. Therefore, if there is anything that we are doing that will hurt or affect our brothers and negatively impact them, God is displeased with that and it opens the door for devouring in our own lives. My prayer is that we believers will raise the bar of what is expected in our treatment of our brothers and sisters in the world. Whether we are in the church, in private business or in public service, may believers raise a standard and lead the way to show the world how we ought to treat our neighbours, our brothers.

Prayer

Heavenly Father, we bless Your Name for all that You are to us. Our Father and our God. We thank You for all that You are revealing in this unique gate of time. We thank You for this day of visitation for the African people and just like the children of Israel You promised to bring us out of bondage with great possessions.

Today, we repent for the Edomite curse of not being our brothers' keepers. Forgive us for the sin of tribalism that pits brother against brother. Father, we have borne the judgement of this curse for so long. So today we repent and renounce this sin in Jesus' Mighty Name. May You break the hold of tribalism that empowers corruption in Africa.

Father, we also want to bring our petitions before You for the four hundred years of back payments for the labour of Africans sold into slavery and all the unjust systems that have been propagated in Africa since then. James 5:1-4 says, "the cry of the labourer has come to the ears of the Lord of Hosts."

So we pray that all the payments of labour and resources due to African people and nations will flow back to Africa in a great wealth transfer in these times.

We ask that you will break all the illegal agreements, covenants and contracts that exist for the sole purpose of robbing Africa of her wealth. We ask that wherever the wealth of Africa has been stored up these four hundred years whether it is in secret vaults around the world or in bank accounts, companies or in any kind of organization or system, today we announce in the Name of Jesus Christ of Nazareth that the wealth of Africa must return to its rightful owners in Africa in Jesus' Mighty Name.

Finally, Father, we ask that You will raise a company of Josephs in Africa-men and women who are anointed with the wisdom of God to administer the wealth of Africa for the good of all men and to the glory of Your matchless Name. We pray all of this in Jesus's Mighty Name.

Amen.

9. Mr. Wonderful

"Now you feel no rain
For each of you will be shelter to the other
Now each of you will feel no cold
For each of you will be warmth to the other
Now there is no loneliness for you
For each of you will be companions to the other
Now you are two persons
But there is one life before you."

Apache wedding blessing

In 1999, the world was in a frenzy about the Y2K bug, a computer flaw that was thought could cause problems dealing with dates beyond December 31st, 1999. It was also known as the Millennium Bug. The hysteria about this computer bug, coupled with the general fear of the unknown that a new millennium represented, painted apocalyptic pictures of what would happen when the clock struck midnight on January 1st, 2000. Would you be able to withdraw money from an ATM or would all the power grids fail? Doomsday preppers had their hands full filling underground bunkers with emergency supplies for the New Millennium.

In my own life, I had thoughts about my life and future. I was 21 years old and was preoccupied with my world. Even though I had friends, I hadn't had a serious relationship with any guy.

When I was 15 years old, I attended a youth conference organized by my mother under the Uganda Youth Forum. It was a fun and engaging holiday conference organized by Maama Janet and the Youth Forum, to talk to young people about their spiritual lives and encourage them to make decisions that honour God in every area of their lives including the area of purity. In one of the Youth Conferences, I was greatly touched by the message shared and the many testimonies from various speakers. At the end of the conference, there was a call for young people to sign the little yellow cards as a sign of their commitment to God to remain pure until they married. I was among the many youth who went to the front to sign "my true love waits" card and made my commitment to the Lord. When I signed that card, I kept it in the middle of my Bible so that I would glance at it often whenever I opened my Bible for devotions.

Soon after that event I felt led by the Lord to begin to pray for my future husband. One may wonder, "how do you pray for a person that you have never seen?"

When I started praying for my future husband, it was a simple prayer of faith. I asked the Lord that, when the time was right, He should be the One to bring His choice for me into my life. I prayed this simple prayer on and off for the next six years. Sometimes, I would feel the Lord prompt me to pray more about this matter. Other times I wouldn't pray about it for a season until again I felt prompted to pray about it. My prayers were always very simple. However, there was this complete sense of trust that My Heavenly Father was listening and this was a wonderful part of my life I was sharing with Him alone.

This area of prayer became so real to me that after some years, whenever I prayed for my future husband I called him, Mr. Wonderful. This person called *Mr. Wonderful* became very real as I prayed and trusted the Lord with this part of my life. Other times, I felt the Lord prompt me to write down the qualities that I wanted in Mr. Wonderful. I did this and kept these notes in my Bible or journal.

This went on for years and at different times the Lord would remind me about my prayer and we would spend time talking about that and then move on to another prayer focus. I found in all my years of walking with the Lord, that prayer time with Him is like having a date with Your Father, only that it is Your Heavenly Father that You can't see with your physical eyes. However, in every other way, I always felt very comfortable sharing my heart with God. I felt He understood me completely, and talking to Him always left me feeling stronger and more at peace than I was before. So this area was like any other area of my life that I shared with Him. I also had this sense that God had something really special stored up for me, like a present at Christmas. There was this sense of trusting and waiting on Him for His perfect time.

In the fall of 1999, I attended a small contemporary Christian singers' album signing at a bookstore in Minneapolis. It was a singer that I liked so, after buying his new CD, I stayed behind to hear his talk and watch his performance. He sang some songs from his new album. Then he took some time talking about the whole Y2K situation and encouraging people to not live in fear about "what the future held." He said, "our faith in God must be greater than our fear of what the effect of a number zero will have on our lives." He in essence said God is Lord over time and therefore even the New Millennium was subject to God's will and purpose.

It was an encouraging message and I agreed with it. When I got home, I started thinking about this New Millennium that would begin in a few months. I hadn't given it much thought before and so I just thought about what it meant in my own life. A new millennium doesn't come along very often, so this change of seasons must mean that something powerful and real was taking place spiritually.

A few months later, as my sister Diana and I prepared for Christmas, our parents called us to let us know that they would be in Jerusalem around Christmas time and they wanted us to join them there. Jerusalem! It had always been my dream to visit Israel, the land that Jesus had walked, lived, died and rose from the grave; the land of the Bible. I couldn't believe that we would get the opportunity to visit Israel. It heightened for me the sense that God was preparing something special for me during that season.

Since I was a teenager, I had always had an affinity for Jewish History, first because of my faith and then as an extension of it. My favourite fictional authors were Bodie and Brock

Thoene, who wrote the *Zion Chronicles*, a series of books set in the Second World War and following characters that were facing very dark times whether it was the holocaust or the 1948 war in Israel after the birth of the new state. I also loved reading historical accounts of Israeli war heroes such as Moshe Dayan and others. I also read a book written by Benjamin Netanyahu about his older brother who was killed during the raid on Entebbe titled, *Self-portrait of a Hero: The Letters of Jonathan Netanyahu*[1]. It was needless to say that I was very excited to see and walk in the land of our Lord Jesus Christ.

As the term drew to an end and we prepared for Christmas, my sister and I went shopping to buy a few Christmas gifts for our family members. I recall that while I was window shopping in the mall, I passed by a shop I liked and in the window I saw a pale yellow shift dress. As I admired the dress, I heard the Lord speak, He said, **"that is the dress you will wear when you meet Mr. Wonderful."**

I felt my heart skip as I heard those words. I don't remember if I bought the dress that very day. However, I went back to the shop and tried on the yellow shift dress. It was a perfect fit. I happily bought it and completed my shopping for our family members.

University finally closed for Christmas and Diana and I packed our bags to make the long journey from Minneapolis to Israel. We stopped over in Cairo, Egypt, and then got a short connection to Gaza. In Gaza, we found someone waiting to drive us to Bethlehem where we found that our parents had already arrived. We were overjoyed to be with them again after a long time, and spending Christmas in Bethlehem.

Bethlehem was not at all what I imagined it would be. After years of seeing nativity scenes of Baby Jesus, Mary

---

1 Jonathan Netanyahu. *The Letters of Jonathan Netanyahu: The Commander of the Entebbe Rescue Force.* Gefen Books. 2013. See also Jonathan Netanyahu, Binyamin Netanyahu, Ido Netanyahu, and Herman Wouk. *Self-Portrait of a Hero: From the Letters of Jonathan Netanyahu*, 1963-1976. Grand Central Pub. 1998.

and Joseph, the manger and shepherds, I don't know what I expected. But what I didn't expect was the town of Bethlehem I saw in 1999. It was a small town. It was not very developed and had a few buildings on some streets. There was dusty construction scattered across the town and, generally, it wasn't what I had envisaged. I kept thinking, "Jesus was born here." The Son of God could have been born in the greatest gilded palace in the world, but He chose this small, dusty, simple town. Bethlehem! Isn't it just like God, to show up in all His glory and power amid our weakness and poverty?

On Christmas Eve, we attended a service at the Church of the Nativity, a beautiful church run by Catholic fathers. At night, the temperatures dropped so much that we had to wear warm coats. It was winter in Israel and, as we attended the service, I imagined what it must have been like that first Christmas night when the angels appeared to the shepherds and sang the glorious chorus in the heavens, *"Glory to God in the highest and on earth, peace and goodwill to men. For today born in the City of David is a Saviour, Christ our Lord."*

On Christmas Day we stayed in Bethlehem and spent time together as a family. It was a very special Christmas together, just my sister and I and our parents. The day after Christmas, we shifted to the Israel side of the border through a checkpoint and the difference was felt immediately. The Ugandan Consul in Israel met my parents and we made the short journey to Jerusalem. We spent the day visiting different sites in Jerusalem like the Upper Room where Jesus had His last supper with His disciples and the Church of the Holy Sepulchre where it is believed that Jesus was buried and rose from the grave.

We also were given a tour of the Old City of Jerusalem and walked through the *Via Dolorosa* or the *Way of the Cross*. This is the small winding road along which, it is said, Jesus walked carrying His Cross on the way to the hill called Calvary. The road was so narrow and there was two-way traffic coming and others going. Also, the sides of the road were lined with souks and souvenir shops of all manner of goods and religious artifacts for sale.

The traffic was so tight that we had to hold hands with the person in front of us and behind us so that we didn't get lost in the crowd. In this traffic, a stranger seemed to push himself into our single file from the side. My mother and Diana were in front of my father and then he was in front of me, but this stranger was pushing himself to come in between me and my father. I was very wary of strangers because the security situation in Israel had been very dangerous with many suicide bombers blowing themselves up in the middle of markets just like the one we were walking through. So I was very worried to see this stranger and tried to maneuver myself back into place by going around him and inching forward in the line. I was worried about my father and wondered why this stranger was positioning himself behind him.

As I inched forward, my heart almost stopped. Almost in slow motion, I saw the stranger begin to pull something grey and bulky out of his side pocket. As I felt the blood drain from myself, I became convinced that this stranger was there to cause us harm, so in a second I pushed myself from the side and took up my position behind my father, feeling that if the stranger tried anything, I could shield my father and family from any hurt. It all happened in a split second, although it felt like an eternity and the fear I felt at that moment was very real. When I was back behind my father, the stranger now moved to my right and then entered one of the shops lining the street. He retrieved what He had removed from his pocket and as I passed him I realized that it wasn't a weapon as I imagined but rather a big bulky cell phone! I felt the fear and panic melt away as I realized I had been alarmed for no reason. By the Grace of God, we all got back to the hotel safely, and I narrated the whole tale to my family who laughed. They were so touched that I thought I could "save" them all by being a shield myself. I realized that what I was seeing on the news had gotten into my head and I was seeing danger where necessarily there wasn't any.

The next day, my mother, Diana and I went to visit the Wailing Wall. The Wailing Wall is the last remnant of King

Solomon's temple and people come from all over the world to pray there and hide their written prayers in between the ancient stone blocks that make up the wall. I cannot express the feeling I had while I sat there witnessing this powerful and moving scene of people from every tongue, tribe and walk of life, calling out to the Lord in prayer. It was deeply moving and, as I sat there alone, I felt the Lord's Presence around me. I felt His loving question, **"What do You want me to do for you, My daughter?"**

I waited for a moment and then spoke in my heart, "Father, I want you to bring Mr. Wonderful to walk into the New Millennium with me."

It was a very simple prayer, but I felt that the Lord heard me. I wrote my prayer down on a small piece of paper and, after praying quietly, I stood to make my way to the wall. I finally found a space where I could touch the cool ancient stones of the wall. I placed my hands on the wall and as I closed my eyes and the noise of the people praying around me drowned out, I placed my prayer in between the stone blocks. I laid my forehead on the cool stone wall and just waited for a moment. His Presence was there, the same Presence I felt when I prayed in my room in Minnesota, or Namagunga, in Entebbe or Rwakyitura, my home where I grew up. He was here, wherever He is, the feeling is the same. And wherever He is, is home to me.

It was a deeply emotional experience. When I finished I went back to where I was seated before and waited for my mother and sister to finish their time of prayer before we left together. I had a sense of peace and joy as we left the Wailing Wall.

After a day or so, when my parents were done with their programme in Israel, we prepared to return home to Uganda. I have gone back to visit Israel since then but I will always remember that special Christmas that we spent in the Holy Land. Coming home has always been a celebration; there is indeed no place like home. Our family was reunited and the house was full of noise, laughter and activity. We arrived back home close to New Year's Day, and since it was the new millennium, there were special prayer services planned for the crossover night at the National Stadium. On New Year's Eve, we went with our parents to Namboole Stadium, where there were all-night prayers for the nation as we prepared to cross into the year 2000! At exactly midnight there was a great fireworks display and a lot of singing and celebrating. There was a big cake that was cut and shared with those present. I recall my mother served cake to those around us and also went down to members of the press who were attending the event and served them cake too. Everyone was happy and excited! After that, my father spoke to the nation for the first time in the New Millennium.

The year 2000 had finally dawned and so far as we could tell, there was no global meltdown as the whole Y2K prophets of doom had foretold. Everything was very peaceful.

On the 2nd of January, 2000 a family friend told me that there was someone she wanted me to meet. I was generally hesitant about meeting anyone who I didn't know before, but my friend insisted that all would be well. She asked that I meet her at a local restaurant that was in a quiet suburb of the city. Since I had my reservations about the whole arrangement, I co-opted my younger sister Diana to come along with me. My sister has always been my friend and 'partner in crime'; if there was anyone who could be a good backup in this new and unknown situation, it was Diana. So we devised a scheme, that she would come along with me and if, somewhere along the way, things didn't go well, if there were awkward silences, or we had nothing to talk about, she could come to my rescue and say we had to leave for such and such a reason. So we were all set to go. I went to get ready and the Lord reminded me about my pale yellow shift dress. I dressed up and we left together. I was slightly anxious, but also there was this strange peace over me. Diana and I agreed that I would give her a sign if things weren't going well so that she could activate our backup plan.

We soon arrived at the restaurant and found my friend and the mystery person waiting for us. We said hello and immediately, I felt electricity as we shook hands. He said, "Hello my name is Odrek," and I probably mumbled something in response.

What was supposed to be a short one-hour meeting lasted the whole afternoon. Diana kept waiting for me to give her the sign that I wanted her to activate our backup plan, but none came from me. I was having so much fun that I completely forgot about our backup plan. When I met Odrek, I was a girl who had a lot of defences, and I was quite sure that no guy could successfully make it through all my defences. What was so unexpected about Odrek is that he was so radically different and he simply disarmed all my defences.

First of all, he has a great sense of humour. He has what in Runyankore is called *okuganiza* which in English can be translated to mean witty, wry or sardonic sense of humour.

From day one, he had me laughing until my eyes teared up and my sides hurt. As we got to know each other better, it seemed like my job was to laugh at all his funny stories that he would regale me with.

Another thing that I immediately liked about him was that he was very interesting, and we found that we had so much to talk about. It seemed that our conversations could go on and on, all day and we wouldn't fail to have new things to talk about the very next day. I loved talking to Odrek and it was always very easy to talk to him. I could be myself completely; I found that with him, I could let my guard down.

But the thing I loved most about Odrek, even on that first day, was that he had a great vision for his life. He was doing things that I hadn't seen anyone else in our generation do. He talked passionately about Uganda and the work he was doing as a trainer and mobilizer for the Movement(the National Resistance Movement is the political party that started as a national liberation movement). He shared his dreams about Uganda and Africa and what we young people needed to do to seize our destiny. I had never heard anyone talk the way he talked and it resonated deeply with where I was in my journey and walk with God and my search for my identity as an African. It is a very powerful connection when for so long you think you are the only person who sees things in a certain way or is searching for something deeper in life, and then suddenly you find that someone else is on the same path as you are, asking the same questions and searching for answers just like you are.

Our meeting was like two worlds colliding, almost like fate smiling at destiny. After hours of engaging in conversation, it was getting dark and we had to say goodbye. We promised to keep in touch and meet up again since my holiday would soon be over. As we drove home, Diana made fun of me for how I had hopelessly reneged on our backup plan. "Huh, what plan?"

My head was in a cloud for the next couple of weeks as Odrek and I got to know each other better. We spent every possible waking moment together whether physically meeting up, or talking on the phone. After our initial meeting, we made plans to meet again and then again and again after that. It was almost like we were on a mission to use every day before I had to go back to college, to spend time together. Those early days were a blissful blur; all we wanted to do was be together and talk to each other and each day it was the same plan, "when can we meet?"

As the days to return to college drew closer, we tried to use every opportunity to be together. One day, he asked if he could drive me to Jinja. I agreed to go after asking my mom for permission. She permitted me but reminded me that 8 pm was my curfew time. I agreed and got ready for our out-of-town excursion. Odrek was driving a small grey Honda which I grew to love. It had a small sunroof which we opened to enjoy the fresh air. Our journey to Jinja was amazing, we played all our favourite CDs and sang along.

While in Jinja, he took me to several sites near the source of the Nile, and then we went for lunch at a restaurant. Again we spent hours talking and soon it was getting dark. I was sure that we could make it back home before my curfew time, but we had underestimated the traffic on the highway back to the city. We sat in traffic for hours and as it got late, we were both worried about my mom's reaction. By 8 pm, we were still stuck in traffic somewhere on the highway. Now we were anxiously looking at the time as Odrek tried his best to manoeuvre through the traffic. After 8 pm, my mom called me on my mobile phone; I apologized profusely saying we were struggling through the traffic. She wasn't amused by our lateness and so we drove back in silence.

We finally arrived home after 9 pm and my mother was waiting for us both in her chair in the living room. She was in no mood for jokes, she sat us both down and addressed Odrek pointedly telling him that if this was his behaviour, she would not be his friend at all. She said their rules were for our good and she needed to hear from him that they would not be flouted again. He apologized and took responsibility for not leaving on time. He promised her it would never happen again. And by the Grace of God, it never did. From then on, by 8 pm, we were always back home. Maama forgave us both and we put it behind us.

Soon the time came for me to return to Minnesota for school. In the space of a few short weeks, my life had been completely transformed. My joy was overflowing even as we sadly said goodbye to each other. There was the hope that maybe, one day soon, we would be together forever with no more goodbyes.

I went back to Minnesota and soon got back into the rhythm of school. However, now, so much had changed. It was almost like one part of me was at home in Uganda and the other part was in Minnesota.

Odrek and I talked on the phone almost every day. Many times he called me in the morning and evening. I am not sure how many phone cards he bought and used but he always managed to make the calls. When the phone calls became too expensive, we resorted to emailing, which became a big link for us in those long months of separation. I easily related to the movie, *You've Got Mail* with Meg Ryan and Tom Hanks because checking my email became an important part of life and the expectation of receiving mail was the high point of my day.

Sometimes, I didn't know the great lengths that he had to go to make the calls. One day, as I was waiting for his phone call, I didn't realize that at home in Uganda his office where he usually called me from was fumigated and so he had to ask a good friend if he could use his office to call me. I was supposed to go out for a class but didn't want to leave before talking to Odrek. As such I picked up the phone and dialled his office line. The phone rang and no one was picking. As I would learn later, Odrek, on the other end, heard the phone ringing and ran to pick it up. On the way there he almost fell down the stairs. Thankfully, nothing serious happened to him and he got to his office and called me back.

As I was gathering my books to go out, I got a phone call. The person on the other line was coughing uncontrollably but still trying to have a conversation. We talked for a while and then said goodbye. It was only a few days later that he told me the cause of his incessant coughing! It turned out that he was talking to me while trying to cover his nose because of the fumigation that had yet to settle. It was a funny story that showed us how strange we must have appeared to those around us who couldn't understand what the big deal was about the daily phone calls.

We managed to survive the months of separation during that year; it was not easy at all. One day, about three months into our relationship, Odrek had a shocker for me! It is the last thing I was expecting at that time. In one of those long-distance phone conversations, he proposed to me! I was completely stunned because I didn't see it coming at all.

Even though I knew that I wanted to get married to him, we both agreed that I had to graduate from college first. So instead of an engagement ring, he bought me a sweet promise ring, with a single diamond set in a circular flower design. I wore this beautiful promise ring until the day we got formally engaged and it was replaced with my engagement ring.

Storm Clouds Brewing

Our relationship kept growing from strength to strength as the year went on. We kept our long-distance relationship going by talking endlessly on the phone, writing emails, sending each other more letters, and all manner of gifts via the post.

In the summer of that year, we went home for the holidays and our time was even more special because we had a greater foundation of friendship and knowledge of each other. By this time, my parents and family members had become aware that our relationship was serious and so they all in different ways tried to get to know Odrek better as a person. They wanted to know who this person was; the person who had made such a big imprint on my life in such a short time. My family is very close-knit; we share everything and so there was a real interest in understanding who this "new guy" was.

We had a wonderful summer holiday and soon it was time to return to college for my final senior year. Diana and I returned to Minnesota that fall, she for her junior year and I for my senior year.

As per the tradition that we had now established, Odrek and I kept in close contact over the next couple of months. We grew to be very close and agreed on very many important areas of life. Despite that, there was one foundational area in which we didn't see eye to eye. That was in the area of faith.

Odrek came from a deeply Christian family. His parents were staunch *Balokole* or *born-again* believers who were part of the Great East African Revival. He had grown up around faith and was very familiar with all the values of the revival such as Walking in the Light and Carrying a Spirit of Brokenness or repentance daily. He knew all this very well and had seen his parents practice this daily. However, he had never made Jesus the Lord of his life; he had no personal commitment to Christ. There is a big difference between knowing about God and knowing God. It doesn't matter what our family background is or how devoted to God our parents or grandparents were, what the Lord desires is for each generation and each person to have their encounter with Him. This was a big issue between us.

I was completely sold out to Jesus and my life revolved around my relationship with the Lord. We started finding that things that were foundational to me were not to Odrek and our differences grew, mainly rooted in our different foundations. Odrek completely respected my beliefs but, to him, they were simply that: my beliefs. He didn't necessarily subscribe to them. He wouldn't ask me to change my beliefs for him but he wasn't going to change his beliefs for me either.

So there we were, stuck in "no man's land". Neither of us was willing to budge from our positions. It led us to have disagreements on big and small things. As this stalemate continued, I grew very anxious about our relationship. I knew that I loved Odrek with all my heart, but if we couldn't reconcile the most important part of our lives together, I knew we would grow apart with time. I was terrified of sharing my life with someone with whom I couldn't share the most important part of my life. What a lonely life that would be! Because of these differences, our relationship suffered.

Later that year, we agreed to take a break to think through what was going on between us. It was very hard and sad to do so. However, it looked like there was no other way. My family members and friends all weighed in and tried to advise me on this decision. I was simply paralyzed and didn't know what to do. That situation dragged on for months. Soon, our communication went silent and it seemed that all was lost.

One night when I was back in Minnesota, as I was preparing to go to sleep, I felt the Lord call me to sit with Him. I moved from the bedroom that I shared with my sister Diana, to the living room of our small apartment. It was late at night and so all was quiet and still. Outside the living room window, I could see the city lights twinkling in the night. The red neon signpost of the building adjacent to our apartment kept glowing with the words, "Gold Medal Flour." This was an old historic building from the days when Minneapolis was the hub for flour milling, and the company Pillsbury ran the mills in what was called the warehouse district.

I sat in silence as I watched the neon sign lighting up the signage with the city skyline as the backdrop.

Then the Lord spoke to me. He said, "**Didn't I tell you long ago that if you would trust Me, I would always lead you on the right path.**"

I had learnt over the years not to talk back to God, I had walked with Him long enough to recognize He had a track record of keeping His Word.

I answered, "Yes Lord."

He said, "**Do not be afraid to marry Odrek. He is My choice for you! You prayed a long time ago for Mr. Wonderful and this is the man I prepared for you.**"

I listened in silence to His Voice; it was like medicine to my soul. I asked the Lord about all the differences we have and the fact that we did not agree on the most important aspect of life.

The Lord answered, "**I will reveal Myself to him**."

Then He said, "I **want you to put Your trust in Me, not in yourself, or in Odrek; not in your parents or family members. Put your trust in Me and I will bring it to pass.**"

I felt the peace of His Presence floods my heart. And what a refreshing feeling it was. I realized how tense and afraid I had been in trying to make this decision. I was so afraid of making a mistake that I loaded myself with anxiety and fear. The Lord reminded me about how I had trusted Him when I was 15 years old at the youth conference, and how I had trusted Him over the years as I prayed for Mr. Wonderful. I realized that somewhere along the way after I met Odrek and our relationship was blossoming, I had taken my eyes off of God and put them on myself and Odrek. I was looking for answers in the wrong place. My answers always came from above, from God, not from myself or other people. I could hear the Lord waiting for my response.

I cried to Him, "I trust You, Father. Please forgive me for trying to do this on my own. I surrender to You now. I trust Your choice for me, Your love for me."

God's peace filled the room; the weight I had been carrying on my shoulders for months simply slipped off. I was free. Tears of joy washed my face, and I felt like our little living room was awash with a golden hue, a glory cloud. His Presence was there. I could feel it.

I went to sleep that night with firm faith that all was well. I didn't know what would happen or what the future held for Odrek and me. However, I had a firm trust that God was in control and that He would take care of it all. I had peace.

On the other side of the world in Uganda, my mother, who had been praying for me, felt the Lord's leading to call Odrek and speak to him. My mother considered Odrek her friend and was saddened to see us having problems. She had a conversation with him on the phone and let him know that she was praying for us and wanted to send him a book to read. Odrek thanked her and promised to read the book when he got it. He respected both my parents, but at that point, he wasn't sure that our relationship could be restored.

The book my mother sent him was a trilogy by author Francine Rivers called the *Mark of the Lion*[2] series. This fictional Christian trilogy traced the story of a young slave girl called Hadassah as she sought to live her life for God in a decadent Rome.

It was a weekend when Odrek got the books and so he had time to stay home and read them. I believe the Lord was behind this because Odrek, who had never before read any Christian literature, stayed home the whole weekend and read those books. And something powerful happened, as he relayed to me later. This came at the end of the first book in the trilogy. By that time, he was so convicted by the story and the powerful witness that it was for the Lord Jesus Christ that he knelt by his bed, alone in his apartment, and called on the Name of the Lord for the very first time. He repented of his sins and asked the Lord Jesus to come into his life! It was a Sunday and he didn't know anyone to call

---

2 Francine River. *The Mark of the Lion Series*. Tyndale House Publishers. 1993.

to share the experience except one of his friends, a Christian, called Steven Asiimwe. On the call, he told his friend that he had just given his life to the Lord. It was November 12th, 2000. On the other hand, his friend Steven, the only member of his circle of friends who was a believer, revealed his side. It turns out that Stephen had been praying for Odrek for a long time. Following the conversation, Steven came to visit Odrek and brought him a Bible. They prayed together and Odrek rejoiced in his newfound relationship with the King of kings and the Lord of lords.

*****

Back in Minnesota, I did not know about the events taking place in Odrek's life. I had never preached the gospel to Odrek and I had not even overtly prayed for him to give his life to the Lord. The Lord had done it all and He deserves all the glory!

A few weeks later, Odrek sent me an email. This was the first email I had received from him since we took our "break."

My heart skipped a beat when I saw his name in my inbox; I quickly opened the mail and soon burst into tears as I read the contents of his brief message.

In essence, the letter shared that Odrek had his encounter with the Lord Jesus Christ, alone in his apartment. He had surrendered his life to Jesus as His Saviour, Lord and King. He then said that, whether we ever got back together or not, he wanted to let me know that he had found the Lord; Jesus had captured his heart.

He quoted 2 Corinthians 2:4:

> *"For out of much affliction and anguish of heart I wrote to you with many tears, not that you should be grieved, but that you might know how much more love I have for you.." – Amplified Bible*

As I continued to read his letter, tears flowed freely down my cheeks. I felt God's mercy and grace wash over me like a tide, and an avalanche of His love overcame me. I couldn't stop myself from crying; it was like a dam that had burst open, and I just cried tears of complete wonder and joy.

God had done it! He had done what seemed impossible. He had touched Odrek's heart on His own when he was so far away from me. With this, God showed me, yet again, that He is God; there is none like Him, awesome in power and majesty! God didn't need me to touch Odrek's heart. All He wanted was for me to trust Him and surrender to Him. He purposefully had me out of the way thousands of miles away in Minnesota so that He could have one-on-one time with His son, Odrek. I was completely blown away by this God that, whenever it seemed like I knew Him well, He went ahead to surprise me in a whole new way.

The rest as they say is history. We had a glorious reconciliation and have never looked back since then. That December, my sister and I stayed in Minnesota instead of travelling home as we usually did. The Christmas break was very short and, to add to that, we both had a lot of work to do during the break.

I invited Odrek to come and visit us in Minnesota and he agreed to come. We spent two wonderful weeks together as I introduced him to my friends there and the little world in which we lived. For the first time I was the one driving him around everywhere, because at home in Uganda, he always drove me in his little Honda car. Now I could drive him around in our little 10-year-old Audi car that we all shared. He couldn't get used to the fact that I was driving on the other side of the road, and kept clutching the dashboard as he worried that I was driving too fast on the highway.

I took him to see a Harlem Globetrotters game that was on tour and visit the city of Minneapolis. We went ice skating with my sister and our friends but he didn't seem to enjoy it very much. We went to our church, Bethlehem Baptist, pastored by the legendary John Piper. There we listened to his sermons that had a high theological and philosophical style of preaching which Odrek relished. We also did fun things like go and together take glamour shots. These were studio pictures where you could change and wear "glamorous outfits." We still have those pictures framed in our home today and our children marvel that we both looked so young at the time. Overall, it was a very special time and I know it was the Lord who made it so special. We both had peace with God and with each other; we entrusted our future to the Lord and so every moment was truly precious. After New Year's Day, Odrek prepared to return home. As we said our long goodbyes at the airport, we looked forward to a new year and all that God had in store for us.

Heaven on Earth

After my graduation in May of 2021, I returned home full of hope and expectation about the next season that the Lord had for me. I felt my cup was full. My four years in Minnesota changed me and helped me mature spiritually, emotionally, intellectually and socially. I went to Minnesota as a wide-eyed girl who had never been away from home apart from boarding school. I returned home more mature, independent and clear on God's purposes for my life.

Coming home was a wonderful blessing. Nothing could compare with being back in my country amongst my people. I wasted no time catching up with all that had happened with my family and friends while I was away. Both my older brother and sister were married and expecting their first babies within months of each other. It was an exciting time, I couldn't believe that I would soon be an auntie and I threw myself wholeheartedly into helping my sister prepare for her little bundle of joy.

My parents welcomed their first grandchild in June of 2001, shortly after I had returned home. The excitement at home was palpable as we got news and pictures from my mother who was with our brother and sister-in-law. A baby boy! Diana and I, at home, were over the moon with excitement.

Soon the couple and baby returned home from the hospital and we got our first look at our nephew, a big baby boy called Ruhaamya. There was a lot of fussing about the new baby by all members of the family. My mother spent time in those early months giving support to Charlotte and Muhoozi as they adapted to life as new parents.

A few short months later in October, I was with my sister, mother and family members on a long night at the hospital in Kololo as we waited for the birth of her baby. Finally, after a very long day and night of labour, Natasha delivered a healthy baby girl in the early hours of the morning. It was all joy and thanksgiving as we held the baby. This was yet another blessing, a bundle of joy and the first baby for Natasha and Edwin; a little girl called Nsaasirwe.

By this time Diana had returned to college for her final year and so I was the one left to do auntie duties.

God had blessed our family with a double portion within a few short months of each other. I spent those first early months helping my sister out, babysitting and just being there for her. I love babies and so having my niece and nephew was a dream come true.

*****

In August of 2001, I registered my own company to deal in grain trading and other forms of agri-business. My parents encouraged me to go into business as opposed to looking for a job with the UN, something I had wanted to do. Aside from that, I needed to learn how to be self-sufficient. Theirs was foresight! I cannot thank them enough for pushing me in that direction. As I speak today, I have been an entrepreneur all my life, and have never earned a paycheck from anyone. I have been my own boss from day one and it is a decision that I have never regretted. In spite of the challenges and stress sometimes associated with being an entrepreneur, I would have it no other way now. It is the life I have become accustomed to and it is a life that has been a blessing to me and my family.

Those first months and years of setting up my business were stressful. Everything I learned about business, I learned on the job, through first-hand experiences and truthfully I made some mistakes. I had so much responsibility from the very first day that I sometimes felt overwhelmed. At 23 years of age, I had employees to pay, taxes to remit and new opportunities to follow. It was very engrossing. Being an entrepreneur is very different from working in a 9 am to 5 pm job because you never really leave the office. Your work follows you into your home. You think about your work all the time, especially if there is a problem or situation at work; as the leader of the business, you can't just do your bit and wait for the boss. You are the boss and so the responsibility is on your shoulders.

Odrek too left his job at the Uganda Revenue Authority. He went out on his own for the first time, starting his own company TERP Media around the same time. So we were both very busy working and setting up our very young businesses with all the accompanying headaches and stresses.

Odrek always encouraged me to not back down or be discouraged in my work. Even when I felt like the challenges I faced were insurmountable, he always believed in me and encouraged me. As such, I always felt like we were a team. The rest of the year passed in a flurry of activity; our relationship was going from strength to strength. Meanwhile, I was working full time and, any spare time I had, I spent babysitting my little niece. It was a busy, happy and exciting time, full of the promise of a new season. The year came to an end quickly.

I got the biggest surprise on the 2nd of January 2002, when Odrek officially proposed to me. It was our second anniversary since the day we first met. I said yes with all my heart, with shock and unspeakable joy. I felt like I was walking in the clouds; I couldn't believe that this was happening to me!

Our journey started long before we ever met, but for me, it started when I committed to trusting the Lord with the matters of my heart when I was 15 years old. As I looked back all I could see was the path of His glory and the imprint of His Grace. God had done it all; He had been with me every step of the way, guiding, encouraging, correcting, and loving me. God had been more than faithful to me! Over the years, I have become acquainted with how He moves and works and there is nothing like His signature style. That is why King David could say in Psalms. 27:4, *"This one thing I ask, this one thing do I require, that I may dwell in the house of the Lord all the days of my love and gaze on His loveliness."*

God is beautiful and everything He does is masterfully beautiful! Every time I think He has topped what He did the last time, He comes and overwhelms me by surpassing the last wonder He performed. That is what my journey with Him has been: Heaven on Earth!

Our wedding date was set for the 20th of July that same year and so the following months were a blur of activity in preparation for our big day. My first thing was to ask the Lord to take control of everything. I wanted Him in the driver's seat. I was simply coming along for the ride. I wanted to just step back and see the Master at work, and He graciously answered my prayer. Through all the weeks and months that followed, I was just being carried along by His Grace; I was completely at rest and glowing with the reflection of God's love for me. I was very aware that God blessed me not because I was good or deserving but because He is good, He is a good Father.

The month of July finally came and our years of waiting to "be together" would soon come to an end and a new journey would begin. A few weeks before the wedding, I went to a jewellery store in Kampala to engrave our wedding bands with some inscriptions. I had planned to inscribe some romantic prose or quote from Shakespeare or Song of Solomon in the Bible. I recall vividly that the Lord spoke to me just as I was entering the shop in that still small Voice that I knew so well. He said, **"Who are you going to enthrone in your marriage?"**

Because I was in a public place, I couldn't speak out loud, but I answered from my heart. I said, "I'm not sure I understand Lord."

He said, **"If you enthrone your husband in the marriage, he will have to keep the marriage. If you enthrone yourself, then you will have to keep it. But if you enthrone Me, then I will be the keeper of your marriage."**

I felt convicted by His words and answered, "I want to enthrone You, I want You to keep my marriage. Forgive me, Lord"

He said, "**Have you not tasted and seen that I am good?**"

I said, "Yes Lord, You have been so good."

He said, "**All you have seen and known of Me up until now is only a taste of what is yet to come. You have only tasted, but from now on you will experience the fullness of who I AM.**"

His Words overwhelmed me. I felt the full force of what He was saying hit me. I blinked back tears and swallowed the knot I felt in my throat.

Then He gave me the inscription that He wanted me to write on my wedding band. It was Psalms 34:8, ***"Taste and see that the LORD is good, blessed is the one who takes refuge in Him."***

That scripture is what I engraved on my wedding band and God has more than proven true to His Word. I quickly called Odrek on my mobile phone as I stood in the little jewellery shop and asked him if he had a scripture he wanted to be engraved in his wedding band. He said in Joshua 24: 15, ***"As for me and my house, we shall serve the LORD."***

I knew that something had transpired that day. We had effectively given the LORD the reins of our marriage and asked Him to take complete control. I can testify with all truth that God is a worthy steward of whatever we entrust to Him. He is God and there is no unrighteousness in Him.

Our wedding day dawned and God's peace covered me like a shawl, His Presence was there, and He was in control. Every aspect of the day was beautiful. Having all my family, friends and loved ones together was a wonderful feeling. My younger sister Diana had recently graduated from university and was home to stay, and my best friend Nukuri travelled from Pittsburgh to be with me on my special day. All my friends from school and the Bencho Gang reunited to be my bridesmaids. Our dear friend Rev. Arthur Rouner (RIP) made the long journey from Minnesota to be a celebrant in our wedding service. He preached the sermon and gave us the prayer blessing after we exchanged our vows. We had so many of our family and friends present. It was only my brother Muhoozi who was missing because he was attending a military course in Egypt that year. Even though I missed him dearly, I was glad that his beautiful wife Charlotte and their young son were with us to share this special time.

The whole day was bathed in a golden hue. It was a perfect day! From the beginning to the end, it was a day unlike any other; the most beautiful day of my life. I was so thankful for my loving family, my father and mother, who gave me my roots and also wings to fly. I always recognized that so much of who I am is because of who they are, and so much of what I have been able to do in my life is because I stood on their shoulders. I very much appreciated each and all my wonderful friends, who had brought laughter, love and camaraderie along the way, each of them with all their unique gifts and personalities.

I was thankful for the new family I was joining from that day onward. Odrek's father had gone home to be with the Lord before we met and so I only knew his mother who became my mother-in-love. I was blessed to become part of a family that, above all, loved the Lord and had a strong heritage of faith as a foundation.

I was thankful for Odrek, my very own Mr. Wonderful. He had made this journey the most beautiful journey of my life. I loved and honoured him for being the man that he is, a man after God's own heart.

I was thankful to my Heavenly Father, my story is, our story, His and mine. I couldn't understand why my wedding day seemed golden to me; everywhere I looked it seemed like there was a golden hue painted over the natural colour of the day. I asked the Lord about it and He answered, **"It is My anointing, I have smeared my Anointing over the whole day."**

God gave me His promise from Deuteronomy 11:21, *"That your days may be multiplied, and the days of your children, in the land which the Lord swore unto your fathers to give them, as the days of heaven upon the earth."*

God's blessing on our wedding day and life together as

husband and wife is not unique to us in any way. God is no respecter of persons. His promises are for "whosoever will". That means He welcomes all to become His children and experience His goodness. As I write this book, Odrek and I are in our 21st year of marriage. The only way I can describe our journey together with the Lord is that it is like the days of heaven on earth and I cannot thank God enough for all that He is to us.

10. The Call

And Jesus said to them, 'Come follow Me (as My disciples, accepting Me as Your Master and Teacher and walking the same path of life that I walk), and I will make you fishers of men." – Matthew, 4:19, – Amplified Bible

Marriage and motherhood agreed with me. God blessed us with our firstborn son Mumutiine and our daughter Kendagaano in quick succession soon after we were married, and for me, motherhood was complete bliss.

I loved spending every waking moment with our children, bathing, feeding and playing with them through the simple routines of the day. While they napped, I got some time to go to the office and check on things, otherwise, I worked from home. In the evenings, I loved taking the children out in the garden and putting all their little toys out on a mat so we could all enjoy some time in the sun. Odrek usually returned home later in the evening and he would spend some time playing with the children before I prepared them for bed. Every day it was more or less the same simple routine and I immersed myself in the baby world with complete relish. I wanted nothing more than to look after my little family and build a home and life together with my husband Odrek.

I was twenty-seven years old and was content with where my life was going. I envisaged a quiet family life at home and then growing our businesses at work. I never wanted anything more than that. At that time, I saw all the uncertainty and bumps of new undiscovered paths as a thing of the past. Or so I thought. I didn't know that God was about to throw me the biggest curve ball and send me in a direction that I never dreamed I would take.

The Vision

In 2005 God started speaking to me in distinct visions about the destiny of Africa. At first, I didn't find this unusual because this was a topic that surrounded me from my college years. It was something I thought of, prayed about and discussed often with Odrek. The vision was very vivid and clear. I saw the continent of Africa, and it was very dark. Then I heard the Lord's Voice say, "**out of what was called darkness will come a great Light.**" The Lord went on to say, "**This Light will come from within you.**"

Then I saw a silhouette of someone blowing a shofar or rams horn, as they did a small Light started shining in Uganda. At first, it was a very small, almost insignificant light, but it soon grew in strength and intensity. As it increased in strength, it started to emanate outward in concentric circles, soon spreading over the whole nation. Wherever the Light landed became a focus for further expansion of light outward, until the whole country was ablaze with white-hot light. Then the light started emanating out of Uganda into the regions surrounding Uganda and eventually spread to the whole continent. When the continent was filled with incandescent light then the light started going out to the nations of the world.

I asked the Lord, "Why is the Light coming out of Uganda? Is it because I am a Ugandan and you are speaking to me?"

The LORD answered, "**No, Uganda is the heart of Africa and just like a man's life is changed when his heart is changed, as Uganda aligns with my redemptive purposes, it will have a domino effect on the rest of Africa.**"

Finally, I asked the Lord, "who is that person blowing the trumpet or shofar."

The Lord answered, "**You are the one blowing the trumpet**."

Then the vision ended.

I kept having this same vision on and off for the space of one year from 2005 to 2006. The feeling that the Lord was calling me to something new and profound grew stronger and stronger. In my heart, though, there was the struggle to remain in the place of comfort that I felt I was just beginning to settle into.

For a long time, I tried to ignore the Voice, hoping that it would fade away. Instead, it kept growing stronger and stronger. I knew that the Lord was asking me to do something. However, I didn't know what it was. I felt Him leading me on, but I could not tell where He was leading me.

This situation continued until the summer of 2006 when Odrek and I travelled to Atlanta, Georgia. Odrek left a week ahead of me because he was transiting through another city where he had some work to do; I stayed home to settle my children in at my sister Natasha's home where they were going to stay for the duration of our trip. Our children were one and two and a half years old, respectively, so leaving home wasn't very easy. Finally, I started my trip to Atlanta on my own. On my long flight to the U.S., I felt the conviction of the Lord the whole way. I was reading my Bible on the plane and could sense His Presence around me. It was almost like He was seated, in the chair next to me, talking to me. I felt there was a struggle in my spirit, like the Lord was leading me but my flesh was resisting His lead. Finally, I heard Him speak; He said, **"You are going to have to make a decision, you can either follow Me or choose your path, but you can't do both."**

I thought long and hard before I answered the Lord. I had learnt from experience that talking to God was serious and I never wanted to speak presumptuously or without careful prayer and thought.

I said, "Lord, You know that all my life is already Yours. I don't understand what You are asking of Me Lord but, whatever it is, I am already Yours, and I do not want a life without You or a road that You aren't walking with me."As I spoke, I felt His peace. I didn't understand what it meant but I felt somehow that God received my answer and it pleased Him.

For the rest of my journey, there was peace and silence. I met Odrek in Washington D.C. and then we travelled to Atlanta together. We had a wonderful time resting and just doing simple things together before we started meeting people and going out for different programmes. On the weekend we drove out of the city to a suburb called College Park to the World Changers Church International church pastored by Pastor Creflo Dollar and his wife Taffi. I had been a partner with Creflo Dollar ministries for a while sending my tithe faithfully to their branch in South Africa. Pastor Dollar's messages impacted me greatly and it was a powerful experience to be in the atmosphere of praise, worship and the Presence of God with thousands of other believers.

As soon as we entered the large auditorium, I felt hit by the Power of the Presence of God. He was here, His Presence Overwhelming! Odrek and I sat high up in the overflow balcony throughout the service; I sat listening with rapt attention. I cannot explain what happened during that service, but it was only then that I understood what the Lord was speaking to me about through the vision that I had been seeing for the past year.

The Light was the Gospel! It was the Light of the gospel coming out of Uganda going out to the nations and filling the continent with Light! I understood that it is the Word of God that transforms. His Word, spoken into the dark void that was the earth, brought Light forth and creation came to be. His Word is the Light that pierces the darkness and the darkness cannot overcome it. His Word is what Africa needed to hear! We had for centuries heard the words of other nations and our own words, but the Word that had the power to transform us was God's Word.

The revelation hit me! I felt overcome by His Presence as I wept in worship. I understood what He was asking of me, what He was calling us to. To proclaim His Word to the continent, to declare as it says in Isaiah 61 the "acceptable year of the Lord, the year of the Lord's Favour."

When the service ended, Odrek and I went to the bookstore and bought as many books and CDs written and taught by Creflo Dollar as we could find. We stayed on, long after other congregants had left; it felt like we were spiritually hungry and suddenly we found ourselves in a lavish banquet of all manner of spiritual food.

When we left the church, we walked in silence on the street the distance from the church to the main road where we could hail a taxi to take us back to the hotel. I will never forget that walk because Odrek and I were both lost in our thoughts. We walked in silence for a while and then started to share what we both felt in the service. Odrek knew what I had been experiencing throughout the previous year and he encouraged me to wait on the Lord's signal. He kept saying that God would reveal what He desired of us.

As we walked from the church that evening, I shared that I felt I understood the meaning of the vision that I had been seeing. I said that I believed the Light was the Gospel going out of Uganda to the nations. We kept talking as we walked and Odrek said, "We always support the gospel being preached at home whenever we can. We give and we support people who are serving God."

All he said was true, but I felt there was more the Lord was asking of us.

Then I shared how I felt so strongly in the service that there was a connection between the vision and the gospel message going out and that the Lord wanted us involved in this in some way. I also told him about my experience on the plane when I felt the strong conviction of the Lord that there was a direction He was leading us and I was resisting His nudge.

As we neared the top of the road that led to the Church, we stopped and continued talking right there in the middle of nowhere. Finally, we agreed that, even though we didn't clearly understand what the Lord was speaking to us about, we would surrender to God's will, whatever it was. We were open to God, whatever He asked of us. Feeling a sense of peace, we continued on the highway and caught a ride back to the hotel. It was after this agreement between the Lord, Odrek and I that I first saw the name, *Covenant Nations Church.* It appeared like a sign in the air and I wrote it down. It was the first time I realized that God wanted us to start a church. A church! What?

*****

I had always known that I wanted to support the work of the Kingdom in one form or another, especially in giving. I felt that giving was my responsibility and I endeavoured, as much as I could, to give to the local church and also other ministries that blessed me like Creflo Dollar Ministries. However, I had never in a million years dreamed that God would ask me, of all people, to start a church. As I came to this realization, I had a million reasons why I was sure the Lord had picked the wrong person. I was sure the Lord had somehow made a big mistake and I needed to let Him know how unsuited I would be for such a role.

First, I was a woman, a wife and a mother with young children. My responsibilities at home kept me so busy that I barely had time to do anything else. Surely, God could find a man who didn't have to care for young children to do His work. Second, I wasn't a church person. Didn't church people have to go to seminary, wear a collar and be deeply theological? I was none of the above, so God must be mistaken, I felt. Third, I was terrible at public speaking. I couldn't even imagine that God could pick me for something like that. I loathed speaking in public and I couldn't imagine that the Lord wanted to torture me by asking me to do that for Him.

Fourth, I was a businesswoman and I was very happy running my business and working together with my husband. We had so many ideas of what we wanted to do together in our work and I couldn't imagine that I could juggle being a mom, working and also being involved in church.

Finally, what I thought was the greatest obstacle was my family background. If, and this was a big 'if', we went ahead with what we felt the Lord was speaking to us, it would mean that we would open ourselves up to the world in a way we never had before. My parents' political positions as President and First Lady, I felt were a big deterrent because it was always there lurking in the background. If we did start a church and people came to church, would they be part of the church because it was "the first family" church or because God called them there? Would people come to church to pray and seek God or to see the names or faces they expected to find there?

I didn't have the answer to that question, but I felt very uncomfortable with the whole scenario. I kept pleading with the Lord, "please pick someone else; there must be so many other better-suited people, men of God who can do Your work without any encumbrances."

I felt God couldn't have found a more unsuited person for this assignment. However, as our days in Atlanta came to an end, it seemed that the seed of Covenant Nations Church, that the Lord had planted, was already beginning to sprout. This is something I cannot easily explain in the natural sense. The working of spiritual things is counterintuitive; it is like a river flowing upstream and, therefore, it is difficult to describe. As long as God's Word has gone forth and there is an agreement, all other rational matters seem to be suspended. What matters is that His Word is received and believed. At the time God spoke to me in the church service at Creflo Dollar's church, I felt like I completely understood what God was saying. But afterward came the avalanche of questions, this did not appear possible.

Every time I prayed, I asked God to please take this away from me and I would gladly do anything for Him as long as He took this away. I would serve any church, and do anything for any of His pastors, leaders and ministers if He would only take this away. We left Atlanta and God didn't take it away. He put more fuel on the nascent fire that had begun to burn. By the time we arrived home, it seemed all established; a *fait accompli*, although we had not shared this with anyone else. It only existed between the Lord, Odrek and me, although already it seemed like it was a big thing.

We joyfully reunited with our children and I hoped that God would speak and say, "Oh sorry! I forgot you have these babies and you are up most of the night changing diapers and feeding them so I'll get someone else to fulfill this assignment."

I waited and waited for such a signal but nothing changed. A few weeks after we returned from Atlanta. As Odrek and I were talking about what we should do next, we decided to put three fleeces out for God. If God answered us on all three fleeces, it would be a confirmation that this was indeed God.

The first fleece was that we called our family friends together and shared with them what the Lord had been speaking to us about and what we felt He was asking us to do. My secret hope was that they would say, "Have you lost your mind? That's crazy you can't do that. you aren't qualified to be a preacher of the Gospel." To which I could go back to God and say, "I tried God, but your people don't think I'm cut out for this."

We called our family and friends together on a weekend and they all gathered in our office at home. After catching up, Odrek and I shared with them what the Lord had been speaking to us about for a year or so and what He felt He was asking us to do.

Without exception, every person in the meeting said this was an answer to prayer and that they, too, had been in a season of transition where they had been seeking God for their own lives. There was joy and excitement in the room as everyone agreed that this was God speaking and that they all wanted to help. I felt fear in my heart as I realized my exit clause was completely dashed. There was relief in confirmation and seeing that God was speaking. However, there was a deep sense of fear of what we were getting into. I remember I said, "I don't know anything about the church; I don't even know how services are run."

Almost in unison, our friends and family all said, "we will help you."

Then I asked, "where will we have the services?"

Here, some said we could rent a hall in a hotel or a small conference facility. There was no agreement over this as others brought up other venue options. Then Odrek spoke up and asked, "why not have the services here at home?"

There was silence in the room as everyone thought about it for a moment. The suggestion suddenly seemed perfect. "Why had we not thought of that before," they all said. Our home had a big garden where we decided to put an outdoor tent and chairs for the meeting. It was all settled; the church would start at home. The last thing we discussed was the date for the first service. The month of July was winding down and so we all agreed that the first service would be held on August 1st, 2006.

The meeting that was supposed to pack the whole church thing away neatly had, instead, given it wings. By the time the meeting ended, everyone was excited and looking forward to the inaugural service and the planting of **Covenant Nations Church.**

Our meeting ended late and everyone went home happy. The seriousness of what was happening wasn't lost on me. I knew that I wasn't the one driving the train, but I was scared at how fast everything was moving. I knew absolutely nothing about preaching. Over the years I had shared messages in fellowships with my friends. I loved the Word of God, both teaching and sharing it, but I wasn't a professional at all. I knew neither Greek nor Hebrew. My knowledge of Church History and theology was scant at best. All that I knew of these, I learnt from walking with the Lord from the time I was a child, but surely that didn't qualify me for this work?

God answered the two other fleeces that we put out just as He did the first one. As the date August 1st, 2006 drew closer, we sent out messages to our friends letting them know that there would be a service at our home on the first Sunday of August. To our great surprise, friends and strangers alike responded happily saying they were excited to come and worship with us.

I sought the Lord about what He wanted the first message to be based on and He spoke so clearly, "The Power of the Holy Spirit." That was our first message and I preached from the Book of Ezekiel 37 and the Valley of Dry Bones.

The first Sunday dawned bright and clear and we opened our gates to allow people to come in for the service. Everyone, from the ushers to the worshippers was drawn from family and friends and it only added to the close-knit feeling of the service. Everywhere I looked I saw my husband, my mother, my sisters and my friends. There were also strangers, people I had never seen before in my life and they were all welcomed with the same warmth as all the others. As we started our worship service, the small CD player we were using blew up, probably because of a faulty connection to the speakers. After that, we had to sing hymns using printed worship sheets and do so in our natural voices. It wasn't a smooth operation, but I could feel His Presence through it all.

Before the service I had spent time in prayer just crying to the Lord reminding Him that this was His service and that if He didn't show up, it was all for nought. I had nothing to give the people; what they needed was Him. He had to come, He had to be present. I felt warmth around me as though He was giving me a warm hug. He was there. He was with me.

When I stood up to preach the Word, I asked that we start with a word of prayer. I was very nervous. However, as I prayed, something strange happened. I felt the power of the Holy Spirit take control; the anointing of God began to flow through me. He empowered me to do what I could never do on my own. I spoke with boldness and conviction that wasn't my own. I could feel His Spirit flowing through me; the words I spoke were not my own; the focus and presence of mind weren't my own. The Holy Spirit had taken over; I was merely a vessel but He was in control. I could feel His Spirit flowing through me, His Word going forth not by my effort but by the power of God, and it was having an impact on the congregation. I would hear people respond with quiet "Amens" here and there, but more than that I could feel the power of God flowing in the service. It was my first time encountering the anointing moving through me that way. It was very beautiful, the most awesome experience.

As I concluded the service, I asked that we all stand up to pray and everyone did. We prayed a simple prayer asking for the Lord to resurrect the dead and barren places of our lives, and of our city and nation. We called forth the Spirit of God to breathe His life into us, our families, marriages, our city and our nation.

When the service was over, people spent time greeting each other and sharing how they felt about the service. It all felt very new and different. After greeting as many people as I could, I excused myself while my husband remained behind to see that everyone left and the parking was cleared. I went to our room in our house and simply sat on the bed. I was exhausted. I felt like something had gone out of me. Even though I was tired, I was content. I felt great peace! God had done it! Again He did it! With Him all things are possible! I had preached my first sermon. It was a miracle to behold!

Afterwards, I asked myself, "how am I going to manage to preach services every week for the rest of the year?" It seemed completely impossible. I recall that I bought a new notebook for my sermon notes. After our first Sunday service, I looked at my notebook and wondered how on earth I would find the sermons to fill that one notebook. Again God did the impossible! God not only provided the Word for each week, just like He did for the children of Israel in the wilderness, but He also provided the daily, weekly, and monthly manna from Heaven to feed His people. Years later as I was cleaning out one of my closets, I found a stack of notebooks all filled with sermon notes that I had made over the years. As I write this today, I have preached the gospel thousands of times over the past fifteen years, all over the country and even internationally. I have shared the Word with all manner of people, leaders and peasants, rich and poor, learned and the uneducated. God's Grace has been sufficient every single time and His anointing has never failed to break the yoke. Every time, before I get up to preach, I cry to God with the same desperation that I prayed that first day I preached to our first congregation. I say, "God, these people haven't come here to see me; they have come to encounter You; I have nothing to offer them unless You come through. It is You they need; please come and touch Your people; speak through me; I am just Your vessel." And every time without fail, God comes, He speaks, He touches His people, He breaks and He binds, He encourages, guides, heals and restores.

I do not know why He chose me. I still feel unqualified for all the same reasons I had when we started. But I accept that He knows all and He chose me for a purpose. It is not for me to question God, but rather to serve Him with all my heart and to be pleasing to Him.

So you don't want to go to church anymore

I wasn't prepared for how much my life would change after the planting of Covenant Nations Church. I had walked with the Lord since I was a child and remained in fellowship with family and friends who were believers, but getting involved with the church was something very different. I had imagined that, because we were all professing Christians filled with the Holy Spirit, all would be sweetness and honey. I thought all our relationships would be true and lasting and our words would be kind and full of love. I was shocked to find that it wasn't necessarily so.

On the one hand, there was the excitement of starting something new, and all the hopes and dreams that we all shared as a team. Meeting together was pure joy; we all looked forward to our Wednesday night meetings that we held at my husband's office in town. These meetings always ended late and we often stayed talking to each other in the parking lot before going home.

Sundays were a celebration, simple but very powerful. As we all gathered, our little children went to Sunday school which was taught by my older sister, Natasha. Worship was led by my younger sister, Diana and many other friends. Our elders were our friends and fellow believers Nicole and Claude Tshani, Sam and Anne Muhanguzi, Dr. Joe and Joanne Okia, Mr. and Mrs. Asiimwe and our honorary elder Maama Janet Museveni. Years later our elders' council expanded to include Mr. and Mrs. Kagina, Mr. and Mrs. Kaguhangire and Mr. and Mrs. Vellasamy. Our first church administrator was my dear friend Nukuri, who helped us during those early days and was of great support to me. Just like the Christians in the book of Acts, we had "all things in common." Fellowshipping together was pure joy and God kept moving in our midst.

On the other hand, there were a lot of challenges I faced in this whole new role. People in the church are still people. I had to learn that through experience. As the church congregation grew, and we faced more administrative, logistical and governance questions, there would be differences of opinion and how to settle those differences with the love of God. There were also disagreements between people, although Christians don't express their dissatisfaction in the same way as secular people. Often Christians couch issues with spiritual phrases like, "we should pray for so and so..." or "I feel like God is saying..." And there were also those in the congregation who had a legalistic spirit who viewed and categorized people according to levels of righteousness based on their lives or choices.

I felt like all these and many more expectations were placed on me to fulfill. I needed to be strong but not too strong, friendly but not too friendly; I needed to be spiritual but not too spiritual, fiery but not too fiery, gentle but not weak, and knowledgeable but not too knowledgeable. And the list went on and on, as I tried to fit the invisible list that I felt I was being measured against.

From church leadership in the city and nation, I received a lukewarm response. I was warmly received and even nurtured by Pastor Robert Kayanja and Mrs. Jessica Kayanja of Miracle Center Churches; I visited Miracle Centre Cathedral often and even shared a message there once. I also appreciated Apostle Alex Mitala who was the General Overseer of the National Fellowship of Born Again Christian churches in Uganda. He received me with kindness and encouraged me as I took my first steps into ministry. Dr. John Mulinde of World Trumpet Missions is a kind and godly servant of God, he has always been very warm and receptive to me and we have worked together many times over the years.

Some pastors viewed me with suspicion and doubts in those early days. After all, what was I doing in the church? Why had I come? Had God sent me or was there some other more convenient reason for all this? Was it political? I was told that some leaders thought I was sent by my father to mobilize the evangelical Christians for political purposes.

Often, the first question that other ministers of God had when they met me was, "how or why did you become a pastor?"

The underlying question they were asking was, "why would someone in your position become a pastor?"

I was always shocked to hear that this was a general sentiment that people had; it was almost like only those who had no other options should serve God. I felt grieved to hear this very low bar that we set in the service of God. In my opinion, serving God is the highest calling and, if I had any fears or reservations, it was because of the great responsibility to stand and say, "thus says the Lord."

There was this time I was called to a meeting with one of the pastors in the city. I asked some of our elders and my friends to come along with me as I was going to attend another conference after that. I went to this meeting with an open mind and with no ulterior motive. I went simply because I was invited and didn't think too deeply about the purpose of the meeting.

When I arrived at the venue, I found the senior pastor and other leading pastors of that church sitting together in the office. We were invited to sit down. After brief introductions, the pastor went on to berate me for not being under the right authority to start a church on my own. We listened as he went on with his attack on us. I felt like I was hit with a sledgehammer. Questions ran through my mind. Is this why I was invited? To be scolded like a child in front of other pastors, our elders and my friends. In my throat, I could feel a hard lump forming. I swallowed hard and answered when I was given an opportunity to speak, "I would never do this if the Lord hadn't called me; for me, it is a sacrifice of obedience to Him. There is nothing else I seek."

The pastor said that if God had sent me, He would have told me to start a ministry under the pastor's church. I agreed, "I said if the Lord told me to come under your authority, I would gladly do so, but He didn't. I must follow what the Lord asks of me."

One of my friends who was with me asked, "is that really the Lord speaking or is it you?"

The pastor answered, "it is the Lord."

The meeting ended soon after that. I left feeling like my face was on fire. When I entered the car, I felt hot tears pour out of my eyes. I wanted to cry to God, "is this what You send me into; to people who reject me, and question the legitimacy of my calling."

I didn't have time to cry much because I soon arrived at the conference venue where I was supposed to share a word. Imagine my state of mind coming into that conference. On the one hand, a leading spiritual father in the city had shredded me to pieces, and on the other hand, I was asked to share a word from the Lord. I will be eternally grateful for the anointing because I cannot count the number of times I have stood up to preach when I am physically or emotionally drained, but as soon as I get up to speak, the anointing of the Holy Spirit takes over and does what I am unable to do.

Jesus said it this way, *"Do not be anxious about what you will have to say, for at that moment the Holy Spirit will give you the words to speak."* - Mark 13:11.

After I shared a brief message, at the conference, I sat down in the front row with other guests. It was a big meeting in a tent and I could see delegates from around Uganda, Africa and the world.

The next speaker was a pastor from Ghana. I do not even remember his name or the theme of his message. All I remember is that, halfway through the message, he pointed to me and said, "My sister, I have a word for you from the Lord." I wanted to shrink into my chair! I was still stunned from my first meeting with the other pastors and now this Ghanaian pastor wanted to share a word with me. He asked that I stand and come to the front. I reluctantly obliged. What he proceeded to share was almost like the Lord brought a giant eraser to obliterate all the words I had heard earlier that day in the meeting with the pastors. I bowed my head as the prophetic words he spoke reaffirmed God's call on my life, His purposes for me and the fact that He had sent me to do His work. Instead of being beaten down, I was edified, God sent this man all the way from Ghana at that exact moment to speak into my life. I received that word as a balm to my spirit, even though I was still emotionally wounded. The pain and confusion of questioning my legitimacy as a servant of God was for the moment quelled.

Soon after that conference, God sent another friend and a spiritual father to encourage me. Reverend Arthur Rouner, my dear friend from Minnesota was travelling through Uganda on his way to Rwanda where he was holding reconciliation retreats. He liked to call and check on us during his brief stay in Uganda and so we went out to lunch. Arthur asked how the ministry was going and I shared with him my recent episode with the city pastors. The wounds were still fresh in my heart although my spirit was stronger. Arthur went on to encourage me as a father encourages a child. I felt as though he cast his mantle over me and said, "often, people fight the new thing God is doing. Don't be deterred. Keep going."

Those words and encouragement from a spiritual father healed my heart. I was amazed that God would take the trouble to send His servants from all over the world to speak into my heart and encourage me.

*****

After the first year of serving God as a pastor, I was completely burnt out, emotionally scarred and ready to throw in the towel. I felt that I just couldn't do it. I had my life and my family needed me. I felt like I had done what God asked and I just couldn't continue.

One day, as I spent time alone with the Lord in prayer, I was asking the Lord to release me from this assignment. I cried, "Lord, I have tried but it is just too hard. I cannot be what Your people need. I am not the right fit for this work."

The LORD answered me gently but firmly, **"who told you that you had to conform to an external standard?"**

I was stunned by His question, "I am trying to be what they all want me to be and it is too hard."

He again said, **"I have never asked you to be anything but yourself; I never sent you to be what people want you to be."**

I said, "Yes but they are Your people and I have been trying to do what they want."

The Lord spoke, **"That is not what I called you to do. I sent You to speak My Word, anything else is not from Me."**

I went silent. The truth of His Words sunk into my heart. He was right. He had never asked me to carry all the burdens I was carrying, trying to be all things to all people. I was trying to conform to some external standard to be what I thought I needed to be a pastor. God had never asked me to do that.

He spoke into my heart, **"I am with you and as long as You follow My Voice, you will succeed; if you try to follow the voices of men, you will fail and be broken in the process."**

With these words, I felt the weight of the burdens I was carrying fall off my shoulders. His peace flooded my heart. For the first time in a long time, I felt like myself again. I have been serving the Lord for many years now and His Word is indeed true, as long as I have followed His Voice, He has blessed His work and I have experienced His peace.

*****

The stormy season of my early days of ministry subsided and I continued working. I still had a lot of growing up to do but I never again questioned my calling or got swayed by pressure from people. I am glad that over the years the Lord has given me many great friendships amongst my fellow pastors, too numerous for me to list. I have worked with many pastors on outreach programmes in the city and nation. Uganda is blessed to have many great servants of God, both men and women. We have seen great breakthroughs and healing of our land as we have prayed together in agreement. I believe that is the real reason that the enemy fights against unity in the church because he knows the blessing that God releases when the church is united.

Years later, I ran into the pastor who had called me for the painful meeting in our early days. I had long forgiven him and had no hard feelings. I was in a busy international airport with my three young children and I recognized him at a distance. Our eyes met across the busy airport hall. I bowed my head in greeting. He responded in the same way and then we moved on. My attitude towards those who are spiritual fathers, whether in Uganda or any other country, has always been one of genuine honour. I honour God's servants because I honour God and always want to be pleasing to Him. I also want to learn as much as possible from any leader that the Lord brings into my path.

*****

Life as a wife, mother, pastor and businesswoman is indeed a very busy life, but God has blessed us on all fronts.

We soon outgrew our little house church and went on to rent a hall in a hotel in the neighbourhood. A few years later, we moved again and rented a house that had a garden where we pitched a bigger tent for the church services. This lasted for a few years until we outgrew it. Then we renovated a warehouse in a property that Odrek and I own and the church is located there today. By the Grace of God, Odrek and I bought ten acres of land on the outskirts of the city and gave it to the church. The plans for the construction of a training centre for ministers and sanctuary are now underway for that land. We have come a long way from those early days, but our God has been consistently faithful.

Ordination

In March 2018, I was blessed to visit Redemption Camp in Nigeria with my mother, Maama Janet. I had never visited

Nigeria before nor had I heard of The Redeemed Christian Church of God before that time.

My mother had met a Nigerian Christian who visited her and gave her a devotional called *Open Heavens*,[1] written by Pastor Enoch Adeboye of the Redeemed Christian Church of God. Maama Janet was so blessed as she used the devotional that she asked her Nigerian friend to send her some more copies to share with our family. This kind gentleman graciously obliged and Maama Janet shared copies with each of us her children. From the time I started using this devotional, I was greatly encouraged in my walk with God. I had not found a devotional in the recent past that challenged my faith as much as the *Open Heavens* devotional. It was through this devotional that I became familiar with the life and ministry of Pastor Adeboye.

When my mother invited me to join her on her trip to Nigeria, I happily agreed. Visiting Nigeria for the first time was quite an experience. My husband had travelled to Nigeria numerous times for work, but this was my first time.

We landed in the chaotic scene that is Lagos, a sprawling metropolis that is home to millions of people. Pastor And Mrs. Adeboye were hosting Maama Janet and her delegation that I was part of during our stay at the Redemption Camp. The church officials picked us up from the airport and drove us to Redemption Camp, approximately an hour from the airport. We went through the highway traffic, aggressive driving of the motorists, loud noises and street vendors which is an assault on the senses.

However, when we drove into Redemption Camp, the atmosphere dramatically shifted. What is called Redemption Camp is, for all intents and purposes, a city. It has its electricity grid, water sanitation centre, roads, shops, banks, schools, a university, hospitals, and homes well planned into estates on streets beautifully named like Holiness Highway, Peace, Joy, Glory and many more. The atmosphere in Redemption Camp is as close to a heavenly city as I have ever experienced. Inside

---

1 Pastor E. A. Adeboye. *The Open Heavens.* RCCG Publishing.

the camp, life is calm and pleasant; the Presence of God is tangibly felt everywhere. It is a truly remarkable place.

We arrived at our guest accommodation and were received by Mrs. Adeboye, whom everyone endearingly calls 'Maama G. O.'(Maama General Overseer) Pastor Adeboye in turn is lovingly called, 'Daddy G. O.,' (Daddy General Overseer).

Mrs. Adeboye is a wonderful woman of God, kind, loving, gracious and the perfect hostess. She made us feel completely at home in our guest accommodation and, before she left, we all knelt to pray together. Maama Janet and Maama G. O. are the same age, both born in 1948. They became very good friends during our visit and their friendship remains strong today.

Pastor Adeboye is a great man of God; a humble man who operates under an Elijah mantle and anointing. God has used Ps. Adeboye to do great things not only in Nigeria but also in the rest of the world. Our time at Redemption Camp was glorious and life-changing.

The purpose of our visit was to attend the Holy Ghost Congress, a large gathering of millions of believers from around Nigeria, Africa and the world. We saw Christians who had travelled from Asia, Europe and the Americas. It is unlike any other congregation I have ever attended, not only because of the size and scope, which is mind-boggling but especially because of the outpouring of the Holy Spirit accompanied by signs and wonders and amazing testimonies.

We arrived in the morning and rested in preparation for the service that started in the evening and would last into the wee hours of the morning. In the evening we got ready to go to the auditorium for the service. When I say auditorium you need to imagine a building that is 3 km wide and 3 km long. The auditorium can hold millions of people sitting comfortably in neat rows as far as the eye can see. On top of this, there are other auditoriums and viewing centres that hold the overflow crowds. When the mass choir of 6,000 begins leading worship, you feel like you have gone to heaven; it is a glorious atmosphere. The lavish outpouring of worship to God by millions of people is an awesome experience that reminds us how big God really is and how we ought to give Him the praise that is befitting who He is as God of the Universe.

After an extended time of praise and worship, the Word was shared by guest pastors and then finally, by Ps. Adeboye. This was after midnight but because we rested during the day, we were wide awake and alert for the message. Ps. Adeboye shared a powerful message and then invited people to share the Lord's supper. I think sharing Holy Communion with millions of believers from all around the world was such a beautiful picture of the Body of Christ. So many times, we bring God down to our small little level. We think God is our God alone, but when you are gathered with so many Christians from all walks of life, from different tribes, nations and tongues, you understand that there really is a global Body of Christ and sharing the Communion is an act of faith connecting us to the power of the Cross, Jesus' Body and the Blood. After communion, we had time to pray individually and corporately. This too was an experience unlike any other, hearing millions of voices raised to God was beautiful. After the offering was given, the service was closed and then everyone was dismissed. It is hard to describe the number of people leaving the service and yet miraculously there was no stampede and no one got hurt. It is truly by the power of the Spirit because people simply walk in an orderly way to their cars or vans or whatever transportation they came with.

When we arrived back at the guest house it was almost 5 am. Maama Janet and I were filled with joy as we shared the highlights of the night. As the sun rose, we went to sleep anticipating what the next day would bring.

The programme for the next day was similar to that of the first day, only that there was no Holy Communion offered. The Friday service was the main Holy Ghost service of the whole congress and so there were more people than even the day before. The whole auditorium was completely packed to the rafters, including the overflow auditoriums. The praise and worship were legendary and it felt like the entire roof would be blown off by the power of praise being lifted. Maama Janet was asked to share her testimony which she did to great shouts of Hallelujahs! and Amen!

The Word shared by Ps. Adeboye that evening was even more powerful than that of the day before. As we all prayed together after the service, I felt the Lord's Presence enthroned above our praise and worship. I realized, for the first time, how great, mighty and big God is. He is great and greatly to be praised! I felt ashamed that I hadn't offered Him the praise that was fitting for who He is as God. I felt my worship had been small and poor. I knew that had to change, that I could never again worship God at my level but rather I needed to raise my faith and worship Him as He deserved to be worshiped. The service ended again in the wee hours of the morning and we again returned to our guest house aglow with the glory of God.

The third day of the congress dawned and we again slept in to rest up for that night's evening service. In the evening we drove to the auditorium expectant about what the Lord would do; this was our last night and we wanted it to be a special time.

The atmosphere that night was electric. As the praise and worship were lifted, I felt we were entering another dimension. God's Presence was so strong in that service, the air was pregnant with a breakthrough. The third night of the Congress is called the anointing service. Ps. Adeboye preached a very strong message about Samson and the power of the anointing. As I was listening to the message I felt the Lord speak to me, He said, **"Today is your ordination day."**

"What?" I thought to myself in light of the message Ps. Adeboye was sharing which showed the tragic results in the life of Samson because of sin. Ps. Adeboye cautioned, "do not come for anointing unless you are going to commit to holiness in life. The anointing is dangerous in the face of sin and consumes completely."

As I heard the message, I was very reluctant to go and be anointed knowing the great responsibility that it placed on my life. Even after all the years of walking with God and serving Him, I was still afraid of letting go, of surrender. The message continued and I felt like I was glued to my seat. Finally, I heard Ps. Adeboye up at the pulpit say, "the Lord is telling someone that if there is something you see in my life that you want, you can ask the Lord and He will give it to you."

As I sat in my chair I knew that Word was for me. I answered the Lord in my heart saying, "Lord, I want to finish well."

At that moment I felt the Lord accept my request, He would help me run my race; He would help me finish well. It is so important to me that I can run the race that the Lord has set for me and finish well. So many times I have read accounts of great men and women of God who started with so much promise, gifting and even anointing, but somewhere along the way, they changed, they forgot God, they were seduced by the world and lost their way. Those stories grieved me deeply; they also scared me. My highest ambition and desire is to finish well and I needed to hear from the Lord that He would help me finish strong.

Ps. Adeboye then said, "remember what you are wearing today because when you receive the anointing oil, you will experience a change in your life."

I stood up with the rest of the congregation and moved to the front to be anointed. When I knelt and felt the oil on my forehead, I knew that God had ordained me as His minister. I went back to my seat and just felt His glow all over me.

As the service closed, we were allowed to gather around the altar to bring our petitions to the Lord. I found some space at the altar and knelt, all around me I could hear people's voices lifted in prayer. I stilled my heart and closed my eyes. I brought my prayers and petitions to the Lord and felt like the Heavens were opening. It is difficult to find the right words to describe the experience at that moment, but it is almost like heaven kissing the earth. God's Presence enveloped me amongst so many other children of God.

The service was finally closed and we were dismissed with a blessing. The next day we prepared to leave for the airport but not before our dear friend Maama G.O. came to say goodbye to us, and she and Maama exchanged gifts. After our glorious days together, we were now friends, brothers and sisters, sons and daughters in the Lord. What a privilege to find God's family everywhere.

As we drove to the airport, I realized why the Lord had brought me all the way to Nigeria; it was to ordain me as His minister and servant. Since then I have continued to be blessed by the ministry of Ps. Adeboye. God has spoken to me many times through him and I count him as a spiritual father. I pray that God will grant him and Mrs. Adeboye many more years of life and health to serve God and lead His people.

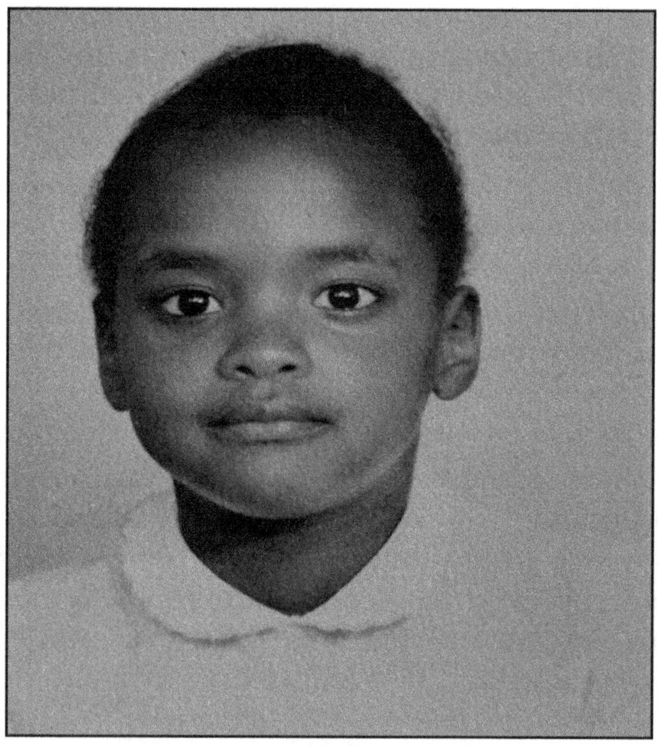

Early years around age 4

My earliest picture with my parents, my brother Muhoozi and sister Natasha & my uncle Caleb Akandwanaho in Tanzania

On a school trip in Primary 5. It is the year I encountered Jesus

As a teenager with my parents on my first trip to Iran and China

Climbing the Rwemengo hill in Ntungamo with my father

With Maama Janet at Redemption Camp in Nigeria

At home with my parents

As a teenager looking after cows with my father. The cow we are petting was the first cow I called my own. A gift from my father, it had a red colour called "Gaju" in Runyankore

The White Council

Mzee and Maama anointing the land in Bunyoro after the "Light up Bunyoro for JESUS" mission.

The "Light Up Luwero for JESUS" mission.

With the 3K's on my graduation day

The 3Ks together

With my brother Muhoozi and sister Diana

At age 13 I couldn't get enough of reading the Bible. I had an insatiable hunger to grow closer to Jesus

Graduation day in Minnesota

3Ks on my graduation dinner

With my best friend, Nukuri at the University of Minnesota

With my brother Muhoozi when he visited us in Minnesota

School days with the Bencho gang

The weekend at the lake that changed everything

At home at the Wailing Wall in Jerusalem with family and friends

Dancing and praising God in the prison in Argentina, to my right is my cousin Dr. Joe Okia and to my left a dear friend, the late Graham Power

With the Bencho girls in Rwakyitura

With Odrek a few months before our wedding

Our wedding day

Our first dance as husband and wife

Sightseeing in Greece on our honeymoon

Sightseeing in Santorini with Odrek on our Honeymoon.

At home with my family

At home with my family

With Odrek and our family visiting Santorini, Greece.

With Odrek at the cylinder bell that was rung daily to change the mindset of people in Canaan Farmers School, Korea.

With Odrek visiting Yoido Full Gospel Church in Korea

With my friend Julie Wang in Korea

At the memorial of the founder of Canaan farmers school in Korea

Sharing the Word at Makerere Full Gospel Church

When the Holy Spirit moves often people cannot contain their emotions. Here a woman was jumping for joy at the "Light Up Bunyoro for Jesus" mission

Bishop Lwere preaching the Gospel.

Sunday morning at Covenant Nations Church

Our first Sunday service at CNC, August 2006. My husband Odrek's Bible is in the chair in the first row

Meeting some young friends in Turkey

With Maama Janet at an evening service in CNC

Some members of our CNC Governing Elders Council

Meeting President Bum IL Kim the director of Canaan Farmers School, Korea

Preaching the Gospel at a crusade in Uganda

Sharing the word of God at a Conference

Leading repentance at the All Nations Convocation in Jerusalem

Speaking at the All Nations Convocation in Jerusalem.

The Buikwe mission.

Welcoming Ps. And Mrs. Adeboye to Uganda in 2019.

Receiving the Jerusalem flag from Rev. Rick Ridings and his wife in Jerusalem

When the Holy Spirit moves...

When the Holy Spirit moves...

When the Holy Spirit moves...

When the Holy Spirit moves...

When the Holy Spirit moves...

When the Holy Spirit moves...

When the Holy Spirit moves...

When the Holy Spirit moves...

When the Holy Spirit moves...

Apostle's Bunjo, Batambuze and other pastors praying for me after a mission

With the pastor of the transformed prison church in Argentina. He was a prisoner but he was more free spiritually than many free people because of his love and passion for the Lord Jesus

Praying for the cleansing of the source of the Nile

Dr. Selwyn Stevens pouring anointing oil at the source of the Nile

My friend and intercessor Jerry praying at the source of the Nile

With Maama Janet at the transformed prison in Argentina

Talking with my dear friend Arthur

My dear friends Arthur and Molly Rouner visiting CNC

With Pastor Tom Hess in Jerusalem

William Seymour

Young men with their hair cut in the Enshunju style. This hair style was popular in Ankole & northern Rwanda

11. Good Hair

We don't go "natural," we RETURN. "NATURAL" is where it began. – Unknown.

Good hair. I'm sure many women have heard that phrase mentioned in passing, maybe about the hair of a friend, sister, mother, or daughter. It is a ubiquitous term that encompasses all aspects of hair qualities such as length, texture, colour, softness and more. Beyond the simple description of hair quality, however, the term carries within it a deeper connotation of the kind of hair that is desirable. If there is "good hair" then there is, by extension, "bad hair." And people who have hair that is deemed "bad" must find a means to make it "good." "Bad hair" goes by many euphemisms such as "kinky", "nappy" and in our vernacular *kaweke*. Some may not deem the topic of hair to be of spiritual importance, but I have found, on my journey with the Lord, that the relationship I have with my hair has more to do with understanding and accepting my identity as an African than anything else. In my experience, it has been the grace of God that has awakened and reconnected me to my identity as an African.

It was not my culture. I love my culture and I believe that culture is very important. However, in Africa, we have experienced deliberate historical distortion and the attendant disconnection; we have been victims of external interference, trauma and the resultant collective amnesia. A lot about us, such as our identity and culture, has been lost in the process. Thus, in our very unique situation as Africans, it takes God to bring restoration of what has been lost in a step-by-step manner. It takes God to reveal the hidden things whether it is about our history, our land, or any other pillars of what makes us who we are, what makes us a distinct people. It took God to peel back the layers of ignorance, blindness and identity crisis in the matter of my hair.

Growing up, like most girls in Africa, my hair was natural all through my primary and secondary school years. Sometimes I would let it grow out long and other times I would cut it short. As I grew into my teenage years and young adulthood there were more things I could do with my hair as I finished school and had more autonomy regarding how I wanted to style my hair. Once in a while, I could have my hair straightened and other times, like when I was in university, I had it relaxed (used chemicals to straighten it). Like many other young women, I never thought deeply about my decision to relax my hair. I saw it more as a fashion choice than anything else. My father detested this and that is putting it lightly; he hated his daughters' changing or what he called "denaturing" their hair. He always complained about us looking like Indians when we relaxed our hair. Whenever he said this, I laughed off his comments and thought he felt that way because he was from "the older generation". I just thought he didn't understand that relaxing my hair was simply a fashion choice. My father loathed everything about treated hair, the look, the touch, and the smell. Many years later when I was married and the mother of young children, God brought home to me the truth that what I was doing with my hair was far deeper than a mere fashion statement. When my daughter, our second born, was around five years old, she liked to play with dolls. I always tried to ensure that the dolls I bought for her had some physical features similar to her own, whether it was brown eyes, brown skin, or black hair. I was intentional about this because I wanted her to play with dolls that resembled her.

Sometimes she would get dolls as gifts from friends or family that were different from our preferences, some that had white skin or blonde hair. On one such occasion, she was combing one of her doll's hair and I was sitting next to her. This doll had straight blonde hair.

As we sat together she said to me, "I wish my hair was like Barbie's hair." Immediately, the African mother lioness rose in me and I assured my daughter that she was a beautiful African princess and her hair was as beautiful as African hair should be. It was black, thick and long. My children all call me "Imma" and she said, "but Imma's hair looks like Barbie's hair and I want my hair to look like Imma's and Barbie's."

I told her that my real hair, my natural hair, looked exactly like hers. And then I reminded her about her grandmother, my mother's hair which was natural and looked just like hers. I will never forget her response when she said, "oh no! Ginga's(grandma's) hair looks like that because she's old, that's what happens when people grow old." She then went on to list all her aunties - my sisters and friends and everybody she mentioned all had straight hair, like Barbie's.

My daughter's words thoroughly cut me through to the heart! I felt that, instead of affirming her identity as a beautiful African child of God, I was part of creating an identity crisis where she was rejecting her beauty for something foreign and different. I remember that, after that encounter, I went and stood outside. I put my hand on my head and I prayed saying, "I make a covenant with you God and my hair that I will not change or denature my hair again; that I will embrace my natural hair and teach my daughters to do the same."

This was many years ago and it marked a turning point in my relationship with my hair. I cannot thank God enough for the freedom He brought into my life and the lives of my children through that one simple decision.

I realized that my father had been right all along. The denaturing or changing of my hair was more than a fashion choice. It was an identity choice and I was causing an identity crisis for my children.

The world had forced a certain image of beauty upon us and we had subconsciously accepted it. My Heavenly Father revealed to me that it is only in embracing how God created us that we experience true freedom. Over time, there have been positive developments, perhaps driven by consciousness similar to my own. There has been a natural hair revolution in Africa and around the world. Natural hair is much more popular now than it was in my growing up days. Many women have rejected the stereotype that you have to have straightened or relaxed hair and there's so much more that is available now for African women to help keep their hair natural.

I believe that it is God moving to restore a part of who we are. So is hair that important? Is it important to God? Does it matter?

Hair as a Mark of Beauty

I want to show you from the Bible that it matters a whole lot. The Bible depicts hair as one of the ways of defining beauty.

2 Samuel 14: 25 talks about one of David's sons called Absalom:

> *"But in all Israel there was none so much to be praised for his beauty as Absalom; from the soul of his foot to the crown of his head there was no blemish in him. And when he cut the hair of his head he weighed it - for at each year's end he cut it because its weight was a burden to him and it weighed 200 shackles by the king's weight." - Amplified Bible*

So here we see that this man Absalom, the king's son, was so handsome there was no blemish on him and one of the things that distinguished him was that he had very heavy, thick hair. His hair was so heavy that its weight was a burden on him and hence he cut it annually; it weighed a lot! Clearly, therefore, hair very much defines beauty. It is something that defines or sets us apart as it did for Absalom.

Song of Solomon 4:1:

> *"HOW FAIR you are, my love (he said), how very fair! Your eyes behind your veil (remind me) of those of a dove; your hair (makes me think of the black, wavy fleece) of a flock of (the Arabian) goats which one sees trailing down Mount Gilead (beyond the frontiers of the desert)." - Amplified Bible*

Solomon in this book is serenading his bride and speaking of her unmatched beauty. One of the things that he highlights is her amazingly thick black hair. I can imagine the sheep with woolly thick black hair that he is describing. King Solomon singles out her thick mane of hair as one of the distinguishing marks of her beauty.

It is very wrong for us to try to get away from the fact that our hair is a part of who we are and it defines us and sets us apart. It distinguishes us, our identity, where we come from, the kind of background we have and the racial identity we have. In both these verses and many other instances in the Bible, hair is defined as beautiful. So I believe God gave us our hair as a mark of glory and beauty.

Hair as a Spiritual Symbol

Another aspect of our hair is spiritual and shows the intimate way that God knows each of us as His children.

Luke 12:7 says:

"But (even) the very hairs of your head are all numbered. Do not be struck with fear or seized with alarm; you are of greater worth than many (flocks) of sparrows." – Amplified Bible

How awesome it is to know that the hairs on our heads are all numbered!

Just like God knows our fingerprint and our eye colour, He also knows our hair so intimately that He numbers it. He knows my hair and He knows your hair. He knows our children's hair; He knows us because our hair is part of that unique identity that makes us who we are. We are not robots, we're not mass-produced, we are individuals and our hair is part of that.

Hair as a Symbol of Covenant

Hair in the Bible was also a symbol of covenant. What you did with your hair would identify if you had a specific covenant or relationship with God.

Numbers 6:5 says thus:

"[In] all the days of the vows of his separation and abstinence there shall no razor come upon his head. Until the time is completed for which he separates himself to the Lord, he shall be holy, and he shall let the locks of hair of his head grow long." – Amplified Bible

I find it intriguing that of all the symbols of consecration that God chose to use, He chose hair. Therefore, a Nazirite, or consecrated one, never cut their hair and wore it long. Examples of Nazirites in the Bible are Samson, John the Baptist and our Lord Jesus. They didn't cut their hair because it was a symbol of their consecration, a symbol of their vow to God.

Hair, apart from being a symbol of beauty and identity, could be a sign of our covenant relationship with God. Cutting hair or growing it long communicated different aspects of consecration to God. In the New Testament, Paul made a vow to God, and when he paid his vow, he cut off his hair before going into the temple to perform religious ceremonies (Acts 18:18).

"At Cenchreae Paul cut his hair, for he had made a vow."

So it is clear this didn't only apply in the Old Testament but in the New Testament as well.

Hair as a Symbol of Glory

Hair according to 1 Corinthians 11 was also a symbol of glory.

1 Corinthians 11:14 -15 says:

"Does not the native sense of propriety (experience, common sense, reason) itself teach you that, for a man to wear long hair is a dishonour (humiliating and degrading) to him, But if a woman has long hair, it is her ornament and glory? For her hair is given to her for a covering." – Amplified Bible

Paul here is saying the hair of a woman is her glory and covering. It is something that God has given to both men and women but specifically to women as a crown of glory. Imagine if every woman or every person was walking around with crowns on their heads, you would probably defer to them and treat them differently. You would probably think they were royalty. Well, according to the Bible, you wouldn't be wrong to imagine that; Paul states that God has given women their hair as their glory or as their crown.

Proverbs 16: 31 says:

"The hoary head is a crown of beauty and glory if it is found in the way of righteousness (moral and spiritual rectitude

in every area and relation in every area and relation)." – Amplified Bible

King Solomon, the author of Proverbs reiterates that our hair is a crown of glory. The very fact that it is situated on our heads reaffirms this.

God gave us hair for a reason. It has a purpose. If we peeled off the skin on our fingers because we hated our fingerprints you would think that is both barbaric and crazy because our fingerprints are what sets us apart as people. According to the Bible, our hair is as unique and as distinguishing as our fingerprints.

African Hair

African hair is unique in that it is the only hair of humanity that defies gravity.

It doesn't grow down as other people's hair grows. It grows up and is attention-grabbing. It is thick and almost always black. African babies almost always are born with a full head of hair, a trait not common in other ethnicities.

In pre-colonial times, African people had a variety of hairstyles and ways of designing their hair. The style of hair a man or woman wore symbolized different things. The hair was a way of defining different age groups, and different brackets of society. It signified family background or social status; if they were married or unmarried if they were older or younger women. Warriors, tribal chiefs, elders and royalty often wore their hair in special hairstyles as well.

There were a plethora of ways of expressing identity through hair.

Hair also had a spiritual significance. African communities understood that there was something spiritual that is connected to their hair. So many times they would not allow just anybody to style their hair. It was a privilege entrusted to close relatives. They felt that if their hair was in the hands of an enemy, it could bring harm to them. There were unique hairstyles for different parts of Africa. Invariably, different hairstyles depended on social norms, geography, climate and soil. The use of beads and earthy colours was also popular in many African ethnic groups like the Masai.

The use of dreadlocks is an ancient practice in Africa. We see dreadlocks and braids on the pyramids, as well as in the Himba tribe of Namibia. Braids and beads were also used among the Fulani in the Sahel region. In East Africa, different ethnic groups had different ways of styling and cutting their hair to show social stratification.

The Banyakore cut their hair in concentric circles called *enshunju*. It was similar to Mohawk This practice was mainly for young men and was popular in Ankole and nothern Rwanda.

With the arrival of slavery and colonialism, African hair and other distinguishing features started to come under scrutiny. Africans who were captured as slaves had to fend for themselves in a new and hostile culture where they were now in the minority and being compared to the majority who were Europeans. The Europeans used racist lenses to demean and demonize the physical features of Africans for their selfish reasons of justifying their oppression of the Africans.

We have seen the negative caricatures of African people whether it is "blackface"[1] or the popular character created by Dartmouth Rice in 1830 which was called, *Jim Crow*. Black Face were minstrelsy shows performed in the northern cities of America after the civil war. The performers were white and they attempted to darken their skin by using shoe polish to create a denigrating picture of African people. African people were depicted as lazy, ignorant, superstitious, cowardly and hypersexual. The message of Black Face was clear, Africans are to be pitied, feared and above all never treated as equals. The character of *Jim Crow* spurned the entertainment industry, but more damaging were the discriminatory laws and practices that became entrenched in the southern states of the U.S. from the 1870s to the 1960s. The Jim Crow laws[2]

---

1 *Blackface: The Birth of An American Stereotype.* Smithsonian: National Museum of African American History and Culture.

2 *Jim Crow Museum: Who was Jim Crow?* Ferris State University.

entrenched racism and discrimination as a way of life for African Americans in the southern states and ensured that the racial hierarchy of whites at the top and Africans at the bottom was maintained and protected by the law.

African hair was described as wild, untamed, woolly, kinky or coarse - in any case, it was depicted as negative as part of the larger rejection of African appearance as undesirable. Negative stereotypes and dehumanization of slaves also extended to their hair. African hair, instead of being seen as a crown of beauty, was seen as something ugly to be covered or altered. African slaves were required to either cover their hair with a wrap or have it straightened using dangerous and primitive practices. Even after the emancipation of the slaves, the negative connotation of African beauty with regard to hair, skin tone and physical traits continued. Natural African women's hair disappeared totally from sight for over 200 years because of the denigration and racist stereotypes attached to it. Slavery and colonialism succeeded in planting seeds of self-hatred and self-rejection in the minds of the Africans.

Since African slaves were kidnapped and torn from their motherland with great trauma and violence, they did not carry with them the combs and implements used for grooming their hair to the new lands. In addition, the lives of slaves did not afford the leisure time for grooming and caring for oneself in the customary way they had done for centuries before enslavement. The slaves were treated as beasts of burden and worked all hours of the day and week. They were granted only a short time to wash clothes and rest, once a week, before all the bone-tiring work resumed. Their hair was neglected and became unkempt, a thing of shame that they sought to cover up.

Willie Morrow, an African American man, wrote a book titled, *400 Years Without a Comb.*[3] The book tells the story of African people in the Americas and the heartbreaking fact that violent disconnection from one's motherland is a disconnection from one's very self. This very real severing of

---

3 Willie Morrow. *400 years without a Comb.* Morrow's Unlimited Incorporated, 1973.

connection manifested itself in the loss of language, culture, traditions and grooming rituals. For these uprooted people, what was naturally passed down from father to son and mother to daughter was lost. As such, the African slaves in the Americas became a rootless people; who didn't know themselves, where they came from and, inadvertently, where they were going. The cruel fact that life as a slave had few if any certainties, family separation became common, increased the sense of being adrift and created a people without any sense of being.

If you add to this mix the exposure to diseases, harsh living conditions, cold climate and cruel treatment by slave owners, it is indeed a miracle of the Grace of God that African peoples survived and didn't become extinct in the Americas. African hair, though, did in a sense become extinct. Since African natural hair cannot be combed with the same combs as European hair, Africans were forced to try and alter the natural condition of their hair by flat ironing, or using dangerous chemicals to try and fit into the grooming world of the Europeans. The voluminous look of African hair was frowned upon, and thus slaves who worked in close quarters with the Europeans were forced to cover their hair or straighten it.

In the 1960s Willie Morrow got a comb as a gift from an African student who was in America and that was the beginning of the African hair renaissance. According to the book, Willie Morrow had more African combs made and started sharing them with people. Equipped with the right comb for their hair, more and more people chose to wear their hair naturally in bi-afro hairstyles. That is why in the 1960s and 1970s, big afro hairstyles became a fashion trend amongst African Americans and around the world. It was in a sense a reconnection with their identity, a way of saying that "black is beautiful."' But also, sadly, it was simply a reconnection with the right kind of comb after 400 years without it.

The African and African American hair care industry is a billion-dollar industry. In the year 2009 Chris Rock, an

African-American comedian, made a documentary called *Good Hair*[4] where he gave the history of the African-American hair care industry and showed that African-Americans spend eighty percent of the market share on hair products even though they are only twelve percent of the population. This is not limited to African Americans, though. The story is the same in Africa.

Chris Rock's documentary showed that African women, whether in Africa or America, use dangerous chemicals in their hair products, these relaxers are chemicals! They denature the hair and break the bonds that make African hair grow as it should naturally. Chemicals like relaxers which are used in these products are at best unregulated. That means it is not clear what their impact is on the body and, at worst, they can cause harm to the user. For sure, they can burn the hair and scalp and it is disturbing to think that we don't know the possible health effects of exposing our skin to these chemicals. According to Willie Morrow, African hair 'disappeared completely' from sight for nearly 300 years. It was rare to see natural African hair in the Americas. It was not that the hair was not growing naturally, but rather that it was being covered. An African woman with straight hair most likely has treated it with chemicals or she is wearing a weave or a wig.

I am not sharing this to shame or embarrass my fellow African women; far from it. I am sharing my journey of discovery with the Lord. It is a journey of healing and restoration and reconnecting with our God-given identity.

I have never seen any other people group or any other ethnic group wear other people's hair. I have never seen Chinese wearing African hair or Indians or Asians doing the same. It is we African people, African women, who either chemically denature our hair, or cover our hair with the hair of others. This journey is to explain why we do that, how we got here and by the Grace of God how we can get back to ourselves.

For 300 to 400 years the subliminal and overt message was,

---

4 *Good Hair.* Documentary Directed by Jeff Stilson 2009. Produced by Chris Rock Production and HBO.

"cover your hair; It is not acceptable; it is offensive." This message is shared on billboards and magazine pictures. It is beamed across television screens where young African children never see girls or women with hair or other features similar to their own. It is communicated at home, where mothers relax their hair like I used to do and communicate to their daughters that they too must be altered 'to become beautiful'.

I am a Ugandan woman and, by the Grace of God, slavery and colonialism are things that are experientially far removed from me. But the vestiges of these great evils are still among us, and we must be intentional about untangling the mess left by those who sought to dominate us physically and still seek to do so psychologically.

> *We do not have sufficient time to delve deeper into other aspects of physical beauty such as skin tone, physical features such as body shape, and facial features. Unfortunately, one of the vestiges of colonialism and slavery is that distinct African features like dark skin and hair texture have been depicted negatively. We have all seen the images of "black face" and caricatures of mannerisms that portray a simplistic and negative image of African people. Darker skin has for a long time been depicted as ugly and this has created an identity crisis in people of African descent. There is an entire industry of cosmetic creams and products to lighten (bleach) the complexion of African women. These creams used over a long time burn the skin and often the person develops a raw red colour akin to the experience of being sunburnt. All this is symptomatic of a deeper problem in the mind and hearts of African people, a disconnection and rejection of self and an attempt to become something different. This problem extends to other facets of life such as the loss of language and to some degree nomenclature. One of the legacies of colonialism has been the local languages being displaced by the English language which at least in East Africa is widely spoken in schools and in the public arena. Oftentimes children in primary school learn in a language*

different from the language they speak at home, this adds to the dilemma because language is the vehicle through which culture is maintained and communicated. If language is lost in the early years, so much of the child's culture is also lost. Therefore, shining a light on our hair is only one aspect of the restoration of our identity that I feel we need to have as African people.

I believe God is dealing with these foundational issues in our time. I can testify that God's way is always better. No matter how deep or longstanding the wound or the pain, His Blood was shed to make a Way for us. Even after 400 years, Jesus' sacrifice can bring complete restoration. The Bible declares that 'he whom the Son sets free is free indeed!' (John 8:36). Praise the Lord for true freedom through Jesus.

What does Jesus' Africa mean? It simply means that, as we come into a closer walk with God, He re-connects us back to who we are, to who He created us to be. There was a disconnection somewhere along the way and He has come to repair the breach. He repairs the places that were broken and one of the places that were broken for African women was; our hair, our crown, our glory, our beauty and our identity.

May the Lord who reveals what is hidden, bring true healing to our hearts and restore the crown of glory to African girls and women everywhere.

Prayer

Heavenly Father, we thank You for Your Word and for the way You are speaking to us in this season. Lord, we pray for this area of our lives as African women that may seem trivial and unimportant and yet it is loaded with negative emotions and stereotypes.

Father, we ask for forgiveness for ourselves and for generations of African women who have been running away, not knowing why, from who we are. Please forgive us for unintentionally passing on these messages to our children, our daughters especially that they are not beautiful, that they are not good enough, and that they need to be changed in some way.

Father thank You for how You are reconnecting Africans to their beauty, dignity and the crown of glory You have given to each of us in our hair. Thank You for showing us that the hair You gave us is uniquely ours and distinguishes us from other people groups. For so long our natural hair had disappeared, but now Lord You are resurrecting and restoring the image of African hair.

Father, we pray that You will heal the deep wounds in African people and people of African descent all over the world, the deep wounds that we carry in our collective psyche. Father please heal us all by the blood of Jesus, and repair the breach. Father, we ask that, in these next years, we will see a complete resurrection and a renaissance of true African beauty, the way You intended it to be celebrated. Beauty that cannot be diminished does not need to conform and that is unashamed. The kind of beauty that isn't afraid to stand out rather than blend in. Father, please heal the hearts of African women and remove the garment of shame. Please give us beauty instead of ashes, the oil of gladness instead of mourning and remove the wrap of weaves, wigs, relaxers and the things that have been covering our heads. Please allow the crown of glory - the natural beauty that you gave to Africans to shine through.

May You be glorified in all Your children in Jesus' Mighty Name.

Amen.

12. Soldier

Soldier, standing along the battleline
Finding comfort in the water and the wine
And your armour still so shiny and so new
But you are dirty, worn and tired
From the battles you've been through

Soldier, keep your eyes straight ahead,
Help the wounded and, though it hurts you, leave the dead
Keep your weapons and your spirit at the ready all the time
Be of courage and conviction
Hit the mark and toe the line

Tonight when all the lights go out
And you lie down to rest
Know that I am proud of you
I know you've done your best
Let Me give you peace, let Me hold you for a while
Yes, you are a mighty warrior
But don't forget you're still My child

Soldier, standing along the battleline
Finding comfort in the water and the wine
Know that I am with you when this old world keeps charging in
I'll be with you and I will see you through to the very end

Soldier, keep My flag flying high
Don't let it fall in battle or be stolen in the night
And above all else, this soldier;
Don't ever lose your battle cry

Because My arm is fighting with you
And I am standing by your side

Tonight when all the lights go out
And you lie down to rest
Know that I am proud of you
I know you've done your best
Let Me give you peace, let Me hold you for a while
Yes you are a mighty warrior
But don't forget you are still My child
Mighty Warrior, You are still My child
You are my child, you are a warrior
Don't forget, you are still My child.

- Song by Phil Driscoll from the album *Warriors, 1994.*

Spiritual warfare is a big part of the Christian walk and part of being a servant of the Lord. The moment you give your life to the Lord Jesus, you enlist in the army of the Lord that is engaged in an epic battle against the spiritual forces of wickedness. Jesus is the Captain of the Lord's hosts and when you get saved, whether you realize it or not, you become a soldier in the Lord's army. Christians today who would like that "we all get along" with evil do not understand that the devil and his forces were defeated hands down at the Cross.

Here is what Colossians 2:15 says:

"When He disarmed the rulers and authorities (those supernatural forces of evil operating against us) He made a public spectacle or example of them(exhibiting them as captives in His triumphal procession) having triumphed over them through the cross." – Amplified Bible

Jesus didn't seek to "appease, tolerate or get along" with the devil. He triumphed and disarmed the powers of darkness and made a spectacle of them. The devil was defeated at the cross and, we as Christians, need to understand there is no middle ground with evil. The Kingdom of God is mutually exclusive with darkness; it cannot co-exist with the kingdom of darkness. As a child of God, you are automatically an enemy of the devil and he seeks nothing more than your annihilation. You may think, "but I am such a nice person" or " I have no enemies."

I can assure you if you are truly a child of God, living your life for Jesus, you have big-time enemies working around the clock to try and destroy you. The fact that they haven't succeeded is because you are protected by the Blood of Jesus, and God has a hedge of protection around you and your loved ones. Angelic forces throng to cover you as you go out and come in. You are a very important person in the Kingdom and you have the spiritual covering to prove it.

By the term 'enemies' I mean spiritual forces, not people. We are taught to live in peace with all people as much as depends on us, so this warfare isn't about fighting with people. It is spiritual warfare and the forces we are fighting are spiritual. These are the words of Ephesians 6:12:

"For the weapons of our warfare are not carnal but are mighty in God for the pulling down of strongholds." - 2 Corinthians 10:4

"For our struggle is not against flesh and blood, but against the rulers, against the authorities, against the powers of this dark world and against spiritual forces of evil in heavenly realms." – Amplified Bible

The Apostle Paul in these verses is talking of a struggle with powers, rulers and authorities. That is the essence of spiritual warfare. When Jesus was about to ascend to Heaven, He gave instructions to His disciples which we now call the Great Commission.

In Matthew 28:18-20, Jesus said:

"All authority in Heaven and on earth has been given to me. Therefore, go and make disciples of all nations, baptizing them in the name of the Father and of the Son and of the

> *Holy Spirit, and teaching them to obey everything that I have commanded you. And surely I am with you always, to the very close and consummation of the age." – Amplified Bible*

Jesus was speaking not only to His disciples who were alive at that time but to every person who would become His disciple through the ages. The Great Commission is for all of us children of God. Jesus said that all authority in Heaven and Earth was given to Him after His death and resurrection. Now He sends us with that same delegated authority to go and make disciples of all the nations. One may ask, "If Jesus already defeated the devil and took back authority, then why do we have to fight battles?"

I will answer that by asking another question, "If Jesus died for the sins of the whole world, why are there still people today who are not saved?"

The answer, of course, is that God through Jesus made salvation available to whosoever will come to the Lord. But in every generation, the gospel still must be preached, people must hear the good news and decide to come to the Lord. God enshrined the free will of humanity when He created us in His image. Every human being has free will and moral agency, we can all choose what we want, and God defends our right to choose even if it means we choose a path that leads to destruction.

The same is true of spiritual warfare. Even though the enemy is a vanquished foe, he continues to deceive human beings to give him access to their lives through sin. Sin empowers the devil to build strongholds in the lives of individuals, families, communities, cities and nations. God has called the Church to take the battle to the very gates of hell and reclaim territory for the Kingdom. His promise to us is sure as He says in the bible, *"Upon this rock, I will build My church and the gates of hell will not prevail against it." Matthew 16:18*

There is no neutral Switzerland in the battle between good and evil. Dietrich Bonhoeffer, the German theologian, author and pastor, who was killed for his stand against Adolf Hitler during World War II put it aptly:

"Silence in the face of evil is itself evil
God will not hold us guiltless
Not to speak is to speak
Not to act is to act."

The battle lines are very clear in the spiritual realm, there are no gray areas. My father once told me that negotiated peace is tenuous, the greatest peace is the one that is gained from the complete triumph over the enemy. I have found this to be true in the spiritual battles of the Kingdom.

Mar del Plata

In 2006, Covenant Nations Church was a very young church. We all knew that the Lord had placed a great call and vision on the church and that this vision was for the cities and nations of Africa.

But how does one reach a city? As we grappled with the big and small aspects of church leadership, God prepared to take us to Argentina to see the template for reaching a city that the church was using there.

A few months later, Maama Janet was invited to be the guest speaker at a conference in Mar del Plata, Argentina, a seaside city that seemed to be at the end of the earth. Maama knew all the work I was involved in with Covenant Nations Church and she thought this would be a good learning experience for me. So she invited me and my cousin Dr. Joe Okia and his wife Joanne to come along with her delegation. When I received Maama's invitation I was a bit reluctant to go. Our children were both under the age of three years, and Argentina looked like it was very far away. However, in my heart, I knew the Lord wanted me to go. As such, Odrek and I agreed that he would stay home with the children with some help from my family and relatives who came home to stay for the week that I would be away.

Our trip to Argentina was long, especially the trans-Atlantic flight from Johannesburg to Sao Paulo in Brazil. I had never flown above the ocean for so many hours, it was a little unnerving looking out of the window and seeing the endless expanse of water beneath us.

After many hours, we were about to land in Brazil's most populous city, Sao Paulo. I was amazed to look outside the window and see the sprawling city below us. We felt like we had just journeyed to the end of the earth and yet here, so far away from home, some megacities were home to millions of people.

We had a short layover in Sao Paolo and then continued on our journey to Argentina. I must confess that all I knew about Argentina was what I had learnt in Geography at school, much of it was about beef rearing on the pampas plains. That and the popular song, *Don't Cry for Me Argentina.*[1] It was popularized by Madonna in the movie *Evita* about the former first lady of Argentina, Eva Peron. So when we landed in Buenos Aires, I was open to seeing the real Argentina. I was surprised to find that Buenos Aires was much more opulent than I imagined it would be. The beautiful old architecture of the buildings spoke of a gilded age that had gone by. Our hotel was a beautiful classical building with ornate gold fixtures and pink marble floors. On the same street as the hotel we were staying in, there were shops selling gold, jewelry and fine gems. The streets had six car lanes and a beautiful piazza where people gathered to eat at cafes and yes even dance to Latin music in the evenings.

The next day, Maama Janet and I and the rest of our team made the long journey from Buenos Aires to Mar del Plata. Again, I felt like we were journeying to the ends of the earth. Argentina is a large expanse of a country with wide open spaces as far as the eye can see. We drove through vast farmlands with little pretty farmhouses decorated with flowers. In the late afternoon, we arrived in Mar del Plata,

---

1 Andrew Lloyd Weber. *Don't Cry for Me Argentina.* Recorded by Julie Covington in 1976 and sang by Madonna in the 1998 film *Evita.*

the beautiful seaside city that was hosting the conference we were attending. That evening, we attended a dinner hosted by the Rev. Ed Silvoso who was the host of the conference. We learnt of the important work his organization called Harvest Evangelism was doing around the world and particularly in Mar del Plata. There were very many new faces and people to meet. Hearing the Word of God spoken in Spanish was a beautiful reminder of how global the Body of Christ truly is.

The Name of Jesus whether it is Yesu, Yesus, or Yeshua always sounds beautiful.

The next day was the opening of the conference, we all attended and Rev. Ed Silvoso shared the paradigm of the city reaching that God had shown him many years prior when he was still a young evangelist. This paradigm focuses on prayer evangelism, repentance, the unity of the Church in the city and marketplace evangelism. Although we knew all these things in theory, seeing them in action was a powerful witness to the absolute authority of the word of God. Prayer evangelism focused on the power of simple prayer to answer and meet the needs of people everywhere. People were encouraged to humbly and respectfully pray for the needs of others wherever they met them whether in the street, the bank or the supermarket. Marketplace evangelism was reaching out to people at the workplace bearing in mind that the New Testament church didn't draw boundaries between the marketplace and the church. Paul often preached to people in the marketplace whether it was at the river where women washed clothes or in the amphitheatre in Athens where philosophy was debated. Finally, the unity of the Church was central to pulling down the strongholds of the city. There needed to be unity, love and interdependence between the spiritual leadership of the city for God's Kingdom to truly come. The session lasted the whole day with different speakers from around the world discussing different topics whether they were from the church or marketplace. All through the conference the word "transformation" kept coming up. We learnt that it was possible to believe and work for total transformation for our cities and nations.

The next day we went to visit a prison that was in the process of transformation. It was unlike any prison I had ever visited before. The first thing I noticed was there were no locked doors. In spite of the fact that all the doors were wide open, the prisoners did not escape. The prisoners, who we were told were hardened criminals, were busy at work making goods out of leather, iron and other materials. They were busy working, and all this with limited supervision. The supervisors handled the prisoners as friends and brothers. In any other prison environment, the tools the prisoners were working with alone could act as weapons to harm the supervisors or guards. However, in this prison, there was only love, acceptance and forgiveness.

We walked around the prison observing and listening as our guides asked the prisoners questions. We learnt that most of the prisoners came there for some crime they committed. When they arrived at the prison, they were transformed when they heard the message about Jesus. They realized that the prison was no longer able to hold them because they were free from the spiritual prisons they had been living in all their lives. They testified that just as God sent an earthquake that shook the prison foundations when Paul and Silas prayed, here too, God heard their prayers and opened the doors of their prisons when they turned to Him in prayer and repentance. It was a remarkable testimony and we soon experienced the earth-shaking power of their prayers when the "pastor" of the prisoners, who was himself a prisoner on death row, led us all in prayer and praise.

I will always remember that moment, when this wonderful man, a brother in the Lord, prayed with such power that we felt the spiritual foundations shaking. When he prayed in Spanish, I felt I understood his heart as he cried out to God. He said the name Yesus, the name I say as Jesus, Yesu or Yeshua. This Spanish-speaking Argentinian prisoner was as much my brother as any member of the Covenant Nations Church.

After the prayer, we all hugged each other and then they started singing songs of praise. We made a chain of praise each person holding the next person across the shoulders as we danced and sang songs of praise. It was the most beautiful, glorious experience I had ever had. These prisoners showed us that the real prisons exist in our hearts and minds; the prisons of hatred and unforgiveness which keep us divided and in bondage. These prisoners we were interacting with were freer than some "free" people walking on the streets. They were working quietly with their hands repaying their debt to society until the day when they would be physically released from prison.

We went back to our hotel very touched by the witness and testimonies (in word and action) of our brave brothers in prison. They convicted us who were free, both spiritually and physically, but who did not live with the same joy and gratitude that they did. We had so much to contemplate after that visit to the transformed prison.

The conference continued and, every day, we were challenged by the power of God to transform a city completely until the atmosphere itself became different. During the conference, I was asked to speak at a session for the youth and share my testimony. Although I was privileged to speak to the youth, I felt I needed to learn more from them than they could learn from me. I shared my testimony simply and gave an altar call; I wasn't sure if they understood me clearly because I was speaking in English and I had a Spanish translator. God confirmed that they all understood my message because when I gave the altar call, almost every young person in the audience came forward for prayer. As they gathered around me; I was extremely touched by the outpouring of the Holy Spirit and their hunger for more of God. I prayed with all my heart for them and their generation, that the Lord would anoint them and use them to do great exploits. They were all such precious beautiful young people I wanted to hug them all and encourage them in their journey of reform and embracing the Lord.

In the course of the conference, Maama Janet was asked to give the keynote address at a dinner where the leaders of the city of Mar del Plata and the spiritual leaders all came together.

Maama Janet thanked Rev. Ed Silvoso for championing the cause of transformation boldly and claiming the city for the Lord. She went on to share with all congregants the work that she was doing as a Member of Parliament in her constituency of Ruhaama in southwestern Uganda. Maama's testimony confirmed that God has His people all across the world at all levels of authority and if His people understand His desire to see the transformation at every level, then we would have very different societies. If God could transform prisoners, why couldn't He transform slums, brothels, schools, universities, hospitals, cities and nations?

The final day of the conference was a wonderful celebration service that was held in one of the big mega churches of Mar del Plata whose Senior Pastor was leading the work of transformation in the city. In that service, we were charged up to sound a battle cry by one of the African Pastors from Zimbabwe called Langston Gatsi. It was a powerful prophetic act to declare war on the powers of darkness in our cities and nation. We were leaving Argentina fully fired up and ready to see our cities and nations transformed.

Our time In Argentina was life-changing; I came into the country 'empty' and I left 'full'. I came with questions about how to reach a city and I left with the biggest testimony and challenge of what God can do if we let Him. Now the ball was in our court; what would we do with this knowledge?

Kampala the City of God.

In 2006, after we visited Argentina, we returned home with faith and expectation of what the Lord would do in our city of Kampala. Mar del Plata challenged us to raise our faith and work to see transformation in our city and nation. We shared all our experiences with the elders at church and the small leadership team. They all agreed that we needed transformation in our city, Kampala, but what should we do? We set ourselves to pray for our city and wait on the Lord to give us a signal as to what exactly He wanted to do in Kampala.

One of the first things the Lord said to us was that we needed to begin to bless the city. He challenged us that almost everything we spoke about our city was negative, grumbling and fault-finding. He showed us that our city was the result of the words that we heaped on it daily through our criticism, grumbling and complaining. We complained about the traffic, the garbage, the taxis and *boda boda (motor bike)* cyclists. We complained about poor planning in neighbourhoods, power cuts and any other thing we found wanting.

The Lord challenged us to begin blessing our city and speaking words of life and gratitude. This took a lot of faith to do because when what you see in front of you is negative, to speak positive words of blessing takes faith. The more we blessed our city, the more we felt sorry for all the negative words we had spoken about the city. The Lord showed us that, when we go to other cities in the world, we bless them with our words and those cities become what the people speak of them. We call Paris the City of Lights, New York the Big Apple, and we bless Dubai and Abu Dhabi, Cape Town and London. But when it comes to Kampala, we reserve only criticism and fault-finding for it. For this, we repented with all our hearts.

The second thing the Lord showed us is that we needed to pray for the City Council. The City Council was the assembly headed by the mayor that was responsible for managing the city. I can confess that in all my years I had never thought of praying for the mayor and the city council. The Lord led us to request a meeting with the Mayor of Kampala who at that time was the late Al Hajji Ssebaggala and his council. I shared what the Lord said we needed to do with our elders and we invited a few other pastors in the city to come and join us to pray for the city. The mayor graciously accepted to meet us and the date was set for us to go to the city council headquarters. I had never stepped foot in the City Council of our city. On the morning day of our appointment, we all gathered as a team and drove to the City Council. I was amazed at how far out of my comfort zone the Lord had led me. Pastor Robert Kayanja of Miracle Centre Cathedral was one of the pastors we invited to come with us.

When we sat with the mayor in his office, I shared that I first wanted to repent to him as a Christian because I had never prayed for him and the City Council. Secondly, many of us residents of Kampala City never blessed our city but spent a lot of time grumbling and fault-finding. I asked for his forgiveness and if he wouldn't mind that we prayed for him. He seemed quite surprised and taken aback by the purpose behind our visit. He responded with thanks and said he had never had anyone ever come to see him to pray for him. I said that was wrong on our part and that I would certainly be praying for him as our mayor.

The mayor was delighted and led us to the large assembly room where the councillors met. We found that the assembly hall was full of all the councillors of the city who had come to meet with us. We were ushered to our seats and Pastor Kayanja was invited to share a word. He spoke a word of encouragement and then prayed for the mayor, the council and the city. The mayor then got up to speak and the highlight of his remarks was when he, a practicing Muslim, started his speech by saying, "praise the Lord."

The room broke out in laughter and the Christians there answered with "Amen."

The mayor thanked us for coming and said we were always welcome to return and that he looked forward to working with us for the betterment of the city. As our meeting concluded, already the atmosphere had shifted from one of contention, negativity and complaining to one of hope and possibility.

After we visited the city council, we reached out to some pastors in the city to hear their ideas about doing a big outreach in the city at the end of that year. We wanted to include as many pastors, ministries and marketplace leaders as possible to create a spirit of agreement over the destiny of Kampala.

The outreach would last three days and incorporate programmes such as cleaning up the city streets and marketplaces, prayer walking in as many streets in the city as possible, and then an open-air meeting for repentance and prayer at Kololo independence grounds.

As we talked about this programme with the pastors we kept stressing that we wanted to see our city transformed and that we needed the elements of repentance, unity in the church and prayer of agreement. Many pastors from all backgrounds bought into the idea and agreed to participate. They supported the outreach with prayer and promotion amongst their members. Covenant Nations Church, a young fledgling church that was just a few months old at the time, was leading this great effort and it indeed took a lot of faith to organize this big outreach. God's Grace and Favour were evident for all to see as we got volunteers from all walks of life to take part in the city cleaning, prayer walking activities, intercession, worship, giving, ushering, and attending to the speakers for the three days of the outreach. As the day for the event drew closer, we thought of what we should call the outreach. The Holy Spirit immediately brought the name, "Kampala the City of God," to mind. Everyone agreed that was the right name for the outreach.

One of the scriptures that we were standing on was Proverbs 11:11, *"Through the blessing of the upright a city is exalted."*

The first day dawned bright and glorious as volunteers came from all over the city to clean city streets and market areas. It was wonderful to see managers and CEOs grab brooms and sweep drainages and collect garbage in neighbourhoods. All our volunteers were wearing white t-shirts with our Kampala the City of God logo. Many bystanders looked on bemused at what the *balokole* (born-again Christians) were up to! After cleaning the streets, other volunteers went on prayer-walking in different neighbourhoods. Prayer walking is simply the act of walking while praying for the neighbourhood, homes, businesses and people in the area. Tracts and fliers were distributed all over the city inviting people to come and attend the crusade at the Kololo grounds at night.

In the evening everyone gathered for the service at Kololo Independence grounds in the centre of the city. There was worship organized by teams from different churches across the city. In addition, we had special songs led by popular gospel artists such as Judith Babirye. On one of the nights,

Judith Babirye sang a much-loved song about the blood of Jesus, and Maama Janet who was at the service that night came onto the stage and started worshipping God with her hands raised in praise. From the very first day, the beauty of the unity of the Body of Christ was evident to all. Our hearts were crying out to God for mercy and forgiveness, asking Him to heal and transform our city, Kampala.

On the first day, I shared a word on God's purposes for cities and nations and how He had a purpose for our City of Kampala and it was up to the church in the city to partner with God to see His purposes established. After the message was shared, there was time for intercession and prayer and we had different pastors lead this time. It was very powerful to hear the prayers of God's people as we all cried out to God for healing, mercy and transformation.

The programme for the second day was similar to the one on the first day. We started the day with different activities across the city, cleaning up sidewalks and streets, marketplaces and prayer walking and street ministry. In the early evening, we gathered again for the second day of the crusade at Kololo. The worship was powerful as all the choirs ministered together ushering in the Lord's Presence. On the second day, we had the word shared and prayer and intercession followed. Every day the sense of expectation in the air grew as we confronted strongholds in the realm of the spirit.

The third day was the last and it would be a little different because we invited the leadership of the city and the government leadership headed by the President and First Lady. The activities in the morning were the same as the previous days, but in the evening we started a little earlier. Our guests and guests of honour arrived on time and were seated. We started the meeting with praise and worship and then I was invited to give a brief synopsis of what the whole three days of city outreach were all about. I briefly shared the background of what the Lord had asked us to do as the Body of Christ in the city. We had brought our prayers of repentance and intercession before the Lord on behalf of ourselves, our families and our beloved city, Kampala. Now we invited the leadership of the country and city to come into agreement with us to pray, believe God and work for a better city. We invited the pastors to again lead the congregation in prayer and repentance for all the sins and ills that plagued the city whether it was witchcraft, idolatry, corruption, poor sanitation, street children, prostitution, poverty and more.

After the time of prayer, we invited the government leadership to share some remarks and, finally, the President was invited to give his speech and oversee the declaration over the city. The President thanked the church leaders for working together and having a heart for the city. He then went on to speak about the kind of city he would like to see Kampala become, a greener, cleaner city with good sanitation where all Ugandans can live in peace and security. Once he concluded his speech, we invited him to unveil the Kampala the City of God declaration that was beautifully framed and presented to him. We read out the declaration and once completed we asked the President and Maama Janet to append their signatures. They signed the declaration and so did many other pastors, government and marketplace leaders.

The three-day outreach was a big success, we felt it in the spirit and the natural. There was a sense that something had shifted, we were expectant, looking forward to what the Lord was going to do. As a young and small church, we had been stretched far beyond our limits. I would continue to learn that stretching the limits of our faith is something that the Lord does often. God usually asks me to do things that would be impossible without His intervention, Grace and help. It is the God-size things that He calls us to because He knows we will look to and rely on Him fully.

We planned and organized the Kampala the City of God outreach two years in a row. After 2007, we felt that the church in the city had awakened to God's heart for transformation. God showed me in a vision, an elite army force establishing a beachhead on land so that the heavy artillery and infantry could come onto the land. He showed us that what He had asked us to do as Covenant Nations Church was to establish a beachhead for the church in the city, for the work of transformation to continue.

A while after our Kampala the City of God outreach, I learnt that the Parliament was debating establishing a "Kampala City Authority" with an Executive Director who is appointed as opposed to an elected official like the mayor. The Executive Director would be a technical person who would be accountable to the government and responsible for oversight and development of the city. I was overjoyed to hear this news and we all prayed for the parliament as they deliberated on this matter. Later on, we heard the good news that the bill to establish the Kampala City Authority was passed. For us who had been involved in the Kampala the City of God outreach, it was an answer to prayer, an intervention by the King of kings in the affairs of our city.

When the new Executive Director was appointed to head the Kampala City Authority, we asked to meet and pray for them and also to give them a gift of the first signed, "Kampala City of God" declaration. Our prayer and hope was that the Kampala the City of God declaration would serve as a kind of spiritual guide or compass to help the new organization navigate its way and fulfill God's purposes for our city. Over the years, we have seen great changes and transformation in the city. There is much more work to be done and the church in the city has a united role to play to provide the spiritual covering and to intercede for the city before God. We continue to pray and work to see Kampala become the City of God, a place of praise on this earth.

Buikwe Mission

In 2012, I saw a vision of a man calling for help. It reminded me of Paul's vision of the man in Macedonia who called to him saying, "come and help us," as quoted in Acts 16:6-10. I soon forgot about the vision. However, a few days later when I was praying for the church, I heard the Lord speak to me clearly saying, **"do not pray for the church, instead pray for Buikwe."**

Buikwe? Where was that? I had never heard the name Buikwe before. When I finished praying, I asked my husband, Odrek, in passing, "do you know where Buikwe is?"

He answered, "it is a district that was formerly part of the greater Mukono area. Why?"

I shared with him what the Lord had spoken to me about while in prayer and how it reminded me of the vision of the man in the Bible calling for help.

After that, I kept praying about Buikwe and what the Lord wanted us to do there. After some days, I asked some of our team leaders to call the local pastors in the district of Buikwe and ask if we could visit them. Many of the pastors in the Bukwe area were part of the National Fellowship of Born Again Pentecostal Churches which was now led by Bishop Joshua Lwere. The bishop and his wife Margaret are good friends of ours and so I called him and made an appointment to go and meet with him. But first I wanted to gather information about what was happening in Buikwe.

We sent a team out to do scouting which soon returned from the reconnaissance mission. The report they shared was harrowing. They said the pastors were overjoyed to hear that God was placing them in our hearts for prayer. They said the major problem they were facing as a community was cannibalism and witchcraft! Cannibalism! Did that happen in this day and age? It seemed like something out of an Indiana Jones movie. How could people in this day and age practise cannibalism? I was incredulous and thought they were exaggerating in some way.

One day, soon after this report, I had a dream and I saw a land in the distance. As I viewed the land I could see a section through the land and I realized that just under the soil on that land was a large dead decomposing game animal. The dead animal was red and it lay just underneath the topsoil. When I woke up I asked the Lord what the dream meant and what the dead animal represented, He answered, **"It is the Edomite spirit."**

I had heard about the Edomite spirit from Arthur Burk, a friend of mine from America whose ministry to the body of Christ focused on teaching and deliverance. I went back to those teachings to understand more about the Edomite spirit. In essence, it is the stronghold that destroys and perverts relationships between people. It is revealed in the book of Obadiah 1:9-15, where God judges the Edomites who were relatives of the Israelites. Instead of helping the Israelites in their time of need, they actively fought against them and rejoiced at their calamity. Tribalism is a result of the Edomite spirit because the relationships between people from different tribes are distorted and perverted to stir up hatred and division.

We kept praying and I met with Bishop Lwere, the General Overseer of the National Fellowship of Born Again Churches and shared with him what the Lord was saying about Buikwe. We agreed to prepare for a 3-day joint outreach mission to the area. We scheduled the date and our church team started the preparatory and logistical work to get things ready for the outreach. We planned to have the outreach during the school holidays so that we could use a local school as the base camp. Working with the pastors on the ground, we invited members of the community and church leadership to come and attend the meeting. Around 1000 people committed to becoming part of the meeting.

When all was ready, I packed my bag to go to Buikwe not knowing what we would find there. I was glad that Odrek and many of our elders made the time to be part of the mission. Those who couldn't stay the whole time endeavoured to make it to one or more of the days of the meeting.

When we arrived, we were touched to see that they had arranged for us special accommodation in the district centre, a short distance from the school where the meeting was held. We had not asked for any special consideration, but our hosts had given us their best place to stay and I was very appreciative. On our first night, our whole team settled in finding rooms for the leaders and worship team. We had one chef who cooked one meal for everyone in the evening and during the day we all fasted and survived on fluids.

The next day, we rose bright and early and after prayer got ready to go for the first day of the conference.

The turn-up for the meeting was very good and we got off to a great start, with praise and worship. First, we heard a report from the local pastors who shared the numerous issues they were facing in the community. Cannibalism was the major problem, they emphasized, and the situation had become so dire that people were afraid to go out walking on the roads at night for fear that they would be kidnapped and killed by the cannibals. I listened intently to the testimonies that people shared; for example, how some street vendors had been attacked one evening and disappeared altogether. It was unbelievable to hear first-hand accounts of such terrible things happening. There was a gentleman I will never forget who got up and started sharing almost casually, that this problem had been part of the community for a long time. Some of the towns and villages were named according to how people were killed by the cannibals. Some were torn apart limb by limb, others were crushed and so on. In Luganda, the names were:

Bubiro - which means the victims are chased;

Kikakanya - which means the remains of the body of the victim would be dried before it is eaten.

It was how he spoke that was shocking, as though he was speaking of the most ordinary run-of-the-mill stories. I was completely dumbfounded.

He said that, although his whole family members were cannibals, he was allergic to meat, and therefore this had saved him from eating human flesh since he was a child.

After hearing full reports from the pastors, it was time to hear the message to be shared by Bishop Lwere. He spoke in fluent Luganda which was the language spoken by most of the residents although there were people from other parts of the country who now lived there. There was a translator for those who didn't understand Luganda well and also a translation from English to Luganda. As the day wore on Bishop Lwere gave an in-depth teaching about the close interconnectedness between some of the cultural practices that people did and their spiritual significance. It was very eye-opening to see how witchcraft and superstition were woven into the small daily routines of people's lives. For example, he shared how women, when cooking banana plantains, would give an offering to a household god called Nabuzaana. Then superstitions like, if you meet a woman in the morning as you go out, that is a bad omen, and because of this you cancel your day's plans and return home. The same was true if you met a dog, or a rat as you walked by the way and it passed by your left side. That too was an omen portending something negative in your future.

The people in the meeting all laughed as Bishop Lwere spoke at length and in detail about these practices that were called "culture" but in truth were superstitions grounded in witchcraft.

By the time the session ended at 6 pm and the meeting was dismissed, I felt like I was carrying a ten-ton elephant on my shoulders. In my mind was one thought, "what kind of people are these?" I felt like I had never felt before; it was internal revulsion. We had a quick dinner and we all retired to our rooms. Some members of our team stayed up to pray but I didn't want to be with anyone. I just wanted to go to my room and go to sleep.

Sleep evaded me that night. I kept tossing and turning most of the night. Even when I tried to sleep, my sleep was fitful. I woke up in the middle of the night gasping for breath. I felt like something was choking my breathing passages. I thought I was dying and knew instinctively that this was related to all the things we had heard in the meeting during the day. This was the spirit that controlled Buikwe. I felt like there was a python wrapped around my body squeezing the life out of my lungs. I cried to the Lord, it was just a whisper, "Jesus..."

Immediately, the Lord answered me, **"You cannot intercede for people whom you despise."**

I knew exactly what the Lord meant. I did despise the people. I thought they were superstitious and primitive to hold to such customs as they did. The Lord spoke again, **"I didn't send you here to judge My people, but to bring My Word of healing and freedom to them."**

" Please forgive me, Father. You are right, I did despise and judge them in my heart. I repent."

In an instant, the pressure I was feeling around my chest dissipated. I could breathe again. I started crying, I was so sorry for my pride and sin, and I asked the Lord to forgive me again and again. He said, **"I forgive you, and tomorrow morning you must ask the people attending the meeting to forgive you."**

"Yes. Lord," I answered. Soon after that, I fell asleep and now there was only peace.

The following morning I woke up bright and early. We prayed together as a team and then returned to the big tent where the people were gathered. As Bishop Lwere prepared to start the meeting, I went and told him I had something to share before we started. He gave me the microphone and I took a deep breath. I spoke in English because I have only a passing knowledge of Luganda. I knelt on the grass and said, "I want to repent to you today, because yesterday while we were learning about the way the culture is connected to witchcraft and superstition, I despised and judged you in my heart. The Lord has shown me that I cannot claim to intercede for people that I despise. I have asked God to forgive me and I ask you also to forgive me."

For a minute, everyone was still and quiet, a little taken aback by what had just happened. No one knew what to expect next. Then suddenly, a woman from the back of the tent stood up and speaking in fluent Luganda, she said, "I want you to know that when I heard you were coming here I came all the way to see you because I hate you and I wanted to look at your face and tell you that I hate you and your family. I wanted to tell you that you have no right to come here and speak to us about anything. But since yesterday when I first saw you and heard you speak, I have felt deep conviction in my heart. God has shown me that I must ask you for forgiveness for hating you."

This woman came to the front of the tent where I was standing and she knelt on the ground with me. She was in tears and I was in tears and I embraced her. The whole tent broke out in choruses of *Tukutendereza Yesu* (Praise Jesus) and Hallelujahs. After that, it was like a dam had burst; person after person came forward to repent to their neighbour for deep feelings of hatred, animosity, anger and unforgiveness. The Baganda repented to the Basoga while the Banyarwanda repented to the Baganda, and Badaama repented to Baganda and vice versa.

There was a man who stood up to repent for holding hatred and bitterness in his heart for over 30 years for something that one tribe had done to his family during the years of civil war in Uganda. This man confessed that he hated all people from a certain region because he felt they were responsible for the pain brought on his family. Even Bishop Lwere repented because he said he lost a close cousin during the war and the commander of the army who was responsible for the boy's killing didn't even give them leave to bury the young man, and his body was left to decompose in the open for a week. He said that even though he had forgiven the commander in his heart, he was deeply prejudiced in his heart against people from the same tribe as the commander. He felt that they were barbaric and inhumane.

There was a great cry that rose from that tent the whole afternoon, as people wailed and cried in repentance before God and to each other. At one point, everyone was lying on the ground crying and weeping to God asking for forgiveness for all our sins against each other. By evening time the weeping and wailing reached a crescendo and then came a great calm. It was a heavenly hush. At this point, we started praying for the Lord to heal and release the land from all the anger, bitterness, hatred, unforgiveness, witchcraft, sexual immorality and shedding of innocent blood. We asked that the Lord would bring judgment against the spirit of witchcraft and cannibalism that had held the land and the people captive for so long. It was a powerful time of intercession as we asked the Lord to send His fire to burn up all the evil altars in Buikwe. We ended the meeting late but knew that God through His Holy Spirit had broken our hearts wide open. We went to our rooms rejoicing and praising God. That night God answered our prayers because, as we slept peacefully, lightning fell from heaven and burnt up several of the altars and shrines in the area.

In the morning the pastors brought us messages about the altars and shrines that had been destroyed at night as God's judgment fell. For example, not very far from where we had camped, there was a tree that was highly revered. Many people who came from the area believed that the god who kept the area resided in that tree. During the storm, lightning struck the tree with such force that the tree was uprooted!

The last day of the meeting was a glorious time of celebration and praise where we shared testimonies, encouragement and endless choruses of *Tukutendereza Yesu*.

Since it was the last day, we needed to close early to give people time to travel back to their homes. We too had to return to Kampala before it became too late. However, this would only happen after we prepared and read a solemn declaration of our agreement as the Body of Christ over Buikwe.

Among those who attended the last day were district and civic leaders. They were greatly moved by the testimonies, the repentance and the reconciliation that was taking place. They concurred that, as a people, they needed to return to the living God.

Our declaration was read out and it spoke words of blessing and peace over the people and the land. We asked that the Lord bring the people and the land back into covenant with Him and that Buikwe would no longer be known for evil, but for good. After the reading and signing of the declaration, we prayed together and then took one group picture in front of our big tent.

Whenever I look at that group picture I see how God sees us through His eyes. He sees us as one people, one family, His children. The Edomite spirit had sought to divide and conquer the people of Buikwe, but the Holy Spirit of God healed and united us through the power of repentance, confession and forgiveness.

What a joyful time it was as we said goodbye to each other. We had become dear friends over those three days, with those who were hated enemies now singing and hugging as one, the children of God.

As we left, the pastors asked us to keep coming back every year to encourage them. Although we haven't managed to have the same kind of convocation in Buikwe yet, whenever I hear about Buikwe it is the good news of all that the Lord is doing there and it warms my heart.

Unmasking the Spirit Behind Freemasonry

The children of God may not wield any physical natural weapons like tanks, planes and artillery, but we are all part of a very big and powerful army: the army of the Lord. The battles we fight are spiritual, but they have repercussions in this natural world. The impact is felt in our lives, communities and nations. Indeed the destinies of entire nations have been steered by the power of prayer, fasting and spiritual warfare.

One of the truths I learned early on as a soldier in the Lord's army is that the spiritual world controls the natural. Many things may seem powerful and entrenched in the natural world, but the truth is they are held by spiritual strongholds. In dealing with natural situations, the Lord has often revealed the spiritual foundations or roots of the issues.

"If the foundations are destroyed, what shall the righteous do?" Proverbs 11:3. This means that understanding the foundations or roots of issues helps when you to deal with those issues spiritually.

In 2018, the Lord showed me a vision of a tall mountain. The mountain was divided into three levels. Two lower levels of the mountain were green and covered with dense vegetation. However, the top of the mountain was barren and bare, with only dry sandy soil covering it. I wondered why there was a difference and asked the Lord, "What does this mountain mean?"

The Lord answered me, **"It is the mountain of the economy in Africa."**

I then asked the Lord why the top of the mountain was so bare. He answered, **"The bottom levels of the mountain have been occupied by the church and so the nations have advanced to those levels. However, the top of the mountain is ruled by a stronghold, and that is why it is barren and bare."**

I asked the Lord what was the stronghold ruling on top of the mountain and I heard one word, **"Freemasonry."**

"What did that mean?" I pondered.

I started searching the internet for teachings on Freemasonry. I knew next to nothing about the society except that it was shrouded in mystery and secrecy. I found some useful teaching on the internet by my good friend and prophetic minister, Arthur Burk. Even as I listened and tried to understand it all, I couldn't see the connection between Africa and what seemed to be a largely European secret society.

A while after that, the Lord showed me a panoramic view of the continent of Africa. As I saw the vision of Africa, the focus zoomed in on the Democratic Republic of Congo, the large central African nation that borders Uganda to the west. As I saw the nation of Congo in the vision, suddenly I saw a large dragon with a long tail and a dark rider wearing a crown. This fearsome dragon with its dark rider kept circling the space over Congo as though it owned and controlled the air space.

I asked the Lord, "what do the dragon and the rider mean?" The Lord answered me, "**that is the king of Congo**."

I was stunned by the answer and kept quiet, listening. The Lord continued, **"You must tell the church in Congo, that all**

their prayers and efforts to be free from that stronghold will not work unless they dethrone that king."

It was all very baffling to me. What did this all mean? However, I started taking note of all these revelations and kept praying for understanding. I also kept researching the history of Congo to get some more clues as to what this all meant.

I called my good friend and elder of CNC, Nicole Tshani and asked her to visit me so we could talk about these revelations. Nicole and her husband Claude originally came from Congo but have been residents of Uganda for many years now. They were part of the founding elders of CNC and have been our friends for many years. Nicole has long carried a burden for her native land and we often spoke of the situation in Congo. I knew that if there was someone I could get more information from, it was Nicole.

She came to see me and we had time to pray and seek the Lord together. I shared with her the vision and the word I got from the Lord. She listened quietly and, when she spoke, her words were measured. She agreed wholeheartedly that indeed the Lord was revealing something for her nation. She said the pastors from Congo needed to hear this message and she would prayerfully send out feelers to see who would be open to hearing from us.

After my time with Nicole, I still didn't know what the connection was between Freemasonry, Congo and Uganda. I asked a few other friends and intercessors to pray over the issue. As I continued to seek answers, through a referral from a friend, I came upon a preacher of the gospel called Dr. Selwyn Stevens who taught extensively on the subject of Freemasonry.

As I listened to his messages, I realized that God has sent us a man who could teach us more on this topic. I took a step of faith and sent him an email obtained from the information I found on his website. It was shot in the dark. I didn't expect him to answer because people don't often respond to random mail sent to their general ministry account.

Miraculously, however, after a few days, Dr. Stevens himself answered my mail! I was truly surprised and knew that the Lord must be in it. He, nonetheless, declined to come to attend a conference in Uganda saying he had a schedule that was fully booked. As I read his mail, a part of me was discouraged, but another part was energized. God had been connecting the dots consistently and I had to believe He would bring everything together. I took another step of faith and sent Dr. Stevens a long letter sharing why we were inviting him to come and speak at a conference in Uganda. I shared the revelation the Lord had given me about Freemasonry and how God had led us to him. After I sent the mail, I prayed and asked God to speak to Dr. Stevens Himself if He wanted him to bring a message to us.

Shortly after that, Dr. Stevens replied and said he had reworked his schedule and that now he could come to Uganda on his way back from a ministry trip to the U.S. This was God's hand again and now we proceeded full-throttle to organize the conference.

Since the Lord had spoken of the African economy, we focused on inviting pastors from the region to attend. With the short notice and very little time we had to organize the conference, we were delighted to get confirmation from pastors from Kenya, Ethiopia, Burundi and Congo as well as our Ugandan pastors. We would have loved to have even more nations attend but there simply wasn't enough time to organize more guests. The conference was slated for September and, as the dates drew closer, a kind of warfare intensified. It seemed as though every day we experienced spiritual attacks in some way. As we invited pastors and guests to attend the conference, we got feedback that the theme of the topic was a "live wire," meaning that it was fully loaded with spiritual warfare and that we best not confront it. To add to that it seemed the big spiritual heavyweights that I was relying on to speak at the conference and help us confront this unknown Spirit were dropping off one by one. Conflicting schedules and prior travel and speaking engagements meant that most pastors, leaders and intercessors I thought would help carry the conference were not there. It was now left to God and us, and I didn't even know what we were confronting.

Amid all the busyness and spiritually tense atmosphere, the enemy attacked. Our youngest daughter was just three years old at that time, and my nanny, called Justine, who had helped look after her since she was a baby, was someone I relied on a lot, especially when I had busy programmes that took me away from home. This was such a time.

One day, I got home to hear the terrifying news that her son, a young man in his early twenties had been kidnapped by unknown men as he left his place of work! As soon as I heard the news I knew that this was the enemy's attack to derail me and the conference. I felt exposed at home and church. What was this we were dealing with? I comforted my nanny and we started the process of informing the police and trying to ascertain what could have happened to her son. The story was that, as he left his workplace, some men in a car approached him and started talking to him, telling him that they were part of an organization that arranged sports scholarships for gifted athletes and that they wanted to sponsor him in one of their schools. The young man, called Felix, loved playing football and despite his initial apprehension, he sat in their car and they drove off. The bystanders thought that the people with the car knew him because there was no scuffle or incident of any kind.

That was all the information we got. The young man's phone was switched off and there was no contact of any kind with him. As we went to bed that night, the whole house was shrouded with worry and anxiety because of not knowing the fate of the boy. The incident happened on Thursday and the conference was set to begin the next week on Monday. That weekend was one of tortured waiting as, every morning and evening, we waited to hear an update from the police.

Finally, on the Sunday before the conference was set to start, I went to church as usual in the morning and returned home in the afternoon. I asked everyone at home if we had heard back from the police regarding Justine's son. No one had anything new to report. The police were searching for the young man and following all the leads but there was no breakthrough yet. That afternoon, I went into my prayer closet and started praying for the Lord to intervene in the situation. By this time I had realized that the disappearance of the young man was a spiritual attack on my household to derail me and my family during this time of heightened spiritual activity. I knew that it was only the Lord who could intervene and prevent this worrying situation from escalating further. I prayed in the Holy Spirit for some time and then started pleading with the Lord to send His angels to release the young man wherever he was and guide him to safety.

As I prayed, I saw an image of a young man bound up in chains in a dark place, then suddenly a giant angel stood before the young man and extended his sword and broke the chains and set him free. This image was so clear in my mind I realized it was from the Lord and I continued to pray with a sense of assurance and peace that the Lord had taken care of the situation. After my time of prayer, I took a nap in my room. Shortly, after I drifted off to sleep, my mobile phone rang. I picked it up in the middle of my sleep and what I heard on the other side of the line made me sit bolt-upright in bed. It was my nanny, Justine, shouting uncontrollably in Runyankore Rukiga. For a minute my heart stopped, as I tried to make out what she was saying. Was she shouting for joy or had something terrible happened? In a moment, I understood her joy couldn't be contained because her beloved son had come home to them, released miraculously by the awesome power of God! I jumped out of bed and fell on my face before the Lord praising Him for doing what only He could do, returning the young man to his mother and family unharmed. What a Mighty God we serve!

Soon, I shared the good news with my family and household and we all rejoiced as more information kept trickling in about the young man's miraculous rescue. Our dear friends and intercessors at church who had been praying for his safe return were overjoyed, God had averted a disaster in the life of the young man and, by extension, all of us who were involved in the situation. The young man was taken to hospital and, apart from the psychological trauma of being kidnapped, he was physically healthy and unharmed.

The story he narrated was harrowing, to say the least. He confirmed that he was lured away by some strangers who detained him in a dark room in an unknown location for some days. He had no idea why they had kidnapped him and he kept pleading with them to release him. They paid no attention to his pleas and he wasn't sure what they wanted from him. It isn't clear if it was a case of mistaken identity or if the kidnappers abducted him to conduct some kind of evil ritual. The young man was kept in the darkroom for a few days and the kidnappers seemed to disagree on what to do with him. Finally, on the day that he miraculously escaped, it is one of the kidnappers who came and untied his chains and told him to urgently run for his life. The young man bolted out of the darkroom and ran out, he was able to run to the main road and catch a motorbike ride back to the city. He used the phone of the motorbike cyclist to call his mother and tell her he was alive!

*****

The weeklong conference started in earnest on Monday. All our delegates from different countries arrived safely and were checked into their hotels. The air was thick with anticipation. None of us really knew what the Lord would do during this conference, but I knew that we had been obedient despite all the odds and all the attacks; we had made it to the conference and now it was in God's Hands. And, as always, God did not disappoint. I learnt a very important lesson about spiritual warfare during that conference that I carry with me always. The greater the breakthrough, the stronger the opposition and spiritual warfare. God wanted to release something big during that conference and so the pushback was equivalent to the level of the revelation and breakthrough God was preparing to pour out.

Each day seemed to build on the one before. The power of God flowed and the anointing was evident as our guest speakers taught and introduced the theme of the conference.

On the Friday of the Conference, all the delegates travelled by car an hour and a half away to the city of Jinja to pray at the source of the Nile. The Lord had instructed us that we needed to go as a group of intercessors to pray at the source of the Nile. As we arrived at the site overlooking the beautiful River Nile, I didn't know what to expect. I had heard how all manners of occultic groups visited the site to perform rituals to gain spiritual control over the waters and the region. There were stories shared about witch doctors who planted trees and dedicated them to evil spirits to defile the land and create a stronghold over the area.

Our goal of travelling to Jinja was simple, to obey God's instructions. Beyond that, I didn't know what to expect. The group of intercessors gathered on a hill overlooking the river to pray in agreement before getting into the boat on the river. The Lord led me to share a few scriptures in the Bible about the meaning of rivers as a source of life, healing and joy. As I shared the Word in which we recognized that we had representatives from different African countries in the region, some of them sharing the same River Nile that has its source in Uganda. We called different representatives of nations and we repented to them on behalf of Uganda.

What followed can only be described as heavenly as a floodgate of tears and repentance followed between peoples from different tongues, tribes and nations. Nation repented to nation asking for forgiveness for the sins of hatred, sectarianism, tribalism and rejecting the other based on our differences. I do not know how much time we spent together on that hill, but I know that, by the time we started walking down the hill to board the boat, the great burden that we had been carrying all week was lifted. God had broken the yoke through the power of forgiveness, love and genuine repentance. The atmosphere changed from one of tears to one of jubilation, praise and spontaneous bursts of worship.

As we boarded the boat, worship continued to swell as worship leaders led the groups in one song after another. It was one of the most beautiful times I have experienced. I realized why the devil is so afraid of unity, it is tremendously powerful and beautiful. When we are united, we win the battle even before we start fighting. The enemy is defeated before we even begin because we are one. That is why Jesus prayed that His Church would be one just as the Godhead is One. God's power is absolute and sovereign because God the Father, the Son and the Holy Spirit are One, united in love and purpose and power. How beautiful if we God's people could be one as the Father, Son and Spirit are One.

When the boat got to the place where the waters of the Nile bubble to the surface from underground springs, the actual spot called the "source of the Nile," our boat idled in the water, as we prayed and did a prophetic act for the cleansing of the waters. Our dear friend Dr. Stevens took salt, water and oil and poured the mix into the water as a prophetic act to signify the cleansing and dedication of the waters to the Lord. Dr. Stevens read out a declaration over the Nile waters enthroning *Yeshua ben Yahweh* as Lord over the Nile and cleansing the waters with the Blood of Jesus.

I will never forget that as he spoke the words of that declaration, I saw the Lord seated on His throne in the sky and I realized that all the fear, all the anxiety about the evil and powers of darkness were a ploy of the enemy to discourage us and to try and get us to give up. I realized that day that there is no contest; God is on His throne, even in the places that the world says have been defiled and dedicated to evil. Even there, when God's people deal with the sin in their lives that separated us from God, the Lord is enthroned in all the earth. The Bible says, "the earth is the Lord's and the fullness of it."(Psalm 24:1-2) This means every tree, mountain, river, valley, and all the earth belongs to God.

What we did that day at the source of the Nile was simply to rededicate the land to God and ask Him to cleanse it and restore it for His purposes. When we returned from the boat, we all looked like soldiers returning from battle, weary but with faces awash with God's glory. There was such beauty and joy and peace in our midst. We knew we had accomplished the task the Lord assigned us to do.

Saturday was the final day of the conference where we planned to have a court session where each nation brought their petitions before the Lord. A court session is a very solemn spiritual act, where God's people present their cases before the Lord and Judge of the Universe and ask that He makes a verdict in their favour. A Heavenly Court isn't something that we take lightly, it is the most solemn and serious type of prayer because you are appealing to the Highest Court, the court of Heaven. If your case is rejected by God, there is no higher court, and there is no recourse. Therefore, appealing to the courts of Heaven requires adequate preparation both spiritually and also naturally.

Each nation was given time to prepare its petition for the Lord. There were things that each nation was asking the Lord to do, given the different histories and situations. I was nervous as I prepared my opening prayer. I felt the immense weight of the moment five African nations would bring their petitions before the Lord. Uganda, Kenya, Burundi, Congo and Ethiopia were each represented by different intercessors who read detailed prayers and petitions before the Lord. Each nation brought repentance for the unique history and sins of their nations against God and the people. Once all nations' petitions were read, Maama Janet, who was present, prayed on behalf of the nations and petitioned for the Lord to answer the prayers of Africa and to heal the land. You could hear a pin drop in the Church as people bowed their heads and knees; some wept quietly, and all felt the weight of the sins of our nations in the Presence of the Lord.

I will never forget that Ps. Nsembe from Congo, a wonderful gentleman and servant of God, knelt before God draped in the flag of his country Congo and cried to God saying, "we know that Your glory has departed from our land, we are all called Ichabod, but please remember us now and return to us and remove our shame."

The Christians from Ethiopia, too, wept and cried to God to remove the reproach from their land of migrants who flee their homes and die on the high seas, the shame of famine, war and the religious spirit. It was such a moving, powerful time as God's people communed with Him and petitioned the Courts of Heaven for a merciful verdict.

After the court session was concluded everyone left for home with a sense of joy. I went home, but my heart was in a state of suspense. We had brought our case before the Lord and I was anxious to hear the Lord's verdict. I tried to sleep that night but sleep failed me. I kept tossing and turning and eventually got up and went to my prayer room. I sat on the floor and waited in silence. "Lord, I'm here," I demurred.

Then I heard Him begin to speak in that familiar Voice I have heard so many times over the years. His Voice was the same, always the same gentleness, stillness and yet weightiness. I found a notebook and began scribbling down what I was hearing. Each word brought joy and elation to my heart. God's verdict was like water to a thirsty soul, and I drank in every word. When the flow of God's Word finished, I looked at the notes I had written down in my notebook. God's verdict was mercy! Overwhelming mercy!

My soul rejoiced, God heard us and He answered with mercy! There was hope; there was hope for Africa!

I fell on my face before the Lord in silent worship. I don't know how long I stayed on my face in my prayer room but when I got up and went back to bed, I slept like a baby.

For the Kingdom and the Lamb

Some may wonder, why spiritual warfare features so prominently in the Christian life, especially if you are involved in ministry. I believe it is because, whether we are aware of it or not, we are all part of this age-old epic battle between good and evil, the kingdom of God and the kingdom of darkness. I once heard the re-known American worship leader Ron Kenoly say, "there is no demilitarized zone." That means you are either on the Lord's side or on the devil's side. There is no sitting on the fence, according to the Bible, if we are not gathering with the Lord, we are scattering. Yes, warfare is part of the Christian life, but after the warfare, there is great victory and peace. King David was probably the greatest warrior King that the nation of Israel ever had. He fought endlessly with Israel's enemies and he enlarged and established the boundaries of the nation. He fought the battles that established peace for generations to come. He was a warrior king, and the Bible calls the Lord Jesus Christ, the "Son of David." I believe that David's life was pleasing to God, not because he fought battles but because he fought the right battles, God's battles and God blessed, prospered and used him greatly. My prayer is that our generation will not shrink away from the spiritual battles that are ours to fight. Once we make a stand for God, victory is assured and God can expand and advance the frontiers of His kingdom on earth further. Every soldier and army has a unique battle cry, at Covenant Nations Church, our battle cry is **"For the Kingdom and the Lamb!"**

13. Remitting the Sins of Slavery

You may shoot me with your words, you may cut me with your eyes, you may kill me with your hatefulness, but still, like air, I'll rise. – Maya Angelou.

Slavery is not an easy topic to deal with. It is emotionally charged, spiritually draining and difficult to discuss. Whenever I share or teach on this topic I feel the weight of our collective history as African people, the descendants of Ham. Our great African history in all its complexity; the glory and the shame, the beauty and the ashes. It is only through the Blood of Jesus and the finished work of the Cross that we can see our past, present and future through the Redeeming eyes of God's Love. My prayer is that the Lord will help to unburden what He has placed on my heart but also that He will impart His vision of Africa and how we look through His eyes of Love.

What is on my heart is not simply about looking back historically but it is mostly about looking forward. This message is about Jesus. Jesus is the central figure of history, of the story of mankind and the journey of humanity. Jesus is the central figure in this story and so even in the context of slavery, Jesus is at the Centre. Not of the sin of slavery, but redemption from it, for all.

I remember hearing a message years ago from the late healing evangelist, Oral Roberts, he talked about Jesus in every book of the Bible. By identifying Jesus in every Book of the Bible, Oral Roberts highlighted the truth that Jesus is the central theme from Genesis to Revelations. I believe that's true in almost every situation in human history.

Therefore, if we look for Jesus, even in the dark, numbing pain of our past as Africans, we can find Him there, and see the Resurrection power of the Cross that triumphed over death and the grave. He can bring light out of darkness and Healing and restoration out of brokenness.

The topic of slavery is too dense in scope to try and do it justice in one chapter, so I will only highlight the Transatlantic slave trade or Triangular slave trade that took place between Africa, the Americas and Europe. However, the Indian Ocean slave routes predated even the Transatlantic trade. This slave trade was through the Indian Ocean carrying slaves from the east coast of Africa. The slaves would be raided by African tribes in the interior of Africa and then they would make the long trek to the slave forts on the East Coast where they were sold to Arab slave traders. The slaves were then taken by ships to Oman and further into the Middle East.

Most of the slaves however, taken into Arabia were made eunuchs to limit the procreation of more African peoples in Arabia so the African slave populations didn't grow as they did in the Americas. The main purpose of the slaves in Arabia was to work as domestic slaves and therefore the Arabs did not desire growth in the number of slaves simply because there was no economic need for a large slave population.

The case was very different in the Transatlantic Slave trade which was driven by the economic demand for slave labour to work the plantations to provide cheap raw materials to fuel the industrial revolution in Europe.

As most evils that have been perpetrated against African peoples by foreigners are; the motivation was purely economic. It justified the insatiable thirst for more slave labour that depopulated the continent and created population centres for slaves in the Caribbean and North and South America. Therefore the volume of slaves traded in the Transatlantic Trade vastly outnumbers the Indian Ocean trade. The number of Africans sold into slavery from the Transatlantic route by records from slave ships is estimated at around 12 million souls. However, some historians posit that this number is deflated on purpose to try and minimize the human cost of the slave trade on the African continent. Other historians put the number as high as 60 million souls which is higher than the population of Uganda today. Whatever, the accurate number, God alone knows but it is staggeringly high and a statistic cannot even begin to capture what Africa lost in the gifts, talents, energy, anointing, mantles and blessing of all those brothers and sisters who were violently taken from their homeland.

The transatlantic slave trade started around the 15th century and continued until the 19th century. The main European powers that were involved in this trade or this evil enterprise were all European countries that were trying to extend their power and their empire. That means the usual suspects of the day; Portugal, Spain, England, France and Netherlands. All these Europeans were travelling west into the "new world" in search of raw materials, new lands and new resources to fuel their empires and their economies. They were in a race to conquer the Americas in search of gold, silver and other minerals. They also wanted to open up new lands for plantation agriculture of the crops they couldn't plant in Europe because of the cold climate. Crops like sugar, tea and cotton could only grow in warmer climates and thus the search for new lands. Once they had planted their flags on the Caribbean islands, South and North America, their next great need was for labour. They had a great need for labour to open up the new lands and to work these lands whether for agriculture or mining.

Labour was very intensive in all of these industries and there was a shortage of people to work these new lands. In the Americas, the local indigenous people of the land were few and lived in small communities. Some of them were hunter-gatherer communities while others lived deep in the jungles in isolated clans and tribal groups. They didn't have the high population centres the Europeans needed.

The indigenous peoples were also very resistant to the European invaders that were coming into their lands. They would resist them by fighting and retreating deeper into the jungles to seek refuge from the Europeans.

The indigenous peoples were also more susceptible to the new diseases that were brought by the Europeans to which the indigenous people did not have immunity. Deadly diseases such as smallpox were known to wipe out entire indigenous communities. Therefore, between the early 16th century and the 19th century there was a hunt for labour to fuel the economic system and more and more the Europeans looked to Africa to provide what they needed.

African societies between the 15th and 19th centuries were highly centralized and thriving population centres with military might, political structures, economic specialization and social stratification.

Any student of African history knows of the Kingdoms found in West, East, Central and Southern Africa at that time. Whether it was Benin, Songhai, Ashanti and Mali in West Africa, Congo and Luanda in Central Africa, or Greater Zimbabwe in Southern Africa. In East Africa, we had kingdoms in Bunyoro, Ankole, Buganda and Rwanda. Their civilizations were organized in highly centralized kingdoms or chiefdoms with clear social structures and economies with the production of goods and labour specialization. Most Kingdoms had military hierarchies, many were wealthy possessing gold and other precious metals in addition to agricultural wealth. There were also strong social structures that regulated everyday life. Dahomey, as an example, was a kingdom in West Africa, which was re-known for its all-female military.

So this notion that Africans were extremely primitive people wandering around in the jungle with bones in their noses is false and part of the narrative created by the Europeans to justify their belligerent behaviour of invasion and conquest of other peoples. They needed to create a narrative of "savages" to justify and soothe their consciences by saying they were coming to "civilize" the "savages." It was after all the "white man's burden" a thankless task cast on him by his superior pedigree to bring "civilization" to the wild child-like peoples of the world. In all these civilizations there was order, structure, and significantly higher population centres than the indigenous peoples of the Americas. They had millions of people who were organized in societies with Leaders/ Chiefs, armies, men, women and the youth. Therefore, through the eyes of the exploiters; Africa was a very attractive place to search for labour.

African people also managed to survive all manner of privations, by the Grace of God they were physically stronger, and did not die very easily due to exposure, disease, brutality, inhumane treatment or even attempts at extermination. For these and other reasons, the African continent was plundered of her sons and daughters for close to four centuries!

Looking specifically at the triangular slave trade - the slave trade between Europe, Africa and the Americas. Slaves would be raided and shipped from

the West African coast to the Americas to work on large plantations, in mines and as domestic servants. They were brought to the Americas to work and provide raw materials for the industries and drive the industrial revolution that was taking place in Europe. The Slaves provided the labour in the Americas, and produced the raw materials which were then shipped across the Atlantic again to Europe to be used in the factories. Finally, the finished products would be shipped to Africa to be sold or exchanged for more slaves and thus the triangular slave trade continued.

The slave traders who were Europeans did not go into the interior of the African continent to kidnap and raid African villages. This was left to the African leaders - kings /Chiefs raided other kingdoms/ Chiefdoms in the interior and kidnapped their people. What is important to understand is that it was African leaders sometimes with the help of Arab middlemen who raided, burned, pillaged, and kidnapped their fellow Africans in the interior of the continent. The kidnapped men and women were chained together to begin the long trek to the coast to be sold to the Europeans.

At the coast, the European slave merchants waited for the aggregating of the slaves as they came from the interior. For the trade to be profitable the slave ships had to be packed to the rafters with human cargo. They wanted to have high numbers so they often waited for different slave raiding parties to bring the people from the interior to the coast. It must be noted that the slave trade was very profitable for the Europeans otherwise it would not have endured for so long.

Many European companies that are in existence today were founded on the proceeds of the slave trade. It is even said that the royal family of England sponsored slave ships, on occasion, because the sizable profits they made from the sale of human beings were too tempting to pass up. The forts that dot the coast of Africa – East, Central and West - are mostly slave forts that were constructed to house the slaves as they went on this journey, first to the coast and finally shipped off the continent. In Uganda we have Fort Patiko in the north, in Kenya there is Fort Jesus on the coast and in Zanzibar, the old stone town was a slave market for Arabs. In West Africa, the coast is dotted with many such forts: Elmina in Ghana and Goree Island in Senegal, among many others.

Goree Island acted as a catchment for many of the slaves that came from the West African coast. It was the slaves' final stop before leaving their homeland forever. Goree Island is now a famous site of pilgrimage for many African-Americans who come to retrace the steps of their ancestors. It is where the infamous door of no return is found.

The slave trade flourished and thrived for so long that it is difficult to calculate the full scale of the loss but we are talking about millions and millions of people. The human cost was staggering. Millions of people died on the high seas, even before reaching the colonies in the Americas. They died in the slave raids. They died during the brutal trek to the coast. They died in the forts where the conditions were terrible, they died on the voyage and more died also on arrival. Those who survived these unimaginable experiences started new and difficult lives in the colonies filled with heartache, inhumane treatment, deprivation, loss of identity and human dignity.

The trek to the coast was truly a 'Trail of Tears' and many towns and villages are named in recognition of these tribulations. Bagamoyo in Tanzania is one such place. It simply means 'Leave Your spirit Here.' This name was given by the slave raiders telling the people they were raiding to leave their spirits there; to give up hope on life, give up hope on ever returning to their homes and families. It was a very terrible experience and we cannot fully grasp the spiritual and emotional trauma to the people, communities and land that this inhumane trade brought.

Once the slaves departed from their homeland they never came back. There was no chance that they could escape and then return to the land of their birth. We know from many real and fictional accounts of the experiences of the slaves, that once the slaves arrived in the colonies they were victims of a very evil system. The dehumanizing system sought to completely strip away their identity and break down the dignity and worth of the victims until they were no better than animals so that they could work as beasts of burden all their lives.

One of the first things that the slave owners did was to forbid the slaves from using their African names. If you watched the movie *Roots*[1] written by Alex Haley; you will remember the gut-wrenching scene where "Kunta Kinte" is being whipped for sticking to his African name and rejecting the European name "Toby" forced on him by his slave owners. Your name is symbolic of your identity - who you are, where you come from, your family and your lineage. In forcing a slave to take on the name of his captors, the slave relinquished his identity to them, and his past, present and future were placed in their hands to control. Today, we see African Americans with names like Clark, Jones or Johnson. That is most likely the name of the slave master that owned them.

Grave mistreatment by slave owners was commonplace: beatings, whippings and even lynchings came with the ugly territory of slavery. Slaves were not allowed to learn how to read or write. All education was forbidden because the slave owners didn't want slaves to have the capacity to think for themselves. All they wanted was simply for the body to work, and the spirit and soul to die. Family structures were completely shattered, and women were routinely sexually abused by slave owners. Rape was common all along the way

---

1 Alex Haley. *Roots: The Saga of an American Family.* Doubleday, 1976.

from the time of the raids, in the forts, in the high seas and the colonies. Families and couples could be separated at the whim of the slavemaster and wives could be violated by slave owners at will and there was absolutely nothing that the husband could do about it.

Many children were fathered by the slave owners, but even then they remained slaves. Parents could have their children sold to other plantations and thus be separated forever. There was no certainty in the life of a slave, save for the certainty of misery, pain and death. For the African slaves, all connection to their past was lost as culture, language and family ties faded. Although some cultural experiences survived through song, dance and oral tradition, especially in the African slaves of south america and the Caribbean, stronger links such as language and hereditary links were lost.

This is a very different experience from immigrant communities that came to the new world. These families were able to retrace the steps of their ancestors back to their original country, village and even homestead. This is because the names, family history, religions, culture and cohesiveness of the society kept the connection to the land of their ancestry for generations. They can reconnect to their past. This was completely lost for the Africans who were enslaved.

Slavery in the Bible

What does the Bible say about slavery? I began by talking about Jesus being a central figure in history and how the Cross is the focal point of all of human history. But how does that apply to something as dark, evil and painful as slavery?

Slavery is present in some way, shape and form in both the Old and New Testaments of the Bible. Slavery was a part of the "World System" at that time and was practised by many civilizations to different degrees. In the Old Testament, the Children of Israel were enslaved in Egypt. Even before and after that, you see that slavery appears in the world. Even before the enslavement of the Hebrews in Egypt, Joseph was sold into slavery by his brothers. In the Old Testament and even the New Testament, slavery was a reality of life in the civilizations in and surrounding Israel.

Exodus 21:16 says thus:

> *"Whoever kidnaps a man, whether he sells him or is found with him in his possession, shall be put to death." – Amplified Bible*

This law in Exodus highlights the point that kidnapping people to enslave them was an evil act that they were grappling with. Otherwise, why else would God address it through the law? We can speculate on the scale and prevalence of slavery at the time, whether it was benign or cruel. However, the fact that it existed in some form is clear.

Leviticus 25:39 says thus:

> *"And if your brother becomes poor beside you and sells himself to you, you shall not compel him to serve as a bondman (slave not eligible for redemption)." – Amplified Bible*

God was very clear from the beginning that enslaving another person in perpetuity was wrong, even if a person became poor and sold himself to survive, there was always the possibility and hope of redemption after the legal time was served, and he could be set free. The principle of a Sabbath rest and Jubilee was enshrined in the law to ensure that even if a person fell on hard times and was enslaved, the door for release and restoration was still open.

God desired that Israel would be a just and equitable society because God is a just God. The law was given to protect the weak, vulnerable and marginalized in society. To steal a person's labour and not pay for it went against the spiritual and moral laws of God. According to God, the labourer is worthy of his wages and therefore it is incumbent upon the employer to pay his labourer a fair wage. Many of the parables that Jesus talked about in the New Testament focused on the relationship between a master (employer) and his servants (employees). The biblical view was that if somebody gives you their labour they are worthy of their hire. Anything else is morally wrong and reprehensible.

Here is what Exodus 21:32 says:

> *"If the Ox gores a manservant or a maidservant, the owner shall give to their master thirty shekels of silver and the Ox shall be stoned." – Amplified Bible*

The Old Testament is a type and shadow of the New Testament. What was foreshadowed in the Old was fulfilled in the New. Thirty pieces of silver is exactly the price that was paid to Judas Iscariot for betraying Jesus. This signifies that the laws governing these matters were active even during the time of Jesus and that He eventually paid the price for slavery with His own life and blood.

But we are jumping ahead of ourselves.

Let us refer to Psalms 109 in the context of slavery and especially looking through the eyes of people who were taken as slaves.

If it is possible, let us put ourselves in the place of the African people who were torn from their lands, and families, from everything that they knew and loved, taken on a trek of death and eventually shipped away to distant lands.

Remember they had no choice in this, they were taken against their will and with great violence.

Let us imagine the fear, horror, and pain; add the physical, spiritual and emotional trauma.

In Psalm 109:1-5, we find these words:

> *"O GOD of my praise! Keep not silence, For the mouths of the wicked and the mouth of the deceit, are opened against me; they have spoken to me and against me with lying tongues. They have compassed me about also with words of hatred and have fought against me without a cause. In return for my love, they are my adversaries, but I resort to prayer. And they have rewarded and laid upon me evil for good and hatred for my love.*

"Set a wicked man over him (as a judge), and let a (malicious) accuser stand at his right hand. When (the wicked) is judged, let him be condemned and let his prayer (for leniency) be turned into a sin. Let his days be few, and let another take his

"Office and charge. Let his children be fatherless and his wife a widow. Let his children be continual vagabonds (as was Cain) and beg; let them seek their bread and be driven far from their ruined homes. Let the creditor and extortioner seize all that he has, and let strangers (barbarians and foreigners) plunder the fruits of his labour. Let there be none to extend or continue mercy and kindness to him, neither let there be any to have pity on his fatherless children. Let his posterity be cut off, and in the generation following let their names be blotted out. Let the iniquity of his fathers be remembered by the Lord, and; let not the sin of his mother be blotted out. Let them be before the Lord continually, that He may cut off the memory of them from the earth! - Because the man did not (earnestly) remember to show mercy, but pursued and persecuted the poor and needy man, and the broken in the heart (he was ready) to slay. Yes, he loved cursing, and it comes (back) upon him; he delighted not in blessing, and it was far from him. He clothed himself also with cursing and with his garment, and it seeped into his inward (Life) like water, and like oil into his bones. Let it be to him as the raiment with which he covers himself and as the girdle with which he is girded continually. Let this be the reward of my adversaries from the Lord, and of those who speak evil against my life. I am gone like the shadow when it lengthens and declines; I toss up and down and am shaken off as the locust. My knees are weak and totter from fasting; and my body is gaunt and has no fatness. I have become a reproach and a taunt to others; when they see me they shake their heads. Let them curse but do You do bless. When adversaries arise, let them be put to shame, but let Your servant rejoice. Let my adversaries be clothed with shame and dishonour, and let them cover themselves with their disgrace and confusion as with a robe. I will give great

praise and thanks to the Lord with my mouth; yes, and I will praise him among the multitude. For He will stand at the right hand of the poor and needy, to save him from those who condemn his life." – Amplified Bible

In reading this Psalm, we notice that there are two groups of people represented, the oppressor and the oppressed; the guilty and the innocent; the slave and the slave trader. One party invokes the strongest words and curses on another party for the great injustice done to them. Looking at it in the context of slavery, the people who were being taken as slaves uttered specific and terrible curses on the people who had sold them into slavery.

Specific curses in Psalm 109:

- **Bad Leaders:** in the past 400 years Africa has faced a crisis of leadership across the continent. From the time of the cultural chiefs who collaborated with slave merchants and colonialists because of their selfish attitudes, myopia and lack of vision, to the present day, when problems of corruption and disunity plague our leaders. Psalm 109 speaks of setting a wicked man over them. Sadly, we continue to experience this curse in a very real way and are still dealing with this foundational issue in Africa. Whether it was Idi Amin or Mobutu Seseko, Africa has seen her fair share of wicked men as leaders.

- **Widows, orphans and the fatherless:** When one looks at the history of Africa, one notices that all the wars, epidemics, diseases, famine, hunger, displacement, instability and economic deprivation have left a great number of widows and orphans in our societies. Even without all the upheavals, there is a deeper problem of irresponsible, negligent and absentee fathers. African women and mothers are celebrated in music, art and culture. We have seen the pictures of the African mother carrying her baby on her back and her load on her head. But where is the African father? What is he carrying? Who is he nurturing? The problems of African youth begin in the home and the curse of fatherlessness, whether it is genuine or self-imposed by men who have lost sight of their role in the family and society, is a festering wound that must be lanced and cleansed.

- **Vagabondism**: The curse of being a wandering people. There are no people on the earth that you find wandering the nations of the world to the extent that Africans do. For whatever reasons, be they political, social or economic, Africans are continually wandering around the world. Oftentimes, they do not stay long enough in a place to take root. Vagabondism means to wander and never be established, never accrue enough wealth to leverage it to make lasting change. This is a spiritual issue that is at the heart of many family, business and societal problems. If Africans are leaving their lands to go to other places, we are courting disaster because a vacuum will always be filled. We must be established in our nations and lands or risk being displaced by others.

- **Beggars and refugees:** Africa has become a continent of borrowers, not lenders.

Whether it's from other nations or International agencies, we see the following:

- **Shame and Dishonor:** Africa experience more shame and dishonour as a people than probably any other people or group on the earth. Whether it is the shame of being conquered and constantly exploited by foreigners or the dishonour of having our wealth plundered and having to borrow money from the very people who have plundered our wealth. Then there is the shame of our internal weaknesses which exposes us to our enemies and those who dream of our destruction. We can write an entire book about this one point alone, but I believe the greatest indignity is being lectured and told what is best for us by former colonial powers as though Africans cannot judge and decide what is in their best interest.

We need not look far to know that both parties that were locked in this terrible dance of slavery, the slave and the slave trader, both suffered greatly. The Africans sold into slavery in the Americas and the Caribbean suffered unspeakable pain, but the Africans on the continent also suffered greatly. The two parties representing two brothers, the two sides of the equation: the slaves who were taken and those who participated in the trade of their brothers and sisters, both have borne the torment of this evil albeit in different ways. Curses that were spoken over the land and her people have been a self-fulfilling prophecy.

But is there anyone who can put an end to this battle, this raging war, in the realm of the spirit, this feud over those who were taken as slaves and those who remained and participated in the selling of their brothers? The only One who can make atonement, the only One who can finally bring peace is the Messiah. The Messiah is the One who stands on the side of the poor and the needy and who can redeem them.

What does the cross have to do with slavery? I have always loved the old hymn "Jesus paid it all." Did Jesus pay for slavery? When we talk about the cross of Jesus Christ, we are talking about the full atonement for all sin - the sin of all humanity.

Matthew 26:14 -16 has this to say:

> *"Then one of the Twelve (apostles), [who] was called Judas Iscariot, went to the chief priests, And he said, what are you willing to give me if I hand Him (Jesus) over to you? and they weighed out for and paid to him thirty pieces of silver (about twenty-one dollars and sixty cents). – Amplified Bible*

Thirty pieces of silver in the Old Testament was the price of a slave. Jesus was betrayed by His close friend, He was handed over by a member of His party, His band of brothers. Judas was not a Pharisee. He was an insider, someone who should have been protecting, serving and supporting Jesus. Instead, he sold Him for thirty pieces of silver. He sold Him for the price of a slave. When he betrayed Jesus, Jesus was bound and arrested. There was a mock trial, staged by the religious leaders where people lied about Jesus and bore false witness against him. There was no real justice. His disciples fled and left Him alone. He was beaten by the violent Roman soldiers and flogged to the point of death.

Psalm 129:3:

The plowers plowed upon My back; they made long fallows.

Picture a field that is plowed. It has long lines made by the plow digging into the land. That is how Jesus' back looked because of the whippings and the beatings. His back had deep, long furrows and His skin was hanging as ribbons. He was taunted, mocked, exposed and ashamed. Jesus experienced everything that a slave experienced and more. From the dehumanization of being sold for money. The fact that there was haggling, and a price arrived at, says that he was not priceless. After the negotiation, money was exchanged for His life as though he was an object and not a person. Jesus experienced the sham of the trial, the injustice, the loneliness, humiliation, fear, isolation, and the pain of the flogging. Jesus experienced it all for us.

Finally, the last point at which Jesus identified with a slave - a person who had no rights was His death on the Cross.

Galatians 3:13 says the following:

> *"Christ purchased our freedom (redeeming us) from the curse (doom) of the Law (and its condemnation) by (Himself) becoming a curse for us, for it is written (in the scriptures), Cursed is everyone who hangs on a tree." – Amplified Bible*

The Bible declares, "cursed is everyone who is hung on a tree". Jesus identified with a slave even at the last point which was death. He identified with the death of a slave because He was hung on a tree.

Slaves have no rights over their lives or their bodies. In ancient Rome, slaves were thrown into the Colosseum to be torn apart by lions and other wild animals for the entertainment of the emperor and the Roman mob. African slaves were treated no better than animals and were often killed by lynching or hanging on trees to inspire fear in all the slaves who heard or saw it.

Jesus identified with a slave even in death when He was hung on a tree and He bore the curse of all who have been hung on a tree. That means He bore the curse of slavery in His own body on the cross.

> Psalm 109:31 declares, *"The Messiah will redeem and stand for the poor and the needy, to save him from those who condemn his life."*

In the Biblical account of Joseph found in the Book of Genesis, Joseph suffered great injustice when he was sold into slavery by his brothers. However, what we don't always realize is that the lives of Joseph's brothers virtually came to a standstill until they repented of their sin many years later. During all those years of separation, they bore the brunt of judgment and the penalty for their sin even in the land of Canaan. The only way that this family could move forward in their lives, was for Joseph and his brothers to be restored. Who could restore and redeem them?

> Psalm 109:31 says: *"it is the Messiah who will redeem and stand for the poor and the needy, to save him from those who condemn his life."*

The Cross is the focal point where those who have been mistreated and those who are bearing the judgment of mistreating others can come together to find atonement, restoration and the remission of sins.

Therefore, the descendants of Africans who still bear the judgment of the curse of slavery, the African peoples on the continent and the descendants of slaves all over the world who still bear in their spirits the woundedness and the curse of slavery, need to get this message. Those two groups, when we come to the cross, and when we come to Jesus who bore in His body the penalty of judgment for the sin of slavery, we can finally receive healing. Both parties can find atonement, healing and restoration through the Blood and the Body of Jesus.

We, as believers in Africa and around the world, must engage in identificational repentance. What does identificational repentance mean? That means that when we repent we identify with the sin of slavery. You might think all this terrible history has nothing to do with you and you are innocent of this evil. You may even think that, if you were alive during the time of slavery, you could never have participated in it. Be that as it may, when we stand in the gap for the sins that our ancestors permitted and even committed, we do not stand aloof or even in the judgment of those sins. The only way that we can repent - truly repent and stand in the gap between the generational sins of our ancestors and our sins - is if we identify with those sins if we "own" those sins as though we had committed them.

The case of Daniel is illustrative here. He was a righteous man, he was an excellent man and a servant of God but when he repented for the sins of Israel he didn't say "they sinned." Instead, he said, "we have sinned." He identified with the sins of his people.

Prayer

Heavenly Father Your word weighs heavy on our hearts, we feel the conviction of the Holy Spirit and today we identify with the great evil of slavery. We confess that our ancestors were willing accomplices and collaborators in this great atrocity. We acknowledge our part as those who sold our brothers and brought a curse on ourselves, our land and our African brothers that were taken from this land.

Father to us belongs the shame of our kings, our princes and our fathers because we have sinned against You. This sin is a stain on us as Africans and we continue to reap the fruits of our iniquities very many generations later.

O, Lord! Our God of mercy, gracious, slow to anger, abounding in mercy and loving-kindness and truth therefore we bring our repentance to you for all that we and our ancestors have done. We repent of the "spirit of Esau" – of selling our birthright, our brothers and sisters for the soup and the sustenance of the day. We beat our breasts and prostrate ourselves before You. We cry to you Father for mercy! Please let the blood of Jesus that washes all our sins and iniquity cleanse and release us from the curses that have bound us for so long.

Father, we also pray that You will restore our relationship with our brothers and sisters of African descent all over the world. Please let Your blood settle the feud and the justified offence that they have held against us in the realm of the spirit. We ask our brothers and sisters of African descent to please forgive the great sin we committed against you by selling you into slavery. Please restore us to true brotherhood through the blood of your Son Jesus Christ.

We also ask that the blood that was spilled on this continent through slavery, the blood that bears witness against us and that cries out for judgment – Lord! That cries out for judgment against us and our land. Father, we are asking today that the blood of Jesus that speaks better things, the blood of Jesus that covers a multitude of sins will cover and atone for the innocent blood that has been shed on this land.

We pray that the cry of that blood will be answered by the blood of Jesus who paid for all our sins in His own body.

Finally, Father, we ask that You will heal the land that has been a witness against us because of all our iniquities. We ask that you will remove the curse on the land of Africa and release the blessing on this great land.

We thank You because we are living in a time of restoration. Thank you, Lord, that we are living in a time of restoration of all things.

We pray all of this in Jesus' mighty name.

Amen.

14. A Troop is Coming

"For this child, I prayed, and the Lord has granted me my petition which I asked of Him." - 1 Samuel 1:27

"As soon as I saw you, I knew an adventure was going to happen." - Winnie the Pooh

I have been privileged to wear many different hats in my life. Of all the hats I wear, one that is nearest and dearest to my heart is that of a mother to our children. I always knew that I would love being a mom. I was that kid who always looked after other people's children. Even when I was very young, I felt the need to mother those who were younger than me, whether they liked it or not. I loved babysitting my aunts' babies and so whenever we had a relative visit us who was a young mother with a baby, I made it my job to become their constant assistant and shadow. As soon as I came home from school I would rush to visit my aunts and help them out with their babies. I loved everything about babies, their sweet smell, and all the paraphernalia that they came with such as cribs, bouncy chairs, bibs and baby bottles. I changed diapers, fed and burped them and then what fun it was to spend the afternoon playing with them.

As I grew up and left home, my interests and passions opened up a completely different world to me. One of academia and intellectual discourse. The world of big ideas that change and shape nations. I found a lot of satisfaction as I pursued knowledge and understanding, seeking out answers to my big audacious goals and questions. After college when my relationship with Odrek was going from strength to strength, a different kind of passion was reignited in me. The passion to get married and have a family of my own.

After Odrek and I got married, we settled into a quiet life as newlyweds. As was my habit, I started praying and talking to God about our dream of having a family. The Lord answered me by showing me a vision of a young man who was speaking and when he spoke his words came out of his mouth as fire. I wondered at that vision and asked the Lord about it. He said, **"you will have a son and My Word will be like fire in his mouth."**

That was not the first time the Lord prophesied to me about my children before they were even born. While I was still in University the Lord showed me a vision of a very sweet light skinned little girl with a big afro and dark eyes. I asked the Lord who that baby was and He answered me, **"That is your daughter."** The Lord later revealed to me that the little girl would be called, *Kendagaano*, which means in Runyankore, "a *child of the covenant.*"

I was used to hearing from the Lord about something before it happened. Sometimes I would realize belatedly that the Lord had spoken to me about something beforehand but I hadn't listened or paid careful attention. So when He prophesied to me about our children in advance, I hid those words in my heart and held onto His promises.

My younger sister, Diana, knowing that I was waiting on the Lord for the blessing of a baby, gave me a gift of some baby clothes. She encouraged me to put the baby clothes in my closet so that whenever I opened my closet, I saw them there and it would serve to reinforce my faith that indeed God's blessing was on the way. I did as she said and every time I opened my closet I saw the little blue newborn clothes and I remembered God's promise to me. **"Your son is on the way."** I felt the Lord's whisper every time I opened my closet and my faith grew.

A few months later, we discovered with joy that indeed God's word had come to pass and our son was on the way.

The kid who had always cared for other people's children was now going to be a mom! Those months as we awaited the birth of our first child were simply heavenly. I planned everything from the baby's nursery to the books and stuffed animals and numerous other baby things I wanted. I also started writing a journal for the baby because I wanted the baby to one day read a daily account of how I felt and what

I was doing while I carried him. Every day was a gift as I watched my tummy grow and started feeling the tiny and then strong kicks of this little person growing inside of me.

Odrek and I were still renting a flat in Kololo, a neighbourhood close to the centre of the city. However, it was our dream to live away from the city centre in our own home that would have a big garden and more space for a family.

As the pregnancy progressed we searched high and low for a home or land that we could buy for our "forever" home. As we looked at house after house, my disappointment grew and the possibility of us finding something we liked and buying it within the few months we had before the baby came seemed very slim indeed. I mentally cancelled the plan of having our own home right then and decided to prepare our little apartment for the new baby. We had one guest room and I painstakingly painted the room in baby blue clouds from the floor to the ceiling. I started decorating the room and looking for curtain fabric to match. I was in full-blown nesting mode, but my husband Odrek wasn't at all comfortable with our arrangement and he kept searching for our "forever" home.

One evening he delayed coming home after work. He arrived long after it was dark and his face was beaming with joy. He announced that he felt he had found our "forever" home. I was not so sure, I had seen enough houses to know that nothing fit our mould, but he seemed convinced. He said he would take me to see the house the next day with the land broker who had found it, a good friend called Tony Kirya. I hesitantly agreed. I was seven and a half months pregnant and felt like a beached whale, but I was interested to see what he had found.

The next afternoon, we made what seemed like a long journey from the city centre to a suburb that overlooked the Lake called Buziga. We branched off the main road to climb the hill where the house was located. It was a murram road that was in very bad condition. We rattled around in the car and with every hump and ditch, I felt contractions tighten around my tummy.

We finally got to the house and I fell in love with it instantly. It was on more than an acre of land overlooking the lake. It had a fresh breeze and wonderful panoramic views of the lake. The house was new and had never been lived in. It was a simple home perfect for our young family and with space to grow. It all seemed too good to be true. I couldn't hide the fact that I liked the house, the land and the neighbourhood. I never liked living in the city centre with all the traffic and noise. This neighbourhood was much more to my liking.

We talked to the land broker and he gave us more background on the owner who was selling. We had a lot to talk, think and pray about. As we drove home, I was excited about the possibilities this home offered us. It was perfect for us, but I was concerned about how much it would cost us. If the smaller houses and lands already cost so much, how much more would this land cost?

As I was mulling over these thoughts I kept wincing at the pain of contractions I was feeling. Since I was still a good one and a half months from being full term, I knew these were Braxton Hicks contractions which I experienced from time to time. But something was strange, they were much stronger than anything I had experienced before. By the time we got home, I wasn't feeling well at all. The contractions were coming stronger and stronger and I didn't know what to do. We decided to call the midwife I had been seeing to come and check on me. She hurried to our home even though it was getting late. On examining me, she worriedly announced that I was in full labour and the baby would be born by morning!

As she spoke those words something rose from deep within my spirit and answered that sentence with a resounding No! I spoke the word "No" out of my mouth but the Source had come from the Spirit of God in my spirit. I said, "My baby will be born full term." The midwife said it was almost inevitable that the baby would be born prematurely in the morning and would need to go in an incubator. I again said, "No, my baby will not be born prematurely."

The midwife asked my husband about his family's medical history and found that his mother had given birth to some children prematurely. So she said, this may be genetic and there is not much you can do about it. Again, I heard the Holy Spirit in me answer, "No."

Things happened quickly after that, the midwife called the gynecologist who prescribed some medication. They also wanted me to go to the hospital, but I pleaded with them to allow me to stay at home and be treated at home. I was confident that the Lord would settle the contractions if I rested at home. The doctor and midwife conferred and finally accepted that I could stay home for that night but they warned that if the contractions started again at night I must go straight to the hospital. We all agreed and they left.

I stayed up late that night; in my heart, I had complete peace. The Lord had not told me anything about my baby being born prematurely and so I didn't feel it was from Him. I trusted that the Lord would bring us through safely. The next morning the contractions had weakened significantly. The doctor came over to check on me and she said even though the contractions had weakened, we were not yet out of the woods. She put me on bed rest for the remaining months of my pregnancy.

I agreed to all the doctor's advice and stayed home mostly for the remaining months. As I prepared for the birth of our baby, winding up my work at the office and working from home, we were also praying about the house and land we had seen in Buziga. By then the owner had communicated the sale price and it was way over what we were looking to pay for a home. To make matters worse, there was a foreign non-governmental organization (NGO) that wanted to buy the house and use it as an office for their agency.

It seemed like it was all over, and that the NGO would get the house. However, in my spirit, I had a firm confirmation that the land would be ours. The Lord gave me a name for the land. He called it "Beulah" from Isaiah 62:4, "It will no longer be said of you, 'Abandoned,' nor will it any longer be said of your land, 'Desolate. But you will be called 'Hephzibah' (My delight is in her), and your land will be called 'Beulah' (Married). For the Lord delights in you, and to Him your land will be married (owned and protected by the Lord.)"

I felt a strong confirmation in my spirit that the Lord had given us the land, but, given the reality, it seemed almost inevitable that we wouldn't get it. So we continued to pray and we made our counter-offer which was lower than what the seller wanted. The seller was a foreigner, who had built the home thinking they would live in the country longer, but then had been quickly transferred to another country and was looking to offload the property. They were a married couple. We made our offer and prayed and waited.

In the meantime, they learnt that we were a young couple with a baby on the way, and the wife took a liking to us. She asked to meet with us and took great pains to come and see us. She was an older woman and she shared with us how much they loved the land and how if they couldn't live in the land, they wanted a family to live in the land and not for it to be an office. We saw the favour of God throughout our interactions with this couple and finally, going against everything that seemed rational, they agreed to sell the house to us. It was a huge testimony to the Grace and favour of God that gives His children more than they could ever ask or even imagine. We paid a down payment and then got a bank mortgage to cover the balance. Within a few short months, the transaction was ready when our baby was born. God had again gone ahead of us and done the impossible.

During my weeks on bed rest, I had time to pray and seek the Lord about this new journey of motherhood that I was about to embark on. I suddenly felt very apprehensive about being a mother recognizing that it was very different from just babysitting other people's children. I realized I didn't even know the first thing about being a mother! What was I thinking? I panicked! How could I be responsible for a whole other human being? What if I made a mistake? What if I messed up? During my panic attack, I heard my voice answer my troubled thoughts, "don't worry, you can give the baby to Ginga."

"Ginga" is the name that our children call my mom, their grandmother. As that thought entered my mind, I felt relief. Ginga, my mom, of course, is the epitome of responsible motherhood. She would know what to do with a baby and she wouldn't make any mistakes, I thought.

God interrupted my self-talk with His calm and still Voice. He said, **"Don't be afraid, I will help you."**

When I heard God's Voice, He stilled the storm that was in my heart. The fear and panic that had gripped my heart melted away. God, my God and Father, the One who had carried me through so many new beginnings and chapters. He would be with me, He would help and carry me into this new chapter of motherhood.

As my due date drew closer, my father phoned me. He jokingly asked me if I was ready to "fight my battle." By this, he was referring to going through the pain of labour. I laughed and said God would help me through it. Since this was my first delivery, I had no clue what he was talking about. He then went on to tell me a story about sheep and goats. He said that the sheep keep quiet even when they are going to be slaughtered, but the goats make a lot of noise. Finally, he concluded, "now you are going to fight your bush war, please be a sheep and not a goat."

I laughed at his analogy, but I got the point. Be brave, be strong. This is your battle.

After weeks of bed rest, on the 9th of November 2003, at exactly 10:30 pm, our firstborn son, Mumutiine Rubanza was born. It is hard to explain the emotion and feeling when a child is born. I'm sure every mother will agree that it is a holy experience. I always felt there were angels in the delivery room when any of our children were born. It felt like there was a clashing of thunder, and lightning, a chorus of "Hallelujahs" and electricity filling the air.

The first night I spent as a new mom with my baby in the room with me was truly a holy night. The hospital had a policy that no one could share the room with me and so, for that first night, I was alone with my baby and God. I remember that the room was dimly lit and his little cot was close to my bed. As I sat gazing at this perfect baby, I was humbled and speechless at the awesome Grace of God. I had no words to articulate my emotions to God. I could feel His Presence with me in the room. He formed a golden halo around me, I felt enveloped in His embrace. The glory cloud filled the quiet room. My journey of motherhood began on a still quiet night in a cloud of God's glory.

Oh and thankfully I was a sheep.....

Exactly seventeen months later, I was back in the hospital. This time, it was to give birth to our second-born child, a beautiful and peaceful baby girl.

Following the birth of our firstborn son, life became a glorious blur. Nights fell into days and into nights again. Our son was a pure ball of energy, so much so that we likened him to the energizer bunny in the battery commercials. He kept us all on our toes running after him as he learnt to crawl, stand and then walk very quickly. He was always running, laughing, jumping and pulling things down from wherever we placed them. Soon we removed all the breakable and delicate objects from our tables because he gravitated to anything shiny and noisy.

Amid all the activity we discovered the happy news that God was giving us another blessing of a baby. Soon the morning sickness was unbearable and I felt that I couldn't keep anything down, including water.

The morning sickness was so bad, I felt that I was dying. Finally, I got some relief when the doctor put me on a drip for some days to regain energy. After the initial stormy months, things settled down and I was happy and full of joy.

The second time around went by so fast because we were very busy with our first born who was still a baby. He learnt to stand, walk and run all during the months of my pregnancy. I kept a journal again so that the baby would know all the emotions and milestones we were experiencing daily. When we learnt that our baby was a little girl, we were over the moon with happiness.

By this time we were settled in our home, Beulah and so I could prepare the baby's room comfortably knowing that this was our home. I relished decorating in all the pastel pinks and whites. I loved looking at baby catalogues and seeing what would go best with my theme for the baby's room.

As the months progressed, I got in touch with a doctor in Nairobi Hospital in Kenya who was recommended to me by a relative. Dr. S. R. Patel was a very experienced doctor and we developed a rapport as I spoke to him and got to know him better. As my due date drew closer, we made plans to travel to Nairobi to be close to the doctor and have the baby there.

One day when we went for a routine checkup the doctor questioned why I looked so tired. I felt very heavy and tired but I imagined it was simply because of how far along I was in the pregnancy. The doctor wasn't convinced and did some tests to check my hemoglobin levels. As he suspected it was very low, so much so that he said I would need to have a blood transfusion after delivery. Again, I felt the Holy Spirit "No!" rise within me. I hadn't heard from the Lord about this and I felt that it wasn't from Him. However, I wanted to cooperate with the doctor. As such I agreed to whatever he advised. I trusted the Lord would carry us through as He had always done and there would be no need for a blood transfusion.

The next week I went into the hospital and the doctor had blood from my blood group ready for transfusion after delivery. As the contractions and labour started in earnest in the middle of the night, I kept praying that the baby would come by morning. It was a long night, in the labour ward I could hear women in different stages of labour; some screaming and shouting for the nurse or doctor. My husband, Odrek, who was with me in the labour ward was very traumatized by the whole experience. He sat outside in the hallway and wrote a twelve-page letter to our soon-to-be-born daughter. He said that, for the first time, he recognized what his mother who had borne seven children went through. He said that he had tremendous respect for women who went through this experience, not just once but again and again. He said if it was up to men, there would be fewer people on the earth.

In all the labour and pain, I could always feel the Lord's Presence beside me, as though He was holding my hand and comforting me. God heard my prayers and at exactly 7:52 am, our daughter Kendagaano Mwangangye was born. A very light-skinned baby who turned beet red when she cried. Dr. Patel who had become a dear friend to us held up the baby and said, "this is where all your blood was going!"

In the freshness of the morning, I heard the clashing of thunder and the lightning in the spirit. I felt as though the room was filled with angels, as God's Presence enveloped us once again. That morning, the doctor checked my blood level and instead of dropping lower as was expected, it had gone up. God made sure that I didn't get a blood transfusion just as I had prayed. It is a long-running joke between my daughter and me that she took way too much blood and oxygen while she was in the womb. Whenever I am scolding her or telling her off, I jokingly remind her that we once shared blood and oxygen and so she should always do what I tell her to do.

After the birth of our daughter, my hands were full. I had two babies at home both under the age of 18 months. My nights were full of night feeds and diaper changes and my days were filled with tummy time and playing together with our active toddler. It was indeed a precious time and I loved every minute of it.

I was extremely thankful that, as an entrepreneur, I could make my own time and didn't have to leave the children at home to go to work. I was able to stay at home with them and only leave for a few hours to have meetings at the office or even schedule meetings at home when it was necessary. The Lord revealed to me, ahead of time as He always did, that our next child would be born when our daughter was four years old. He spoke to me clearly and said, **"When Kiki is four years old, you will have a son, and you will call him Judah because you will praise Me."**

I received that Word and hid it in my heart. I knew that the Lord was giving me time to focus on our very young family. A year after the birth of our daughter, Covenant Nations Church was born in our home and the work of the ministry also needed time to stabilize.

God's Word never returns to Him void but must accomplish what He sends it out to do. When our daughter was entering her fourth year and our firstborn son was five years old, we discovered with joy that we were expecting again; right on time according to God's timetable.

I was now a more experienced mom, but I still always relied on the Lord for His help and Grace to carry me through. I had learnt so far that prayer is the daily partner of a mother. We pray when a child runs a temperature at night or has a bad fall. We pray when they are going to school for the first time or when they are going for immunization. We pray when they don't make friends and we pray when they make the wrong friends. We pray before their examinations and when they are making major life choices. Motherhood is one long unending prayer. But what is amazing is that God answers. He answers the desperate cries for help and the long midnight talks. He hears and He answers. I have for many years kept a prayer journal and I am amazed at the many prayers that God has answered. The seemingly small and insignificant prayers and the big breakthrough prayers. He hears them all, and He gives attention to us whenever we cry out to Him. Sometimes it is just that heartfelt cry from a mother's lips, "Jesus." Or for me, "Yeshua." He hears all. And answers. Always.

My third pregnancy came at a different stage in my life. I was a little older and I had the experience of my first two children who, at that time, were out of their toddler years.

Odrek and I had opted to homeschool our children when we found a system that worked well for us and so it was a peaceful season in our lives. Things at church had also started to stabilize after the first shaky years and our businesses were growing and thriving. Our lives were certainly busy but a little more structured.

My third pregnancy was quiet and peaceful, I didn't have the extreme morning sickness that I experienced with my daughter. There was discomfort but it was bearable. The pregnancy progressed peacefully and when I was around seven months pregnant, I prayed and asked the Lord to help me have a peaceful delivery. I had noticed that things usually got a bit bumpy for me around seven months into my pregnancy. That had been my experience with our older children. I didn't want a repeat of what had happened with the bed rest and the low blood levels and I sought the Lord about it. I heard the Lord answer me. He said, **"Take Holy Communion at home every day until the baby is born."**

This sounded like a strange instruction to me. I usually took Holy Communion at church with other believers and also a few times while attending fellowship with family members. However, God instructed me to take Holy Communion daily for the remainder of my pregnancy. I didn't understand it but I knew His Voice and I was sure He was speaking to me so I obeyed.

For the remaining months, I took communion every day and it was such a precious blessing. As I partook of the Lord's Supper I put my faith in the body and blood of Jesus to carry me through the remaining months of pregnancy and to give me a safe delivery. Every day I prayed and felt my faith grow stronger. God's peace mounted up a defence over my heart and mind and I knew all would be well. I went through the remaining weeks of my pregnancy without incident and, as I came closer to my due date, I prepared for the birth of our baby.

We again chose to deliver our baby at Nairobi Hospital, with the help of our dear friend Dr. S. R. Patel, a wonderful doctor that we had developed a close-knit relationship with since the birth of our daughter. I continued taking Holy Communion until the day I went into the hospital to deliver our baby.

As I went into labour, the doctor couldn't understand what was holding up the contractions. They seemed to start and then stop without any reason. Sometimes they came strong and fast and then they slowed down. This went on for most of the day and by evening nothing had happened. The doctor said the baby would probably be born in the morning. By this time I was quite tired after being in labour since the day before.

My sister Natasha, who had come to the hospital to help me, brought a prayer book. I started praying and asking the Lord what was wrong and for His help. As I prayed, I felt His Presence take over as He had done so many times before. The fear and anxiety of what could be wrong melted away and I felt His peace. The doctor left after checking me and my husband Odrek came to spend the night as my sister went home to get some sleep. It was around midnight and it didn't seem like anything was going to happen during the night. I tried to get some sleep, but the contractions started growing in strength and intensity. At around 2 am, I called the midwife and told her the contractions were coming very strongly. She checked and kept monitoring me. In a few minutes, they were so strong that I couldn't even stand to walk. I knew that the baby was coming soon and they called Dr. Patel. It was very dramatic as they tried to hurriedly wheel me into the delivery room as I was bearing down and feeling the baby coming. My sister, who had just reached home, got a call from Odrek saying that the baby was coming and she dashed back to the hospital just in time to hear the cry of our newborn baby boy!

Our son Judah Nyentsya was born at 3:42 am. I felt the angels that I always felt in the delivery room and the sound of lightning and thunder in my spirit. The glory cloud of the Lord covered the room as we all gave thanks for the safe delivery of our baby. As soon as our son was born, Dr. Patel noticed something strange on the umbilical cord of the baby. There was a knot and he showed it to Odrek as he asked him to cut the cord. He said, "this is probably the reason that the labour was not progressing. It is called a true knot and occurs in one in one thousand babies." He went on to say that if at any time during the labour or pregnancy, the knot had tightened, it would have immediately cut off the blood and oxygen supply to the baby and that would have been the end. Odrek asked how they might never have seen this during the scan. How could they miss it?

The doctor explained that during the scan they always take a section of the chord to check that the blood flow to the baby was flowing well, but because the chord is so long they cannot check the whole chord. In any case, even if they knew there was a true knot, there was nothing they could do to remove it. Odrek asked when this could have happened. The doctor answered that it must have happened months prior when the baby was still small enough to jump and turn around in the womb and get the chord tied in a knot. He asked specifically when he thought this happened and he answered that it must have been by six months.

I recalled that the Lord instructed me to take Holy Communion every day starting at seven and a half months onwards. Later on, when Odrek and the doctor shared this situation with me, I marvelled at the preserving power of God. I understood why the Lord led me to take Holy Communion; it was to preserve the life of our baby while in the womb. As we partake of the Lord's supper we are proclaiming the death of the Lord Jesus in our stead. The great exchange of the Lord standing in our place and taking in His body the punishment that was ours, and we receive the righteousness and justification that is His by faith. As we partake of the blood and the body of Jesus we are by faith appropriating all that Jesus' body represents. Wholeness, healing, deliverance, restoration, peace and so much more. For me, partaking of the Lord's table meant preservation for our baby in the womb, a place that only God could see and protect him. I was so humbled and overwhelmed by the goodness of God, and it gave me a new level of appreciation and love for the blessing of partaking from the Lord's Table. We have shared this remarkable testimony with our son, Judah, as he has grown. We let him know that God preserved him when he was in the womb and that He will always look after him.

With three young children life was beautiful and full. Our older children doted on their baby brother and the larger family of cousins, aunties, uncles and grandparents, church family and friends did so too.

Life became busy with family on the home front, our growing church family and our burgeoning businesses. Our businesses had grown to focus in a big way on agribusiness and in particular dairy farming. When our son Judah was two years old we made the difficult decision to move from the city to live on our farm to supervise our work better. We had a vision of processing dairy products directly from the farm working with our network of farmers and having a processing plant in the hinterland.

Our move to the farm was to give more focus to this work and to actively run the operations while living at the farm.

Our family loved living on the land. The children loved farm life, and the freedom of space, fresh air, no traffic jams and no congestion. They enjoyed playing out till late, camping under the stars, feeding the calves and just exploring the outdoors. Homeschool was a Godsend for us because it helped us give our children the best education at home in those early foundational years.

A few years after moving to the farm, when our children were a little older and the dream of establishing a processing plant was becoming a reality, I felt led by the Lord to return to the city to actively run the church programmes personally. It was a difficult decision to return to the city because I loved our life on the farm, I loved the peace I felt there and the freedom it gave our young children. But I knew the Lord had spoken to me and so we packed up and made the move back to the city.

When our son Judah was four years old, the Lord again spoke to me about blessing us with another child. I dreamt that the Lord visited me in my room and asked me to open my mouth to swallow something with a spoon. When I looked at the spoon as I opened my mouth I saw a beautiful baby girl on the spoon. I knew then that the Lord was telling me to prepare for a beautiful bundle of joy.

A few months after that we discovered the joyous news that we were expecting again. The morning sickness returned with a vengeance and that was our first confirmation that it was a baby girl. In my experience, I found that, for me, my pregnancies for baby girls had a lot of morning sickness. The morning sickness was so bad that I had to ask for treatment to get some relief. After the first trimester things settled down a bit and the rest of the pregnancy progressed smoothly. The baby grew strong and my tummy grew bigger and bigger. By my final trimester, I felt as big as a whale. As always God gave me the strength to work at church until the 9th month. Our church family had a wonderful prayer send-off during my last Sunday service before my leave started. It was a wonderful time filled with prayers and blessings from all our friends and family at church.

God gave me the strength to work and do all that I needed to do without any trouble and I was so grateful for His blessing all through the pregnancy. As I neared my due date, the Lord kept bringing to my mind Isaiah 66:7. Which says, "Before Zion travailed she gave birth, before her pain came upon her, she was delivered of a son. Who has heard of such a thing? Who has seen such things? Shall a land be born in one day? Or shall a nation be brought forth in a moment? For as soon as Zion was in labour, she brought forth her children. Shall I bring to the moment of birth and not cause to bring forth?" says the Lord. Shall I who cause to bring forth shut the womb? says your God."

I knew the Lord was communicating something to me but I tried to ignore His Voice. I knew He was telling me that something would be different with this delivery. After walking with the Lord for all these years, I can feel when He is sending me a message, and He was sending me a message but I didn't want to receive it. During my last doctor's appointment, the doctor told me that the baby was very big and he was concerned that delivery would be difficult. By then I was experiencing contractions on and off. He advised that I go home and return the next week and if the contractions were still coming strong, he would recommend a caesarean section.

I had never had a c-section and I didn't want to have one. I kept praying that I wouldn't need to have one but deep in my spirit I knew that the Lord had already told me that this would happen. We went home for the weekend and I spent time taking long walks around our neighbourhood. The following Monday, we returned to the doctor's office and he did a full check. After the physical examination, we met with him in his office. He told us that he felt the baby's size and the fact that my blood pressure was unstable made him feel that the best option was to proceed with the c-section. He insisted that his first concern was for the health of the baby and my health and he didn't feel it was safe to wait for labour to start naturally. He said it wasn't part of his initial plan but the baby needed to be delivered that very day.

His words hit us like an avalanche. I had never had a c-section and didn't know what it entailed. I was used to having our children naturally and was very concerned about the procedure. However, in my heart, I knew the Lord had already told me this would happen and as such I felt that this was His plan for me this time. I slowly accepted the doctor's plan and we were immediately taken to the ward to be admitted. I had the greater part of the day, to pray about what was going to happen. In my heart, I felt this strange unexplainable peace. I knew that the Lord was in this even though I couldn't understand why. My husband called my mother, sisters and prayer warrior friends and asked them to pray for us. He let them know it was going to be a c-section and asked them all to pray. By evening, I was wheeled into the cold theatre room where local anesthesia was administered. I remember vividly being placed on the operating table and not being able to feel anything from the neck down. As I blinked and squinted in the bright light of the operating room, I felt all alone and helpless. During natural labour there was the sense of being a participant in the process of bringing a baby to birth, there was something beautiful and powerful in all the blood, sweat and tears. But in this sterile and cold environment where I couldn't even move my body, I felt alone and afraid. I spoke in my heart, "Lord I'm alone here."

He answered me immediately, **"I'm here with you."**

I choked back tears, "I can't do anything, I am helpless."

He answered, **"I will do it all.**"

I felt His Presence in that theatre room as I had never experienced Him before. At the point of my greatest weakness, I experienced His strength and saw His glory. I realized the truth of the scripture that says, "My grace is sufficient for you for My strength is made perfect in weakness. When I am weak, then I am strong."(2 Corinthians 12:9)

Before the operation began, my husband was ushered in dressed from head to toe in the blue theatre scrubs. He spoke to me reassuringly as the doctors began the procedure.

In a few moments, as they lifted our newborn baby girl and we heard her piercing cry, I felt the presence of angels in the room in a greater way than I ever had before. There was the peeling of thunder and lightning that reverberated in my spirit. Our beautiful baby Gigi Hadarah was born at exactly 5:55 pm. She weighed in at over 4 kgs, the biggest baby born in the ward and the biggest of our babies. I felt tears of joy rolling down my cheeks as I heard her beautiful strong cry. She was gorgeous and I couldn't stop crying.

The doctor spoke to me after the operation and confided that he was happy that we agreed to the c-section as he advised because he found that the baby had shown signs of distress and that he was glad we opted for immediate delivery. He also said that the baby was so big and with my blood pressure being unstable, he knew it would have been difficult to have the baby naturally. I was so overjoyed at the birth of our baby that I didn't even think about the procedure anymore. The doctor expressed again his surprise at the size and weight of the baby, he asked me if all my babies were that big. As I began to answer his question, I felt the Lord speak into my spirit. He said, **"It is the weight of My glory."**

And how true that was! Our daughter was carrying the weight of God's glory and God ensured that she had a safe delivery despite all my concerns.

Our daughter was the talk of the whole maternity ward as midwives came to see the big baby that was born. The midwives cooed over Gigi and talked about how beautiful she was. We were filled with joy unspeakable and full of glory.

A few days later when I returned to the hospital to have my wound dressed, I could see that the mood in the doctor's office was subdued and low. As the midwife changed my dressing I could sense the heaviness in her spirit. She was usually a jolly and effervescent person but that day she was quiet and sad. I finally asked her if there was anything wrong. She sadly shared with me that a woman, who was due at the same time as me, was scheduled to have her baby delivered by c-section. She said that all seemed well and routine, but by the time they did the procedure they found that the child had died in the womb and they had to remove the lifeless baby. I was speechless as she narrated the sad story of this woman and her loss. I knew that if it weren't for the grace of God this could be me, and I was more grateful than ever for the Lord's hand that constantly guided, directed, preserved and protected us. I knew that the Lord allowed me to have the c-section for the preservation of my life and that of our daughter. He who sees the end from the beginning always knows the best route to take to get us to where He wants us to be.

It reinforced the importance of allowing the Lord to lead me even when He seemed to be leading in an unusual way or in a path that we had never walked before. As long as the Lord is leading, we can be sure He will get us to the place He wants us to be. As I returned home, I felt deep pain for that other woman who had lost so much. I was beyond grateful for the blessing of our beautiful daughter, and for my Heavenly Father who delivered her miraculously. Her life is a testament that when the Lord's anointing is upon you, you carry the weight of His Glory.

The birth of each of our children was always as unique as the child born. Motherhood has been one of the greatest gifts and blessings in my life and it is a journey I have given myself wholeheartedly to. As our children have grown out of the baby years and into the teenage years, I have continued to witness the Grace of God as He has proven that He is truly the All-Sufficient God. His Grace is more than enough, for every situation and every season. Life is a relentless journey moving us from the place of birth until we finally return to the God who gave us life. It is like standing on those moving escalators you find in airports, it keeps moving even when you are standing still. The older I grow, I realize that every day, our lives are moving whether you stand still or run, your life is moving somewhere. It is up to us, therefore, to make up our minds to embrace the journey, the process, the growth and change and allow God to work in our lives through all these changing seasons.

There is so much for us to learn through all the different seasons of life if we will open our hearts to receive the miracles that God has in store for us. Whether it is in the sleep deprivation, midnight feeding and diaper changes of new motherhood, the busyness and activity of the toddler years, or the homework, spellings, times tables and parent-teacher meetings of the childhood years and the growing pains of teenage years. Each season has a gift that God holds out for us, and we must grow, change, learn and be transformed in the process. Just like the caterpillar that is transformed into a beautiful butterfly through a process of pressure and change, so we must allow God to mould us and change us through all the seasons of life. As a mother, I started out thinking I was the one to teach my children everything, after all, I was the mom now.

Over the years, though, I have found that even though God has placed me in the position of teacher, and I do teach them so much, I have also learnt so much from each of my children. Each of them has a gift, a grace, an anointing from God that He has blessed them with to be a blessing to others. I have learnt that so often it is in the chaos of the ordinary, that life happens, that the beautiful diamonds in the rough are revealed. Being a mother demands all of your focus, time, energy, attention, love, patience, forgiveness and so much more. It is endless hours of doing seemingly the same repetitive activities day in and day out. And if you don't pay attention, you can miss the miracles happening every day in the mundane. Whether it is a child taking their first steps, saying their first words, or learning to read, write or ride a bicycle; those moments and the millions of tiny seemingly insignificant moments of the journey of a mother cumulatively added together, create a beautiful tapestry of a life well loved.

These last two years have been a very difficult season of feeling like God is stretching me far beyond the limits of my comfort. I found myself anxious, emotional and apprehensive about my children growing up and leaving home for the first time. I cried many tears as I watched old home videos, and looked at old photo albums. In my mind was only one thought, "how quickly did the time go by.."

The separation anxiety of having my children leave home made me realize how strong the bond between a mother and child is. How much of yourself you give away to this little person who eventually grows and when they are leaving home, they take your heart with them. "Did I over-invest in my children?" I thought. Then one day the Lord answered my internal thoughts through the teachings of a great Christian speaker called Sono Harris who has already gone home to be with the Lord.

After sharing a very humorous story of her separation anxiety when her eldest son got married and left home, she said, "Don't be afraid to give your heart away to your children, so that when they leave home and start their own lives, you have something to lose."

As I listened to her speak I realized that my separation anxiety was not a sign that there was something wrong, but rather that there was something right. I had given myself away to my children and I had so much to lose because I gave them my whole heart. As painful as it was, I was so happy that I gave them all of myself from the very beginning. It doesn't make it easier, but it does mean there are no regrets. In the words of the great comedic genius Jerry Seinfeld, when he was asked if he wanted to go back and do his hit comedy show all over again, he answered, "No, what would I do differently?" He meant he had given 110% of himself to the show when it was made and there was nothing he would add or take away from it. It was his magnum opus, his life's work. Motherhood, for me, is like that, and I thank God that His Grace has been sufficient for me every single day since my troop invaded my life and painted it all with broad strokes of beautiful colours.

15. The Need for a Return

"At Basel, I founded the Jewish State. If I said this out loud today, I would be answered by universal laughter. Perhaps in five years, and certainly fifty, everyone will know it." – Theodore Hertzl, First Zionist Congress. Switzerland 1897

The summer of 2020 was a watershed moment in global race relations following the brutal killing of George Floyd. The world watched in transfixed horror at the violence and turmoil in America following the killing of an innocent man that was recorded by a bystander. This video clip went viral and people from all over the world watched the death of an innocent man right before their eyes. This wasn't a movie, it was real life and this was a real man crying out for help and receiving none.

In the days following the incident the city of Minneapolis, where George Floyd was killed descended into absolute chaos with protestors clashing with police every day and rioting, looting and burning the city.

The protests also spread to many other major cities in America. This was all happening against the backdrop of the global pandemic of Covid-19 which had kept most people and cities in lockdown mode for months. The fact that so many were willing to risk going out to protest during a global pandemic speaks to the sense of shock and horror that everyday people felt.

This is not the first time that the world has seen images of African American men and women being harassed and even killed by the police in America. Over the past couple of years and, especially with the coming of smartphones and social media, one horrific moment can be captured by a bystander and beamed all over the world in a matter of minutes.

We have all seen the hashtags reminding people of the lives of innocent African American men and women that have been tragically and senselessly snuffed out by law enforcement that abuse their authority.

They are far too common to ignore or call isolated incidents. #Philando Castile# #Trayvon Martin #Sandra Bland #Ahmed #Aubry #Eric Garner #Michael Brown and sadly the list goes on.

And what about the city of Minneapolis which became the epicentre of this race war? If there ever was an unlikely suspect in the war between the races, it would be Minnesota. How do I know this?

Well, Minnesota, and Minneapolis in particular, was my home for four years. I attended the University of Minnesota located in the Twin Cities of Minneapolis and St. Paul.

For four years, I lived, studied and made lifelong friends in that city. I grew as a person, spiritually, emotionally and intellectually. The core of my beliefs about my country, Uganda and my continent, Africa and our place in the world were formulated in their most nascent form in Minnesota. I sought answers, both through knowledge and through deep times of prayer and soul searching in Minnesota.

The earliest European immigrants who settled in Minnesota came from the Nordic countries, especially Sweden. Americans in Minnesota tend to have the same culture and outlook as the Scandinavian people, which is humane, embracing people from all walks of life and very philanthropic. The United States opened its doors to more than 100,000 Somali refugees at the height of the civil war in Somalia. Today, the largest Somali population in the U.S. resides in Minnesota. The area they reside in Minneapolis has such a high Somali population that it is popularly known as "Mogadishu," after the capital of Somalia.

The Somali community had access to education, many young Somalis went on to study up to the university level, and recently one such immigrant rose to the rank of Congresswoman representing her area and her people. Representative Ilhan Omar immigrated to Minnesota as a refugee at a tender age; she now represents her congressional district, courtesy of the large number of voters from her community.

I remember the Somali community of Minneapolis well because I volunteered to teach English as a second language to the older Somali women who spoke only their native language. During my time volunteering, I spent many afternoons with these wonderful old ladies who were trying to adjust to their new lives in a new country.

There is one memory I have involving the Somali community and the Minnesota weather that I cannot easily forget. It was winter and Minnesota winters are legendary; I had concluded my afternoon session with my students and they all hurried to their homes. I took some time to clean up the class and gather my teaching materials. As I did this, when I looked out of the window, I realized there was a blizzard coming in. I had no car and knew that there wouldn't be any public transportation during a blizzard. Zero visibility meant that driving would be dangerous for motorists.

I couldn't stay alone in the community centre indefinitely for the whole evening; so I said a prayer and started the arduous journey back to the university campus on foot. The whole landscape was white with snow covering signposts, roads, cars and buildings. I knew that if I made the wrong turn there was a very real danger of exposure to the cold and possible frostbite. I kept praying and asking God to lead me to the main highway where I could find my way back. That day I experienced the guiding Hand of God, directing my footsteps and leading me to safety during a blizzard. When I arrived safely at my dorm, my friends couldn't believe that I had walked the whole distance on foot in a blizzard. That was the Grace of God.

In my final year, I also got to meet with some of the elders of the Somali community to interview them for my dissertation which was focused on the development of two African nations post-independence, Somalia and Botswana.

Uganda has been lauded internationally for our government's policy toward welcoming refugees and we host refugee communities from many countries in our region, including Congo, Rwanda, Burundi, South Sudan, Somalia and Ethiopia.

In Uganda, refugees from other African countries such as Rwanda and immigrants from non-African countries such as India have been able to rise to leadership positions such as Members of Parliament, Cabinet ministers and other high-ranking positions of Government. That being said, the rapid integration and rise of the Somali community in Minnesota are noteworthy and commendable.

I recall fondly the many lifelong friends I and my family made in Minnesota. One such friend was the late Reverend Arthur Rouner and his wife, Molly. They were dear friends of my parents, who had spent their lives serving God as pastors of a Church in Suburban Minnesota. Rev. Arthur felt the call to begin doing mission trips to Africa in the mid-1980s to help support vulnerable communities in Uganda. His work brought him to Uganda and he was introduced to Maama Janet Museveni who was at that time doing a lot of work for orphans under her charity UWESO(Uganda Women's Effort to Save Orphans).

Rev. Arthur Rouner and his congregation, committed to supporting Maama Janet Museveni's work in UWESO (Uganda Women's Effort to Save Orphans) and did so for many years. His commitment to missions in Africa ultimately brought misunderstandings between him and his church leaders who asked him to choose between his role as a Pastor in America and his mission work in Africa. Rev. Arthur made the bold choice to serve God and continue his work in Africa and was asked to resign and hand over his pastorship in the church. He spent the last 25 years of his life serving refugee communities in Africa working for reconciliation in many communities that had experienced civil war like Rwanda, Burundi, South Sudan and the cattle-raiding tribes In western Kenya and Eastern Uganda.

I can go on and on talking about the many good people that I came to know personally and the many others that I have heard of and seen the positive and uplifting work they do from a distance: however, the point I am trying to make is that the lives, purpose and actions of these people seem to be wiped out in one moment when the evil actions of one man are all we can see.

Therefore, this place and these people should not and cannot be judged by the evil actions of one man. Their cumulative history cannot be reduced to the murderous actions of one policeman.

The presence of good people in any society doesn't negate the very real issues of injustice and racism that exist in the system. It just means that the system determines who benefits and who doesn't, based on the colour of your skin.

So, what recourse do we have? Why is it that it seems that even with all the protests and activism and effort that well-meaning people put in and the passage of time, the same old problems keep cropping up? Someone said, "the more things change, the more they stay the same."

Why do things stay the same? How can young African Americans still be protesting police brutality in 2020 when their great-grandparents built America with their unwillingly given slave labour?

Is it possible that we are asking the wrong questions and looking for change in the wrong places?

The Bible declares in Psalm 11:3: "*If the foundations be destroyed, what shall the righteous do.*"This simply means that if the foundations of the building are wrong, the building may go up and look tall and shiny on the outside, but any shaking will reveal deep cracks and instability on the inside. You cannot build on the wrong foundations. The Passage of time doesn't legitimize the wrong foundations.

The year 2019 marked the 400th annual milestone of the slave trade in America and I was privileged to attend a special prayer breakfast at the African Union in Addis Ababa hosted by President Uhuru Kenyatta of Kenya. He invited other African leaders including our own President Museveni to attend and speak on the topic of "the Return, marking the 400th anniversary". The theme for the prayer breakfast was "2019 the Year of the Return." This spoke of the 400-year commemoration of the Atlantic Slave Trade that saw the forceful and violent removal of millions of young Africans from Africa to work as slaves in South America, the Caribbean and North America.

During the breakfast, there were representatives of the African American faith community led by Bishop Claude Alexander and the U.S. government with Dr. Jendayi Fraser, a former Assistant Secretary of State for African Affairs.

In their remarks, both speakers spoke of the need for African Americans and people of African descent all over the world to begin the spiritual, emotional, social, economic and even physical return to the land of their ancestry, Africa.

Some of the ideas they put forward were:

- Cultural exchanges with students from Africa and African Americans;
- No visa requirement for any African Americans returning to Africa;
- Promotion and networking of African business with African Americans especially with a goal towards trade and partnership to enhance cultural linkages;
- Tourism promotion for both Africans and African Americans to better understand the others' culture and history.

The year 2019 was called the *Year of the Return* and many people of African descent from around the world made the pilgrimage back to Africa some even took on secondary citizenship in the lands of their ancestry. In his remarks to his counterparts during the prayer breakfast, President Yoweri Museveni submitted that whereas cultural and economic linkage was good, the real focus must be on the political and economic integration of Africa. His firm position was that it is only when the African continent is strong, that the people of African descent around the world will be able to have a more formidable and secure position. Therefore, the focus of African leadership must be on the political and economic integration of the weak and balkanized states of Africa that were carved up by the colonialists. It is only in our unity that we can begin to project our unique worldview, with policies and positions that reflect our interests as Africans. His Address to the General Assembly was a prophetic call to African leaders to integrate or be defeated by the world powers that have always sought to divide and conquer us.

African people were scattered all over the Americas as a result of the collusion between the bankrupt African chiefs and the white thieves. The original weakness was here in Africa and is still here.

Honest confrontation of our past is the beginning of the healing and I believe that the full restoration of Africa and her sons and daughters will come in phases. The role of the African Church is pivotal in discipling the nations to move at the moment that we are living in. A unique Gate of time that probably only comes by once in the history of a people. I believe this is such a time.

The African Church must be able to hear what the Spirit is saying in this time and season. The Great move of God that generations of Africans have been praying and waiting for is upon us and the Church must be prepared to carry this move in the spirit realm so that it is birthed into the earth realm. God is always looking for people to stand in the Gap to be able to midwife and birth His plans and purposes, if those people are not in a position or are distracted or ignorant of what the Lord's will and purpose is, they miss their moment of visitation. That is an indescribable tragedy and my prayer has been that Africa should not miss her moment of visitation. The responsibility of the Church is to do spiritual warfare to see the Will and Purposes of God prevail on the earth.

God prophesied to Abraham what would happen to his descendants in Egypt saying in Genesis 15:13-14:

> *"Know positively that your descendants will be strangers dwelling as temporary residents in a land that is not theirs, and they will be slaves there and will be afflicted and oppressed for 400 years. But I will bring judgement on that nation whom they will serve and afterwards, I will bring them out with great possessions." – Amplified Bible*

Here, the Lord was speaking about the bondage of the children of Israel and the fact that people can be strangers and temporary residents in a land even when they have been there for 400 years. Is it possible that African Americans and people of African descent all over the world have been strangers and residents in the lands of their bondage and is it possible that that is precisely the reason why after all these years, the large majority of people remain on the fringes of the society, never fully possessing the inheritance and promise of the land as their very own? Is it possible that there is a great Return on the horizon for people of African descent to return to the land of their ancestry and find peace for their hearts, souls and minds? Is it possible that as we pass through this great gate of time, the 400-year milestone, the ancient doors and foundations of peoples, lands and nations that have been silent for so long, can no longer hold the blood and guilt in those foundations? Is it possible that we are living through a time of Exodus?

Acts 17:26 declares:

> *"And He made from one common origin (source, blood) all the nations of men to settle on the face of the earth, having definitely determined their allotted periods of time and the boundaries of their habitation(their settlements, lands and abodes). So that they should seek for God, in the hope that they might find Him, although He is not far from each one of us." – Amplified Bible*

In essence, this scripture declares that all the peoples of the earth come from one common origin or family and that God pre-determined the lands that He had given to the peoples of the earth and there is a redemptive purpose that is unlocked when people understand their relationship with God and their relationship with the land God has given them. I believe that God created this Great continent of Africa for African people and that there is a redemptive gift that is unlocked when African people in their land are reconnected to their relationship with God and their relationship with the land He gave them.

What does that mean for the people of African descent who were carried away as slaves?

I would like to answer that by looking at the case of the Jewish people after their dispersion around the world in A.D. 70. When the Romans under Titus sacked and destroyed Jerusalem, the Jewish people were scattered to the four corners of the earth. They were dispersed to Europe, the Middle East and North Africa.

They dwelt in those lands for over 1000 years, continuing to practice their faith which remained largely intact despite the great pressure to renounce Judaism and convert to other religions. The land of Israel was occupied by foreign powers for centuries and was left barren and desolate. But the Word of God prophesied about a nation being born within a day in Isaiah 66 and God's Word cannot return to Him void. At the turn of the last century, a young Austro-Hungarian Jew, named Theodore Herzl was restlessly searching for his identity and purpose. Even though he was heavily assimilated as a European Jew and didn't even practice Judaism seriously, he constantly felt the sense of being an outsider or the "other." As he travelled around Europe, he noticed that the condition of the Jews was the same wherever they settled, no matter how successful they were, how many achievements, how much money, or how great a contribution they made to the countries they lived in. He recognized that antisemitism, much like modern-day racism against blacks, could only be stemmed by ending the homelessness of the Jews and establishing a sovereign state.

Initially, he sought the support of powerful Jewish families like the Rothschilds and other world leaders to support his dream; but soon found that no one thought his dream plausible. It was laughable, a Jewish State established out of thin air? Impossible! Why even the Jews themselves thought Herzl's grand visions of the future were suspect. Herzl went on to found a political mass movement around an annual meeting called the Zionist Congress. Many who would become the leaders of the future Jewish State were first enlightened by Herzl's Congress.

When Herzl died in 1904, a 17-year-old boy living in a Polish village wrote, "The sun is gone, but its light will shine again, the seeds of renaissance which he sowed in our hearts will not remain frozen forever!"

The teenager's name was David Ben-Gurion and, 44 years later, he would stand under the portrait of Herzl and read out Israel's Declaration of Independence.

The Jewish State was only founded after the horrors of the Nazi concentration camps; it meant that the world could no longer turn a blind eye to the dark depravity and hatred of antisemitism and the Jewish people could no longer simply hope that their neighbours would not harbour antisemitic sentiments towards them. Simply put, we cannot legislate against the sentiments that people have in their hearts. No matter how good, how successful, or how great a contribution to society that you make, there will always be people who harbour prejudice, who are afraid, who are small-minded, intimidated by growth and success and motivated by bigotry and hatred. Just as God's Word declared the Jewish people, were restored to their homeland after so many centuries and a nation was born in a day.

The African Return

Isaiah 45:2," I will go before you and level the mountains to make crooked places straight, to break in pieces the doors of bronze, and cut asunder the bars of iron. And I will give you the treasures of darkness and hidden riches of secret places, that you may know that it is I, the LORD, the God of Israel, Who calls you by your name." One of the saddest places on the coast of West Africa is the infamous Gore Island which acted as a last point connection to the land of Africa for the slave ships that were bound for the Americas. During the trans-Atlantic slave trade, slaves were raided in the interior by African slave traders and brought to the coast where they were sold to the Europeans and held in large forts until the number required to fill the ships was acquired. They were then loaded onto the slave ships like cargo and set sail never to see their homeland again. In Gore Island which acted as a catchment slave fort for slaves raided off the coast of West Africa, the door of no return symbolized the last connection that they had to the land of their birth.

Once the door was closed, it was never opened from the outside in, meaning people never returned home to Africa from slavery. In 2019, as many people of African descent made the long pilgrimage to Africa, and many came to Gore Island, they symbolically opened the door of no return from the outside. This action was to show that the sons and daughters of those who were never meant to return had finally come home. The scripture in Isaiah 45 declares that God will break down the doors of bronze and cut asunder the bars of iron (chains). In the years following the civil rights movement and the post-colonial independence in Africa, many people of African descent sought to relocate to Africa, whether for study or cultural and spiritual reasons. Dar-es-salaam University became a hotbed for intellectual discourse among young African scholars and people of African descent coming to Africa in search of Pan-African ideals. Walter Rodney, the great African American author and thinker who wrote the book, *How Europe Underdeveloped Africa,*[1] spent time in Africa for study and discourse with African intellectuals and leaders. The question of a return to Africa was very real and tangible at that time for many. However, I do not believe they were able to fulfill their dreams because there is an appointed time for everything. I believe that this is the time to reawaken the desire for a return and restoration of Africa's sons and daughters to their land.

Re-integration:

Some of my earliest memories are of growing up as a child in Sweden, a country that my family fled to as refugees during the years of civil war in Uganda. On arrival in Sweden, we

---

1 Walter Rodney. *How Europe Underdeveloped Africa.* Bogle-L'Ouverture Publications, 1972.

were welcomed into a camp where we lived for 6 months and began to learn the language and we children started school. There were many other families in the camp and each family was assigned a modest cabin, there was a communal dining area, a school for the children, a play area and some other recreational spaces. The purpose of the camp was to begin the absorption of refugee families into Swedish culture and society. Being very young, I and my siblings quickly picked up the language and culture of the Swedish people, their norms and habits became our own. One of the strange habits I picked up was spitting, something that was quite common and acceptable. It was commonplace for people to spit in the snow as they walked or even in mid-conversation. My mother scolded me for this habit and I had to quickly drop it, but children are like sponges and can absorb and adapt quickly to their environment.

One of the primary goals of the African return should be:

Define the demographic that can be easily integrated into society (ages 18-35 yrs)

Determine the areas that they will be engaged in the economy (agriculture, IT, services)

Determine the incentives for individuals to immigrate such as land, education, training

Absorption and integration policies

Is Africa able to receive her people back?

This is a question which will no doubt be on the minds of Africans. If the countries and governments of African nations are struggling to find employment for their nationals, why would they invite the burden of more people to provide for?

Again I feel here that we are asking the wrong question. It is similar to a parent choosing to neglect a child simply because he is residing in another location. The child is still part of you wherever they may be living and planning for the proper immigration and integration of whoever has a desire to do so is not only necessary but also incumbent on us to do so.

The African Union at the continental leadership should begin to table this question and debate it on a regional and continental level. The African Union and individual nations can prioritize those returnees to whom they want to offer citizenship. This can be based on investment (Income level), skill set or age and begin to incentivize them with the benefits that would be offered to returnees. Another matter is the re-settlement of returnees, a lottery system can be created to ensure that no one region is overburdened with too much immigration at one time. The key is to have a united vision and agreement on a continental level to ensure that people who do wish to return are absorbed into their homeland as quickly as possible.

Conclusion:

I opened this chapter writing about the tragic and senseless loss of too many lives of people of African descent through gun violence and police brutality particularly in the United States. In hearing all the rhetoric back and forth, it seems that the only options put forward are those that try to mitigate the problem of racism. However, I am offering another option, a homeland for people of African descent to return to. Africa is their home and they should have the option to return to their home. This is an offer that only we as Africans can bring to the table, these are our brothers and sisters, being killed in broad daylight, and the solutions that are proffered do not deal with the deeper problems and origins of the violence. As Africans, we must own our part in this problem, which is the historical roots of slavery which began here in Africa. It was in Africa that the problem started when we sold our people for trinkets. Therefore, I believe that we must rise to the occasion with humility, repentance and take responsibility for this grave evil. The wounds must be healed here with our brothers and sisters and the door must be flung open for a great return.

I leave you with the words of Isaiah 60:

"Arise, shine for your Light has come, and the glory of the Lord has risen upon you.

See, darkness covers the earth and thick darkness over the peoples;

But the Lord rises upon you.

Nations will come to your light

And kings to the brightness of your dawn.

Lift up your eyes and look about you.

All assemble and come to you

Your sons from afar

And your daughters are carried on the hip.

Then you will look and be radiant,

Your heart will throb and swell with joy

The wealth of the seas will be brought to you,

The riches of the nations will come

Herds of camels will cover your land

Young camels of Midian and Ephah

And all from Sheba will come bearing gold and incense

And proclaiming the praise of the Lord.

All Kedar's flocks will be gathered to you,

The rams of Nebaioth will serve you:

They will be accepted as offerings on My altar and I will adorn My glorious temple.

Who are these that fly along like clouds, like doves to their nests?

Surely the islands look to Me;

In the lead are the ships of Tarshish bringing your children from afar, with silver and gold;

To honor the Lord your God, the Holy One of Israel

For He has endowed you with splendor.

Your gates will always stand open, they will never be shut, day or night;

So that people may bring you the wealth of the nations;

Their kings led in triumphal procession.

For the nation or kingdom that will not serve you will perish, it will be utterly ruined.

The glory of Lebanon will come to you,

The juniper, the fir and the cypress together, to adorn my sanctuary;

And I will glorify the place for my feet.

The children of your oppressors will come bowing before you; all who despise you will bow down at your feet and will call you the City of the Lord, Zion of the Holy One of Israel.

Although you have been forsaken and hated,

With no one travelling through

I will make you the everlasting pride and joy of all generations.

You will drink the milk of nations and be nursed on royal breasts.

Then you will know that I, the Lord, and your Saviour,

Your Redeemer, the Mighty One of Jacob.

Instead of bronze, I will bring you gold and silver in place of iron

Instead of wood, I will bring you bronze and iron in place of stones.

I will make peace your governor and well-being your ruler.

No longer will violence be heard in your land,

Nor ruin or destruction within your borders,

But you will call your walls Salvation and your gates Praise.

The sun will no more be your light by day nor the moon shine on you,

For the Lord will be your everlasting light and your God will be your glory.

The sun will never set again, and your moon will wane no more

The Lord will be your everlasting light and your days of sorrow will end.

Then all your peoples will be righteous and they will possess the land forever.

They are the shoot I have planted, the work of My hands, for the display of My splendour

The least of you will become a thousand, and the smallest a mighty nation.

I AM the LORD*; In its time I will do it swift*ly."

16. Marrying the Land

"You shall also be so beautiful and prosperous to be thought of as a crown of glory and honour in the hand of the Lord, and a royal diadem(exceedingly beautiful) in the Hand of your God.

"You shall no longer be termed Forsaken, nor shall your land be called Desolate any more. But you shall be called Hephziba(My delight Is in her), and your land shall be called Beulah (married); for the Lord delights in you, and your land shall be married(owned and protected by the Lord).

"For as a young man married a virgin O Jerusalem, so shall your sons marry you; and as a bridegroom rejoices over the bride, so shall your God rejoice over you." - Isaiah 62:3-5 – Amplified Bible.

Many years ago, I was visited by a dear friend and fellow intercessor for Uganda and Africa. As the visit came to an end, she asked if we could pray together. This wasn't unusual, because many times after visiting with a friend and if they are Christians, we often like to begin and close our time together with prayer. So she prayed and her prayer would have been quite normal and unremarkable, except that she prayed for something that truly resonated with my spirit. She prayed that young people would be "married to the land" and as a result feel the Grace and call of God to fight for, defend and develop the land God had given us.

Our time together ended but her remarkable prayer stayed with me.

What did it mean to marry the land?

Without even knowing it, her words struck a deep chord within my spirit. I felt my spirit receive those words even though I didn't fully understand what they meant.

In my travels across the world, I have encountered diverse cultures and peoples and seen the close-knit relationship that people have with their lands. Whether it is the cold temperate climates of Europe, the desert dunes of Arabia, the tropical rain forests of Africa or the vast open steppes of Eurasia, it is clear that people will adapt to the lands they dwell in no matter how harsh or inhospitable the lands may be.

I recall visiting the archipelago that is Venice with my husband some years back. As we marvelled at this city that seemed to be floating on water, we visited theatres and museums to learn more about the history of the city. I remember one theatre production we attended that chronicled the history of the city from its earliest days. The play told of a festival that was held in the city to marry the people of the city to the waters because they recognized that the prosperity of the city relied heavily on the water that brought merchants, traders and visitors to the city. I had never seen anything like it. However, during the festival, church leaders, political leaders and Venetian citizens all came together and threw gold rings into the water as a symbol of marrying the water and becoming one with the land. After the ceremony, the church leaders would bless the people and so solemnize the event.

As I watched the play, I was reminded of my friend's prayer and wondered if carnal people could recognize that there is a unique relationship between the people and the land and this relationship should be celebrated.

It took me many more years to fully understand what the Lord truly desires for us as His children concerning the land He has given to us as an inheritance. But first, let me share my testimony that brought this truth home to me.

From the time Odrek and I got married, we knew that we both shared a deep love for the land and, in particular, living a country life. So we invested a lot of time and money as soon as we were married to begin to develop our home in the country. When we started, our land was traditional farmland operating according to the traditional ways that our culture and people had done for generations. We worked for a long time to bring order and to put some simple systems in place to make the land sustainable economically. However, in all this, we didn't have a clear vision for the farm; we only hoped to create a nice second home for our family that we could visit during the holidays. Needless to say that it was a constant struggle, year after year, to manage the farm and sustain it with the income generated by our businesses in the city. Despite all the discouragement and seeming bottomless pit of needs the farm represented, we still nursed the hope that one day, it would be sustainable.

One Easter holiday, I visited the farm with our two young children. I always loved the Easter holidays, because the land seemed to be coming alive again after the short dry season that lasted from January to March. In March the early rains usually begin to fall, and the land is refreshed and renewed. These rains continue until late May when the long dry season sets in. This lasts until mid–August when the long rainy season begins. It brings heavy downpours that fill up dams and provide the much-needed water for the new planting season. This cycle continues every year and, even though you are aware of it in the city, it has more impact and meaning to life when you live on the land. Although I love and see the purpose of every season, I particularly enjoy the short rains because they are gentle rains that refresh the land. When I am at the farm during this time, I can hear the cooing of the birds at dusk which is my favourite time of day. I hear the high-pitched cry of the bulls as they seek out mates and ward off other bulls that seek to invade their territory. The crickets and frogs croak and sing out their harmonies and the young calves and cows moo and low at each other. The land comes alive and it is as though everything is singing praises to God, thanking Him for sending the showers of rain to refresh the earth.

During one such time, I visited the farm and was going about my chores when the head of the farm staff came to speak to me. Technically, he wasn't the head of the staff. He was a soldier called Ochora who helped out with some things around the farm. He was responsible and so the few staff we had, tended to look to him for leadership in our absence. Ochora brought me a long list of needs for the farm. I felt a sense of weariness overtake me as I looked at the long list of farm needs, ranging from cattle drugs to barbed wire for fencing, and a myriad of other things. I looked over the list then, with a sigh, I asked the question, “Ochora, isn’t there something we can sell from the farm to take care of these expenses?” He then answered me with such confidence and assuredness as though he was Einstein explaining the theory of relativity.

He said, “there is no single income on this farm.”

His words seemed so heavy and final that my spirit revolted against them. I thought to myself, “Why? How?”

I took the list and said I would handle it, but that day I went into my room and cried to the Lord. I stood in the centre of our bedroom and asked God to send His Spirit from the north, the south, the east and the west and to breathe life into the dead bones of our land as it says in Ezekiel 37.

I couldn’t understand how this beautiful, green, fertile land could have no income at all. It seemed wrong somehow and yet I knew that was the case and it was the same with many of our neighbours in our community. The land was very rich but the productivity was so low that there was hardly anything coming out of it. It was a bottomless pit of expenditure, for food, and upkeep of staff and animals, but there was no productivity.

That night I had a dream. I saw a bird’s eye view of our farm as though I was an eagle circling it from above. Then I drew closer and, as I did, I saw a convoy of trucks coming out of the farm. As I zoomed in to look at the trucks, I could see that the trucks were full of boxes carrying goods out of the farm. In the dream, my bird’s eye view zoomed in closer to see what was written on the boxes that were in the trucks. I saw the name, *Tomosi’s Farm*.

I realized in the dream that all these trucks were coming out of the farm filled with boxes of produce going out to feed the world. I was amazed at this revelation in the dream.

When I woke up, I knew that the Lord had answered my heartfelt prayer. I knew that the barren unproductive land would produce and take products to the world.

Later on, I shared this dream with my husband, Odrek and we continued to pray and think about what this could mean for us. It gave me a renewed sense of hope, that the sense of outrage and revolt against our unproductive land was just and right. God didn't want to see our land poor and barren. He gave us this beautiful land to produce abundant food to feed our country and the world.

From that time on, we started calling our farm, Tomosi's Farm, after Odrek's father and the founder of the farm. His father was the one who started the farm many years before and laid the foundation for what the Lord was revealing to us.

We continued struggling with maintaining the farm for a few more years. One year, Odrek and I took some time off to pray and seek the Lord for the direction of our businesses. We took time out and booked ourselves into a hotel for a weekend with the sole purpose of praying and seeking the Lord. Our businesses had been growing and doing well, but we needed a sense of direction and clarity on what we needed to focus on as our flagship enterprise. That weekend was a turning point for us because, by the end of the weekend, the Lord had spoken to us clearly that He wanted us to focus on agriculture and, specifically, dairy farming. Up until then, we had only kept the farm as a kind of token family inheritance. We hadn't looked at it as a business and, definitely, not as our flagship enterprise. But the Lord's word was clear to us: agriculture needs to be the focus and the flagship. He reminded us about the dream He had shown me years prior and how He would fulfill it if we would be faithful to do our part.

Again, the excitement and joy I had felt before returned. The Lord had reinforced and re-confirmed His word to us. Now we had to step out in faith. But what were we to do?

Our family was growing and we had welcomed our third baby into our world. Work at the office was very busy, and my work at church was busy too. Where on earth would we find the time to start a new venture in agriculture? I kept wondering!

It seemed impossible, even before we got started, but as things are usually with God, it makes more sense to your spirit than it does to your mind. So we accepted His Word and received it in our spirits even though we didn't know how we would practically do it.

Following our prayer retreat, we made a crucial decision to focus more of our investment on the farm. Many team members in our company couldn't understand why we would take hard-earned money and invest it in the "village". A village is a village, they thought. What significant return could come from there? It was a clear case of "can anything good come out of Nazareth?"

We persevered and focused on building the infrastructure at the farm. Odrek worked on opening up the farm and making a network of roads across the land. We dug dams and separated paddocks. We cleared the land of weeds and thorny bushes. We invested in mechanization and bought new tractors and coolers for collecting milk. In all this, we didn't have electricity at the farm and so we applied for rural electrification. This is a programme which helps to extend power to rural areas, where the applicant pays an initial amount and the government subsidizes the cost of setting up the power lines to that location. We could only apply for rural electrification by proving that we needed power at the farm for industrial and not domestic use. It took a while, but after some years, we got the approval for rural electrification and for the first time, we had power lines set up within the farm. The power lines went through our farm and continued to provide power to the school and trading centre close to our land.

It was a big breakthrough and now we had all the necessary ingredients for our dairy processing to be established. We had power, water and a growing network of farmers that were selling milk to us daily. Every day, these farmers would bring their milk on bicycles, motorbikes and cars to our collection centres that were scattered around the district. The milk would be chilled in coolers in collection centres until the milk trucks would come to collect it and take it to the city to sell to the processors. Even though our milk supply was increasing, our dream was never to sell raw milk but rather to process milk in the hinterland and not in the city.

Our dream was to have dairy products leaving the farm and going out into the wider world. All the processors of milk were located in the city to avoid the problems that we were grappling with such as power, water, infrastructure and so on. However, the main source of dairy products was located in our region, the area known as the cattle corridor where the majority of dairy and beef comes from. Therefore, we had the incentive to establish a processing plant in our region, not only for the jobs and other trickle-down economic benefits but also for the quality of the product. The quality of milk that has to spend 48 hours in transit from the country to the city to be processed is lost along the way. Often, milk would arrive in the city spoiled and would have to be poured or be turned away at the gate. We wanted to have the milk move from the farm to the processing plant in a matter of hours so that we ensured that the quality of milk was high. Everyone we spoke to about this dream thought this was impossibly difficult. Why not just process in the city like the others?

At this time, we began praying that the Lord would bring us investment partners to establish a processing plant in the hinterland. We had bought another piece of land close to our farm. It was on the main road and an extension of the farm. During this time, a strange thing started happening; we started receiving visitors to the farm from all over the world. I cannot count how many dinners we made and hosted for possible investors that came from all over the world. These investors had heard what we were doing and wanted to come and see the potential of this project. When they visited the farm, they often spent the night in our guest cottage, we made them dinner and made a presentation. Then we would take them around the farm and, if time permitted, we would take them to visit some of our partner farmers in the community. Finally, they would plant a tree around the farm in commemoration of their visit. This same scenario played out weekend after weekend and with one possible investor after another.

Many times it would look very promising, and then fizzle out along the way. Despite all this, we soldiered on, splitting our time between the city and the country, week after week. On one occasion, we received visitors from Israel who seemed quite serious about the intention to invest in the agricultural sector. We went through the usual procedure that we did with all our other guests. These visitors seemed genuinely interested in the potential of our project. They listened intently to our plan and asked pointed questions as we toured the farm and visited other farmers. In our final meeting, they spoke to us candidly, they said they would want to partner with us. However, the scope of the project was simply too small and it would never work.

We were devastated by this news, it seemed that our tireless efforts over so many years were in vain. Hearing from people much more experienced in agribusiness that our project was not viable was very disheartening. The day after those Israeli investors left, the Word of the Lord came to us like cool rain after a blistering hot day. He said to us from His Word, ***"Do not despise the day of small beginnings." -* Zechariah 4:10**

He spoke with compassion but strength, **"Don't be discouraged, those who seem strong now started the way you are starting. Don't stop the work, keep on moving."**

"But Lord, what if no one ever wants to partner with us? How will we manage all this work?"

The Lord answered us, **"I will be with you, don't be afraid, keep on working**."

And so we continued struggling against price wars within the dairy sector, staff issues, underwriting the business and splitting time between the city and the country.

Two years after the visit of our friends from Israel, they returned to visit us again. They were amazed at how much the business had grown over the years and realized the potential of the project. This time they said they wanted to partner with us and we began discussions for a joint venture.

More than ten years after the Lord gave me the dream of the trucks coming out of the farm with products going to the world, we successfully launched our dairy products in the Ugandan market. These dairy products are now exported to countries in the region and feeds millions of people. The Lord more than proved Himself, in that He gave us the dream, nursed it even when it seemed doomed to die, and brought it to fulfillment.

Our dreams for productivity aren't restricted to only our land. However, we see this as something that needs to happen everywhere in Uganda and Africa. When God through our work, sweat, toil, prayers and love, makes the barren land fruitful, it is a fulfillment of God's promises to us. I believe that God wants all our land in Uganda and Africa to become the Garden of Eden, a place of delight and fruitfulness. However, it is only in our partnering with the Lord in this great assignment that we will see this come to pass.

This is the true meaning of "marrying the land."

Korea and Canaan Farmers School[1]

In 2019, Odrek and I visited South Korea for the first time. It was a wonderful learning experience as we traversed this unique country. I had been interested in visiting Korea after meeting a dear friend called Professor Kim whose father and family were the founders of the re-known Canaan Farmers School in Korea. This remarkable family, so internalized the truths of God's Word regarding work, that they were instrumental in reclaiming barren land and making it productive again. Their model of work was so successful, that the government of South Korea used their model of work and mindset change as the blueprint for the national programme

---

1 Kim Yong Kyi. *The Unique Canaan Farm of Korea*. The Greatest Light Publishing Co., 1984.

of poverty eradication in the rural areas, dubbed "Saemaul Undong."

Professor Kim visited Covenant Nations Church and told of the remarkable story of his family's journey from poverty which mirrored the South Korean nation's journey out of poverty towards prosperity and industrialization.

I was touched by how much adversity their family had faced and the harshness of the conditions of their land. If people don't work, and produce enough food to take them through the winter, they starve. This isn't the case in Africa and, especially, not Uganda where the climate is so mild, the soil so fertile and the rain so abundant that, even if you don't produce enough food, you can always live off the wild fruits and vegetables that the land produces. In Uganda, you can sleep under the stars for 365 days a year and you won't die of exposure. It might not be comfortable but your life wouldn't be in danger.

When we visited Korea, and we drove from Seoul to Canaan Farmers School in the mountains, I was struck by how much of the country was mountainous. Every inch of land in the valley below was covered with rice paddies. The land is in limited supply with most of it being mountainous and unsuited for arable farming. As such, they use as much land in the valley for agriculture as they can.

When we visited Canaan Farmers School, I felt ashamed of myself as a Ugandan and an African. We arrived at the school at night and the air was cold and chilly. We were shown our modest accommodation in the school where we would be staying for the duration of our visit. As I lay awake that night in that cold room, I felt the Lord speak to me.

He said, "**You have gone all over the world searching for answers to your questions, thinking that there is some secret or mystery that will solve all your problems as Africans. You are looking for what you already possess. The answer is within your heart. You already know what you ought to do, but do you do it**?"

I have never felt more ashamed of myself as an African as I did that night in Canaan Farmers School, for I came face to face with my ineptitude as an African. This ineptitude isn't a matter of capacity, but rather the will to do the things we ought to do. I saw our brothers and sisters in Korea doing so much more with so little, compared with how much we have in Africa that we do so little with. I remembered the parable of the talents in the Bible where the Master, who represents the Lord Jesus, praises the servant who multiplied his talents and rebuked the servant who buried his talents. Jesus called the servant who buried his talents wicked. I believe that is how the Lord sees us when we bury the talents He has bestowed on us.

I realized that the Lord had allowed me to go to Korea to look at myself in the mirror of His word and to see that there was no secret I would learn; there was no great new technique for me to imbibe. No, God took us there to show us that our poverty is not of materials but of spirit. We are rich and greatly endowed, but we are blind to all our blessings, and we go with empty hands to those who are truly poor and we ask them to give to us. The whole time we stayed in South Korea, I kept silent and just listened. I was chastised and didn't have anything to speak or to ask.

We were honoured to meet the founding member of Canaan Farmers School, President Bum Il Kim who told us of their mindset change teachings and how that was the catalyst of their rural transformation in Korea. As we discussed these matters, he said something that confirmed what the Lord had spoken to me the night before. He said, "Uganda and Africa can be much greater than Korea. You are very rich, but it is in the mind." And he pointed his finger to his temples. I nodded in agreement, I knew exactly what he meant. It should be Africa teaching the world about the best farming practices. We have the highest percentage of arable land in the world. It should be Africa feeding the world, not getting handouts from such poor countries like Japan, Korea and the Nordic countries. Isn't it a mystery how a country that is under snow for half the year can give to a country that is blessed with sunshine and rain all year long?

On our final day at the Canaan Farmers School, a young man called Simon, who was our guide, took us on a tour around the school, showing us how their training programme runs. We ended our tour at the bell which always rang to wake up the students to start the day. The bell was a simple gas cylinder that was suspended on a metal rod and they used another rod as the gong to hit the cylinder. During their training, they rang the bell three times to awaken the mind, the body and the spirit. Their mindset training teaches that it is only when the mind, the body and the spirit are awakened that true transformation can take place. They rightly believe that it is the slumber of the body, the mind and the spirit that allowed for subjugation and even colonization by other forces. Therefore, it is only when the whole human being is awakened from this slumber that they can reclaim their land.

I was profoundly impacted by my journey to Korea, not because there was something new I learnt that I didn't know, but because the Lord showed me how poor my spirit and mind had been. How weak my resolve was, how quickly I became discouraged, and how much about my country I took for granted. How many talents had I been given by God and how many of them were still buried in excuses?

I prayed that the awakening I experienced there would stay with me forever so that, by His Grace, we could work hard to create and expand the Garden of the Lord in our own country, the same way our Korean brothers and sisters had worked to do so from Canaan Farmers School.

Israel and the Kibbutz Movement

When I was still in school, I greatly enjoyed reading about the history of Israel. I am not sure why I was so drawn to the nation of Israel. It could have stemmed from my faith in God. I also loved reading historical fiction and my favourite Christian author was called Bodie Thoene who wrote extensive fictional accounts about the history of Israel. Later on, my interests expanded to the political history of Israel and so I read a lot about its founders like David Ben-Gurion, and their leaders like Yitzhak Rabin, Golda Meir, Moshe Dayan and the founding father of Zionism, Theodor Herzl.

I also enjoyed reading about the country's contemporary political leaders like Benjamin Netanyahu. I recall reading Benjamin Netanyahu's book called *A Place Among the Nations*,[2] which chronicled his own life's journey through the political upheavals of Israel's nationhood. One story that stayed with me was when Netanyahu described his military training as a young man in the Israeli Defense Forces. He said part of their training was to get to know the topography of the land. To do this, they would walk across the land on foot filling their water bottles in the Jordan River and then pouring the same water into the Mediterranean Sea on the other side of the country. He said that, in doing that, they walked the length and breadth of the land. They came to know and love their land so dearly that they were prepared to die for their country.

There are two things, I believe, that cultivate a love for the land God has given us. The first is working the land, making it produce food to sustain the people of the land. The second is fighting to defend the land God has given us. In the case of Israel, the people are taught to do both from a very early age. Each Israeli citizen must serve in the military for at least 2 years in their youth and is part of the country's army reserve.

Second, the founding fathers of the nation, the people who asserted themselves and settled the land were all involved in the Kibbutz movement of reclaiming the land through agriculture. After the Second World War Jewish immigrants poured out of Europe in search of a homeland after the horrors of the holocaust in Hitler's Germany. Many immigrated to the newly- established state of Israel, a tiny country sandwiched between larger Arab countries.

These immigrants were professionals; they were doctors, lawyers, engineers, writers, and musicians, all coming from

---

2 Benjamin Netanyahu. *A Place Among the Nations: Israel and the World*. Bantam Books, 1993.

the capitals of Europe. However, when they landed in Israel, there were no professional jobs available. There were only agricultural jobs in the socially organized kibbutz where people lived communally and worked the land. It is very humbling for a medical doctor, a lawyer or an engineer to take up a plough and work the land. But that was what the country needed to be reclaimed. No country has any kind of development without reclaiming the land through agricultural work. The land must be worked by the people of the land and reclaimed so that it can begin to produce so that it can feed the people.

The founder of Canaan Farmers School, Kim, articulated this clearly when he said, “If the land is not reclaimed through agricultural work, it remains a wilderness and wild.”

Every country that has experienced rapid industrialization and technological advancement has first reclaimed the land through agriculture. What is popularly known as Silicon Valley today was formerly the Santa Clara Valley which was filled with fruit orchards. The hi-tech hub of Tel Aviv was the first agricultural land farmed by the first settlers. This is true of Korea, as well, as I have already narrated through the *Saemaul Undong* movement, which led to the reclamation of rural lands through agriculture. All these nations that have become technology hubs had to first be reclaimed through agriculture. The land became the foundation upon which to catapult their development.

Israel became what it is today, an advanced industrialized nation with nuclear capabilities, based on the reclamation of land through agriculture.

I must reiterate that no country can advance and develop without first dealing with the agricultural sector in a serious and focused way.

The benefits are not only economic but social as well. When the land is worked by its people, it is reclaimed, it is in a sense married to its people. It is when you work your land, you walk it, you smell and touch the soil, you know the scent of the soil when the rain first falls and the refreshing feeling that it brings. Over time, a bond is created between people and their land. This is a gift from God and it is an important part of our development as people.

Who should be involved in Agriculture?

There is a paradox that I see in Africa and that we also confronted when God led us to seriously invest in agriculture. Those who should be involved in agriculture run to the cities and those who remain on the land cannot bring significant change to the land. What do I mean by this? By reclamation of the land, I do not mean that we should go back to working with hoes and simple farm tools.

I believe that each generation has something new to add to the building blocks of our society. A benefit that our generation has is that of modern education. We have had more investment in education in our country over the past decades than ever before. The result is that we have a more educated workforce now than we had a generation ago. As such, as a country, we should reap the dividends of this investment in every sector, especially agriculture. When children return home with university degrees, they should help their parents improve the family business on the land. They can do this by upgrading it using the new knowledge they learnt in school. Whether it is coffee farming, growing fruits and vegetables, banana plantains, or dairy and beef farming, the younger generation can improve and build on the foundations already existing. The educated have more to offer and more to bring to the table, be they farming or business techniques than their parents have. As such we need to encourage more educated young people to get involved in agriculture as a way of reclaiming the land and hence fast-tracking the development of the nation.

Sadly, though, many young and educated people despise the land and would rather spend their lives in air-conditioned buildings looking for the few jobs available in the cities. Our young people are running away from the vast work that is before us in reclaiming the land in the countryside to crowd in the city looking for office jobs; jobs that may not even exist.

Focus on the land could also help avoid catastrophes of the kind we see in news releases as young people venture out to seek greener pastures across the world. In this respect, it is heartbreaking to see the large numbers of young Africans who risk their lives on boats in the oceans in search of work as migrant labourers in places such as Europe. Meanwhile, they leave behind their lands which are their spiritual and natural inheritance. My prayer is that we will hear the wake-up call from God in our bodies, minds and spirits so that we can return to the land and commit to working the land so that all the barren places in our country can become fruitful.

Ethiopia - Coming Full Circle

When I was around six years old, there was a devastating famine in Ethiopia. At the time, my family was in Sweden in exile because of the political instability in my home country, Uganda. I vividly recall that every night on the news, they would beam terrible images of skeletal Ethiopian babies and children. These horrifying images of children with distended abdomens, and flies buzzing around their mouths and eyes, haunted my young mind. I kept thinking if I could carry the food from our table to Ethiopia to give to those babies and children so that they wouldn't be so hungry. The American pop singer Michael Jackson, and music producer and promoter Quincy Jones gathered a group of musicians to record a song that later became famous titled, We Are the World. The objective was to raise money for relief aid to be sent to Ethiopia.

I remember seeing and hearing this song playing on TV and the radio over and over again. As food aid was sent from countries around the world, again images of African mothers, fathers and children being handed bowls of rice were beamed into living rooms all over the world. Sometimes, there would be pictures of bags of food being dropped from helicopters to hungry families on the ground below. These bags would often burst on impact with the ground spilling the precious food into the dust, and the people would gather the food from the dust to eat.

These images stayed with me and always made me question why we didn't have enough food to feed our people as Africans. Even in my childlike mind, it felt very dehumanizing to see my fellow Africans depending on handouts of food just to survive. I have always felt deeply offended at people and organizations that use images of hungry Africans, especially children, to raise money for relief efforts. It is dehumanizing to the image of Africans and, especially to the children. I become very disturbed when I see Christian organizations that claim to be doing good, exploiting the images of hungry children to raise money to help those very same children. The famine in Ethiopia in the 1980s was very severe, but hunger and lack of food security are problems that we haven't completely eradicated in Africa.

My father has spoken extensively on the need to integrate markets in Africa for the sake of dealing with the demand and supply of goods and services. There are products where we have a comparative advantage to produce in Uganda, but we need a wider market to sell those products. The dairy sector is one such area, where we have an oversupply of dairy products in Uganda and a shortage of dairy outputs in the region.

I travelled to Ethiopia in early 2019 to research the market and the possibility of supplying the Ethiopian market with our dairy products. The city of Addis Ababa, including its outer suburbs, has a population of over five million people. Ethiopia has a population of over 100 million people. However, the consumption of dairy products is much lower than should be the case simply because the supply is inadequate. When I visited the supermarkets in Addis Ababa, I was amazed to find that there was a rationing of milk products. A family could only buy one packet of milk, and by midday, all the milk was gone and the shelves were empty. When I compared this to my own family of six where the consumption of milk is

20 litres every couple of days, I knew that we needed to find a way of getting our products into the Ethiopian market.

That said, the dream of exporting our milk from Uganda to the markets of Eastern Africa confronted numerous bottlenecks and barriers. Most of these barriers are, again, within our minds as Africans, where it is easier for us to import things from Japan and Saudi Arabia than from our region. Infrastructure is also a problem; it is hard to lift a product from one region to another so that it arrives at the destination market competitively. There is an urgent need for organization and streamlining of our laws, tariffs and regulations to make business and movement of products easy. There are a whole host of challenges to confront but this task isn't impossible; it is a necessity if we are going to survive as distinct entities, people and regions.

In 2019, we tested our products on the Ethiopian market and the reception was very positive. When I met our potential distributors in Addis Ababa, I shared with them that I have a specific interest in having our products in Ethiopia. I told them that it was time for Africans to work and do business together to ensure that we had food security for future generations. I narrated how the famine in the 1980s affected me and how we can solve our problems as Africans if we work together.

We continue to work towards this goal of seeing the walls in our minds and our systems melt away to allow us to build a stronger union as African people: spiritually, socially, economically and politically.

Revelation of the Sons of God

There are several lessons that I have learnt from the Lord in dealing with the land and restoring barren land to fruitfulness. It is too dense a topic to deal with in detail here, but suffice it to say that as Christians we need to have a better understanding of what the land represents, what has happened on the land through past human activity and how we can cleanse the land through prayer.

All land has experienced defilement in one way or another. This defilement comes through strife, quarrels, jealousy, hatred, breaking of covenants and shedding of innocent blood. We shouldn't be surprised to hear that the land is defiled by human activity, in the same way, that land can be cleansed or blessed by righteous human actions. In the Old Testament, God required that the land have a year of rest after every seven years to allow it to replenish its resources. The Sabbath rest for the land ensured that the vitality of the land would be conserved for generations. God also advised the elders of Israel what they should do if the land was defiled by the shedding of innocent blood.

Here are the words from Deuteronomy 21:6-9:

> *"And the elders of that city nearest to the slain man shall wash their hands over the heifer whose neck was broken in the valley. And they shall testify, our hands have not shed this blood, neither have our eyes seen it. Forgive, O Lord, Your people Israel, whom You have redeemed, and do not allow the shedding of innocent blood to be charged to Your people, Israel. And the guilt of blood shall be forgiven of them. So shall you purge the guilt of innocent blood from among you, when you do what is right in the sight of the Lord." – Amplified Bible*

As Christians, we have a new covenant that is ratified in the precious blood of our Lord Jesus. Therefore, we do not have to rely on the blood of bulls and cows for sacrifice. However, our faith must be in the finished work of the Cross and the perfect sacrifice of our Lord Jesus Christ. As we cleanse our land through prayer and plead the blood of Jesus, we can cover our land, homes, offices and whatever belongs to us with the blood of Jesus and thus cleanse it from any defilement.

Finally, God shows that land can be a witness against us if our actions go against the Principles of God's Word. Joshua 24:27 has these words:

> *"And Joshua said to the people, see this stone shall be a witness against us, for it has heard all the words the Lord has spoken to us; so it shall be a witness against you, lest*

you lie and deny your God. So Joshua sent the people away, every man to his inheritance." – Amplified Bible

Moses echoed those words in Deuteronomy 4:26:

"I call heaven and earth to witness against you this day that you shall soon utterly perish from the land which you are going over the Jordan to possess. You will not live long upon it but will be utterly destroyed."

God's Word is very clear that sin defiles the land and robs its people of the right and authority to dwell in that land. In Numbers 35:33-34, we have it that:

"So you shall not pollute the land in which you live; for blood pollutes the land, and no atonement can be made for the land for the bloodshed in it, but by the blood of him who shed it. And you shall not defile the land in which you, in the midst of which I dwell, for I, the Lord, dwell in the midst of the people in Israel." – Amplified Bible

The same Word of the Lord came from the Prophet Jeremiah, in the book of Jeremiah 16:18:

"Before I bring them back to their land, I will doubly recompense and punish them for their iniquity and their sin, because they have polluted My land with the carcasses of their detestable idols and with the abominable things offered to false gods with which they have filled My inheritance." – Amplified Bible

God's Word is very clear that He doesn't want us to defile the land that He has given us through our sins and that if we continue to do that, we lose the very rights to that land.

However, as Christians who have a new and better covenant, God hasn't called us to merely not sin in the land but, more so, He has called us to heal and reclaim the land through prayer and positive action to make it fruitful.

I close with the words found in Romans 8:19-20:

"All of creation waits expectantly and longs for God's sons to be made known (waits for the revealing of their sonship).

For the creation was subjected to frailty, not because of some intentional fault on its part, but by the will of Him Who so subjected it, yet with hope. That nature (creation) itself will be set free from bondage to decay and corruption (and gain an entrance) into the glorious freedom of God's children." – Amplified Bible

I pray that our generation will rise and take up our God-given mantle to heal, restore, reclaim and make the barren lands of Africa fruitful again to the glory of God.

17. The Joseph Company

"If you want to be the best leader you possibly can be, no matter how much or how little natural leadership talent you possess, you need to become a serving leader." - *John C. Maxwell*

I am a firm believer that every word from the Lord comes with a level of personal responsibility. I have a responsibility to discharge this message as the Lord has given it to me and, by the grace of God and by the help of His Holy Spirit, I have been doing that through the chapters of this book and other avenues the Lord has made available to me. However, once that Word goes forth and is imparted, there is a responsibility transferred to the reader. What do you do with what the Lord is speaking to you? In the last chapters, we prayed that God would raise a Joseph Company. What does it mean to be part of the company of Josephs? What does it mean to be part of a Joseph generation?

In my humble opinion, I believe it means to be a person of destiny; a person who is called and anointed by God to solve specific problems in the different spheres of our society.

Seven major spheres of society or mountains mould and shape the nation. They are the mountain of family, the mountain of the Church, the mountain of Education, the mountain of Media, the mountain of Culture and Celebration, the mountain of Economy and the mountain of Government.

I believe each of us is called to serve on at least one of these mountains in our societies. Some people are called to serve on more than one mountain. But wherever we find ourselves, regardless of our calling, these mountains affect our daily lives and we need to constantly intercede and ask the Lord to send out reformers to make disciples of these mountains.

To disciple or influence a mountain doesn't necessitate being in a position of authority. A stay-at-home mother, looking after her family is influencing the mountain of the family; a pastor serving in God's House is influencing the mountain of the church; a teacher helping to impart lifelong skills to students is influencing the mountain of education. As such, regardless of the positions we hold in life, whether Chief Executive or custodial worker in an organization, we can all make a difference and influence the mountains the Lord has stationed us on.

Take the example of Joseph, one of the twelve sons of Jacob, who had a unique journey with God that prepared him to be a great influence in the world. I firmly believe that God sees a Joseph in each of us. The question is, "do we see a Joseph in ourselves?"

Joseph received a vision from God early in his life, which was very clear about the purpose of God for him. He realized that there was something unique that he was supposed to accomplish in his life. In his dreams, he saw symbols of his family, brothers and parents bowing down to him. This was easily interpreted as Joseph having a calling that would elevate him above his brothers and even his parents. We must note that these dreams were not from Joseph. He did not make these dreams up and he probably didn't even want them. God is the Dream Giver. He alone knows the design and purpose of each of our lives. When God reveals His purpose or dreams for us, we have two options; we can reject or embrace His dreams. In the case of Joseph, he embraced God's dreams for him and that made all the difference.

Throughout the Bible, it is evident that people who embrace the vision of God for their lives at a young age usually attain success early in life. Examples include Joseph, David, Daniel and ultimately our Lord and Saviour, Jesus Christ. Knowing the vision or purpose of God is the springboard for successfully fulfilling the will of God for our lives. Joseph went through many trials, tests and setbacks on his journey to fulfill God's dream for him. These tests were not unique to Joseph, indeed anyone who will be used by God will experience these same tests to different degrees.

1. The Identity Test.

Joseph, as the favoured son of Jacob, probably imagined that he would live out his life in Canaan, alongside his father and brothers. But there is a dramatic twist in the plot when his brothers, motivated by envy and jealousy, sell him into slavery. Here, he is rejected by the people that he loves and trusts. The very people he expects to protect and defend him ultimately betray and sell him into slavery. Here is what the Bible says in Genesis 37:19-20:

> *"And they said one to another; see, here comes this dreamer and master of dreams. So come on now, let us kill him and throw his body into some pit; then he will say (to our father) some wild animal has devoured him; and we shall see what will become of his dreams!" – Amplified Bible*

Joseph was rejected by his family and the rejection was not only of him but also of God's vision for his life. They imagined, erroneously, that if they got rid of Joseph, they could kill the dream. However, they would find out later, through great pain and heartache, that if the dream comes from God, it cannot be killed. The purpose of God preserved Joseph's life and kept propelling him forward to the fulfillment of destiny.

The fundamental test of rejection, especially by the people that you love, respect and admire, is a test of *identity.* If our identity is found in people then when those people reject us, we will experience an identity crisis. This is because we cannot see ourselves outside of this group of people.

Mercifully, Joseph's identity was tied to his relationship with God. When his family rejected him and committed the ultimate betrayal, he was deeply wounded, even devastated. However, he was not destroyed. Even though his status in life, his home, his country and his relationship had changed, his relationship with God remained constant. Therefore, Joseph was able to remain who he was; his identity in God was untouched and it enabled him to be resilient and rise above the tough situations that he faced.

So, what is our identity based on? Is it based on our education? Family? Status in life? Is it based on material possessions or physical appearance? Is it based on success or achievements? We must understand that if we base who we are on these externalities, then if anything changes we will have a crisis because what we have tied our identity to has been shaken.

Ephesians Chapter 1:6 says thus:

> *"(So that we might be) to the praise and the commendation of His glorious grace (favour and mercy), which He so freely bestowed on us in the Beloved." – Amplified Bible*

This scripture declares that we have already been accepted in the Beloved, in Jesus Christ. Therefore, if Jesus has already accepted us, no amount of rejection in the world can affect who we are. We are the accepted, not the rejected because we are in Christ. If we know that we are already accepted in Christ, then our identity will be strong, firm, and unshakeable.

We must know who we are in Christ and that our identity rests in Him and Him alone. It is only then will we be stable and fixed. This is because we are building on a firm foundation that doesn't shift or change.

2. The Integrity Test

Joseph was rejected by his brothers who sold him into slavery in Potiphar's house. There, he served as a faithful steward, although he faced great temptations. For example, he was tempted by Potiphar's wife to sleep with her and when he refused her advances, she lied and slandered his character, falsely claiming that Joseph had assaulted her. Joseph was arrested and imprisoned, in essence for doing the right thing.

There is no doubt that, here, Joseph faced the test of his integrity.

Anyone who will be used by God will be tested in the area of their moral integrity. Whether it is the temptation of the lust of the flesh, the lust of the eyes or the pride of life.

1 John 2:15-17 has this to say:

> *"Do not love or cherish the world or the things that are of the world. If anyone loves the world, love for the Father is not in him. For all that is in the world – the lust of the flesh (craving for sexual gratification) and the lust of the eyes (greedy longings of the mind) and the pride of life (assurance in one's own resources or the stability in earthly things) – these do not come from the Father but are from the world (Itself). And the world passes away and disappears, and with it the forbidden cravings (the passionate desires, the lust) of it; but he who does the will of God and carries out His purposes in his life abides (remains) forever." – Amplified Bible.*

The lust of the flesh relates to sexual immorality, the lust of the eyes relates to money or mammon, and the pride of life relates to power. Those are the three major areas in which we face temptation. Looking through the long lenses of history, we see that leaders, whether Christian or secular, have been brought down because of temptation in these three areas. Great empires and powerful people have been destroyed by the power of temptation in these three main areas: immorality, money and power.

Joseph was seduced and tempted to sleep with Potiphar's wife. Thankfully, he rejected her advances and was able to overcome that temptation. As powerful as the temptation might have been, Joseph was only able to overcome it because he possessed a fear of the Lord that was greater than his fear of Potiphar's wife and what she could do to him.

In Genesis chapter 39: 9 Joseph says:

> *"He is not greater in this house than I am; nor has he kept anything from me except you, for you are his wife. How can I do this great evil and sin against God?" – Amplified Bible*

Joseph looked at this temptation in the context of sinning against God, and because he had a reverential fear of God, he ran away from this temptation.

I believe that only when we have a reverential fear of the Lord that is higher than any other fear that we may have, can we confront and overcome temptation. We must put a higher premium on our relationship with God than on any other relationship on earth. Temptations will come to all people whom God seeks to use and whom God is preparing for service – in whatever capacity. Joseph saw his service in Potiphar's house ultimately as a service he rendered to God and that he was accountable to God. This is a profound truth that is lost on many believers today, for it is sad to say that, often, Christians are found to be wanting in their service whether it is to God or man. Joseph could not stretch his hand out to do wrong because he feared God and felt that he was God's steward. How amazing it would be if Christians, today, would have the same practical approach as Joseph wherever they may be, be it in the public or private sector; to be Christian in deed and not in name only; to be people whose actions and lives speak for themselves as children of God. Joseph was such a man.

Many times we go through tests and don't recognize them as such. I imagine that Joseph didn't, at the time, recognize his situation as a test; he most likely thought of it as a terrible setback. It is only in God's equation where a setback is a setup for promotion.

3. The Waiting Test

The third stage of the process in the life of Joseph is one that I think many believers and many people who are on the journey with God can relate to. That is the waiting season. In this waiting season, it is very easy to question whether God's Word, God's promise, God's vision, God's dream is true or will ever come to pass. In the Bible, we see other stories of men and women of God who experienced a season of waiting in their lives. During this time, we often feel like God and society have forgotten us.

Moses waited 40 years in the wilderness as he led the children of Israel out of Egypt. I'm sure those were lonely years when he must have questioned God's plan for his life. Abraham waited for God's plan to materialize for 25 years. Those years are part of the process - the waiting, the silent years, the lonely wilderness time where it is easy to question God. Where is the dream? Where is the vision? Where are all those prophecies that I received?

The test in the waiting season is faithfulness. God desires to see our hearts and if we will be faithful to Him when it looks like He is not answering our prayers when it looks like He has forgotten us, when everybody else has forgotten us and when it looks like the promise is not going to come to pass. There is always that question, "Did God really speak to me?" If He spoke to me then why am I here? Why am I in this situation? Why am I alone? Why am I still waiting? Why has the promise not been fulfilled yet?

As someone who has experienced my waiting seasons, let me encourage you. Don't give up. Remain faithful to God. It is a test of your faith and it is part of the process.

In the end, God is always vindicated; He always promotes; He always remembers and establishes His children when they are faithful. Every season, every stage of the process has its hardships, its difficulties and the season of waiting is not any different.

Romans 4:19,20:

> *"He did not weaken in faith when he considered the (utter) impotence of his own body, which was as good as dead because he was about a hundred years old, or (when he considered) the barrenness of Sarah's (deadened) Womb. No unbelief or distrust made him waver (doubtingly question) concerning the promise of God, but he grew strong and was empowered by faith as he gave praise and glory to God."* – *Amplified Bible*

Abraham could have doubted God in that season. It was only natural to doubt or question God. However, the Bible says he did not waver or give way to unbelief. Instead, he was strengthened in faith being completely convinced that God was not only able and mighty but He was faithful to do what He had promised.

My encouragement to you is that God is not only able, He is not only mighty enough, but He is also faithful to honour the promise He made to you. Whatever you are waiting on God for, He is faithful and He will come through for you. Joseph went through those stages in the process and anyone who is used by God will go through such a process. I believe it is a kind of purification process to prepare you and me for our service; to prepare us for our assignment and our calling.

Am I a Joseph?

It is important to question where we are going in life. Imagine, you get on a train to go to a specific city. You are seated in a comfortable chair, and you have a great book to read. The train may even have a great meal service. You meet an interesting person in the next aisle and strike up a conversation. You are having a great time. About two hours into your journey, the conductor speaks on the intercom, announcing that you are almost getting to your destination. But alas the city he announces is the wrong destination for you! You realize that you mistakenly got on the wrong train and that you have travelled in the opposite direction to where you originally intended to go. The journey was comfortable and even pleasant until you realized you were on the wrong train!

This is a simple story to demonstrate that God didn't create us to simply have the "good life' but rather the "God life."

You may be comfortable in your life, and everything may be moving along at a pleasant and predictable pace. But are you on the train that God assigned you? Have you looked at your ticket to make sure you are where He wants you to be? Have you checked that the train you are on is headed in the direction that God wills for you?

Whose Dream Am I Living?

The vision for our lives must come from the Lord. He is our creator and He alone knows the plans that He has for us.

You may be like Joseph or like David who received their visions from God early in life. You may even be like the prophet Samuel who was dedicated even before he was born. Or you may be like many other people who came into their calling a little later in their lives; people who, maybe, had to change direction somewhere along their journeys.

When Jesus called the disciples they were all fishermen. They had probably thought that they were going to be fishermen all their lives; maybe their fathers had been fishermen or they lived in fishing communities. It is possible that fishing was all they had ever known. When Jesus met Simon Peter he said, "from now on you will catch [fish] men."(Luke 5:10) Jesus, in calling Peter, was telling him that, 'your life is going to take a different path.'

Paul was a lawyer and Pharisee before he became the apostle to the Gentiles. However, God had another plan for him. As such Paul had to align himself with the plan and the purpose of God. We see the same with Moses, who came into his calling much later in life.

You could be someone who has always known what God's vision for your life is. You could also come into that vision much later. Indeed, you could, right now, be questioning God, saying, 'what is Your vision for my life?'

The most important thing is that the vision comes from God, the vision is not our own. Therefore, it is only through your relationship with Him that He can reveal to you what His vision is for your life.

The first thing in being a Joseph is to have God's vision. We need to seek God if we do not know what it is He has for us. If we are fighting with God about that vision and purpose; if we are trying to go our way, we need to spend time with God and align our lives with His vision.

Intimacy With God

Daniel 11:32 says:

".....but the people who know their God shall prove

themselves strong and shall stand firm and do exploits (for God)." – Amplified Bible

The word "know" as used in this scripture, speaks of intimacy. Knowing God is not just knowing about God and His existence. It denotes more than attending church services or doing religious activities. Knowing God can only come from having a relationship with Him as Father, experiencing Him and developing unshakable confidence in His character.

There is no way that we will come to know God if we don't spend time with Him. We must invest time in prayer and Bible study, and learn to commune with God. Take the example of Joseph. When he was in prison, he didn't have any weekly fellowships or Sunday worship services to take part in. He didn't have the support and the luxury of fellowship with other believers. All he had, in all those years, was his relationship with God.

David said in Psalm 42:7, "the deep calls to deep" and I believe that means that the deep places in God's heart call to the deep places in our hearts. Knowing God in an intimate relationship is to relate to Him one-on-one. That is where we create deep reservoirs, pools of refreshing for our spirits; that is where our real relationship with God is built. David's strength and relationship with God were forged in the early years of his life as he was on his own tending his father's sheep. It was there that he learnt to worship God. It was there that he experienced God as his Shepherd.

How could David have known this? He experienced it. He realized that God looked after him with the same tenderness and care that he looked after his father's sheep. Such intimacy is priceless and we can draw on that for years to come.

Hearing From God

One of the questions my children asked me when they were younger was, "How do you hear from God? How do you know God's Voice? Does He speak audibly? How do you know it is Him and not your own voice?" These were tough questions coming from young minds.

My only answer was to pose a question to them, "if Imma or Daddy were out and called on the house phone, how would you know who was calling?" They would laugh and insist that, of course, they could tell our voices apart because they knew us well. I answered that is just the way it is with God; when you know God, you begin to recognize His Voice. His Voice becomes familiar to you, just like a parent's voice.

What is interesting is that when you are intimate - when you know someone well - you can hear the person clearly, and decipher when it is their voice or not. It is very important to be able to hear from God. To be a Joseph, you need to be able to hear from God.

Let me share with you two scriptures, one is from the life of Joseph and the second is from the life of Daniel.

Genesis 41: 15-16 has the following words:

"And Pharaoh said to Joseph, I have dreamed a dream and there is no one who can interpret it; and I have heard it said of you that you can understand a dream and interpret it. Joseph answered Pharaoh, it is not in me; God (not I) will give Pharaoh a (favourable) answer of peace." - Genesis 41:15, 16.

This is very critical. Pharaoh told Joseph he had heard that Joseph could interpret dreams and Joseph was clear in pointing out that it was God who gave him the power and thus was able to interpret the dreams. Joseph wants to make the point that he doesn't have this innate ability to decipher dreams. Rather, it is through his relationship with God and the fact that he hears from God. His ability to hear because of God was the answer to Pharoah's dilemma.

Our ability to tap into God's mysteries, secrets and wisdom for every situation, is what sets a 'Joseph' apart from everyone else.

God gave Joseph the answer to the biggest question of his life. Many of us are going to confront or are confronting similar, and perhaps, big questions, big decisions, and big problems. On our own, we are not able to solve these problems. However, from this account of Joseph's life, we see that the critical component is God and our ability to hear from God.

In our own lives, we can also say with confidence that God will give us the answer for whatever situation we may be facing.

Daniel 2:19, 26-28, says:

> *"Then the secret was revealed to Daniel in a vision of the night, and Daniel blessed the God of heaven. The King said to Daniel, whose name was Belteshazzer, Are you able to make known to me the dream which I have seen and the interpretation of it? Daniel answered the king, The (Mysterious) secret which the king has demanded neither the wise men, enchanters, magicians, nor astrologers can show the king, But there is a God in heaven who reveals secrets, and He has made known to king Nebuchadnezzar what is that shall be in latter days (at the end of days).*
> *– Amplified Bible*

Daniel was a son of the nobles of Israel, who was captured and brought to Babylon with other young men to serve in the king's palace. He dedicated himself to the Lord's service even while in a foreign land. He possessed an excellent spirit from the Lord. Daniel was confronted with the problem of first reminding the king of his dream and then interpreting the dream. This was a very tricky situation to be in and the consequence of failure was certain death in ways that only a Babylonian king could conjure up.

The Bible states, however, that the secret was revealed to Daniel in a vision in the night and Daniel blessed the God of heaven. Daniel recognized that God was the One who revealed the vision.

Daniel was the only man in the entire kingdom with wise men, enchanters, astrologers and soothsayers who could interpret the king's dream.

In today's language, wise people would be represented by economists, scientists, lawyers, doctors, political thinkers and analysts. The wise men in Daniel's time did not have the answer. Even today, many so-called wise men do not have the answers to the ills of our societies.

Daniel 2:28 says:

> *"...but there is a God in heaven who reveals secrets and He has made known to the king what it is that shall be in the latter days your dream and the visions in your head upon your bed are these but as for me this secret is not revealed to me for any wisdom that I have more than anyone else living but in order that the interpretation may be made known to the king that you may know the thoughts of your own heart." – Amplified Bible*

Amazingly, Daniel essentially confessed that he was not different from any other man; he was not smarter, not wiser, and didn't possess some innate ability to do what he was doing. Daniel confirmed that God had revealed the meaning of the dream. The stories of Daniel and Joseph, separated by centuries and in completely different social, economic, political and spiritual environments, arrive at the same conclusion; 'it's not me it's God.'

Therefore, to be a 'Joseph' in this season - in this generation - we need

to be able to hear from God because God is the determining factor in solving the complex problems our societies face.

What Is My Purpose?

The word "purpose" is one of the commonly misunderstood and overused words today. Often, it is used interchangeably to mean: talents, disciplines, areas of focus, and passion. So what exactly is 'purpose'? What does it mean?

Every person has a calling and an assignment in their life and is confronted with a specific problem to solve. Note that God's assignment often presents itself as a problem.

At the beginning of Creation, God put Adam in the middle of the Garden of Eden and commanded him to "tend it."

The assignment often appears as something that needs to be fixed, tended or solved. Sometimes it is a very dire problem like the situation with Joseph that was about dealing with food security. In his case, Joseph's life training prepared him to deal with the enormous problem of worldwide famine. Often, the difficulty and intensity of the training are commensurate with the size and scope of the assignment of God. The bigger the assignment, the more difficult the training. Oftentimes, the assignment of our lives will be dealing with just one problem which may have different facets. However, it is usually just one issue that God has called us to focus all our energies on. For example, the problem that catapulted Joseph to his destiny was one of food security. In the same way, God has called us to be problem solvers. We need to embrace the problem that God has created us to solve.

Many times when we see a problem, our first instinct is to run away from it. However, I believe that if God brought something to you, as he brought to Daniel and Joseph, He desires to partner with you knowing that, His wisdom, working through you, can help you solve the problem. As He helps you solve the problem, He is glorified and you fulfill your purpose in life. Fulfilling one's purpose brings a deep sense of contentment, meaning and joy.

After God has revealed His assignment for your life, the next thing that He does is to give you a God-given strategy. As you tap into the wisdom of God He downloads His solution. These solutions are usually profoundly simple. For Joseph, He instructed him to store up a portion of the harvest from the seven good years to feed the world during the seven bad years. Joseph followed God's strategy and it worked! What is interesting is that there were very many wise and educated people in Egypt. However, it was only through the wisdom of God that this strategy for the salvation of the nation was revealed. Therefore the solution does not depend so much on our skill, our ability or our education.

Of course, it is good to have skills, abilities and education and to apply ourselves as needed. However, God is not limited to those things.

Many times, even in our history as a country, God has given our leaders divinely inspired strategies. It can be a natural strategy such as the war against HIV/AIDS or it can be a spiritual strategy as many of our spiritual leaders have had spiritual strategies in attacking spiritual situations.

What I want to make clear is that God reveals the problem and then He gives a strategy to confront the problem. Looking at the examples of Joseph, Daniel and Moses, God gave them lifelong assignments and they spent the rest of their lives dealing with their respective problems. Their entire lives were spent managing and growing the solutions and the resources for the respective problem. We don't hear about Joseph doing any other thing, except being a steward in the house of Pharaoh. We don't hear Daniel doing any other thing except being a leader - a governor in Babylon. That call to serve God is a lifelong call and that assignment is a lifelong assignment.

The Spirit of Fear

Finally, I believe that people who have come out of lengthy bondage, or being under a stronghold of oppression, need to confront fear. The children of Israel had been slaves for 400 years, roughly four generations. Fear was a constant issue they faced because all they had known for so long was slavery. In some instances, their fear of the enemy was greater than the enemy itself.

Joshua 10: 24 says:

> *"When they brought out those kings to Joshua, (he) called for all the*
>
> *Israelites and he told the commanders of the men of war who went with him, Come, put your feet on the neck of these kings. And they came and put their feet on the (kings') necks. Joshua said to them, fear not nor be dismayed; be strong and of good courage. For thus shall the Lord do to all your enemies against whom you fight." – Amplified Bible*

Just picture it, these were the children of slaves who had known no other life. They were fighting against and displacing kings who had been ruling these lands for generations. Joshua called his commanders and had them put their feet on the necks of their enemies. This is a vivid picture of what

God wants to do for His people as they trust and obey Him. In essence, the slave would overthrow the master, and the subjugated would put his foot on the neck of the oppressor. The slave would rule over the king. I believe Joshua, also a former slave, wanted to give his people confidence, boldness and courage. The battle they were fighting was psychological, spiritual and physical. It was a battle with their past and a way to establish a new present and better future. God charged Joshua and the people to be strong and courageous because, from then on, they would displace and overthrow the oppressive kings.

That is a word for all of us today. Our God is effectively putting our feet on the necks of oppressive strongholds, principalities and systems that have been ruling on the mountains of our lives and our nations. The Lord is saying, "Thus will I do to all your enemies." Therefore be strong, do not be afraid, and be of good courage, for the Lord will give you overwhelming victory over your enemies in Jesus' Mighty Name.

Prayer

Father, we thank you for this word that has gone forth to awaken and stir up the Gifts, dreams and visions in the lives of your children. I pray that You will confirm the vision and call on the lives of Your children that are reading this book. I also pray that You will empower them to embrace the problem that You destined them to solve in their generation. Please help us all to hear Your voice clearly and bring heavenly strategies to the circumstances we face. I pray that You will release into the marketplace the movers and shakers of this generation - the Joseph company that will be shepherds, priests and gatekeepers in our society. In Jesus' Mighty Name, Amen.

18. The Crossing

Through all the days that eat away
At every breath that I take
Through all the nights I have lain alone
In someone else's dream, awake

All the words in truth that were spoken
That the wind has blown away
Oh, it's only You that remains with me
Clear as the Light of day

O siyeza (oh I'm coming), o siyeza (oh I'm coming)
Sizofika webaba noma (you know the tide is turning)
O siyeza, O siyeza (I'm telling you the tide is turning)
Siyagudle lomhlaba (gonna make this crossing)
Siyawela lapheshaya (over this dark land)
Lulezontaba ezimyama (gonna touch your face)
Lapha sobheka phansi (gonna lay me down)
Konke ukhulupheka (in that green field of grace)

A punch drunk man in a downtown bar
Takes a beating without making a sound
Through swollen eyes, he sways and he smiles
Cause no one can put him down

Inside of him a boy looks up to his father
For a sign or an approving eye
Oh, it's funny how those once so close and now gone
Still so affect our lives

O siyeza, o siyeza
Sizofika webaba noma
O siyeza, o siyeza
Siyagudle lomhlaba
Siyawela lapheshaya
Lulezontaba ezimnyama
Lapho sobheka phansi
Konke ukhulupheka

Take me now
Don't let go
Hold me close
I'm coming home

– Song by Johnny Clegg and Savuka from the album *In My African Dream,* 1994.

As indicated elsewhere in this work, in 2019, I was privileged to join my father on a trip to Addis Ababa, Ethiopia. He was going to attend the African Union assembly and I was going to meet some potential distributors for our dairy products. I had accompanied my father before to Addis and even spoken at the Prayer Breakfast at the African Union. I can describe the African Union only as African Heaven because it is there that you understand how vast and diverse Africa is. All the languages, nations, cultures and dressing styles are so beautiful to behold. It is wonderful seeing the pictures of the founding fathers of the Organization of African Unity which later evolved into the African Union; Kwame Nkrumah of Ghana, Emperor Haile Selassie of Ethiopia, Sekou Toure of Guinea, Mwalimu Nyerere of Tanzania, Mzee Jomo Kenyatta of Kenya and others.

I was not aware that 2019 marked a historical milestone in our spiritual, social and political journey as African people. I would learn during the visit that the African Union and people of African descent around the world were marking the 400th anniversary of the first African slaves arriving in America and the beginning of the Trans-Atlantic Slave trade. I attended a prayer breakfast hosted by then-Kenyan President H.E. Uhuru Kenyatta, which was attended by other presidents including my father. There were delegates from all around Africa and the Americas, mostly church and political leaders. I learnt that the year 2019 was named "The Year of the Return." Many symbolic events were planned on the continent and in the diaspora to commemorate this milestone and the long journey of African peoples from slavery to freedom. I was greatly moved to learn this aspect of the history of African people as it resonated deeply with what the Lord had been revealing to me spiritually since 2017. I wanted to learn as much as I could and make as many contacts from the African diaspora to facilitate this discussion further to prepare for the gate of time that was approaching later in the year.

I also learnt that my father was going to make a keynote presentation to the plenary session on the importance of African integration for the survival of the African people. In the hotel room, I listened to my father as he read out his speech to see how much time it would take because he was given a specific time allotment to speak. As I listened to his speech, my spirit resonated and responded profoundly to his words. I realized that his was not simply a political speech, but more so a prophetic call to the nations of Africa and the African people to unite or perish. I understood that the Lord had allowed me to go to Addis not only to do my own business but to provide spiritual support for my father as he prepared to give this landmark address. I wasted no time in calling our intercessors at home, family and friends and asked them to pray for Mzee as he prepared to give this speech. We agreed in prayer that he would have enough time to read the speech in its entirety and not an edited version. We also prayed that there would be a spirit of agreement among the leaders in response to his speech. Finally, we prayed for God's favour and anointing on Mzee and the words he would release that day. We recognized the power of agreement and how necessary it was for there to be an agreement so that the words he spoke would be received and accepted.

I kept speaking to our intercessors and friends and family back home and kept them all abreast with the programme of the day and the specific time Mzee would be speaking. I was privileged to sit right behind him in the great plenary hall and prayed in my heart the whole time he was speaking. It was one of the most powerful and poignant moments I have experienced. You could hear a pin drop for the entire duration of his speech, everyone sat in rapt attention.

I recalled reading a book by author David McCullough, titled *John Adams,*[1] which chronicled the life of the second President of the United States. The author described the moment John Adams rose to make an impassioned bid for the independence of the colonies from the English crown. According to the book, the atmosphere was electric and there was a strange hush in the entire room. It also says that when John Adams rose to speak, he spoke with such power and conviction that he didn't understand where it all came from. In the margin of the book, I wrote the word "anointing" to explain the unexplainable sense of power, ability and might to do what you couldn't do on your own. The anointing is God's spiritual enabling to do what we cannot do by ourselves.

In that plenary hall, I felt that same sensation, the hush and stillness of the room, the electric atmosphere, the force and power of Mzee's words as he spoke to the leaders of Africa. When he completed his speech, he received an amazing response. I can only liken it to when a boxer wins a great title or championship and everyone jumps into the boxing ring and he is completely swamped and swallowed up by those seeking to congratulate him. I remember Sylvester Stallone's *Rocky* movies where the crowds would just inundate him after winning the title. This is similar to what happened when my father completed his speech and we rose to leave. People of all languages, colours and nationalities swarmed around him shaking his hand, hugging him and congratulating him on articulating the needs, desires and aspirations of an entire people. It was awesome and beautiful

---

1 David McCullough. John Adams. Simon & Shuster, 2001.

to behold. I was so greatly moved, and I felt tears well up in my eyes. I realized then that Africa is beautiful, so beautiful and unity is beautiful and that is why the enemy hates unity and seeks to constantly drive a wedge between brothers.

I share Mzee's speech in its entirety in this chapter because it is more than a speech, it is a prophetic call. And the prophetic must be received by the church and prayed over and incubated by people of faith to see it come to pass. I believe that African integration and unity will be realized by the Grace of God. However, we as the Church must receive this vision and internalize it in our prayer closets and our hearts, speaking to God about it and then to each other in His house for it to become a reality. May the Lord bring forward what seems so far away, and unite Africa under His banner of love.

A Paper on Africa's Economic and Political Integration Delivered at The 32nd Ordinary Summit of The African Union Heads of State In Addis Ababa Ethiopia.

President Yoweri Kaguta Museveni

Africa is the origin of man, four and a half million years ago. All human beings only lived in Africa until about 100,000 years ago. The last ice age ended 11,700 years ago. Before that, people could not live in many parts of the North of our Globe. Therefore, the European Stock (Europeans, Americans, Canadians, Australians), the Asians, the Arabs etc., are all former Africans.

They lost the melanin in their skins on account of their living in cold climates, with little sunshine, where melanin is not required.

Africa is the pioneer of civilization. The Egyptian civilization which started around 5200 years ago, around 3000 BC, is one of the earliest civilizations of the human race.

The three great religions of the modern world were succoured by Africa in one way or another. These are Christianity, Judaism and Islam. Baby Jesus was hidden in Egypt when King Herod started killing all the infants. This is found in the Book of Matthew 2:13-14 in the Bible. Before that, in the year 1567 BC, the Jews had been saved from starvation when one of the children of Jacob, Joseph, who had been sold into slavery by his brothers, took them into Egypt where there was plenty. This is found in the Book of Genesis_Chapter 42 verses 1-10, in the Bible.

Yet, this Africa of many firsts in the history of the human race has faced calamity after calamity in the last 500 years. These calamities have included: the slave trade, colonialism, genocide in some cases, neo-colonialism and marginalization. Why has this been so?

Africa, which had achieved many firsts for the human race, had some internal weaknesses which made it difficult for its people to respond to the threats that emerged after 1453 AD. This was the year the Ottoman Turks, people coming out of Central Asia, captured Constantinople, the capital of the Eastern Roman Empire. By doing so, they blocked the overland silk route which had been pioneered by Marco Polo in the years 1271 to 1368. Since Marco Polo, silk and spices had been coming through this route. Now, that route was closed and Western Europe was cut off from the products of the East, that they had come to treasure.

A frantic search for a sea route to the East by the Europeans started, led by Portugal. Better ships were, eventually, built and the Portuguese got to Sierra Leone in the year 1460. In 1498, Vasco Da Gama went around the Southern tip of Africa and, on Christmas day, landed at Natal, hence the name of that place up to now, coming from the Latin word, *natalis* (Natal) which means origins/beginnings or birthday.

A few years earlier, in 1492, Christopher Columbus, working for the newly United Kingdom of Spain (Castille and Aragon United in the year 1479), had reached a whole new continent, America, whose off-shore Islands, the Caribbeans, he mistook to be the Islands of the East, hence the eventual name of the West Indies.

Therefore, on account of the pressure created by the Turks on the Europeans, the Europeans burst out of their homelands and started accessing the lands of Africa, America and Asia through the Atlantic and the Indian Oceans.

This is when the weaknesses of Africa and the Americas came to the fore. The indigenous populations of the Americas could not withstand the afflictions of the European invasion and many of them perished; they were exterminated and their lands were taken over by the immigrants from Europe. Hence, the Europeans became the Americans. Those who did not perish were marginalized.

Since the Africans do not die easily, they survived the 500 years of foreign invasions but had gone through many privations: slave trade, colonialism, in some cases genocide, etc.

Why couldn't Africa defeat these invasions? Indeed by 1900, the whole of Africa had been defeated, except for Ethiopia which defeated the Italian invaders in the battle of Adwa in 1896. According to our analysis, it was not because of a lack of courage or the will to resist. It was, mainly, on account of political balkanization. The African population is only divided into four linguistic groups. These are the Niger-Congo (Bantu and Kwa), the Nilo-Saharan (Hamitic, Nilotic and Nilo-Hamitic), the Afro-Asiatic (Arabic, Tigrinya and Amharic), and the Khoisan (so-called bushmen in Southern Africa). Therefore, the entirety of the African peoples is either similar or linked. I can pick words that are similar to the ones in my dialect, Runyankore, in the Bantu dialects, all the way from Cameroon to South Africa. 2000 miles away in South Africa, for instance, the Zulus and Xhosas greet: *Saubhona,* which, I suspect, means: "I have seen you". This must be from the verb: *kubona* – meaning "to see". In my dialect, Runyankore, the verb *kubona* means to find something that has been lost. In Swahili, however, the verb: *kuona* means exactly what it means in the South African dialects. That is within the Bantu cluster of dialects. Even between clusters – e.g. Niger-Congo versus Nilo-Saharan — you find similarities. The Nubians of Southern Egypt and North Sudan, apparently, use the word: *Nina* to mean "Mother".

In many of the dialects of the Bantus of the Great Lakes, the word for Mother is *nyina*. Amazing. The Somali word for cow is *saa*. In the Bantu dialects of the Great Lakes, the word *saa* is specifically and exclusively used for cow-dung (*obusa, amasha, amasa, etc.)*. Therefore, these African peoples are either similar or linked. Indeed, if you use the word "nation" to mean a people from a common ancestry or a common heritage, you can say that the entire African population of 1.3 billion people today, is comprised of only four nations: the Niger-Congo, the Nilo-Saharan, the Afro-Asiatic and the Khoisan.

What, then, was the problem? Why couldn't Africa defend itself against the invaders? Why is Africa still weak today? According to our study, the answer lies in political balkanization. By the 1400s, Africa was governed by small Kingdoms, Chiefdoms or, sometimes, by segmentary arrangements (the rule of age groups).

The Europeans tried to swallow China but it was too big to swallow. They tried to swallow Japan; it was too big to swallow. They tried to swallow Ethiopia but it was too big to swallow. The African Kingdoms and Chiefdoms were swallowable when confronted by the more organized groups from outside. The gradual defeat of Africa from 1400-1900, caused serious distortions which are captured in many studies we have made.

Apart from the slave trade and other haemorrhages inflicted on the African societies, there was also the gradual destruction of the artisan classes (the blacksmiths, the carpenters, the copper smiths, the medicine men, etc.) and replacing their products with the imported ones. Even with the primitive societies, they always produced their own food, their own clothes, their own weapons (spears, bows and arrows, etc.) and means for their own shelter (housing materials). It may only be the Africans of the colonial and neo-colonial eras that depend on the food, clothes, weapons and building materials of others. All this was a consequence of the distortions emanating from colonialism.

Nevertheless, by a combination of factors, African countries regained their independence, starting with Egypt in 1922, Sudan in 1956 and Ghana in 1957. What were these factors? These were: Africans refusing to be exterminated like the American Indians [Natives] and the Australian Aborigines; the resistance by the African freedom fighters; the support of the socialist countries such as the USSR and China; and the wars among the imperialists – the so-called 1st and 2nd World Wars – which weakened them very much to our advantage. In 1994, the last part of Africa under foreign control, South Africa, regained their political freedom.

What, however, is amazing is that many of the African political elite, the intellectuals, the other social leaders etc., have not bothered to investigate the cause of our near extinction in the last 500 years and to look for ways of how we can immunize ourselves against any and all threats against our survival, our sovereignty, our security and our prosperity in our land. That is how we come to the two issues that we regard as crucial for our future. These are the political and economic integration of Africa. Our view is that African integration means three things: prosperity, security and fraternity. We cannot guarantee our prosperity if we do not solve the issue of the market. When companies or families produce products (goods) or services, how many consumers will buy those products? If a product does not have enough buyers, the business will fail. In Uganda, recently we had a big crop of maize. We produced 5 million tonnes but Uganda consumes only 1 million tonnes. The prices collapsed. Many farmers will move away from maize in the coming seasons. This is just one example. Many others can be quoted across Africa. We, therefore, need economic integration to provide a market for our producing families and companies to be assured of a market on principles of competitiveness. The integrated African market will not only stimulate production in Africa, [but] it will also enable us to negotiate credibly with the other big markets such as the USA, China, India, Russia, European Union, etc. It is good that, recently, we agreed on the Continental Free Trade Area (CFTA). Let us implement its provisions. It is the way to prosperity and part of the answer to under-development, poverty and joblessness.

However, economic integration, even if it creates prosperity for our individual countries, will not answer the issue of strategic security against global threats. The Americans are talking of four-dimensional superiority: superiority on land, in the air, at sea and in space. Recently, President Donald Trump was talking about creating a Space Army. Many African countries do not yet have even a capable army on land, let alone air, navy or space. What is the future? Even when our individual countries become first World or Middle-Income countries, they cannot, individually, have the strategic capacity to defend themselves against the global superpowers. In the Second World War, the first victims of aggression were the developed but small countries of Europe: Holland, Belgium, Denmark, Poland, etc.

Israel, technologically, is a superpower. However, strategically, Israel would be hard-pressed to survive in the Middle East without the partnership of the United States. Therefore, in the end, size also matters. That is why, therefore, we say that, in addition to economic integration, where feasible, political integration is very crucial. The present 54 States of Africa, even when they are developed, may not be able to guarantee our future against greedy global powers. The attack by the Western countries against Libya was a shame to Africa. That is why, therefore, for 55 years, I have been in the footsteps of Mwalimu Julius Nyerere on the issue of the East African Federation (the political integration of Kenya, Tanzania and Uganda). The EAC has since expanded to include Rwanda, Burundi and South Sudan. These people are specific groupings of the African peoples comprised of the Interlacustrine Bantus (the Bantus of the Lakes) and the Interlacustrine Nilotics, Interlacustrine Nilo-Hamitic and Interlacustrine Cushitic. These groups have great similarities in dialects and also linkages among different clusters. Above all, they have the good fortune of having the de-tribalized dialect of Swahili. The six countries are working on the issue of Confederation and, ultimately, Federation. The politically united States of

East Africa, with a present population of 170 million, which will be 878 million by 2050, with one million square miles of land territory, would be equal to India in land area. Such a unit would be cohesive, around Swahili, as well as a centre of gravity for African security. It would be capable of any task – to defend Africa, if necessary, on land, at sea or in space since that is what others want.

We should, then, look across Africa. Which other areas have such similarities and linkages? How about Southern Africa? How about Central Africa? How about West Africa with its cross-border peoples of the Hausa, Fulani, Yoruba, Akan, Mandigos, etc.? How about North Africa with its people that are Arabic speaking and, mainly, Moslems? How about the Horn of Africa with its confluence of the Cushitic and the Semitic peoples of this area? I would not die from blood pressure if the present 54 States of Africa, the former colonies, were replaced by 10 or so States, each about the size of India. When the British forced independent tribes of our area into a Uganda, they, definitely, did a good thing. If Uganda is a better product than the "Republic" of Ankole, my tribal area, why shouldn't the Union of East Africa be better?

Is it correct to deify the colonial political architecture of the 54 present countries (52 of them former colonies) and rule out the possibility of a rational re-organization to achieve optimum results? Two colonies of the Dutch – Orange Free State and Transvaal were united with the two British colonies – Cape Town and Natal to form the Union of South Africa in 1910. Everybody is happy with the Union of South Africa. Why can we not improve on what the colonialists did? In 1912, defeated Africa, and initiated a strategic counter-offensive against the invaders when the patriots in South Africa formed the African National Congress (the ANC) which also attracted the great Mahatma Gandhi.

The counter-offensive gathered momentum, including the 5th Pan Africanist Congress of 1945 where our elders like Nkrumah, Kenyatta and others vowed to free Africa from the disgrace of foreign rule, acting in coordination. It has, therefore, been an oversight to allow that strategic counter-offensive to peter out after independence. We need to re-ignite and develop that counter-offensive.

Finally, the main point is that the people we are trying to bring together, as pointed out earlier, are either similar to one another or linked. They all belong to the four clusters according to language: Niger-Congo, Nilo-Saharan, Afro-Asiatic and Khoisan. They are fraternal groups. When Muammar Gaddafi was alive, I did not agree with him on the issue of a continental Government now. With trading, I can trade with everybody.

However, political integration needs more intimacy. The people should either be similar or compatible. That is why I prefer Mwalimu Nyerere's strategy of Regional Federations where feasible. Mzee Kwame Nkrumah preferred a continental Government, like Muammar Gaddafi.

Therefore, the integration of Africa means three issues: prosperity; strategic security; and fraternity. There are longer and more illustrated documents dealing with this issue.

The African leaders since independence, need to be careful not to share the historical condemnation like the one we heap on the pre-colonial chiefs who, for almost 400 years, certainly in the case of the Great Lakes, concentrated on rivalries among themselves, even after Vasco Da Gama had passed by the East African Coast. Instead of uniting our people, they were busy fighting one another with their obsequious subjects heaping pseudo-praises on them.

When the Europeans were ready, after the Berlin Congress, they penetrated the continent and picked up many chiefs like grasshoppers. Europe, America and Asia are now going towards the 4th Industrial Revolution – the use of intelligent machines. In Africa, we have not even gone through the first and second Industrial Revolutions – the use of steam engines and electricity. Yet, the economic and political integrations are crucial stimuli for these changes. African leaders, therefore, need to work hard so as not to share the fate of the pre-colonial tribal chiefs that let down their people.

I thank you.

Monday, February 11, 2019

19. The Glorious Church

"Imagine yourself as a living house. God comes in to rebuild that house. At first, perhaps, you can understand what He is doing. He is getting the drains right and stopping the leaks in the roof and so on; you knew that those jobs needed doing and so you are not surprised. But, presently, He starts knocking the house about in a way that hurts abominably and does not seem to make any sense. What on earth is He up to? The explanation is that He is building quite a different house from the one you thought of - throwing out a new wing here, putting on an extra floor there, running up towers, making courtyards. You thought you were being made into a decent little cottage, but He is building a palace. He intends to come and live in it Himself." - *C. S. Lewis.*

When the Lord called me to the ministry seventeen years ago, the overarching vision He gave me was of a transformed Africa. As I started preaching the word the Lord had given me, many believers didn't fully understand or agree with the message. Initially, they felt that the church should focus on preaching salvation through Jesus Christ alone.

What did the church have to do with the destiny of nations? My response was and still is everything. I believe that if you want to know the direction that the nation is going, you need to listen to what is being preached in the pulpits of churches. Someone once said that 'where the pulpit goes, so goes the nation.'

The nation is dependent on the church fully understanding its role and participating in it. When the church is silent and disengaged from society, we are not shining the light of Jesus in the world. The world becomes a dark place. I believe that the church has everything to do with the destiny of the nations.

In Matthew chapter 28 verse 18 Jesus had final parting words to His disciples as He ascended into heaven; what we call the Great Commission is a powerful statement about what God's expectation of His Church is.

Mathew 28:18-20 says:

> *"Jesus approached and, breaking the silence, said to them, All authority (all power of rule) in heaven and on earth has been given to Me. Go then and make disciples of all the nations, baptizing them into the name of the Father of the Son and of the Holy Spirit. Teaching them to observe everything that I have commanded you, and behold I am with you all the days (perpetually, uniformly, and on every occasion), to the (very) close and consummation of the age. Amen (So let it be)." – Amplified Bible*

Jesus, clearly, tells His disciples that the fundamental assignment He is giving them, and all who will believe that will come after them, is to go and make disciples of all nations. What does the word 'nations' mean? Nations mean people groups. He was not talking necessarily about nation-states as we know them today, but rather people groups.

Acts 1: 8 says:

> *"But you shall receive power (ability, efficiency, and might) when the Holy Spirit has come upon you, and you shall be My witnesses in Jerusalem and all Judea and Samaria and to the ends of the earth." – Amplified Bible*

Jesus here is reiterating the Call to go and preach the gospel to the ends of the earth, but then He adds that this assignment can only be accomplished through the power of the Holy Spirit.

The Holy Spirit is the custodian of the Church, the power, and the life force behind the Church. Without the Holy Spirit, the Church becomes dry bones of religious activity and eventually burns out. The Holy Spirit is the One that brings life, spirit, and the breath of God into the body of Christ.

In Acts 1:8, Jesus again emphasizes that He is sending the Church out to the different people groups or nations of the world. The people group of Judea was the Jews and the people group in Samaria was the Samaritans, a mixed ethnic group that had been brought to Israel after the invasion of the Assyrians when the northern tribes were carried away into captivity.

The Apostle Peter was called to be an apostle to the Jewish nation and he stayed within the boundaries of his call. Peter became the leader of the council of the twelve that remained in Jerusalem and was consulted on major issues of church doctrine.

The Apostle Paul, who was called an apostle to the Gentiles, had much more success with the Gentles than the Jews. Being a Jew, he desperately wanted his fellow Jews to come to the saving knowledge of Jesus Christ.

However, God raised him and anointed him to preach the gospel to the Gentiles. After countless clashes and upheavals coming from the rejection of the gospel by the Jews, Paul finally focused fully on preaching the gospel to the Gentile nations.

The call of Covenant Nations Church (CNC) on my life has been primarily to be a witness, preach the gospel and make disciples among African peoples - African nations. I believe that every believer is called to be a witness to those around them and so all of us as believers are called to be witnesses to our families, our friends, and our places of influence. But beyond that, there are specific assignments that God gives to different churches and different peoples.

For Covenant Nations Church, the primary mission and focus that the Lord has given to us from the beginning has been Africa. The point is that if every believer was fulfilling their specific assignment in the Great Commission the world would be a very different place.

Our God is a multifaceted, Omnipresent, Omniscient God; He can release His power, anointing and Grace into the lives of His people to confront the challenges of our times.

Therefore the Church of Jesus Christ is not supposed to be hidden away from society but rather to be right in the center, leading and ministering to the nation spiritually. The Church is to be like a spiritual and moral guide, a compass for the people, a north star to help the nation navigate its way by the Word of God and the leading of the Spirit.

Without the Word of the LORD guiding a nation, the nation falls into a dangerous state similar to the time when the prophet Samuel was born as it says I Samuel, *"The word of the LORD was rare in those days..."*

The Church is not meant to be a relic of the past, some religious institution from the Middle Ages but rather to be ahead of the nation. You cannot lead if you do not know what ails the people and if you are disconnected from the culture. The church must be relevant to our times. I am always struck when I read the gospels by how unafraid Jesus was to confront challenging situations. He faced situations squarely, whether it was religious hypocrisy, adultery, pride, greed, avarice, or complacency. Whatever the situation, Jesus met it head-on. He ministered by the shores of the sea of Galilee, in the synagogue, to the woman at the well, blind Bartimaeus on the street, Nicodemus at night, the tax collectors and sinners. Jesus met them all. He spoke about what ailed the nation. He healed, He comforted, He taught, and He was relevant.

Jesus was a great teacher and often taught principles through parables. He said it in a very beautiful way as recorded in Matthew 5:13-16

> *"You are the salt of the earth, but if the salt has lost its taste (its strength, its quality), how can its saltiness be restored? It is not good for anything any longer but to be thrown out and trodden underfoot by men. You are the light of the world. A city that is set on a hill cannot be hidden. Nor do men light a lamp and put it under a peck measure, but on a lampstand and it gives light to the whole house to all in the house. therefore Let your light so shine before men that they may see your excellence your moral excellence and praiseworthy, noble, and good deeds and recognize and honour and praise and glorify your Father Who is in heaven." – Amplified Bible*

Here Jesus is clearly saying that in His Church, His body is not supposed to be hidden away going through old dusty books, on the outskirts of society and the outskirts of culture and the nations. He said the Church is supposed to be the salt- that means you preserve it. Further, the Church is supposed to be the light to the nation. It means that, if the nation is struggling in the dark, then it is due to the failure of the Church to bring that matter to light. He said that the Church is a 'city on a hill', which means that people should be able to look to the Church as an example for society. I believe God wants His Church to be a planet shaker and a nation-reforming church.

Steve Jobs, the founder of the technology giant Apple, had a goal and mission in life. He is quoted as saying, "We're here to make a dent in the universe. otherwise why even be here."[1] Interestingly, Steve Jobs could have a vision - a plan to be a shaker - to make a "dent in the universe" in his sphere of technology and succeeded in doing that through his company. Today Apple is one of the most successful companies in history and is well on its way to becoming a trillion-dollar company, richer than many nation-states.

How much more should the Church of Jesus Christ be a planet shaker and a reformer of nations through the preaching of the gospel?

Part of the answer may be found in Joshua 3-17:

> *"Joshua commanded the people: When you see the ark of the covenant of the Lord your God being borne by the Levitical priests, set out from where you are and follow it. Yet a space must be kept between you and it, about 2000 cubits by measure; come not near it, that you may (be able to see the ark and) know the way you must go, for you have not passed this way before. And Joshua said to the people, sanctify yourselves (that is, separate yourselves*

---

1 Film Pirates of Silicon Valley directed by Martyn Burke, 1999 and based based on *Fire in the Valley: The Making of the Personal Computer* by Paul Freiberger and Michael Swaine.

for a special holy purpose), for tomorrow the Lord will do wonders among you. Joshua said to the priests, Take up the Ark of the Covenant and pass it over before the people. The Lord said to Joshua, This day I will begin to magnify you in the sight of all Israel, so they may know that as I was with Moses, so I will be with you. You shall command the priests who bear the Ark of the Covenant, When you come to the brink of the waters of the Jordan, you shall stand still in the Jordan. Joshua said to the Israelites, Come near, hear the words of the Lord your God. Joshua said, Hereby you shall know that the living God is among you that he will surely drive out of the Lord of all the earth is passing before you into Jordan! So now take twelve men from the tribes of Israel, one from each tribe. When the soles of the feet of the priests who bare the Ark of the Lord of all the earth shall rest in the Jordan, and the waters of the Jordan coming down from above shall be cut off and they shall stand in one heap.

"And when the who bore the ark had come to Jordan and the feet of the priests were in the brink of water – for the Jordan overflows all its banks throughout the time of harvest.- Then the waters which came down from above stood and rose up in a heap far off, at Adam, the city that is beside Zarethan; and those flowing down toward the sea of Arabah, the salt (Dead) sea, were wholly cut off. And the people passed over opposite Jericho. And while all Israel passed over on the dry ground, the priests who bore the ark of the covenant of the Lord stood firm on dry ground in the midst of the Jordan, until all the nation finished passing over the Jordan." – Amplified Bible

In this scripture, Joshua had taken the helm of the leadership of Israel and was preparing for the conquest of the Promised Land. There are striking similarities between this time and the New Testament church.

This is an amazing account of the charge of the priesthood going before the nation. The Ark of the Covenant which was the symbol of the Presence of God in the nation went ahead.

Moses and Joshua were always very clear that the Ark - the presence of God - led the nation. The people didn't move or decide unless the presence of God led them there first. In every situation, the Presence of God was very key and the priests who ministered to God and who were responsible for the ark were central to leading the nation. What is interesting, and worth emphasizing, is that the priests were not hidden away in a sterile monastic building. No, they were in the trenches with the people, going ahead of the people.

The nation needed to cross River Jordan and the scripture is clear on this, "*as soon as the soles of their feet touched the waters of the Jordan the waters opened.*" So the Lord used the priesthood to open the way for the nation to cross over. The priesthood even went ahead before Joshua and the army. It is the primary role of the church to open the way for the nation through prayer and spiritual warfare.

Something else to note is that the priests didn't just go ahead, they waited in the water until the whole nation had crossed over to the other side of the river. That means they provided spiritual oversight and care for the nation. Once all the nation had safely crossed over, the priests carried the ark to the other side of the Jordan and the waters returned. They had succeeded in their mission. How had they succeeded? The answer: the nation had crossed over.

That is a very clear picture of what the Great Commission means by discipling the nation. The way you know that the Church is successful is when the nation is discipled, in other words, ministered unto. It is not successful by how many people attend the church, how many buildings it owns, or how rich it is. This is well and good but the ultimate litmus test of the success of the Church is the condition of the nation.

2. The battle for Jericho

In Joshua chapter 6:2 – 6, we get the following:

"And the Lord said to Joshua, See, I have given Jericho, its king and mighty men of valour, into your hands. You shall march around the enclosure, all the men of war going

around the city once. This you shall do for six days. And seven priests shall bear before the ark seven trumpets of rams' horns, and on the seventh day you shall march around the enclosure seven times, and the priests shall blow the trumpets. When they make a long blast with the rams' horns and you hear the sound of the trumpet, all the people shall shout with a great shout; and the wall of the enclosure shall fall down in its place and the people shall go up (over it), every man straight before him. So Joshua's son Nun called the priests and said to them, Take up the Ark of the Covenant and let the seven priests bear seven trumpets of rams horn's before the Ark of the Lord." – Amplified Bible

What is interesting about this account is that it is a war scenario, there was the commander of the army, the top military brass, and the soldiers. Yet, astonishingly, there was the church in the midst of them. It was a full worship team with instruments and priests carrying the Ark of the Covenant.

The seven priests carrying the seven rams' horns went before the Ark of the Covenant - the presence of God was again key in leading the nation into battle.

Here is a question for you and me: how many battles are our nations facing? Are they physical battles, political battles or economic battles? When the presence of God is not in our midst we lose battles unnecessarily. How many times do we fail simply because the presence of God is not going ahead of us?

In the account of Jericho, God's people were right in the middle of the battle, they were doing spiritual warfare to open the way. They did spiritual warfare for seven days as they marched around Jericho. They were in essence spiritually mapping the city. As they marched around, there was intense intercession, prayer and laying spiritual claim to the land. Once the spiritual work was done, the natural battle was just a walkover because the difficult part was concluded in the realm of the spirit. Many times when the spiritual work is done it is easy to get a victory.

3. Moses and the Amalekites.

In Éxodos 17: 10-13, we have the following:

> *"So Joshua did as Moses said and fought with Amalek; and Moses Aaron and Hur went up to the hilltop. When Moses held up his hand, Israel prevailed; and when he lowered his hand, Amalek prevailed. But Moses' hands were heavy and grew weary. So (the other men) took a stone and put it under him and he sat on it. Then Aaron and Hur held up his hands, one on one side and the other side; So his hands were steady until going down of the sun. And Joshua mowed down and disabled Amalek and his people with a sword." – Amplified Bible*

Moses was a mighty prophet of God who provided spiritual leadership over the nation when he held up his hands in prayer and intercession. This act is a vivid portrayal of spiritual warfare. It is lifting our hands in prayer over the circumstances of our lives. When Moses' arms were raised in prayer, Israel prevailed; when he lowered his arms Amalek prevailed. Moses' arms were heavy and so the other two men, Aaron and Hur, helped with holding up Moses' hands until the battle was won.

Again we see here that this was a battle situation but the priesthood of God - the Church of God was in the heat of the battle. Moses, who operated in both spiritual and natural capacity, was praying for the battle to be won.

Spiritual warfare is intense and tiring. Moses, not Joshua, got tired and weary from holding up his arms in prayer all day. This is what happens with people engaged in spiritual warfare. They can experience burnout and discouragement. They need support, encouragement and refreshment to maintain their watch over the nation. Moses was a great man of God but he too needed support from other spiritually-minded people so he could fulfill his assignment.

How do we know that Moses succeeded in his assignment that day? The answer is that the nation was victorious, they broke through. If Moses hadn't succeeded in his role as a priest and an intercessor for the nation, the nation wouldn't have broken through.

How many times do we see our nations not succeeding simply because there is no one standing on the hill with their arms uplifted towards God, there is no one taking up that spiritual position, and there is no watchman on the walls?

Ezekiel 22:30 says thus:

> *"And I sought a man among them who should build up the wall and stand in the gap before Me for the land, that I should not destroy it, but found none." – Amplified Bible*

The position that Moses took on a hilltop was symbolic of a position of spiritual oversight, which the Bible calls a "Watchmen on the wall." It means that you get a bird's eye view because you're seeing not just in the natural realm but in the spiritual realm. In this respect, the church must awaken to its role. It is crucial. The church isn't supposed to be separated from the nation but instead should be engaged in the discipling of the nation.

The history of the children of Israel clearly shows us that when they had a strong priesthood with the worship of God, and walked in the laws and the Covenant of God, they were invincible. Consequently, no army could stand against them because God fought for them. However, when the priesthood failed in their role to lead the nation in the true worship of God, the nation fell into judgment, war and turmoil.

Judgement always begins in God's own house because He expects His Church to lead the nation in the path of righteousness.

4. Eli and His Sons

1 Samuel 2:27-35 reads as follows:

> *"A man of God came to Eli and said to him, Thus has the LORD said: I plainly revealed Myself to the house of your father, when they were in Egypt in bondage to Pharoah. Moreover, I selected him out of all the tribes of Israel to be*

my priest, to offer on My altar, to burn incense and to wear an ephod before Me. And I gave to the house of your father all the offerings of the Israelites made by fire.

"Why then did you kick, trample and treat with contempt My sacrifice and offering which I commanded, and honour your sons above Me by fattening yourselves upon the choicest part of every offering of My people Israel?

Therefore, the LORD the God of Israel says, I did promise that your house and that of your father should go in and out before Me forever. But now the LORD says, Be it far from Me, For those who honour Me I will honour and those who despise Me shall be lightly esteemed." – Amplified Bible

God was very displeased with the sons of Eli because they despised God's offering and there was sin in the house of the Lord. To make matters worse is that, when God judged the priesthood, the nation also suffered for the sins of the priests. When the Ark of the Covenant was stolen by the enemies of Israel, the nation was defeated in war. God is very serious about His house and places great authority on the priesthood to disciple the nation. His house must always be a lighthouse and a beacon to the people, positioned above all other mountains so that the nations can flow to it. The house of God must be a place of truth, light, holiness, the love and fear of the Lord and prayer.

When God's priesthood is what it should be, then the nation can also be what it is meant to be.

I believe that the African church must awaken to her role in discipling the nations of Africa in truth, holiness, and the fear of the Lord; ultimately, this can be the greatest hour for the church in Africa and the world.

5. The Sheep versus the Goats

In Matthew 25:31-34, we have the following words:

"When the Son of Man comes in His glory (His majesty and splendour), and all the holy angels with Him, then He will sit on the throne of his glory. All the nations will be gathered

> *before him and He will separate them (the people) from one another as a shepherd separates his sheep from the goats; And He will cause the sheep to stand at His right hand, but the goats at his left. Then the King will say to those at his right hand, Come, you blessed of my Father (you favoured of God and appointed to eternal salvation), inherit (receive as your own) the kingdom prepared for you from the foundations of the World. – Amplified Bible*

When the LORD Jesus Christ returns in triumph and glory, He will judge the nations and separate them according to what their response has been to the Gospel. The sheep nations are those that would have aligned and embraced the Gospel of the Lord Jesus Christ and the goat nations are those that have rejected the gospel.

The responsibility of discipling those nations into sheep nations is firmly in the hands of the church, being led and empowered by the Holy Spirit. The fact that there are goat nations means that there are nations where the Gospel has been rejected. The fact that there is judgment means that there was a conscious choice made to be either a sheep or goat nation. The role of the church is unavoidable, and the responsibility is awesome. God would not call us to an impossible task. May God grant us the grace to rise to the assignment He has placed before us, and give us the strength to fulfill it to the glory of His Name.

Prayer

Heavenly Father, we come to You on our own behalf and on behalf of the church in our nations. We want to stand in the gap and repent of all our sins. Father where we have been short-sighted, selfish, ignorant, blind, or if we have focused on building our own kingdoms, please have mercy on us. Where we have been competitive, jealous of one another, neglecting the primary commission and assignment that You gave to us to disciple our nations, Father we pray and ask for forgiveness. Where there is sin in the church whether it is sexual immorality, pride, disunity, the love of money or corruption - Father we ask for forgiveness and we plead for mercy.

Father, we ask You for mercy because You have called us to a high calling. We are Your body and the Lord Jesus is our Head. You have given us a great and awesome responsibility to partner with You, to be led by Your Holy Spirit to disciple our nations so that they can be sheep nations.

Father, we are living in a time of great shaking and we ask for mercy for the church in the world. Any sector of our societies remaining in bondage is an indictment on the church.

Father, we ask for mercy and forgiveness and we ask that the blood of Jesus will cleanse and sanctify the church in every nation. We pray that You put Your salve on our eyes so we can see and help our leaders by giving spiritual covering. Help us to be true Watchmen on the walls of our nations and to be able to warn our nations of danger and sound the alarm on the day of trouble.

Father, we ask that the church be the light, the salt, the city on a hill so that our nations on that final day can be sheep nations. That is the greatest calling that You have given to each of us. It is impossible without Your help and the empowering of the Holy Spirit. We ask that You help us to walk in love and holiness by Your grace. May we be a church that is, truly, without spot or wrinkle.

May we be that glorious church that You have called us to be in the mighty name of Jesus. Amen.

20. Rebuilding Africa's Walls

"And if you spend yourselves in behalf of the hungry. And satisfy the needs of the oppressed, then your light will rise in darkness, and your light will become like the noonday. The LORD will guide you always; He will satisfy your need in a sun scorched land. And will strengthen your frame. You will be like a well-watered garden, like a spring whose waters never fail. Your people will rebuild the ancient ruins and will raise up the age-old foundations; you will be called repairer of broken walls, restorer of streets with dwellings."
- Isaiah 58:10-123.

In times gone by, the strength of a city or kingdom could be measured by the physical condition of the walls and gates of that kingdom or city. If the walls, gates and towers of the city were strong and built up, it meant that the people were safe in case of invasion from external enemies. We know that the Great Wall of China served as an impenetrable defence against invasion from the North. It was only when the Mongols were able to successfully breach the Great Wall, that they had a chance to invade and topple the dynasty.

The city of Jerusalem had twelve gates and a strong wall that guarded the city. Different gates had different functions which their names sometimes alluded to. The strength of each gate and the condition of the gates and walls of the city catalogued the strength, prosperity and security of the kingdom. The city of Jericho could only be conquered and possessed by the children of Israel by breaching the walls. This happened when the walls were supernaturally breached and broken down. The book of Revelations also gives us a glimpse into the New Jerusalem which the redeemed saints of God will possess as an everlasting home. The New Jerusalem, as described in the Book of Revelations, also has walls and twelve distinct gates named after the twelve apostles of the Lord.

Jesus also highlighted that hell itself has gates, but made it clear that these gates would not be able to overpower His Church. Psalm 24:7-8 declares that:

> *"Lift up your heads, O you gates; and be lifted up you age-abiding doors, that the King of glory may come in. Who is the King of Glory? The Lord strong and mighty, the Lord mighty in battle." – Amplified Bible*

The Bible is clear that there are natural gates and walls that we can see and touch physically, and there are spiritual gates and walls that we may not be able to see and touch but still have a profound impact on our lives.

God called and commissioned the prophet Ezekiel as a watchman over the house of Israel, as it is written in Ezekiel 3:16-17:

> *"And at the end of the seven days, the Word of the Lord came to me; son of man, I have made you a watchman to the house of Israel; therefore hear the Word of My mouth and give warning from Me." – Amplified Bible*

Ezekiel spent his entire life in exile amongst the Jews who had been carried away into Babylonian captivity. He could never be a natural watchman on the walls of the City of Jerusalem. In this instance, therefore, God was commissioning Ezekiel to be a spiritual watchman over the nation of Israel. He was calling him to stand in the gap as an intercessor and prophet to the nation. God would show him things in the realm of the spirit, and God wanted him to do two things; first to pray and intercede for the nation and, second, to warn and continually speak God's Word to the people.

Note that the word "watch" or phrase "keeping watch" is a spiritual discipline that involves prayer.

Jesus told His disciples during the most critical and tormenting night of His life, as is written in Matthew 26:39:

> *"My soul is very sad and deeply grieved so that I am almost dying because of sorrow. Stay here and keep awake and watch with Me." – Amplified Bible*

When the disciples failed to stay awake in prayer, Jesus reprimanded them by saying, *"What! Are you so utterly unable to stay awake and keep watch with Me for one hour? All of you must keep awake and watch and pray, that you may not enter into temptation. The spirit indeed is willing but the flesh is weak."* - Matthew 26:40-41.

Going back to the prophet Ezekiel, we see that the watchman bore a great responsibility before the Lord. God held the watchman accountable for the nation and the people and was duty-bound to warn and speak the Word of God faithfully to the nation and the people. Here are the words as written in Ezekiel 33:2-6:

> *"If when he sees the sword coming upon the land, he blows the trumpet and warns the people; then whoever hears the sound of the trumpet and does not take warning, and the sword comes and takes him away, his blood shall be upon his own head. He heard the sound of the trumpet and did not take warning; his blood shall be upon himself. But he who shall take warning shall save his life. But if the watchman sees the sword coming and does not blow the trumpet and the people are not warned and the sword comes and takes any one of them, he is taken away in his perversity and for his iniquity, but his blood I will require at the watchman's hand. So you, son of man, I have made you a watchman for the house of Israel; therefore hear the Word of my mouth and give them warning from Me." – Amplified Bible*

These scriptures confirm again that there are spiritual walls and gates over nations and the strength of those gates determines the protection over the people. The scriptures also confirm that God has commissioned certain people to be spiritual watchmen over the walls of cities and nations. Even as we have physical guards and defence of buildings, cities and nations, so too do we have spiritual protection. The scripture is therefore clear, we need strong spiritual walls, gates and watchmen to guard and protect our nations from any spiritual attack which may finally manifest as physical destruction.

Nehemiah: A Builder in God's Kingdom

What I find interesting about the Bible is that God often calls His people to one single assignment all their lives. This is very different from our 21st Century's perspective where we are all trying to do it all. Moses was called by God to deliver the children of Israel from bondage; King David was called to fight the enemies of Israel and establish the kingdom; Mary was called to be the mother of the Lord Jesus Christ; Paul was called to be an Apostle to the Gentiles, and Peter was called to be an Apostle to the Jews. What is also interesting Is that many people stumble onto their assignments from God.

Take the example of the good doctor Luke in the New Testament. Luke was a doctor and a Gentile, he travelled with Paul on some of his missionary journeys. No doubt he heard the accounts of Jesus' life and ministry from the apostles and early church members. Because he was a doctor, and his mind worked in a very logical and detail-oriented way, he did extensive research from those who had a first-hand account of Jesus' life and the early church. Then he wrote the most detailed and extensive accounts of the life and ministry of Jesus and the early church which we have today as the Book of Luke and the Book of Acts of the Apostles. Those two books are seminal accounts of the life and ministry of Jesus and the early church. The two books are read by billions of Christians all over the world daily and bring strength, courage and conviction to continue the work of the Great Commission.

That said, I do not think that when Luke was writing and researching those books, he recognized the gravity of what he was doing. It was probably a side-show of his life and medical work. He probably did it in his spare time when he didn't have patients to treat or when he didn't have travelling engagements. But the sideshow became the main show according to God's divine agenda. It is possible that God created Luke with his intelligence and brilliant mind for him to write the gospel of Luke in such a detailed manner.

God trained him as a doctor to provide an in-depth and well-researched perspective of the life and ministry of our Lord Jesus Christ.

I feel the same way about Nehemiah. Here was a man who had been elevated to the position of the king's cupbearer in the court of King Artaxerxes. He was at the height of his game as a politician and government official. He served the king and was in the presence of the king and queen daily. He had succeeded as an exile in a foreign land and that, in itself, speaks to his character, diligence and work ethic. He must have thought that God's plan for his life was to serve the king and be a good citizen. Then out of nowhere, he got news about his home country and city. Suddenly his perfect world was not so perfect. The world that he had left behind caught up with him in Persia. Probably over the years, Nehemiah had come to terms with his life as an exile. Maybe he had made up his mind to prosper in the foreign land. He had tried hard to forget his homeland and the city of his ancestry and, for a time, it had worked. And then his destiny collided with his reality and he had to make a choice. He could ignore his heart and the deep call of the Spirit of God in his life and stay in his cushy life in Persia, or he could answer the call and return to the land of his ancestors to make a difference.

These are the words in Nehemiah 1:2-4:

> *"Hanani, one of my kinsmen came with certain men from Judah, and I asked them about the surviving Jews who had escaped exile and about Jerusalem. And they said to me, the remnant there in the province who escaped exile are in great trouble and reproach; the wall of Jerusalem is broken down and its gates are destroyed by fire. When I heard this, I sat down and wept and mourned for days and fasted and prayed before the God of heaven." – Amplified Bible*

Nehemiah was a government official in the superpower of the day, Persia. He served a great king Artaxerxes and possibly Queen Esther. He had gained valuable experience in the administration of people and resources from the most successful empire of its day. Is it possible that God gave

Nehemiah this training to equip him to manage and steward the rebuilding of the wall of Jerusalem and post building recovery of the nation?

I believe it is. Often, what appears as a diversion or a sideshow is the main show and everything else was simply the training ground, preparing us for the assignment.

The Problem

We have seen in previous chapters that oftentimes, God's assignment presents itself as a problem. Nehemiah's heart was broken over the state of affairs in Jerusalem. The walls of the city were broken down and burnt. As a result, the people were in a perilous position; they were exposed to grave danger, reproach and trouble. Nehemiah responded in prayer, which is the place where we must always begin. He took time to fast, pray and seek the Lord. He was overwhelmed emotionally by the news of the situation of his brothers and sisters in Jerusalem. After prayer and repentance for the land of Israel and the city of Jerusalem, God divinely orchestrated an open door. The king asked Nehemiah why he was sad.

This is significant because the Bible tells us in Proverbs 21:1 that, *"the heart of the king is like a river in the Lord's hand; he turns it in whatever direction He wishes."*

We know the story in the book of Esther when God made sure the same king Artaxerxes couldn't sleep for him to call for the books to be read before him at night. It was in the reading of these books that the king was reminded of the good deeds of Mordechai, Esther's uncle and the very man that the wicked Haman had planned to hang in the gallows the next day. God can make a king lose sleep and He can make a king recognize that his servant is sad and offer him help.

That is exactly what happened. As Nehemiah narrated the situation in Jerusalem, the king asked him what help he needed from him. The wheels were in motion and soon Nehemiah found himself on his way to the land of his ancestry to rebuild the walls of his nation.

True Leadership

When Nehemiah arrived in Jerusalem, he privately toured the entire perimeter wall of the city to see for himself the level of damage. He realized that the situation was indeed as bad if not worse than the reports he had received while in Persia. The task ahead of him seemed insurmountable: the people were weak, few and demoralized. There was a complete lack of leadership and the people needed to believe that they could indeed change their situation. Nehemiah 2:17-18 says thus:

> *"Then I said to them, You see the bad situation we are in - how Jerusalem lies in ruins, and its gates are burned with fire. Come let us build the wall of Jerusalem, that we may no longer be a disgrace. Then I told them of the hand of my God which was upon me for good and also the words which the king had spoken to me. And they said, Let us rise up and build! So they strengthened their hands for the good work." – Amplified Bible*

What I find interesting in this account is that the remnant in Israel saw that the walls were broken down and the gates were burned, but they never lifted their hands to deal with the situation before Nehemiah came. God had to call Nehemiah and empower him to come and deal with the fallen and burnt-down walls of Jerusalem.

Ponder this: Nehemiah did not possess any special qualities or gifts that placed him above the remnant in Jerusalem. What was different was that the Lord called him and gave him a vision of the restoration of the walls of Jerusalem. Fully empowered, Nehemiah could see something that all the people could not see. They could only see the physical walls broken down and burned, but only Nehemiah could see what God was showing him, which was that the walls and gates were going to be rebuilt. Without a vision, people stumble around in the dark, even when the way may seem apparent and obvious before them. Every person who desires to be used by God needs to pray for clarity of vision to be able to see what God is revealing at that time.

The Opposition

As soon as the people had set themselves to work in unity, the worms crept out of the woodwork. Sanballat and Tobiah were foreigners who had somehow maneuvered into positions of leadership in Israel as a kind of caretaker government. They immediately felt threatened by the arrival of Nehemiah because the more he strengthened Jerusalem, the more tenuous their situation became. Some people prosper only by keeping others weak, poor and divided. It is a sad and dangerous ideology that pits people against each other and believes that for one group to prosper, one must impoverish another group. This is the party to which Sanballat and Tobiah belonged, an illegitimate government that was in place to simply tax and milk the land and the small remnants of the meagre possessions they still had. Nehemiah was a definite threat because he came with the blessing of the king of Persia whom they claimed to serve as representatives. Nehemiah was sent by the God of Heaven and Earth and he could not be stopped by illegitimate leaders.

The initial response of Sanballat and Tobiah was to laugh at the people and scorn their efforts. They mocked the people with their words and showed them to be insignificant. Such a situation is usually the first port of call of those opposed to the will and purpose of God. First, they will laugh, scorn and ridicule you. Then if that fails to deter God's people they will react in anger and rage.

Nehemiah 4:1-3:

"But when Sanballat heard that we were building the wall, he was angry and in a great rage, and he ridiculed the Jews. And he said before his brethren and the army of Samaria, What are these feeble Jews doing? Will they restore things at will and by themselves? Will they try to bribe their God with sacrifices? Will they finish up in a day? Will they revive the stones out of the heaps of rubbish, seeing they are burned?

"Now Tobiah the Ammonite was near him and he said, "

What they build - a fox climbs upon it, he will break down their stone wall." – Amplified Bible

One might wonder why Sanballat responded with such rage, after all, he was benefitting indirectly from the efforts to rebuild the wall. Why was he so violently opposed to what appeared to be in everyone's interests?

There are many Sanballats in the world today. I am speaking of the celebrity philanthropists who travel the world virtuously prescribing the measures to create a more just and equitable world in their eyes. They cry and weep about the destitute in Africa and love to take pictures of African children with potbellies and flies. They give in-depth interviews about the need to "do more" to help poor Africa. They recount moments of epiphany when they realize how "blessed" they are when they see the misery of poor hungry African children. It is virtue signalling at best and these same do-gooders are the very same people who will bare their fangs if the poor African endeavours to unite and seek an equal stake in the profits of the raw materials extracted from their countries.

When African nations speak of unity and a unified position concerning economic and political integration, foreign policy, security and defence, those same do-gooders react with the same rage as Sanballat did. They mock African leaders who seek to unite and rebuild the broken-down walls of the continent. They belittle and minimize efforts by nations to forge a way forward despite the many pitfalls and international opposition. This minefield is represented by international organizations such as the World Bank, the International Monetary Fund and the United Nations. All these organizations, founded after the Bretton Woods Accords following World War II, had one goal and one goal only. That was to preserve the balance of power with Western countries led by the new superpower, the United States and her cousins the former colonial powers of Europe Great Britain, France, Germany and the smaller European countries at the top of the pyramid. Africa and Asia only feature in this pyramid as a source of raw materials which must remain cheap at all costs to maximize the profits in the industrialized countries.

Therefore, the international order had and continues to have a vested interest in keeping Africa weak, poor and divided because only then can they keep the stream of raw materials flowing cheaply out of the continent. Therefore, on one hand, they give their donations in the guise of "aid" while the other hand extracts far greater resources and profit through institutionalized robbery.

Are these not the modern-day Sanballats and Tobiahs? For they seek to govern over Africa with her broken-down walls and balk at the slightest notion that Africa's walls can ever be rebuilt.

Conspiracy

In Nehemiah 6:1-4, we get the following words:

> *"Now when Sanballat and Tobiah and Geshem the Arab and the rest of the enemies heard that I had built the wall and that there was no breach left in it, Sanballat and Gershem sent to me saying," Come and let us meet together at Hakkephirim in the plain of Ono." But they intended me harm. And I sent messengers to them saying, " I am doing great work and I cannot come down. Why should the work stop while I leave it and come down to you? And they sent to me four times in this way and I answered them in the same manner." – Amplified Bible*

When Sanballat and his cronies realized that Nehemiah was not deterred in any way in the work of rebuilding the wall they hatched a conspiracy to kill Nehemiah. By the Grace of God, Nehemiah wasn't fooled by their efforts to get him to come and meet them in an isolated location. This most likely saved Nehemiah's life. But they were ready to kill him and any other people who might have stood in the way of their desire to maintain a stranglehold on the nation.

Africa has too many stories of assassinated leaders whose lives were truncated because they represented revolutionary ideals that were incompatible with the profit-driven motives of the powers that be. They are usually taken out directly and supplanted by weak puppet regimes or weakened and isolated by relentless international attacks. The purpose is to ensure that Africa remains weak and that her walls are broken down to ensure that the raiding and mining of natural resources continue.

The only thing to fear is fear itself

In Nehemiah, 6:5-9 we get these words:

> *"Sanballat for the fifth time sent his servants to me with an open letter in his hand. In it was written," It is reported among the nations and Gershem also says it, that you and the Jews intend to rebel; that is why you are rebuilding the wall. And according to these reports you wish to become their king. And you have also set up prophets to proclaim concerning you in Jerusalem, "There is a king in Judah." And now the king will hear these reports so come let us take counsel together. Then I sent to him saying," No such thing as you say has been done, for you are inventing them out of your own mind." For they all wanted to frighten us thinking," Their hands will drop from the work and it will not be done." But now O God, strengthen my hands." – Amplified Bible*

What is interesting about this passage is the lengths to which Sanballat was willing to go to block Nehemiah's work of rebuilding the wall. He in essence lied and tried to intimidate Nehemiah into a meeting with him. What was the purpose of the meeting? Well, we have already seen that there was a conspiracy to kill Nehemiah. If that didn't work, I believe Sanballat wanted to try and buy Nehemiah out. Sanballat was a corrupt and deceitful man and probably thought that he could compromise Nehemiah with bribes and thus end the work. Thankfully, Nehemiah was a true reformer, a servant of God who couldn't be bought and, so, that too failed. The goal of Sanballat was to stop the work of rebuilding the walls at all costs. He knew that if the walls of Jerusalem were rebuilt, the land would be secure, settled, and the people would prosper. If the land prospered, Sanballat's role would soon be questioned and the shackles of control he wielded over them would be cast off.

Here are the words from Nehemiah 6:10-14:

> *"Now when I went into the house of Shemiah the son of Delaiah, the son of Mehetabel, who was confined to his home, he said, 'Let us meet together in the house of God, within the temple. Let us close the doors of the temple, for they are coming to kill you. They are coming to kill you by night.' But I said, 'should such a man as I run away? And what man such as I could go into the temple and live? I will not go in.' And I understood and saw that God had not sent him, but he had pronounced the prophecy against me because Sanballat and Tobiah had hired him. For this purpose he was hired, that I should be afraid and act in this way and sin and so they would give me a bad name in order to taunt me." – Amplified Bible*

Finally, the last weapon that Sanballat had against Nehemiah was the weapon of fear.

Fear is a very real spiritual weapon that the enemy uses to paralyze us or to move us to act in ways that are contrary to God's will. Fear is a spirit and can only be countered spiritually. What is so astounding and shocking is that the house of God is not always a haven for God's people. If the house of God is led by people who are carnal or simply religious, they can be the most dangerous enemies of all. Remember, the Lord Jesus was crucified not because the Romans wanted to kill Jesus, but because the religious Jews, the Pharisees and keepers of the law were desperate to get rid of Jesus. The religious spirit is dangerous, indeed, because it cloaks itself in legitimacy and self-righteousness but, at its core, it is opposed to the will and purpose of God.

When the Church is compromised it is a big breach to the spiritual walls of the nation. The religious spirit can only be discerned by true children of God who know their God intimately. That is why Christians must have an intimate relationship with God because only then can we discern what is of God and what is of the enemy.

Jesus said, in John 10:5, "*My sheep hear my Voice and the Voice of a stranger they do not follow.*"

Those Who Know Their God Will Do Great Exploits

The defining characteristic of the true sheep is the ability to hear from God for oneself. Nehemiah could hear from God and he discerned that the person who was supposedly a "prophet" was hired by the enemy. I cannot stress enough how important it is for Christians to have an intimate personal relationship with the Lord; then and only then will we be the true reformers that our communities and nations need today.

But to fully understand the African context, we must go back a little further in our history and see how the spiritual walls of Africa were broken down, and by the Grace of God in so doing, learn how we can work to rebuild her walls again.

Breaking Down of Uganda's Walls

I am going to use Uganda as a case in point. Although the histories of the different countries in Africa vary, there are overarching similarities that can be drawn, especially concerning the way "religion" was used as a means of subduing, classifying and dividing peoples. In studying our Ugandan history, I am shocked at the extent to which religion was a tool used by the colonizers in partnership with their missionaries to extend their imperial mandate. Simply put, the French missionaries actively sought to advance the goals of France just as the English missionaries wanted to establish British rule. This is vastly different from the new testament template we have from the missionary journeys of the Apostle Paul and the New Testament Church. The Apostle Paul, whom we can safely call the greatest missionary of all time, had only one goal and that was to preach about Christ.

> *"Now I make known to you, brothers, the gospel which I proclaimed to you, which you have also received, in which you also stand, by which you are also being saved, if you hold fast to the message I proclaimed to you, unless you believed to no purpose. For I passed on to you as of first importance, what I also received, that Christ died for our sins according to the scriptures and that He appeared to Peter, then to the twelve, then He appeared to five hundred*

brothers at once, the majority of whom remain until now, but some have fallen asleep. Then He appeared to James, then to all the apostles, and last of all, as it were to one born at the wrong time, He appeared to me. For I am the least of the apostles, not worthy to be called an apostle because I persecuted the church of God. But by the Grace of God I am what I am, and His grace to me has not been in vain, But I laboured even more than all of them and not I, but the grace of God in me. Therefore, whether I or those, in this way, we preached and in this way, you believed." 1 Cor. 15:1-11; – Amplified Bible

Paul was very categorical about the essence of the gospel that he and the early Church preached and believed in. It centred around the death and resurrection of Jesus Christ and the new life of the Christian as a new creature in Christ.

This is what he writes in 1 Corinthians 1:23:

"But we preach Christ crucified, unto the Jews a stumbling block and unto the Gentiles foolishness." – Amplified Bible

Paul was outspoken against the Christian Jews who tried to bring the Gentiles under the Law or to in a sense Judaize them.

In Galatians 2:14-16 & 19-21, Paul writes thus:

"When I saw that they were not acting in line with the truth of the gospel, I said to Peter in front of them all, " You are a Jew, yet live like a Gentile and not like a Jew. How is it, then, that you force Gentiles to follow Jewish customs?

"We who are Jews by birth and not sinful Gentiles know that a person is not justified by the works of the law, but by faith in Jesus Christ. So we, too, have put our faith in Christ Jesus that we may be justified by faith in Christ and not by the works of the law, because by the works of the law, no one will be justified.

"For through the law, I died to the law so that I might live for God. I have been crucified with Christ and I no longer live, but Christ lives in me. The life I now live in the body, I live by faith in the Son of God, who loved me and gave

Himself for me. I do not set aside the grace of God, for if righteousness could be gained through the law, Christ died for nothing!" – Amplified Bible

Paul called out the Apostle Peter, for being hypocritical and trying to force upon the Gentiles, the customs and laws of the Jews. Paul declared that faith in the Lord Jesus Christ was the only way to justification and so trying to make the new Gentiles into Jews through the law was a counterfeit of the Gospel. Paul remained true to the foundational truths of the gospel as they revolve around the Person of our Lord Jesus Christ and that is what he preached on his many missionary journeys. He didn't work with the "government of Israel" to extend Jewish interests abroad. In fact, to the contrary, he was constantly persecuted by the Jews until he turned his full focus to reaching the Gentile nations. The Apostle Paul was an ambassador of the Lord Jesus Christ and he represented the Kingdom of God, operating in the ministry of the Holy Spirit with attesting signs and wonders. This is why he was very effective, he never built any physical schools or buildings, but the impact of his life and ministry is seminal to the spread of the gospel.

In my study of the Protestant and Roman Catholic missionaries who came to Uganda at the invitation of Kabaka Muteesa, I find many differences in the overall approach of the two missionary camps. While Paul was more focused on spreading the gospel, those who came to Uganda were advocates of colonial powers

Martin Luther and the Reformation

To understand the differences between the missionaries and the Apostle Paul, we must understand the impact that the Reformation had in Europe. Martin Luther, the humble monk, with his simple revelation from the Bible, brought down the Holy Roman Empire and forever split the Church, and in the process birthed the spiritual awakening called the Reformation. Martin Luther did not set out to do any of these things. As a devout monk, he desperately sought to know and serve God but was constantly beset with tormenting fears of hell and his own sinful life. Christians today cannot fathom that some things we take for granted were once far removed and inaccessible to ordinary people. Examples include access to the Bible, the Lord's Supper, worship in church and the ability to directly confess our sins to God and receive forgiveness and release from guilt,

Superstition and religious rituals focused on punishing the physical body by inflicting pain as a path to justification and sanctification. A good example is flagellation which was a terrible ritual of flogging or beating one's body to uplift the spirit. There were other less severe customs like spending hours kneeling on hard stone floors so that the knees bled and formed callouses. The Bible was only read at mass by a priest and in Latin which was not understood by the masses. This meant that God's Word was completely out of reach of the majority of people. Even the learned monks didn't have easy access to the Word of God. The interpretation of the Word of God was the monopoly of the priests.

On top of this, there was the matter of the sale of "indulgences." In the 1500's the Church in Rome had committed itself to great building projects like the construction of St. Peter's Basilica and other similar projects of significance. These projects came with an exorbitant price tag which could not be met by the tithes from the people. Indulgences were simply certificates issued by the Church or its representatives in exchange for money. The sale of indulgences extorted money out of people to "buy" freedom for the souls of dead relatives out of purgatory. It was said that, as soon as the sound of the gold coin hit the offering bowl, a soul was freed from purgatory. Here, the Church preyed on the spiritual ignorance and emotions of people in pressuring them to buy indulgences and get certificates stating that the souls of their dead relatives were released from purgatory. Apart from the numerous building projects, there were also the lavish lifestyles of the popes, cardinals and bishops of Rome to sustain. The money for such also came from the sale of indulgences.

In 1509 when Martin Luther wrote his ninety-five theses, the pope sent his emissary to Germany with a wagon full of indulgences in a bid to fill Rome's coffers with gold. It seems unbelievable today, but the sad truth is that without preaching God's Word, darkness and superstition get free rein. The excesses of the Church in Rome were financed by the rich provinces of Germany where Martin Luther lived and so the sale of indulgences was a very real evil that Martin Luther encountered.

This, in a nutshell, was what life was like for people in the 1500s when Martin Luther started seeking God. He was so tormented by fears of hell and his mortality and eternal damnation that he was driving himself crazy with fear. In his search for God, he had a dramatic encounter in a field where his life was saved from a bolt of lightning and, from that moment, he realized that God had saved his life for a reason. He started searching the scriptures and came upon the verse in the book of Romans 1:17:

> *"For in it the righteousness of God is revealed from faith to faith; as it is written, The just shall live by faith." – Amplified Bible*

It is said that this revelation came to him while he was in his "cloaca" which can be translated as a toilet. Martin Luther had a heated study situated at the top of a tower where the "out house" or cloaca was located so whether he was actually on the cloaca or simply in his study in the cloaca tower, he often mused that God would give him his greatest revelation in the most unexpected place.

This is what he writes:

> *"The Holy Spirit gave me this art in the cloaca. At last by the mercy of God, meditating day and night, I gave heed to the words, namely, 'In it the righteousness of God is revealed.' As it is written, 'He who through faith is righteous shall live.' There I began to understand that the righteousness of God is that by which the righteous lives by a gift of God, namely by faith. And this is the meaning; the righteousness of God is revealed by the gospel, namely the passive righteousness*

with which the merciful God justifies us by faith, as it is written, 'He who through faith is righteous shall live.' Here I felt that I was altogether born again and had entered paradise itself through the open gates. Thus a totally other [different] face of the entire scripture showed itself to me. Hereupon I ran through the scriptures from memory. I also found in other terms an analogy, as the work of God, that is, what God does in us, the power of God, with which He makes us strong, the wisdom of God, with which He makes us wise, the strength of God, the salvation of God, the glory of God. And I extolled my sweetest word with a love as great as the hatred with which I had before hated the word 'righteousness of God.' Thus that place in Paul was for me truly the gate to paradise." - Martin Luther.

The author Eric Metaxas has written an excellent treatise on the life of Martin Luther[1] and the dramatic encounter which began the Reformation in Germany and from there spread to other parts of Europe, notably England which would later become the colonizer of Uganda. The impact of the Reformation cannot be overstated. On the occasion of the 500th anniversary of the Reformation, the people of Germany unanimously agreed that there was no figure more central to the identity and consciousness of the German people as Martin Luther. They honoured him by putting his picture on their paper currency to mark the anniversary.

Eric Metaxas writes on pages 96-98 that:

"This is the earthshaking insight that gave Luther the solidest [most solid] of all foundations in scripture upon which to base what may well be reckoned the greatest revolution in human history. But by jesting in 1532 that it happened in that most humbling and humiliating of places - 'upon the toilet' - Luther made it a perfect illustration of his theological foundation. That is because it is in keeping with everything he knew about the incarnated God of the Bible. The specific point here is that the infinite, omniscient

---

1 Eric Metaxas, *Martin Luther: The Man Who Rediscovered God and Changed the World.* Viking Press, 2017.

and omnipotent [C]reator God of heaven did not descend to earth on a golden cloud. He came to us through screaming pain, through the bloody agony of a maiden's vagina, in a cattle stall filthy with stinking dung.

"This is how humans enter the world, and if God would enter the world as a human being, he must enter it that way. It was the only way to reach us where we are and as we are, and because of His love for us He did not shrink from this approach, vile and difficult as it must be. Luther saw in this the very essence of Christian theology.

"God reached down not halfway to meet us in our vileness but all the way down, to the foul dregs of our broken humanity. And this holy and loving God dared to touch our lifeless and rotting essence and in doing so underscored that this is the truth about us. In fact, we are not sick and in need of healing. We are dead and in need of resurrecting. We are not dusty and in need of good dusting; we are fatally befouled with death and fatally toxic filth and require total redemption.

"If we do not realize that we need eternal life from the hand of God, we remain in our sins and are eternally dead. So because God respects us, He can reach us only if we are honest about our condition. So it fits well with Luther's thinking that if God were to bestow upon him - the unworthy sinner Luther - such divine blessing, it must be done as he sat grunting in the 'cloaca.' This was the ultimate antithesis to the gold and bejewelled splendour of papal Rome. There all was gilt, but here in Wittenberg, it was all Scheisse. But the refuse in its honesty as refuse was very golden when compared to the pretense and artifice of Roman gold, which itself was indeed as refuse when compared to the infinite worth of God's grace. That was cheap grace, which was only to say, it was a truly satanic counterfeit. True grace was concealed in the honesty, in the unadorned refuse of this broken world, and the devil's own refuse was concealed in the pope's glittering gold."

The author's language may be a bit crude but it draws a stark contrast between the two, the earnest seeking of the reforming monk and the corrupt excesses of Rome. It was from this that the ninety-five theses were posted on the doors of the castle church in Wittenberg. Luther did not intend or expect his ninety-five theses to be the spark that lit the wildfire that would bring down the Holy Roman Empire and split the church forever. He could not have foreseen such events; he merely wished to have a wider discussion about the major areas of concern that he had. He wished to effect change quietly from within, but God had other plans. The printing press had been invented and it is on the wheels of the press that the theses spread like wildfire consuming everything in its path and stirring up a spiritual reckoning that would forever change the world. The Reformation that began in Germany would spread to the rest of Europe, dividing the continent and dragging the nations of Europe out of medieval times into the modern era.

Even though the Reformation was, evidently, the work of God to bring revival and awakening to the world, it split the church and created two camps, the Roman Catholics and the Protestants. England broke away from the Roman Catholic Church and embraced the Reformation for both political and religious purposes. This was the time of Henry VIII who was King of England in 1509. He had greatly desired a male heir to stabilize his throne, but his wife Catherine of Aragorn had only produced one child who lived past infancy, a daughter called Mary.

When it was clear that his wife Catherine couldn't produce a male heir, Henry VIII became interested in another lady, Anne Boleyn. Since England was under the Roman Catholic church, the king was forbidden to divorce his wife to marry another. When the pope refused to give the king permission to marry, Henry VII went ahead to declare the Act of Supremacy which made him the head of the Church of England. This schism with Rome had a far-reaching impact and continued the bitter divisions in Europe between the Roman Catholic church and those they viewed as rebels and heretics, the Protestants.

Fast forward 300 years later when Britain had become a great naval power and was seeking to expand her sphere of influence into Africa. The divisions of the Church in Europe were exported to their colonies as rival camps of missionaries began to compete for dominance in the colonies and protectorates. While in Europe, the divide was still bitter, the boundaries were set mostly across nations; Germany and Britain were Protestant while France, Portugal, Belgium and Spain were Roman Catholic. In Africa, and Uganda in particular, the competing camps were vying for influence in the same nation, often in the same region. This heightened tensions between the missionary camps and even brought them to sporadic wars.

Religious Wars in Uganda

In 1875, Henry Morton Stanley, a journalist and explorer, visited Buganda for the first time and was welcomed at the court of Kabaka Mutesa. Upon the advice of Stanley, Kabaka Mutesa wrote a letter to Queen Victoria of England inviting her to send missionaries to Uganda. It is unclear what Muteesa's entire set of motives was, but he must have thought that he stood to gain something from having the Europeans in his kingdom. Maybe he was looking for guns and the superiority that firepower would give him, or maybe it was prestige and backing against his arch-rival Kingdom of Bunyoro.

Whatever the reason, Mutesa wrote a letter of invitation to the Queen of England which was duly published in the Daily Telegraph newspaper in 1875. Two years later, in 1877, the first group of missionaries arrived. They were protestant missionaries sent by the Church Missionary Society (CMS). These were Shergold Smith, Rev. C. T. Wilson and O'neill. Their leader, Alexander Mackay, joined them a year later.

Roman Catholics arrived in 1879 and they were called the White Fathers. They were led by Rev. Father Simon Lourdel, along with Brother Amans Delamas, Father Leon Livinhac and Father Leon Barbot.

In the subsequent years, many more missionaries arrived in Uganda and the camps of the Roman Catholics and the Protestants continued to grow. To say that they were camps isn't an overstatement, for that is the way they saw themselves. They never looked at each other as brothers in arms but rather as competitors fighting for supremacy in the region and the continent. It was only for brief interludes when they had to unite to fight against the Mohammedans (Muslims) that they found some common ground. But once the Mohammedans were repulsed and subdued the Christians returned to their sectarian battles.

In 1890, Captain Frederick John Dealtry Lugard arrived in Buganda. He came as a representative of the Imperial British East African Company. Lugard was born in India to missionary parents and lived most of his life in the far-flung reaches of the British empire, from East Africa to Burma to Nigeria. The Imperial British East African Company was a chartered company that paved the way for the annexation of East Africa by the empire. His book, *The Rise of Our East African Empire,*[2] gives great insight into his methods and motives as an agent of the British Empire. The word "our" denotes that the audience Lugard was referring to and addressing was European, and specifically, British. I am sure he never imagined that generations later, Africans would read his book and use it to gain insights and speak of building a very different kind of kingdom. But I digress.

Captain Lugard was known for many things, topmost of these was his pioneering of the system of administration called *Indirect Rule.* In a layman's language, Lugard saved the British Empire money and lives by buying the collaboration of kings and chiefs and making them subservient to the interests of the company and eventually the crown. The collaborators who capitulated to Lugard's demands were rewarded with "protection" and special status, a gift from

---

2 Captain John Dealtry Lugard. *The Rise of our East African Empire: Early Efforts in Nyasaland and Uganda.Vol.2*, Forgotten Books, 2012.

the Queen of England. The kings and chiefs who collaborated were propped up by the company and empire and those who resisted, and fought for independence and freedom were punished and destroyed. It was the age-old strategy of divide and conquer, and for reasons that we have already studied in previous chapters, it worked very effectively.

I will not focus on Lugard's role as a precursor to the colonial annexation of Uganda but rather on his interaction with the missionaries and the situation that he as a secular man observed.

By 1890, the Berlin conference had already ceded large tracts of land with its peoples, nations and kings to different European powers. East Africa was shared between Britain and Germany.

Here is what he says, in part:

> "*Mgr. Hirth, on my first arrival, had cordially offered me his support and told me that, now that Uganda was ceded by 'international agreement' to the influence of Great Britain, he and his party would cordially recognize the company's administration. This declaration, I fully believe, to have been sincere at the time; but the reader will judge from the subsequent events to what extent he acted up to this promise. But Mgr. when saying this, also added that up to the time of the Anglo-German agreement Uganda had been 'no man's land,' and that it was perfectly legitimate for anyone to establish an influence, with a view to ultimate political supremacy. That he had worked with this view hitherto, I understood him candidly to admit. And herein, it appears to me, lies the solution to the whole matter. French-made arms had been imported into the country, and there were very many of them in Uganda, and these must have been brought by the Fathers, for, so far as I know, there is no trade in French arms on the East African coast. The R. Catholics had been taught to desire French supremacy, and their faction had adopted the title of Wa-Fransa. But supposing that Mgr. now wished to undo all this, and accept the British administration, the work of years could not be*

> *undone in a moment, nor could the Fathers persuade the whole faction to resign the aims they had themselves fostered, though they might explain the change to some of the most intelligent chiefs. Unfortunately, the faction opposed to them was 'English.'*
>
> *"How far a similar policy of creating a political influence in favour of British rule had been promoted by the Protestant missionaries, I have no accurate means of knowing. Doubtless, they were a little behind the Fathers in their desire to secure in Uganda the supremacy of the nation to which they belonged, for General Gordon, speaking of the Ugandan mission, says that, 'as it is composed, it is more secular than spiritual' and accordingly writes to indicate the political attitude the mission should take. Mackay's letters prove him to have been a most zealous promoter of British supremacy.; and Mr. Gordon's actions upon and subsequent to Mr. Jackson's arrival indicate that the missionaries apparently considered that they were the representatives of British interests. I do not believe, however, that they ever imported any arms, or had any definite political schemes. On arrival, I was looked upon by the Fransa party as an addition to the hostile camp. The British flag was regarded as the standard of the Wa-Ingleza; the French flag as the standard of the Wa-Fransa. Had the Germans taken over Uganda, they would have been unwelcome to the R. Catholics, as being Protestants; but their flag, at least, would have been looked upon as neutral. This feeling was very strong among the peasantry in the outlying districts. Later, when I went to Buddu, the R. Catholics refused me food, on the ground that I was English, saying they would only supply Frenchmen." - Lugard p.66-67.*

This of course is contrary to the spirit of Christianity. The Bible is clear that, in Christ Jesus, the dividing wall was broken down and that there is now no longer Jew nor Gentile, slave nor free, male or female. But all have been made one in the Lord Jesus Christ. It is very sad to see that the church, instead of being a unifier, was an instrument to divide people along sectarian and nationalistic lines. That goes against the very grain of what St. Paul, as a missionary Apostle, taught and modelled. Therefore, in Uganda, and Africa in general, the missionaries failed in that regard, something that was evident to a secular man like Captain Lugard who duly recognized that they had strayed from the basic tenets of their faith.

The Apostle Paul addressed sectarianism in 1 Corinthians 1:10-13:

> *"But I urge you and entreat you, brethren by the Name of our Lord Jesus Christ, that all of you be in perfect harmony and full agreement in what you say, and that there be no dissensions or factions or divisions among you, but that you be perfectly united in your common understanding, and in your opinions and judgements. For it has been made clear to me, my brethren, by those of Chloe's household, that there are contentions and wrangling and factions amongst you. What I mean is this, that each of you says, I belong to Paul, or I belong to Apollos, or I belong to Cephas (Peter), or I belong to Christ. Is Christ divided into parts? Was Paul crucified on behalf of you? Or were you baptized into the name of Paul?" – Amplified Bible*

The obvious answer to Paul's rhetorical questions is no. No, the body of Christ is not divided and no human being died on the Cross for our sins apart from the Lord Jesus Christ. Paul's point is very clear, those who operate in a spirit of sectarianism have not genuinely encountered the Lord Jesus Christ. If they had, they would seek harmony and unity with their fellow brothers.

Jesus had Himself set the precedent for His disciples when they too, in their overzealous fervour, sought to clamp down on people ministering in Jesus' name.

> *"Now John answered Him saying, 'Teacher, we saw someone who does not follow us casting out demons in Your Name, and we forbade him because he does not follow us. But Jesus said, 'Do not forbid him, for no one who works a miracle in My Name can soon afterward speak evil of Me. For he who is not against us is on our side.'"*

The basic premise of Jesus' statement is that even though someone isn't necessarily your follower, it doesn't make the person your enemy. As long as your goals are the same, you are on the same team. How different Church history would be if we listened and lived by Jesus' instructions.

Here are Lugards' words:

"I, therefore, endeavoured to separate, in the minds of the people, the two ideas of religion and nationality. I always spoke of the R. Catholics as the 'Wa-Katoliki' and the Protestants as the 'Wa-Protestanti,' refusing to acknowledge the terms 'French' and 'English,' for we were all English now (I said). - Lugard p.68

He continues,

"The Land was divided into two hostile camps, and every evildoer was championed by his faction. Mwanga, of course, chose the stronger-the Wa-Fransa; they had more white men than the Wa-Ingleza, more arms and more people. He dare not punish one of this faction, lest he should alienate himself from them. I will ask the reader to pause and try and realize the difficulty of my position. In order to gain the confidence of the Wa-Fransa, it was necessary to treat them precisely as the Wa-Ingleza, though the bulk of the one faction was bitterly hostile to me, while the other was loyal." - Lugard p.69

"I think it not improbable also, that the R. Catholic chiefs thought they might obtain arms through the medium of the French mission; for, as I have said, it appears beyond doubt that as long as Uganda was under no European protection, and the prohibitions to import them, and the Waganda could not, of course, appreciate the difference made by the international prohibitions. In writing thus, I must leave my reader to form his own conclusions as to whether it is fitting that missionaries should be the importers of arms, either for the purpose of gaining a political ascendancy for their own party, or for any other motive. For my part I think it is not; for it appears to me impossible, that anyone who has lived in Africa should not appreciate the incalculable

harm done by the import of arms. At the same time, it must be remembered that according to Mr. Jackson, Pere Lourdel had openly advocated their introduction, in order that the Christians might be able to annihilate the Mohammedans." - Lugard p.75

There is a juxtaposition between the attitude of the missionaries versus the Biblical teaching and what Jesus espoused. We find this in Matthew 22:36-40:

"When asked what the greatest commandment was, Jesus answered, 'Love the Lord your God with all your heart, mind and soul and the second; love your neighbour as yourself. On these two commandments hang all the laws and the prophets.'" – Amplified Bible

Jesus' statement is very clear, what matters to God above all, is that we walk in love. The Bible even says those who know God, true Christians, will be known by their love (John 13:34-35). It is love, and not earthly power, that characterizes God's people. When we walk in love, we disarm the powers of darkness and gain spiritual authority.

Violence and War

With all the sectarianism that existed in the Corinthian church, it did not descend into physical violence and war. The Christians in Corinth disagreed on questions of faith and doctrine such as which apostle was superior, sexual immorality, marriage, eating meat, head coverings for women, spiritual gifts and the Lord's supper. Even though their sectarianism earned them strong condemnation and correction from Paul, they never sought to take up arms against each other.

It is unbelievable for Christians today to imagine that missionaries would encourage their "converts" to fight and kill people based on faith. It simply doesn't make sense spiritually. The Lord Jesus came to this earth to make a way for us to become children of God. The only way that we can become children of God is if the gospel is preached to us, and we believe in our hearts and confess with our mouths. That is what the Bible says, there is no other avenue of making disciples. War is not a means of proselytizing and bringing people to the Lord. That is why Jesus told Pilate that if His kingdom was an earthly kingdom, his disciples would have fought to keep Him from being arrested. But Jesus did not come to establish an earthly kingdom, but rather a spiritual heavenly kingdom. The missionaries were wrong to try to establish the kingdom of God using earthly tools such as violence and political intrigue. The seeds they sowed into the people and culture of Uganda, and Africa in general, have had devastating effects for generations. However, we need to recognize that they were simply copying and pasting the religious climate that had existed in Europe for centuries. The European powers had fought bloody religious wars for years going back to the Crusades against the Ottoman Empire and the Wars with Spain that culminated in the Spanish Armada in 1588.

Back to Captain Lugard and the clash of missionaries and their converts:

> "*Men came running in to say that some Wa-Ingleza, returning from Chagwe, had been attacked by the Wa-Fransa of Salo-Salo's place, and two killed. Again the war drums beat, and the armies assembled for war in an incredibly short time. The king, I was told had already sent to arrest the murderers, and he begged me to go to Katikiro to try and prevent hostilities. The Wa-Ingleza were dejected and exclaimed that it was always the same story, fresh outrages and no satisfaction-fresh provocations to war. I told them not to be fools, but to come out with me and help to stop the battle. Coming out of the Katikiro's house I found the whole country up once more, and huge crowds of the Fransa faction collecting on the hills with a large red and white flag (which was I understand, the French flag)" - Lugard p. 84*

On matters of violence, Bible instructs us thus in Luke 6:28-29:

"Implore blessings upon and pray for the happiness of

those who curse you and implore God's blessings upon those who abuse you. To the one who strikes you on the cheek, offer the other cheek also, and from him who takes your outer garment, do not withhold your tunic." – Amplified Bible

The Lord Jesus' example in praying for his executioners is the ultimate example for the Church to fight our battles with spiritual weapons not with the weapons of this world.

Sectarianism

From the book of Genesis to Revelations, the relationship between God and man is framed as one of choice. God created man in His image, this means that human beings are different from animals and we are also different from angels and other spiritual beings. We are made in God's image and one of the key traits that differentiates us from other created beings is that of free will. Human beings have the incredible gift of agency or free will. God built into our DNA the ability to choose what we want in life and He defends our right to choose even if that choice is against Him.

God does not force anyone to believe or follow Him. He sent His Son to make a way for us to become children of God through the sacrifice of His life and blood. When the gospel is preached, God presents to us the choice that we all have, to either receive the Lord Jesus in our hearts and become reconciled to God or to reject the Lord and be separated from God. This choice has eternal significance but the Almighty God still gives us the freedom to make that choice. One day, all flesh will stand before the judgment seat of God and answer for the choices we made while here on earth. Those who accepted Christ will enter into eternal joy in heaven and those who rejected Christ will enter into eternal damnation. It all depends on our choices here on Earth. Religious liberty is something that God takes very seriously, and it is His nature to bring freedom. This freedom is not to be abused or taken for granted, rather it must be recognized as an immeasurable gift of God and guarded jealously.

> *"The Wa-Ingleza demurred because they said that the real Christians in the country were a very very small minority, and the rest would go over in large numbers to the religion, or rather a faction, of the king, whatever it might be(and he nominally is a R. Catholic, or French). They had only been deterred so far by fearing to lose their places and estates. Now, if these restrictions were removed, the English political party would be decimated, and then, if trouble arose, and the parties turned out to fight, the 'French' would not be restrained, but would go for the small residue of Protestants left and destroy them. At present, one reason for the maintenance of peace, had been that the two parties were so evenly matched, that all knew that a war would be the destruction of the whole country." - Lugard p.98*

He continues:

> *"Had the questions really been one of liberty of conscience and religious toleration, nothing could have persuaded me to favour anything but an absolute freedom of creed. It was, however, not a religious question, though it is easy, by substituting the names Protestant and R. Catholic for Ingleza and Fransa, to make it appear so." - Lugard p.97*

He adds:

> *"So far as the comparative toleration of the two sects is concerned, I am quite convinced that it is erroneous to say that the R. Catholics were animated by a spirit of toleration and wished for absolute liberty of conscience while the Protestants wished to coerce the people into following their religion. All these evictions were produced solely by religious intolerance, and the attempt to force the dwellers on an estate to follow a particular creed; and in this matter as I have said, the R. Catholics had taken the lead." - Lugard p.98*

> *"The Fathers looked on Protestantism as a heresy which they were bound to combat and expose. On the other hand, I myself discussed the question of toleration at*

various times with Protestant chiefs, and I understood them to say they their missionaries had taught them that every man should be allowed to worship God in his own way. My own subsequent action will prove I think, that I included them all, Moslem as well as Christian, in my own doctrine of toleration, leaving God to judge which was acceptable to Him." - Lugard p.99

"I emphatically pointed out that the British flag had no reference whatever to religion. I fail to see how a national flag can be said to have any religious signification. That the Wa-ingleza accepted it only proves them to have been the political faction loyal to British rule; that the Wa-Fransa refused it, does not show that they as R. Catholics were opposed to us but that as being the "French" party, they would not fly the flag of the "English." - Lugard p.125

"Again in his letter to me Mgr. states that during the last six months of 1891, the fort in Kampala was exclusively Protestant, and our chiefs never had access to the representatives of the Company. While Mgr. thus vehemently asserted that during Williams' tenure at Kampala, gross partiality had been shown to the Protestants, the English missionaries, as I have shown, complained in terms equally loud and indignant of the bias shown to the R. Catholics. No evidence could be more conclusive of Williams impartiality. It is not therefore to be wondered that the "converts" of either religion were animated by the instensest rancor and hatred of each other, since their "teachers" showed such narrow-mindedness." - Lugard p.323

Let's see what Paul says about such in 1 Cor. 3:17:

"Now the Lord is the Spirit, and where the Spirit of the Lord is, there is liberty (emancipation from bondage, freedom) – Amplified Bible

The Lord Jesus Christ Himself declared that His mission on earth was to set the captives free. And in Isaiah 61:1 we find these words:

> *"The Spirit of the Lord God is upon Me, because the Lord has anointed Me, to preach the Gospel of good news to the poor; He has sent me to bind up and heal the broken hearted, to proclaim liberty to the captives and the opening of the prison of those who are bound." – Amplified Bible*

One of the litmus tests of spiritual awakening and revival is that it always comes with the loss of spiritual chains with a resulting impact on the social, economic and even political lives of the people. This was evident in the East African revival, where the born again believers shunned many spiritual and social ills such as witchcraft and superstition, backwardness, polygamy, drunkenness, smoking tobacco, domestic violence and male chauvinism. These and many other spiritual bonds were loosed and there was a dramatic shift in the social, cultural and political lives of the people. The same can be attested to the revival in South Korea, and the reformation in Germany and Britain, which was exported to the United States of America through the pilgrims and Puritan settlers in the American colonies. Where the Spirit of the Lord is, there is liberty because wherever Jesus is preached, chains are broken and captives are set free.

It can therefore be deduced that the missionaries who came to Africa, carrying the Bible, relied on human strength, rather than spiritual authority, to gain religious superiority. The Gospel is not preached through man's power but rather by the power of the Holy Spirit. We rely on the power of the Holy Spirit, as Jesus admonished the disciples in the book of Acts 1; the Gospel is preached as God intended, by the power of the Holy Spirit with confirmation of signs and wonders. In all the places the Gospel was preached in the New Testament, the results were the same: people turned to God in repentance and the power of darkness was broken. Even when the disciples faced persecution, they never resorted to violence or the promotion of sectarianism. In fact, they actively fought against any kind of factionalism and sectarianism. Wherever the Gospel was preached, people were set free.

Trusting in the arm of flesh opens a veritable can of worms. Unfortunately, the missionaries who arrived in Africa looked at violence and sectarianism as tools or vehicles to spread Christianity. Indeed I wonder what the Christianity they preached was because it does not bear resemblance to the message in the Bible. As a result, the missionaries opened a dangerous door and gave authority to the wrong spirit to operate in the communities and people they sought to convert.

Schools, Hospitals and Religious Sectarianism

In writing about this approach of early missionaries in Africa, it is not my intention to give the missionaries a bad rap. For someone to leave their home country and travel a great distance to another unknown land, there obviously must be some deeper spiritual stirring and devotion to a cause higher and greater than oneself.

Many of the missionaries knew that danger and possible death awaited them in the new lands they were going to, but still, they went. This is lauded and commended as evidence of their firm commitment to the Lord and the work of missions. The missionaries did many good deeds in Uganda and other parts of Africa. They built schools and hospitals and invested in the social advancement of the people they served. I attended a former missionary school, Mt. St. Mary's College Namagunga and can attest to the spiritual devotion of the Catholic nuns who expended their lives in our education. In previous years, the best schools in the country and hospitals were those founded by missionaries. This is a good legacy that we must commend and celebrate.

However, in writing on the subject of the missionaries' shortcomings, I seek to highlight the immensity of the spiritual authority given to the Church to build the walls of the nation and the nations. It is to the Church that the Lord has given authority to disciple and lead the nation spiritually on the right path.

As it is written in Matthew 16:18-19:

> *"On this rock, I will build My church and the gates of hell will not overpower it or be strong to its detriment or hold out against it. I will give you the keys of the kingdom of heaven; and whatever you bind (declare to be improper and unlawful) on earth must be what is already bound in heaven; and whatever you loose (declare lawful) on earth must be what is already loosed in heaven. – Amplified Bible*

The Lord Jesus Christ gave this power to the Church and it comes with great responsibility. If the Church looses a spirit of sectarianism or corruption or sexual immorality, these evils are permitted to operate in the land. God holds the church accountable because God has given His Church authority to bind and to loose.

I believe that through the spirit of sectarianism that was present amongst the missionaries, this same spirit was loosed and given permission to wreak havoc in the nation. From 1962, when Uganda gained Independence from Britain, sectarianism based on religion and tribe became the dominant force in the politics of the nation. I am not a historian, but from the 1960s through to the 1980s politics in Uganda and much of Africa was defined along the lines of religious and tribal sectarianism. In Uganda, political parties formed strong religious alliances that formed a deadly marriage of convenience.

There was the Uganda People's Congress (UPC) led by Dr. Milton Obote, who was a Langi and a Protestant, and Democratic Party led by Benedicto Kiwanuka, who was a Muganda and a Catholic. Kabaka Yeka was a monarchist political movement, led by the Mengo establishment. Even though it had intense internal rivalries, the majority of the members were Protestants and they eventually allied with UPC because they too were Protestants.

The feud between the Protestants and Catholics was the main reason that Benedicto Kiwanuka of DP was rejected as the candidate for the position of Prime Minister. Instead,

Mengo backed Dr. Milton Obote who succeeded in becoming the first Prime Minister of Uganda and executive head of the government.

After Independence, Obote and Muteesa continued to fight over the position and status of Buganda within Uganda and especially the matter of the return of the two "lost counties" of Buyaga and Bugangaizi to Bunyoro. After Buganda lost the referendum and the counties voted to be returned to Bunyoro, the tensions between Obote and Muteesa continued to escalate. These tensions culminated in the 1966 crisis and the suspension of the Constitution, the exile of Kabaka Muteesa and the declaration of Uganda as a republic with Milton Obote as the President.

More than fifty years after Independence, the legacy of religious sectarianism that was sown into the very foundations of the Church in Uganda has been difficult to fight and overcome. God has continued to move through different waves of spiritual awakening that have touched different parts of the country. The growth of the Pentecostal Churches that focus more on the move of the Spirit has also helped to dilute the sharp sectarian feuds. In the last thirty years, the NRM government has promoted a government based on ideology and not identity and has fostered political expression along the fundamental pillars of Pan-Africanism, patriotism, economic and social development, and unity.

I believe that God has intervened divinely to set Uganda and Africa back on the right track. However, it is sad that instead of laying the right foundations that the nation could spring from, the church was instead a tool to sow contrary seeds that the nation has had to recover from. My prayer is that in the years and generations to come, we as the Church will only work to be an instrument in the Lord's hands to disciple the nations into God's perfect will.

Divide and Conquer

The Bible is clear that we, as believers, must seek to live in peace with our brothers at all times. Unity and brotherly love are foundational beliefs with great benefits and blessings to those who uphold them. Proverbs 6:16-19 declares, *"These six things does the Lord hate, yea seven are abominable unto Him. A proud look, a lying tongue, and hands that shed innocent blood. A heart that devises wicked imaginations, feet that are swift in running to mischief, a false witness that speaks lies, and he that sows discord among brothers."*

Sadly, the Gospel was used to further the political aims of the British Empire, rather than the spiritual aims of the Kingdom of God. These political aims couldn't be actualized if the African leaders and chiefs worked together in unity. Unity would have been a barrier to the success of their mission. On their part, it was imperative that the British break down the relationships and bonds that the African leaders possessed to build new bonds of loyalty to the British crown. In Lord Lugard's own words, he wrote:

> *"At this time a messenger arrived from Kabarega, the powerful king of Unyoro, to treat for peace with Mwanga. He was entirely opposed to Europeans, and I knew his proposal to be insincere. We found later, as we anticipated, that he had sent a large army to cooperate with the Mohammedans. I, therefore, advised Mwanga at present to have nothing to say to him, and declined to negotiate myself, till he should send a properly accredited envoy with adequate proposals and guarantees." - Lugard p.114*

Lugard actively worked to bring a wedge of division amongst the kings and chiefs to ensure that no leader could unite with his fellow leader outside of the colonial structures the British wanted to build. The missionaries were part of this and followed along with the political intrigue of setting brother against brother. Those who collaborated with Lugard were rewarded, while those who fought against the foreigners were punished and disenfranchised. By the time Lugard left Uganda in May 1892, he had effectively neutralized an entire nation by pitting brother against brother.

The question that I keep asking is why this policy was condoned by the Christian missionaries. I believe it was because the missionaries saw themselves as representatives of their home governments spreading a kind of cultural Christianity that came along with adopting the names, language and culture of the European power they called home. They did not see themselves primarily as representatives of the Kingdom of God, sent to preach the Gospel of the Kingdom that is above any national government or interests. The missionaries represented their nations and when there was a conflict between faith and nationalism, they capitulated to the national interests of their countries. This was in complete contradiction to what the Apostle Paul advocated for in Philippians 3:5-7:

> *"circumcised on the eighth day, of the people of Israel, of the tribe of Benjamin, A Hebrew of Hebrews, in regard to the law; a Pharisee, as for zeal, persecuting the church, as for righteousness based on the law, faultless. ... But whatever were gains to me I now consider loss for the sake of Christ. – Amplified Bible"*

The Apostle Paul in essence meant that his national identity as a Jew was submitted to his first identity as a Christian. He was promoting the Kingdom of God as a missionary and, as a result, the effects of his ministry were the character of the kingdom which are righteousness, peace and joy. Sadly, the same cannot be said of the legacy of the missionaries in Uganda and Africa.

Darkest England

When the Lord called me into ministry in 2005, He showed me a vision of a light coming out of the heart of Africa and He said, *"Out of what was called darkness will come a great light."* I found it interesting that the Lord showed through that statement that He never called Africa "dark." The association with Africa and darkness has been a long one. Whether this "darkness" described the lack of knowledge that the European powers had of the interior of the continent and their desire to "open" it up or the technologically backward peoples they encountered whom they eventually subdued and conquered; I cannot tell. The title "dark continent" has been used to describe Africa for generations as the superstitious, weak, poor and backward place where Africans dwell. But was this the reality on the ground when the Europeans first came? Certainly not!

Of the cultivation of the land in Uganda Lugard writes:

"The plain here, at foot of Rwenzori was of excessively rich soil. I have never seen anything like the cultivation. As far as the eye can see endless acres of plantation extend, all looking most luxuriant- bananas, grains and beans. They say they are independent of the seasons here; the dew is so heavy and the soil (a light black loam) so rich, that as soon as one crop is gathered, they plant another. The huts are well made, and the people go about the fields unarmed - a rare thing in Africa - with only sticks in their hands. When going on a journey, they carry spears with diamond-shaped blades, but poorly made. The hoes are of iron. The fields are wonderfully well kept, not a weed to be seen. I am told that a vast quantity of food is grown, in order to be exchanged for salt. It is a wonderful granary and if we had the salt lake we tap all this endless supply." - Lugard p.180

He continues a few pages later:

"The soil was everywhere extremely rich, and the heavy dew and rainfall made the vegetation most luxuriant. Though this should be the driest time of the year, we experienced daily rain and thunderstorms, as we marched below the peaks of the great mountain, against which the rain clouds broke." P.193

Of the Salt trade he writes;

"Everywhere were piles of salt, in heaps covered with grass-some beautifully white and clean. On our right was the salt lake, about three-quarters of a mile in diameter, at the bottom of a deep crater-like depression.

"Much as salt is appreciated by us, it seems to be even

more coveted by the Africans. On Nyasa and everywhere I have been in Africa, a pinch of salt was the greatest treat you could offer a visitor. He would slowly consume it by damping his finger and licking it with the utmost gusto, and apparently would never stop as long as he could obtain the luxury." - P.168

Of the roads, he writes:

"We had an excellent broad road made by the constant traffic to the salt lake." - P.166

Of the cattle keepers Lugard writes:

"In colour they vary, as do the Somalis, some being very pale, others black. Some are remarkably handsome men. They wear loose skin, beautifully cured, thrown over their shoulders and so are mostly naked, but the women are clothed." p.158

Of the livestock, he continues:

" These were of a fine breed, large straight-backed, without humps and with prodigious horns over two feet long. The sheep also were large and well-bred, of the fat-tailed species. They also keep a fine and powerful class of dog, which they used in herding cattle.." p.159

Lord Lugard's account, and indeed those of many other explorers and European travellers through Africa during the 17th -18th centuries are of civilizations that had centralized forms of governments, organized trade, economy, agriculture, burgeoning industry, social stratification and the beginnings of an exchange system. Africa, from their description, was by no means dark but filled with glorious beauty and light. The Europeans were taken aback by the extreme wealth of the African soils, minerals and the infinite possibilities Africa offered. Coming from their own poor countries where scarcity of food had brought down monarchies (the French Revolution is an example), Africa was not dark but filled with brilliant light.

In Lugard's own words:

"Yet what else has the civilized world hitherto imported?

Are the natives better, wiser, or happier men, for the possession of beads, brass, iron, and copper ornaments, tawdry-looking glasses and mouth organs? But here in Uganda, Usoga, and Unyoro, there are no fictitious wants to supply or wants to create. Farthing-looking glasses, and Birmingham stuff- warranted to break soon, and to want replacing-are not in vogue. The people are fully clothed in bark cloth, which though admirable indoors and in fine weather, is no better than a sheet of wet paper when damp. To replace this with sound good cloth at fair rates, to supply the house utensils, the coinage, even writing paper (Which they really want) is a fair aim of commerce; and in return, the starving 'civilization' of our cities may well tale of their superfluity of food, and the grain which the country can provide. Not that I include myself among those who say we should take nothing out because we brought nothing in (nothing useful at least). While misery and want exist in 'darkest England' we must find food and scope for Industry for our people, even if we create wants in Africa to do it. But the absurdity of it, is that the cloth we bring to E. Africa is mostly not English at all, but American and Indian. Some cloth is imported from England to Nyasaland, but it is proverbial for short measurements, and for being plastered with 'size' to make weight and deceive by appearances, as Livingstone pointed out long ago. The biscuits are German, the oil, I believe, Russian, the matches Swedish; yet we talk of opening up English markets by our African companies!" – Lugard." - P. 141

Writing in his journal Lugard has a moment of truth where he confesses to himself that Britain doesn't have anything to offer Africa, but rather it is Africa that holds the keys to sustaining Europe. England was going through the industrial revolution with all its dark misery of workhouses and poor houses portrayed in Charles Dickens's *Oliver Twist.* At the time, the industrial cities of Birmingham, Manchester and Liverpool were dark and miserable places where the poor and working-class masses lived in dire poverty, hunger and working in inhumane environments. But to justify their greedy grasping for African resources, they had to create a narrative that the Europeans were coming to "protect" Africa and to "put the countries in order." To do so, they had to deceive the African chiefs into thinking that there was something of value that they were getting in exchange.

Of the treaty with Ankole Lugard writes:

> *"I greatly pleased them by consenting to go through the full ceremony according to their own rites and I founded upon our mutual pledges the treaty which I submitted to England. I had this treaty read and most carefully translated to them. Its main provisions were that the British were to be free to pass through Ankoli, or to build and settle in it, and that the king would do all in his power to suppress the import of arms and powder, by the Waziba traders in German territory to Kabarega and the Mohammedan Waganda, and would seize and confiscate all he could. In return, I gave him a flag and [a] copy of the treaty and promised him the protection and the alliance of the company. We exchanged presents, and the ceremony was complete, and this large country of Ankoli was added to the company's territory." - P.160*

Lugard must have been very pleased with himself, to gain so much in exchange for so little, or more precisely nothing at all. Lugard played the chiefs and kings against each other and in the process a company subdued a whole country. Whatever the British lacked in basic human decency they more than made up for in shrewd calculation and machinations. They were masters of the strategy of divide and conquer, and sadly the church was an active participant in this game of conquest.

Rebuilding Africa's Walls

At the beginning of this chapter, we presented how God sent Nehemiah to rebuild the walls of Jerusalem. Through this historical analysis, I have been making the case that the church was actively involved in the breaking down of the walls in Africa. The missionaries paved the way for the annexation of Uganda and many other parts of Africa. They were partners with their home governments because they had misplaced loyalty to their earthly government rather than the heavenly government to which we as Christians belong. The Apostle Paul, who was the greatest missionary of all, did the true work of a missionary, which was to preach the Lord Jesus Christ. As such he left a legacy of faith in all the places he travelled to and we still hold to that legacy through the New Testament Epistles.

I have also emphasized that my purpose in analyzing our history is not to give the missionaries a bad rap. It is only the Lord who sent them who can judge their actions ultimately. We are all responsible for our actions, not those of others. In tracing our history as the church in Uganda, my goal was to show where and how the spiritual walls were broken down. I hope that if we can understand how the walls were broken down, we can know how God wants us to rebuild the walls of Africa.

The major problem that I see as contributing to the breaking down of the spiritual walls in Africa, was the spirit of sectarianism in the Church. This spirit remains today, in the traditional denominations and even, to some extent, amongst the Pentecostal churches. I believe the Lord has given the church authority to bind what is unlawful and to loose what is lawful as the Lord Jesus declared.

It is time for the Church in Uganda and Africa to bind the spirit of sectarianism and loose the spirit of unity.

In my journey as a pastor over the last 17 years, the Lord has always led me to work in unity with the church and church leadership. I have willingly submitted to church leadership and always sought to work in agreement with other leaders because that is when blessings are released on the church and nation. In the last few years, God has opened more doors for me to work with pastors and church leaders in the region of East Africa and the world. I believe God is raising watchmen on the walls of the nations of the world and, as we join together in unity, mutual submission, honour and love, the spiritual walls of Africa will be rebuilt.

As the spiritual walls of Africa are rebuilt, I believe the nations will be stronger and more united. The barriers to our working together will diminish and there will be greater blessings released to our nations and communities. I pray that the Lord will breathe into the Church in Africa, a new spirit of unity to heal the divide, and to close up the breach and broken down walls. May the Lord raise the spiritual walls of Africa in this generation so that we will never again be the slaves of Sanballat and Tobiah.

References

Lugard, Frederick John Dealtry. *The Rise of Our East African Empire: Early Efforts in Nyasaland and Uganda*. London: W. Blackwood, 1893.

21. Testimonials

Epilogue

I once heard someone say that the Book of Acts is the only book of the Bible that is still being written. God includes the church of all ages in the Book of Acts because as long as the Holy Spirit is still on earth, there is still work to be done to advance God's Kingdom.

We began the journey of this book considering our history as African people after the notorious 1884 Berlin Conference that carved up Africa into fifty-four states/countries. I said, right from the beginning, that the purpose of this book is not to point fingers or trying to pin blame on anyone. The objective of this book is to help us, as Africans and, in particular, the Church in Africa, to take responsibility. However, in order to take responsibility in a meaningful way, I believe that we need to first understand what happened in the past - spiritually, emotionally, psychologically and materially. In understanding what went wrong, we can then make peace with the past through the Blood of Jesus, and close the door to the pain and trauma that still lingers on. When we close the door to the past, having come to terms with its reality, we can then embrace the present and work hard for the future that we all want to see for ourselves, our children and our children's children. For me, writing this book is my small contribution to the work of rebuilding the walls of Africa that were broken down and burnt. May the Lord help us all to become repairers of the breach and restorers of streets to dwell in.

I am very thankful and encouraged to know that there are many other reformers whom God has already planted on the mountains of our societies. They are all doing their part to rebuild Africa's walls. Here are some of their testimonials they have presented. I hope you will join us in this journey.

Rebuilding the walls on the Mountain of Education and Sports

In my book, *My Life's Journey*, I mention how God called me into politics to serve our country. This was in my parent's home area, known as Ruhaama County in Ntungamo District, Western Uganda. God confirmed His word by giving me a resounding victory and leading me to accomplish a lot in the ten years I served as a Member of Parliament.

It is during that time, that I came face to face with the ruins and devastation of our education system as I toured several schools including my former primary school, Kyamate, which had transitioned into a secondary school without any additional infrastructure.

Before serving in the Ministry of Education and Sports, I served in the Karamoja Sub-Region, a region that had suffered a lot of insecurity, hunger and poor service delivery, and this increased my anguish.

Like Nehemiah, the burden and anguish in my heart translated into a vision to see the broken walls and devastations of the education sector rebuilt. My work in the sector is anchored in prayer; there is nothing I do without inquiring from the Lord. As a result, I have seen our small efforts bear a lot of fruit from rebuilding the spiritual infrastructure of this generation to rebuilding the physical infrastructure.

The giants of our time demand humility in order to understand the Kingdom's agenda and what is at stake. It is with this knowledge that God has equipped and enabled us to fight the sexual perversions that threaten the moral fabric of our nation. We have focused on discipling our young generation through advocacy against agendas like Comprehensive Sexuality Education to formulating a values-based education on sexuality for our children. We have focused on youth summits and conventions to consistently pass on the values of sexual purity and integrity to young people.

God has given us the grace to mobilize resources from partners like the Global Partnership for Education and

Education Cannot Wait to build infrastructure in many of our schools including in our refugee-hosting communities. In line with the government policy of having a primary school in every Parish and a secondary school in every sub-county, we have seen many of our children access education and this work continues.

Our young sportsmen and women continue to raise our flag high on the global scene as they excel in sports and this can only be the favour of God and a confirmation that the ruins and devastations of the education sector are being rebuilt by God himself.

Maama Janet. K. Museveni, First Lady of the Republic of Uganda and the Minister of Education and Sports.

Revisiting the Foundations of Education

When it comes to choosing a school for one's children is one of those times of deep reflection for parents. We were not spared this sometimes agonizing process as we debated the school options for our firstborn child. It took us a long while to decide, but once made, it was to be the school for all the siblings as they started school. As the years rolled on and the siblings joined the school, we soon realized that the values and principles of life we upheld as a family were not being reinforced in school but rather were being eroded.

All curriculum is founded on a philosophy that guides the education process encompassing all aspects of life. Education, therefore, is more than acquiring knowledge. It is a process that forms one for life, teaching beliefs and principles, and imparting values and morals that would help one navigate the entire journey of life. Education shapes the minds of peoples and nations for life and, eventually, development.

In the early part of the 16th Century, Martin Luther, the Reformer, began building schools in Germany to teach children how to read the bible and understand biblical principles. His educational philosophy centred on the home. He, however, insisted on a fundamentally Christian education with the Scriptures at the centre, although he eventually supported state involvement in education with the central role of financing. These principles elevated Germany to prominence and initiated a period of reform that lasted for more than 200 years, taking Germany to the period of the Hapsburgs, a time of economic and political prosperity.

In pre-colonial Africa, education was a way of life, encompassing all aspects of social well-being. The desirable societal traits, social behaviour, knowledge, and skills for productive living were communicated through daily activities in the home and broader societal interactions. The goal was to prepare one for fruitful, impactful, and successful living in society. With the arrival of the Christian missionaries, there was a change in the philosophy of, approach to and structure of education. Education shifted from the home and community to the teacher who then became the primary instructor. In this regard, the teacher replaced the parent and the community into which the child was born. The education focus shifted from raising a productive member of their society where the emphasis was placed on academic progress through reading and writing to producing a human resource that would serve the colonial government in a supportive role.

With the fast-changing culture and societal needs, the education system experienced changes emphasizing academic success at the expense of everything else. This state of affairs has mostly stayed the same.

By the time our third born went to school, we knew it was time to consider a different educational path for our children. We started looking for an education system founded in biblical principles and values, addressing all aspects of life, not just academics, and considering each child's unique needs. On 20th February 2002, we started homeschooling our four children using the Accelerated Christian Education (ACE) curriculum. Little did we know that this journey would lead to the establishment of Vine International Christian Academy (VICA) and the establishment of several other ACE schools that now train thousands of students in Uganda and the East African region.

Along the homeschooling journey, we increasingly realized that our life calling was education. My husband, Dr. James Magara, a dentist, focuses on training young dentists and is involved in leadership and governance training. Together, we have given our lives to equipping and empowering those called to the education sector and into leadership and governance. In 2018, I was appointed the Chairperson of the Makerere University Council and I am currently serving the second term. Serving on the governing council of Uganda's oldest and premier university is a privilege, honour, and an incredible opportunity to mentor and train the students, preparing them to address societal needs and contribute to national development. The scripture God gave me, as I took on this assignment, was Isaiah 58:12, *"Your people will rebuild the ancient ruins and will raise up the age-old foundations; you will be called Repairer of Broken Walls; Restorer of Streets with dwellings."*

My educational journey led me to take an undergraduate degree in education and a master's degree, and, now, I am undertaking a doctoral degree. I have served in various capacities as a homeschooling mum, a coordinator for ACE schools in Uganda, the Principal of VICA, and the Chairperson of the Makerere University Council. These opportunities have allowed me to experience the "broken walls" of our education system and its impact on individual lives and the nation. My life's mission is to contribute to the "rebuilding of the ancient ruins, raising the foundations and repairing the broken walls" of Uganda's education system. A robust, adaptable, and godly education system is a critical driver in Uganda's ability to embrace its God-given destiny and harness its rich potential. I thank God that the Ministry of Education is currently reviewing the Educational Policy, whose findings will inform the nation's education system for future generations. I pray that Uganda's education foundation will be rebuilt, the walls repaired, and the streets as national highways for national development, making Uganda a praise on the earth!

Mrs. Lorna Magara, Principal Vine International Christian Academy and Chairperson Makerere University Council.

Serving the Public Guided by Faith

For the last 36 years, it has been my greatest privilege to serve in the Public Sector in Uganda. Perhaps I follow in my father's footsteps, who was a civil servant all his working life and retired satisfied after a distinguished career.

When I joined the public sector straight out of university in 1986, I mistakenly thought I was entering into a sector that was mundane and predictable. Nothing could have prepared me for the battles ahead. It wasn't long before I realized that Makerere University, where I first began working, President's Office where I worked for three years, Uganda Revenue Authority, where I worked for 22 years and now Uganda National Roads Authority, where I have been working for the last 8 years were my mission field. For each of these placements, there was a specific assignment that required contending for the establishment of the Kingdom of God. That was my commission.

There have been many and significant victories on this mission field but all came at a price. I have been most fortunate in my working career to have had strong leadership teams. We have had to invest a lot in prayer and fasting but also in confronting wrong whenever it presented itself in the name of corruption and mismanagement. Sometimes the Lord led us to do massive human resource restricting at corporate levels to create an environment of integrity and good work ethics. Sometimes we had to defend ourselves in courts of law against some who sued us as a way of intimidating us. Many times, we had to say no to others who, by virtue of their positions, expected favours that were contrary to operational policies. Many times we had to guard our mandate jealously from those who would have abused this mandate.

In every battle, the one thing I felt God required of me was to be accountable at whatever time I would be called to account and, secondly, to take care of the well-being of His people, the staff He had entrusted to me. I don't know where this journey goes next, but I have seen the faithfulness of God and the faith adventure continues.

Patience's well-written personal spiritual journey affirms many of the principles that have guided me in serving the Lord's people.

Mrs. Allen Kagina, Executive Director, Uganda National Roads Authority.

Mountain of Art and Celebration - Rebuilding Africa's Walls

In 2016, during a Sunday service at Covenant Nations Church, as we studied the roots of slavery, I saw an image of an African woman being taken into slavery, on a long, death march from her home. There were lines of terrified, defeated-looking men, women and children along the paths in the bush. The woman had a hollow and sorrowful gaze and she had a wooden clamp over her mouth. That image remained with me. It came at a time when I had a deep stirring inside me to tell a particular story relating to Uganda's history. I had started on the path of telling it through film. Treading carefully with prayer and yet with passion simultaneously. The Lord God was very near to me throughout the process. And how I needed Him!

The assignment, because I felt it was an assignment, was met with much spiritual and human resistance. It has been a hard battle, but praise the Lord that we overcame by the Blood of the Lamb and by the word of our testimony! The film was made. It is titled *27 GUNS*. It tells the story of Uganda's War of Liberation (also known as The Bush War) fought from 1981 to 1986. At the forefront of the liberating army was a young idealist, and a true revolutionary, named Yoweri Kaguta Museveni, my father. With 40 other young men, 27 of whom were armed, they went to fight for the salvation of a nation. Behind them, as their wind, were the prayers of the believers. And, with the Lord as their help and shield, they triumphed.

We continue with the work of testifying of what the LORD has done in Uganda. I believe that what the LORD told Joshua is true for us, that every place that the soles of our feet tread upon, He has given us. "For the Kingdom and the Lamb!"

"For the creation waits in eager expectation for the children of GOD to be revealed," as it says in Romans 8:19. This verse, along with Isaiah 60 and Psalm 24 verses. 7-10 were my propellants during that assignment. This was in addition to a few others that were in connection with my personal life. I believe we are the children of GOD being revealed in these times. I also feel that Isaiah 60 is true for Africa now. Our light has come! And the glory of the LORD is rising upon us. May we not miss our time. May we arise and take the mountains for our LORD with force, with Him as our Help. May we be in our positions on the mountains of authority to cry out.

> *"So wake up, you living gateways! Lift up your heads, you doorways of eternity!*
> *Welcome the King of Glory, for He is about to come through you.*
> *You ask, "Who is this King of Glory? Yahweh, armed and ready for battle,*
> *Yahweh, invincible in every way!" Psalm 24:7-8.*

Recently, the LORD positioned me to launch a cultural foundation through Mzee's prompting. It all started very casually and then began to take on a life of its own. There is a backstory to this, which is that, in the area of Uganda where we come from, Patience and I and our families; where the East African Revival's influence is still being felt; and whose blessings we are still enjoying, there has been a longstanding battle between faith and culture. Why? Like all ancient cultures, ours in Africa, in Uganda and, personally, among the Banyankore, there was beauty and there was evil. Deep and profound songs and poetry, true wisdom shared through proverbs and storytelling alongside immoral sexual practices and pagan worship. During the time of the Revival (1930-1950), with the entrance of Christianity, cultural practices of every kind were frowned upon by those who had converted to the faith. I had the dilemma of trying to correlate what is preeminent in my life, which is my faith in Jesus, the Son of GOD; with the identity, I was born into, in terms of music and art. The Spirit of the LORD reminded me, out of the blue, of this Scripture.

> *"And He made from one man every nation of mankind to live on the face of the earth, having determined their appointed times and the boundaries of their lands and territories. This was so that they would seek God if perhaps they might grasp for Him and find Him, though He is not far from each one of us,"* Acts 17:26-27.

We are all fearfully and wonderfully made. Everything within us, from generations past, and outside of us; in the communities we are born into, comes together to form the intricate tapestries of our unique identities. And in the name of Jesus, every power of darkness that has inhabited the thrones of our identity must relinquish them to the authority of the Most High GOD!

> *"...The kingdoms of this world have become the kingdoms of our Lord and of His Christ, and He shall reign forever and ever!"* Rev. 11:15.

Natasha Museveni Karugire, Writer and Filmmaker.
Director of the Heritage Foundation.

The Korean Experience

Upon reading the Bible verse "Seek first the Kingdom of God and His righteousness" (Matthew 6:33), I am convinced that faith goes beyond mere spiritual growth. It involves the transformation of individuals and society as well. This conviction was further strengthened by my experience with the Canaan movement in Korea, which emphasized that as God became human in the world, Christians should also march into the world and work towards transforming people's lives. The Canaan community in Korea was a living embodiment of this philosophy. Christians in the community dedicated their lives to rebuilding their nation, which was devastated by colonization and war. Their impact on people's lives was immense. As a member of this community, I witnessed how Christians should serve and dedicate themselves to the world. They sacrificed their lives and demonstrated their faith by steadfastly living for three generations. They woke up early and worked hard, believing that even a grain of rice turns spiritual when we think of the farmers' tears and sweat and God's contribution to making the grain. They worked because God works. Wherever they went, barren land turned into fertile soil, and people's lives changed.

I have many colleagues in Africa, some of whom succeeded in changing people's lives while others fell apart. However, I noticed a commonality among the successful ones. They were all leaders who committed to doing small, doable things first and did not give up. Although the commitment to taking small steps may seem trivial, it is a critical component of the spiritual journey. The small farmers who clean every day the community yard make a bigger change than a politician. They teach us that true transformation is built on a foundation of small, consistent actions that eventually lead to significant changes. When we commit to small things, we create a habit of perseverance, which is essential to achieving long-term success. The leaders remind me of Canaan in Korea. They demonstrate through small actions what being a Christian is all about.

My experience with the Canaan movement in Korea and Africa has taught me that Christians have a responsibility to work toward the transformation of their communities. By committing to small, doable actions and persevering until the end, we can make a significant impact on the world. As we march into the world, let us strive to embody the teachings of Christ by working to build a better world for all.

Jangsaeng Kim, Deputy Director, Canaan Global Leadership Centre, Republic of Korea.

On Peace & Reconciliation

Our unique approach to reconciliation was first developed in Rwanda and neighbouring Burundi in the aftermath of the

1994 genocide as a way of rebuilding trust in individuals and communities that were shattered. Our co-founders, Arthur and Molly Rouner, were invited by World Vision to partner with one of their Eastern African leaders to explore what could be done to start the work of reconciliation in these deeply wounded countries. Many NGOs were there providing needed practical support for necessities, yet who was there to listen to their broken hearts and begin the process of reconciling? You can build medical clinics, dig wells, and start schools, all of which were desperately needed. However, if people are still in conflict they will end up fighting over the clinic, the well, and the school. So our work of reconciliation was birthed.

Molly shares about those early days,

It was very early morning. Our room in one of the few functioning hotels in Rwanda had a small balcony. I stood there a long time, looking out at the morning hills of Rwanda. On that first day, I stared at the beautiful hills of Rwanda that had seen such devastating evil in the awful killing time, and I asked God over and over, 'Why have you brought me to this place? I have no skills, no expertise to help these people.' And He said to me then. and repeatedly in the months that followed, 'I have brought you here to go to your knees before them, to ask the forgiveness of these people for what your people of the West did, to divide them from each other.' I went to my knees and knelt before them and asked for their forgiveness.

In our very first *Healing and Reconciliation Retreat,* some thirty people from the Tutsi and Hutu tribes, from many denominations, gathered, and Molly did just that. She pulled out a chair, placed it in the centre of the room, and knelt at the chair, waiting for the stunned circle to come. One by one they began to surround her, lay hands on her and prayed for her...the very forgiveness she had asked. The prayer time went on for hours and hours, with extraordinary truth, confession, repentance and forgiveness. And then there were tears from both men and women. That surprised them, as they had been advised by Rwandan experts that we would not likely receive a warm response for our efforts. Rwandan men do not express their emotions openly.

During this time of prayer, the pastors and the reconciliation team were kneeling at a small table in the centre of the room. The Holy Spirit touched and healed their hearts, and the group's tears puddled over the table. One Pastor brought over a towel to wipe the flood of tears.

The retreat ended with praise and amazement. They all reached to clasp the Cross at the centre of the table, vowing to carry the message of reconciliation to every corner of their ruined country.

After the genocide, there were plenty of ideas about what reconciliation was; what it truly meant. People were pouring in from the West to conduct seminars, workshops, lectures and teachings on reconciliation. Suddenly, there was another answer. The way into the heart is not through information or explanation. What's needed is a way to experience transformation. This was the beginning of our call to be reconcilers.

That call compelled us to continue our unique work of reconciliation for nearly 30 years, bringing hope and healing by renewing individuals, restoring relationships and revitalizing communities through the ministry of reconciliation. Tens of thousands of church, community, and country leaders, as well as vulnerable women, youth, and displaced persons throughout East Africa, have experienced the power and repentance and forgiveness at the cross and the potential for a new future.

We are profoundly grateful to be partnered with many other Kingdom of God co-labourers, including Pastor Patience and Covenant Nations Church in seeking to rebuild the walls of East Africa. The work continues and God will be faithful to complete the work He has begun! ***All this is from God, who reconciled us to Himself through Christ and gave us the ministry of reconciliation. II Corinthians 5:18***

Rev. Dr. Jim Olson, President: Pilgrim Center for Reconciliation; www.pilgrimcenter.org and Molly Rouner, co-founder of Pilgrim Centre for Reconciliation. St. Paul, Minnesota, US.

The Isaiah 19 Highway

We thank God for the nation of Uganda, for the President, and for the wonderful way that they're standing for Israel. We're also grateful for Pastor Patience Rwabogo and her heart for her nation, the continent of Africa, the nation of Israel, and the Isaiah 19 Highway.

We've been involved in Africa for many years, and I have visited 20 nations on the continent. We have also hosted four All-African Convocations between 1997 and 2014.

I remember the first time I went to Ethiopia, Reuven Berger (Israel) and I were ministering to around 300 pastors about Replacement Theology. All of the pastors started weeping, and after that special time, the pastors in Ethiopia started supporting the Messianic movement and Israel in a much closer way.

I also remember being in Uganda numerous times with Dr. John Mulinde from World Trumpet Missions; John has come to our annual event, All Nations Convocation Jerusalem, every year since 1996 and I thank God for his leadership.

We have met with the First Lady- Janet Museveni- numerous times in Uganda and Israel, as well as with her daughter, Pastor Patience. Uganda is one of the Founding Nations of our ministry Jerusalem House of Prayer for All Nations. I remember convening a convocation at the source of the Nile in Jinja, Uganda, for all the nations connected with the Nile. We also convened three convocations in the African Union where we sat in the seats of all the leaders of Africa in 1997 and then again in 2000 and 2010. We had delegations from all of Africa and we sat in the seats of the heads of state and prayed for a breakthrough for every nation of Africa and their governments. Every year at the All Nations Convocation Jerusalem, about 25% of the delegates are from the continent of Africa.

The theme of our Convocation this year is *The Isaiah 19 Highway and All Nations Breakthrough Back to Jerusalem* which reflects our passion for seeing the Isaiah 19 Highway prophecy fulfilled: Egypt, Israel, and Assyria worshiping God together as a blessing on the earth. In 1993, we called a convocation in Cairo, Egypt, where we gathered 30 Jewish pastors from Israel with 70 pastors from Egypt. This was the beginning of the Isaiah 19 Highway movement. We recently celebrated our 30th anniversary at our Tukey convocation this year with Pastor Patience joining for the first time!

We thank God that the Isaiah 19 Highway originates in Africa from the River Nile and especially from Uganda which is the source of the Nile and flows through Ethiopia, South Sudan, Sudan and Egypt. We believe that the Nile is the Pishon and the Gihon, from the book of Genesis Chapter 2, and these two rivers were the southern border of the Garden of Eden. We believe that the significance of this land did not stop with the Garden; that in the coming years, we are going to see God arise from Africa in a special way. We are now in touch with about 3 or 4 nations that are ready to move their embassies to Jerusalem in the next year and we believe that Uganda and all the nations of Africa are going to stand with Jerusalem in increasing ways in the coming years.

Pastor Patience released a wonderful message at last year's convocation about repentance for the Africans themselves selling their fellow brothers and sisters into slavery. We believe that God is going to do deep work from Africa and there's going to be a big release from the South of the Isaiah 19 Highway nations including missions, 24/7 worship & prayer watches, and a great multiplication of disciples and congregations. As we're lifting Yeshua 24/7, it says He will draw all men to Himself, and so we see the Lord drawing people from Africa, Egypt, Israel, and Assyria to Himself to worship Him together, and this region will become a blessing in the whole earth. We pray for the fullness of the redemptive purposes for Uganda, all of Africa, and the Isaiah 19 Highway to come to pass, and we bless the Lord for what He's doing and what He's going to do in and through Africa back to Jerusalem, in Yeshua's name!

Tom and Kate, Founders and Pastors of All Nations Convocation Jerusalem & Jerusalem House of Prayer for All Nations, Mount of Olives, Israel.

Rebuilding Africa's Walls

The concept of a wall entails the act of enclosing and protecting a certain area by means of a fence or barrier. The space within the wall can only be accessed through a door, which serves as the main point of entry and exit. However, the reconstruction of a wall implies its previous destruction, rendering the use of the main door useless, as entry can now be achieved through other means.

In this book, the author explores the factors that contributed to the destruction of Africa's walls. Through a historical account, the author shows how the arrival of European missionaries to Africa, specifically in Uganda, played a significant role in the destruction of Africa's walls. The missionaries' approach favoured secularism, which eventually led to sectarianism and division among once-harmonious communities, due to the partial preaching of the Word of God.

Despite the destruction of the wall, there is still hope for Africa. The author highlights individuals, like Nehemiah, who can take up the challenge of rebuilding Africa's walls. These people are leaders who are aware of the gravity of the situation, and they exhibit true leadership skills despite opposition, conspiracies, and fear. They also rely on God, who calls us to be repairers of breaches.

African servants of God must understand that unity and perseverance are essential to rebuilding Africa's walls on a solid foundation - Jesus Christ. The gospel's simplicity is the key to reconciling man with his Creator and his neighbour. Christians in Africa must also equip themselves with spiritual weapons, as the reconstruction of the wall is primarily a spiritual endeavour.

May the Lord Jesus Christ raise an army of servants of Christ, builders and repairers of breaches, despite our cultural and linguistic diversities. Let us form a kingdom of priests and princes in unity, so that His reign and will may be done on earth (in Africa) as it is in heaven.

We recommend this book by Pastor Patience, which challenges us as servants in Africa of the Great King, Jesus Christ following Ezekiel 22:30, Isaiah 58:12, and Joel 2:17.

Pastor Israel Nsembe Loyela, Pasteur Principal du Centre Evangelique L'Arch de L'Alliance (Ark of the Covenant). AOG Président Honoraire des Assemblées de la DRC, Président de L'Association des Ecole Chrétiennes de la DRC. Directeur National de One Hope Internationale en DRC.

Restoring the Shattered Vase for Use By God and Man

I see Africa as a porcelain vase that was once the envy of the world but was shattered at some stage by foreign interests. In Africa today, we speak Portuguese, English, French, Spanish and Arabic over, and above our African languages and dialects. Often we are unwilling or unable to listen to each other. This is largely because we have failed to cooperate and understand our purpose as created by God. The ignorance of the fact that we were uniquely created in the image of God to fulfill our mandate as Africans, engendered a sense of selfishness in those who took leadership as the decolonization exercise began in the 1950s. Some of our leaders relapsed into tribal cocoons to govern, using sectarian tools like religion to revive past rivalries against each other. They missed an important window of opportunity - a season that God gave us to reconstitute the broken vase.

God has now given our generation a window and some tools to use to restore the vase into the marvel of our nations and the world. On my part as a businessman, that tool is to build an export-led economy that will raise the Gross National Product (GNP) of my country and create jobs for young people so that they can be proud of their continent and have no need to flee to the rest of the world in search of what they can more than achieve at home. We are making four interventions to achieve this.

First, we are approaching the markets of the world with research and appointment of trade representatives so that the brand of Uganda's food, agricultural output, manufacturing, mineral wealth and tourism potential are known and appreciated. We want to end the current blind trade where our farmers and enterprises produce but aren't sure where and how to sell to the world. This way, we are speaking to the world about the human and natural resource capacity God gave us. We welcome the world to participate with us in this so that the blessing of our rich country and continent would be shared equitably and fairly, unlike in the past where uneven relationships with the world were the norm.

Second, we are working hard to improve the standards of our food and products so that our laws and regulations comply with global food, plant and animal safety standards. This is to enable us to create confidence both for our producers and consumers that we mean business; we are a new crop of leaders willing to match good-for-good with the world and are not scared of competition if it will help us fulfill our mandate as Africans.

Third, we are working around the clock to build and strengthen the current infrastructure for exports and expand options for our business community – ports, vessels, roads, trains, aircraft, etc. to ensure we lower the unit cost of export from Uganda and make it easy for the world to taste our food and industrial products. As Cyril Ramaphosa, President of South Africa said recently about Uganda, "It is a mystery at the centre of Africa. Who would not want to source a product from this place?"

Finally, we are taking all strides to build an export credit fund to de-risk entry of Ugandan products into competitive markets both in the region and beyond. Africa needs to save and put all her land and other idle assets to use to build the financial capital for investment in machinery, and equipment and better the skill of our youth and keep us innovative. The starting point is to lower the cost of credit by both the private sector and governments investing in a fund of this nature. A combined effort of these funding options means that we can increase trade with each other using the new tool – the Africa Free Trade Area (AFCTA). Just by trading with each other in the next ten years, Africa can raise intra-trade from less than 20% to more than 35% by 2035 and create new incomes of more than USD500bn – almost the size of Nigeria's GDP! So, imagine if every ten years, Africa adds this kind of income to her accounts. Would we not end the low levels of manufacturing, assembly, and value addition, improve our social economic classes and politically stabilize our continent?

Odrek Rwabwogo, Farmer, Businessman and Senior Presidential Advisor on Special Duties; Chairman, Presidential Advisory Committee on Exports and Industrial Development (PACEID).

Glossary of Terms

Term	Meaning
Balokole	A term used to refer to Born Again Christians.
Boda Boda	A motorcycle that is used to transport travellers usually in short distances around the town or city.
Enshunju	A Runyankore term that means a distinguishing haircut similar to a mohawk, that was reserved for young men in pre-colonial times.
Kanyafu	A Runyankore term referring to a rod used to discipline children. It is usually made from a soft, supple, branch of a tree.
Kaweke	A colloquial term that means hair that is either undesirable either because of texture or colour.
Maama	A term of respect and love for a mother or any woman who is a leader in her community.
Mzee	directly translated as "old man" it is a term of respect and love for a father or any man who is a leader in his community.
Okuganiza	A Runyankore term that means a sarcastic, witty or sardonic sense of humour.
Oweisheimwe	Directly translated as "Having one Father" it is a Runyankore term used by born-again Christians to mean other believers in the Lord Jesus Christ.

Owoluganda	Directly translated as "brother or sister." It is a Luganda term used by born-again Christians to mean other believers in the Lord Jesus Christ.
Tukutendereza Yesu	A popular Christian song sung by born-again believers especially those with roots in the East African Christian Revival. It means "Praise Jesus."

Just as I am

Just as I am, without one plea,
But that Your blood was shed for me,
And that You bid me come to You,
Oh, Lamb of God, I come, I come.

Chorus
Ooh, just as I am, Ooh I come
Ooh, just as I am, oh Lamb of God, I come

Just as I am, and waiting not
To rid my soul of one dark blot,
To You whose blood can cleanse each spot,
Oh Lamb of God I come, I come.

Just as I am, though tossed about
With many a conflict, many a doubt,
Fighting and fears within, without,
Oh, Lamb of God, I come, I come.

Just as I am, You will receive,
Will welcome, pardon, cleanse, relieve;
Because Your promise, I believe,
Oh, Lamb of God I come, I come.

Bridge:
I come to you wretched and blind
In need of healing in my mind
I come to You broken and poor
I am empty, I have nothing more
Oh, Lamb of God, I come

Charlotte Elliott, 1835

Prayer for Salvation

LORD Jesus, I come to You today with a broken and contrite heart. I recognize that I have lived in rebellion against God and rejected the offering that was made for me when You died on the Cross for my sins. Today, I return to You and ask You to forgive me of my sins and wash them away with Your blood. I believe You died on the Cross for my sins and rose from the dead victoriously on the third day. I accept You as my Saviour and Lord today. Please write my name in Your book of life and give me the grace to follow You for the rest of my life. Please take my life and use it for Your glory and from now on whenever I call on Your Name, answer by fire.

In Jesus' Mighty Name.

Amen.

About the Author

Patience Museveni Rwabwogo is a wife, mother, pastor, reformer and entrepreneur. She graduated from the University of Minnesota with a degree in Political Science and Global Studies. She has pastored Covenant Nations Church in Uganda since its founding in 2006. She is passionate about seeing God's redemptive purpose fulfilled in Africa and the nations of the world.

She shares her messages on numerous platforms reaching thousands of listeners weekly. She founded the Edward and Erina Kataaha Bible College in 2022 as a vehicle to train young reformers to go out and shape the communities around them. She has been married to her husband Odrek for over 20 years and God has blessed them with four children. In addition, they work together running their private company called Tomosi Group.

www.ingramcontent.com/pod-product-compliance
Lightning Source LLC
Chambersburg PA
CBHW030944150426
42812CB00072B/3476/J

* 9 7 8 1 9 8 9 9 2 8 2 2 6 *